SAMURAI

and the Warrior Culture of Japan
471–1877

A SOURCEBOOK

SAMURAI

and the Warrior Culture of Japan
471–1877

A SOURCEBOOK

Edited and Translated, with an Introduction, by
Thomas Donald Conlan

Hackett Publishing Company, Inc.
Indianapolis/Cambridge

Copyright © 2022 by Hackett Publishing Company, Inc.

All rights reserved
Printed in the United States of America

25 24 23 22   1 2 3 4 5 6 7

For further information, please address
  Hackett Publishing Company, Inc.
  P.O. Box 44937
  Indianapolis, Indiana 46244-0937

www.hackettpublishing.com

Cover design by Elana Rosenthal
Composition by Aptara, Inc.

Library of Congress Control Number: 2021945313

ISBN-13: 978-1-64792-056-2 (cloth)
ISBN-13: 978-1-64792-039-5 (pbk.)
ISBN-13: 978-1-64792-057-9 (PDF ebook)

The paper used in this publication meets the minimum requirements of American National Standard for Information Sciences—Permanence of Paper for Printed Library Materials, ANSI Z39.48–1984.

∞

CONTENTS

Acknowledgments   xi
Introduction   xiii

SECTION I
The Story of Swords: Understanding the Warriors of Ancient Japan (471–900)

1. An Inscription on the Sakitama-Inariyama Sword   1
2. A Fifth-Century Sword from the Eta Funayama Tomb   3
3. Bright (*yang*) Sword and Shadow (*yin*) Sword   4
4. Sword of Sakanoue no Tamuramaro   7

SECTION II
Warriors and the Court (900–1150)

1. Excerpt from "Tamakazura," *The Tale of Genji*   9
2. Excerpt from *Chūyūki*, the Courtier Journal of Fujiwara no Munetada, 5.20.1108   11
3. "How Taira no Masakado Raised a Rebellion and Was Killed" and "How the Noble Minamoto no Yoriyoshi Chastised Abe no Sadatō and His Followers," from *Konjaku Monogatari*   12

SECTION III
The Wars of the Twelfth Century (1150–1189) and the Creation of a Warrior Government

1. Excerpts from "The Heiji Rebellion," in Jien's Thirteenth-Century History *The Gukanshō*   26
2. An Order (*kudashibumi*) Issued by Taira no Kiyomori   28
3. Civil War in the 1180s   28
4. The Difficulty of Estimating Army Size   31

SECTION IV
The Age of Kamakura Ascendancy (1221–1333)

1. Go-Toba's Order to Chastise Hōjō Yoshitoki	34
2. The Will (*yuzurijō*) of Nejime Kiyoshige	35
3. Hōjō Yoshitoki's Letter to the Shimazu of Satsuma Province	36
4. A Directive (*mikyōjo*) from Hōjō Yoshitoki to Ichikawa Rokurō	36
5. A Rokuhara Order (*gechijō*)	38
6. A Kantō Order (*gechijō*)	39
7. Excerpt from *The Chronicle of Jōkyū*	39
8. Excerpt from the *Baishōron* Account of the Jōkyū War	41
9. The Formulary of Adjudication/Jōei Code (*Goseibai shikimoku*) (1232)	42
10. Letter from Hōjō Yasutoki Concerning the Formulary	60
11. Kamakura Amendments (*Tsuikahō*)	61
12. *Bakufu* Justice: A Case Study	62
13. Hōjō Shigetoki's Letter to His Son Nagatoki	69
14. Excerpt from Takezaki Suenaga's *Scrolls of the Mongol Invasions*	81
15. Legal Amendment (*Tsuikahō*) Concerning Rewards	85
16. Suenaga's Audience with Adachi Yasumori	85
17. Excerpts of Tōgan Ean's Statement of Opinion (*ikenjō*)	87
18. Summons (*meshibumi*) of the Chinzei Eastern Administrator	88
19. Kamakura's Attempt to Dispatch Forces to Korea	88
20. Petition for Reward (*gunchūjō*) by Shami Shukumyō Ōkami Korechika	91
21. Copy of a Letter by Shōni Kagesuke	92
22. The New Laws (*Shin-shikimoku*) of Adachi Yasumori (1284–1285)	93
23. Excerpts from *The Confessions of Lady Nijō*	96
24. Excerpt from "The Light and Shadows of the Day," *The Clear Mirror* (*Masukagami*)	100
25. Kamakura's Response to the Asahara Assassination Attempt	102
26. Excerpts from *Mine'aiki*	103
27. Excerpt from "The Dayflower," *The Clear Mirror* (*Masukagami*)	109
28. Kanesawa Sadamasa Letter (Fragment)	111
29. Command (*ryōji*) of Prince Moriyoshi	112
30. Petition for Reward (*gunchūjō*) by the Monks of Taisanji, Harima Province	113
31. Document of Praise (*kanjō*), Aso Harutoki	114
32. Document of Damages (*funshitsujō*) by the Nun Jikai (Excerpts)	115
33. Copy of Mino Washimi Tadayasu's Petition for Reward (*gunchūjō an*)	115
34. Command (*ryōji*) of the Fifth Prince (Moriyoshi)	116

Contents

SECTION V
The Rise of the Ashikaga and the Life of Ashikaga Takauji (1305–1358)

1. Excerpt from Imagawa Ryōshun's *Nantaiheiki* — 118
2. Ashikaga Tadayoshi Directive (*mikyōjo*) — 121
3. Ashikaga Takauji Prayer (*gammon*), Shinomura Shrine — 121
4. Excerpts from *Baishōron* — 122
5. Copy of a Letter (*shojō an*) by Ashikaga Takauji — 143
6. Mobilization Order (*gunzei saisokujō*), Ashikaga Takauji — 144
7. Ashikaga Takauji Prayer (*ganmon*) — 144
8. Document (*kakikudashi*) by Ashikaga Tadayoshi — 145
9. Reminiscences by Aiba Ujinao — 145
10. Letter (*shojō*) by the Protector Priest (*gojisō*) Kenshun — 146
11. Prayer (*ganmon*) by the Protector Priest (*gojisō*) Kenshun — 147
12. Sutra Colophon Written by Ashikaga Takauji — 148

SECTION VI
Warfare in the Fourteenth Century: Warrior Experiences (1331–1392)

1. An Oath by Members of the Nejime Family — 150
2. A Petition for Reward (*gunchūjō*) by Hatano Kageuji — 150
3. Takeda Nobutaka Document of Praise (*kanjō*) — 153
4. A Cosigned Document (*rensho shojō*) — 153
5. The Letters of the Yamanouchi — 154
6. A Document by Kō no Morofuyu (*hōsho*) — 167
7. Yamanouchi Tokimichi Report of Arrival (*chakutōjō*) — 168
8. Oaths and the Kannō Disturbance — 168
9. Petition for Reward (*gunchūjō*) by Aso Koresumi — 171
10. A Document of Loss (*funshitsujō*) by Tannowa Nagashige — 172
11. Excerpts from "The Battle of Ryūsenji," *Taiheiki* — 173
12. Excerpts from *The Chronicle of Meitoku* — 176

SECTION VII
The Ashikaga Decline and the Ōnin War (1441–1477)

1. Prince Sadafusa's Account of the Assassination of Ashikaga Yoshinori (1441) — 178
2. The Poems of *Ikkyū* (1394–1481) — 180
3. The Ōnin War (1467–1477) — 181
4. The Process of Praise and Rewards: A Case Study — 184
5. Selection from the *Inryōken Nichiroku* Concerning Guns — 186

Contents

6. The *Chronicle of Ōnin* (Excerpt)	187
7. Observations from *Hekizan Nichiroku*	188
8. Kikkawa Mototsune Roster of Wounds	189
9. Remembering the Ōnin War	190

SECTION VIII
The Rise of Regional Hegemons (*Daimyō*) (1450–1557)

1. Ōuchi Laws Regarding Violence	193
2. Ōuchi Regulations for Yamaguchi, 4.29.1486	194
3. Ōuchi Regulations for Yamaguchi, 4.20.1487	195
4. Further Prohibitions Regarding Killing	196
5. Prohibitions of Loitering	197
6. Ōuchi Reverence for Kamakura Law	198
7. More Laws Concerning Violence	200
8. Regulations Concerning Shipping	201
9. Portrait of Hosokawa Sumimoto	204
10. The *Jinkaishū*, Laws of the Date	206
11. Mōri Motonari Oaths	216

SECTION IX
The First European Encounter (1543–87)

1. Ōuchi Yoshinaga's Commendation	223
2. Portuguese Translation of Ōuchi Yoshinaga's Commendation	224
3. Letter by Ōtomo Sōrin	225
4. Photo of Ōtomo Francisco (Sōrin) Saddle with FRCO Monogram	226
5. Photos of Ōtomo Francisco (Sōrin) Cannon with FRCO Monogram	227
6. The Dissemination of Guns: The Example of the Takeda	229
7. Portuguese Recipe for Gunpowder, Given by Ashikaga Yoshiteru to the *Daimyō* Uesugi Kenshin in 1559	231

SECTION X
The Late Sixteenth- and Early Seventeenth-Century Transformations: The Creation of "*Samurai*" (1575–1691)

1. Ōta Gyūichi, *The Chronicle of Lord Nobunaga* (1610)	235
2. Letter by Shimotsuma Rairen	240
3. Toyotomi Hideyoshi's Edict Concerning the Collection of Swords (1588)	242
4. Toyotomi Hideyoshi's Edict Regarding the Separation of Status (1591)	243
5. The 100 Article Code of Chōsokabe Motochika	244

6. A Receipt of Noses	259
7. The Memoir of a Unification Era Warrior, Fukutomi Han'emon	260
8. The *Buke Shohatto* of 1615	264
9. The Revised *Buke Shohatto* of 1635	265
10. Kumazawa Banzan, "Abolition of the Separate Soldier Class"	267

SECTION XI
The *Samurai* of the Tokugawa Era (1603–1867)

1. Excerpts from Arai Hakuseki's *Autobiography*	272
2. Excerpts from *The Book of the Samurai Hagakure* by Yamamoto Tsunetomo	276
3. Selections from *Musui's Story: The Autobiography of a Tokugawa Samurai*	280
4. Selection from *The Autobiography of Yukichi Fukuzawa*	291
5. Selection from *Remembering Aizu: The Testament of Shiba Gorō*	292
6. Two Petitions for Reward (*gunchūjō*) Submitted in 1869	297

SECTION XII
Abolishing the *Samurai* (1868–1877)

1. *The Japan Mail:* Abolishing of the *Samurai* Right to Wear Swords	300
2. Selections from *The Diary of Kidō Takayoshi*	302

Glossary	309
Bibliography	316
Source and Image Credits	324
Index	327

ACKNOWLEDGMENTS

I owe a profound debt of gratitude to several people who helped this book come into being. First, I would like to thank Rick Todhunter for approaching me to do this project, something which I had long wanted to do, and for all his advice and editorial skill. Next, Yoshikawa Shinji aided me greatly in securing images and permissions. He has been a help and inspiration to me for many years. While we were locked down at Princeton, Horikawa Yasufumi aided me with translations of many difficult law codes, letters, and oaths. I learned much from him and truly enjoyed our exchanges, which have immeasurably improved the quality of this book. For securing images at Kyoto University, I am grateful to Iwasaki Naoko, Kido Hironari, and Murakami Yumiko. I also am indebted to Yamada Kotoko of the Saitama Museum for her help and to Roberta Schwartz of Bowdoin College. A special thanks to Elana Rosenthal for her great help in making this a better book during the production process.

Royall Tyler has been a great friend and interlocutor. I have enjoyed our exchanges, both in person during a wonderful few months in Princeton and over email regarding many topics. Royall has been a model for me for scholarly rigor and beautiful prose, and I have learned more from him than words can say. I am grateful for his generosity in allowing portions of his books to be reproduced. I also owe a special thanks to Luke Roberts for generously allowing me to publish parts of his remarkable narrative of Fukutomi Han'emon. Patrick Schwemmer translated the Portuguese version of the 1552 Ōuchi Daidōji document and gave me permission to use it. I have learned much from his erudition. Special thanks, too, to Christopher Mayo for his help with the Ōtomo Sōrin documents and source materials. And with the efforts of Iwasaki Naoko and Yoshikawa Shinji, I could see Ōtomo Sōrin's magnificent saddle in person.

I am especially grateful to Ekaterina Pravilova, for without her help I never could have secured images for the Ōtomo Fransisco cannon. I am in debt to Dr. Sergei Efimov, the deputy director of the Military-Historical Museum of Artillery, Engineering, and Communications Forces, for his photos, permission, and interesting explanation of this remarkable object and its storied history. Kurushima Noriko introduced me to the existence of nineteenth-century petitions for reward. Wada Shūsaku also proved helpful in explaining military documents of western Japan. Finally, Ebara Masaharu earns my thanks for informing me of the existence of this cannon in the first place.

I owe great thanks to Mark Ravina for introducing me to *The Japan Mail* translation of the edict abolishing the *samurai*, as well as his erudition regarding the events of the 1870s. I am also grateful to Gregory Smits regarding the social orders of Okinawa. Jaqueline Stone has always been a source of knowledge and inspiration. I have also learned a tremendous amount from Andrew Watsky. Thanks, too, for Shel Garon's and Federico Marcon's insights and suggestions. And finally, I am grateful to Michael Como, Brian Steininger, and Bryan Lowe for their help in deciphering and translating ancient swords.

My students have been a great help and inspiration for this project. In particular, the graduate students who took my Sources in Ancient and Medieval Japanese History class over the years. Kyle Bond, Gina Choi, Claire Cooper, Antonin Ferré, Megan Gilbert, Filippo Gradi, Joseph Henares, Kentaro Ide, Caitlin Karyadi, Nate Ledbetter, Skyler Negrete, David Romney, Michelle Tian, and Mai Yamaguchi have contributed much to my knowledge of documents, and they have aided in some translations. Undergraduate students in my Origins of Japanese Culture and Civilization course in the spring of 2018, 2020, and 2021 tested out some translations and helped me to improve them, as well as students in my Warrior Culture of Japan course, and the students in Rob Hellyer's Japanese history course at Wake Forest University.

INTRODUCTION

Becoming *Samurai*: The Warrior Culture of Japan

Beginning with sword inscriptions (the oldest known writings related to Japanese warriors), this book is arranged more or less chronologically, proceeding on to works of court literature, diaries, letters, documents, and law codes as well as portraits and picture scrolls. It aims to show that an autonomous and unique warrior culture arose and thrived and explores warriors' roles as fighters, guards, lawgivers, and managers and traces their rise in Japanese society—from bodyguards to marginal provincial figures to autonomous warriors, and finally, in some cases, to provincial magnates and dominant rulers over all of Japan. Included here are such illuminating texts as the late sixteenth-century documents formalizing the creation of the *samurai* order as well as ordinances from the 1870s abolishing that very same order.

A Brief Overview of Japanese History 471–1877

The warrior culture of the earliest centuries covered in this book (471–900) is revealed through inscriptions on five swords, two of which contain the earliest known writing in Japan. They date from the time of the Great King Yūryaku (known then as Wakatakeru) and correspond to a time of extensive immigration to his Yamato kingdom. These immigrants, primarily from the Korean peninsula, brought with them new beliefs, such as their ancestral gods; new technologies, including writing; and a new means of recording time through a Chinese calendar.

The powerful Yamato kings had massive tombs, requiring millions of hours to construct, and undoubtedly controlled extensive armed forces. Some Chinese histories refer to the Yamato leaders as great generals who maintained peace and commanded all military affairs with their battle axes. However, after Yūryaku's time, the tombs decreased in size. In chronicles dating from 712 and 720, Yūryaku is portrayed as being a cruel and arbitrary leader. But we can tell, from looking at his swords, that his reputation began to suffer even sooner than that. One of his swords, which had at some point been owned by a prominent magnate (*kuni no miyatsuko*), eventually ended up in the hands of a far lesser figure—someone who could not afford a lavish tomb but was instead roughly buried on top of another man's tomb. The disgraced Yūryaku's gifts were shunned by the powerful, even in a time when great value was placed on a good sword.

Little is known about the oldest warriors of Japan, save what can be gleaned from these swords, or from images of them made from pottery, known as *haniwa*. In purely material terms, we know these warriors wielded bows and possessed iron swords, and, from the fourth century onward, some wore suits of iron armor, which also protected their horses. Their horses were small, resembling the animals we would now call ponies. Equestrian warriors had obvious advantages in terms of mobility on the field of battle and enjoyed a certain amount of prestige compared to the majority of fighters, who fought on foot. Inscriptions on swords found in the tombs of powerful kings indicate that some descendants of regional magnates (*kuni no miyatsuko*) would travel to central Japan, where they served the powerful kings of Yamato. Though these early warriors most likely came from local elite families, with some serving the Yamato rulers, it seems unlikely that they fell into any well-defined social category.

In the sixth and seventh centuries, the states of East Asia significantly improved their administration. New beliefs, such as Buddhism, came to favor, and a powerful state arose, with a well-defined capital, carefully laid out roads, and an extensive administrative system whereby all men, women, and children were given lands to cultivate. Commoners would pay taxes on agricultural produce, goods in kind, or provide labor. Of the labor taxes, the most onerous was conscription. In principle, one out of every three able-bodied men, aged twenty-one to sixty, would have to serve in the army, although in practice the rate was much lower. Conscripts had to provide their own armor and provisions and could serve in guard duty or on the frontiers of Japan. So burdensome was this duty that many conscripts deserted in order to escape their obligations.

In the seventh century, Yamato became known as Japan. At that time, Japan's rulers adopted the title of *tennō*, heavenly sovereign or emperor, and claimed cosmic universal authority based primarily on their administrative control over revenue and people in the archipelago. Throughout the seventh and eighth centuries these emperors administered Japan with a firm hand, creating provinces, districts, and highways crisscrossing the archipelago, and imposing a countrywide system of taxation.

In 737, a devastating smallpox epidemic decreased Japan's population by a third and strained the elaborate administrative system. An emperor named Shōmu (701–756; r. 724–49) tried to mitigate this epidemic by patronizing temples, having Buddhist sutras read, and otherwise enhancing his Buddhist merit. Most notably, he ordered the construction of Tōdaiji, the largest temple in the world. Symbolizing both imperial power and protection, by the time of the death of his consort Empress Kōmyō in 760, his two swords—named "Bright" and "Dark"—were placed under the Great Buddha altar of this temple.

In 749, significant deposits of gold were discovered in the northern regions of the main Japanese island of Honshu. Unfortunately for the Japanese court, this northern part of Honshu was not under their control, and the inhabitants of that region—known as *emishi*, or barbarians—did not recognize the authority of the state. Resisting the encroachment of the Japanese government, these *emishi* attacked the military forces sent to subdue them and initially achieved great success, capturing and destroying many garrisons and military outposts in the far north. Yet the war between the residents of Honshu and the central Japanese government would ultimately last for another thirty-eight years. In 794, the government finally decided that a conscripted army was not an effective fighting force against the *emishi* and ended the practice of conscription.

Having abandoned conscription and a standing national army, the Japanese government instead turned to a network of small groups of powerful warriors to preserve order in the provinces. A more substantial military force remained in the far north, however. Known as the Six-District Army, this force remained stationed in the gold-rich regions of northern Honshu, although it never did conquer the far northern reaches of the island. The commander of this force—which remained in place until 1189—was the Chinjufu *shōgun*, or the "Pacification General." After 1089, however, actual authority passed to the "Military Envoy (*ōryōshi*) of Mutsu Province," a hereditary position held by a towering northern warrior named Fujiwara no Kiyohira (1056–1128). He and his descendants Motohira (?–1157), Hidehira (?–1187), and briefly, Yasuhira (?–1189), controlled the north through 1189.

The Office of *Sei-i-tai Shōgun* and Changes during the Heian Era (794–1185)

The war in the north was brought to a successful conclusion when Sakanoue no Tamuramaro (758–811) was appointed as the Pacification General (Chinjufu *shōgun*) in 796, and then to the extraordinary and temporary office of *Sei-i-tai shōgun*, or "Barbarian-Subduing General" in 797 and again in 804. Taking command of the situation, he defeated the *emishi* decisively in 802, although skirmishes continued through 811. After his victory, he lived out his remaining days in Kyoto. He was eventually buried with his sword, one replete with gold fittings, a symbol of his successful conquering of the north. Over time, the office of *Sei-i-tai shōgun* would become the core office justifying the Tokugawa shogunate, but originally it was an ad hoc and extraordinary position.

During the tenth century, Japanese governing institutions were simplified. Capital Police (*kebiishi*) provided order in Kyoto, the capital, while commissioned officers, known variously as "Envoys to Pursue and Capture," or "Pursue and Destroy," would quell rebellions. They were most notably successful in defeating two uprisings: one by Taira no Masakado (?–940) in the east, and another by Fujiwara no Sumitomo (?–941) in the west. Masakado's is the more famous of these major revolts and is the subject of some of Japan's earliest-known warrior tales.

Over the course of the Heian era, provincial governors, known as *zuryō*, served as tax collectors who extracted, often arbitrarily, revenue from the provinces. The previously egalitarian society became stratified, and the provincial elites, known as *zaichō kanjin*, or "provincial office holders," assisted their governors in squeezing taxes from the locals.

Although the provincial office holders helped governors tax other residences of the provinces, they themselves were only lightly taxed. As the governors' bodyguards, however, they did have to supply their own armor, weapons, and horses, both for themselves and their closest followers. Dozens of such men—whose descendants would eventually become the Japanese warriors of legend—would serve their provincial governor. In Murasaki Shikibu's classic eleventh-century novel *The Tale of Genji*, the passages describing an encounter with the "Commissioner" accurately portray the general attitude of these warriors to provincial governors.

Japan in the eleventh century also witnessed a political transformation with the rise of "Dharma," or "Retired" Emperors. These men became Buddhist monks but did not renounce the affairs of the world. To the contrary, they engaged in direct administration and oversaw rituals which were thought to be the essence of court governance. The first of these Retired Emperors was Go-Sanjō (1032–73; r. 1068–73). But the position was solidified by Shirakawa (1053–1129), who officially reigned as Emperor from 1073–87. But Shirakawa continued to govern as a Buddhist monarch after his "retirement" and conducted rites demonstrating that he, rather than the nominally reigning Emperor, was sovereign.

Over the course of the eleventh and twelfth centuries, the most powerful warriors remained provincial office holders who helped provincial governors collect revenue. Most governors were clients of the Retired Emperors. Some warriors who lacked strong ties to a governor could escape his depredations by commending and thus placing their lands under the protection of a court noble. In doing so, they created what are known as *shōen* estates.

Introduction

Shōen have been greatly misunderstood by many later historians. *Shōen* were not owned by any single person. Rather, multiple people of differing status could point to the same piece of land, proclaim "This land is my land!" and would all be correct. The most important status-based rights of income were *gesu shiki*, managerial rights, and *ryōke shiki*, or proprietary rights, to these lands. The person on the land who commended the estate became the *gesu* and, as a rule of thumb, would overlook the estate and be entitled to a third of its surplus. The proprietor, on the other hand, secured two-thirds of the surplus revenue and had to be a capital noble. No local warrior could hold proprietary *shiki*; nor could a central noble possess managerial rights. Not until the mid-fourteenth century did these status-based rights of income blur.

The *gesu* remained in a precarious position. He could be divested of his post at any time by the proprietor. In other words, he served at the proprietor's whim. Hence, establishing an estate was usually an act of desperation and one that could well leave unfortunate *gesu* with nothing.

Retired Emperors exacerbated this instability on the land because on occasion they could create estates through administrative fiat, dispossessing powerful provincial office holders (the *zaichō kanjin*) in the process. This instability and uncertainty regarding provincial land rights led to resistance against the dictates of the central court, culminating in the so-called "Genpei War" of 1180–85 and the rise of the Kamakura Shogunate, Japan's first "warrior government."

Animosity regarding the policies of the center focused not on the Retired Emperor Go-Shirakawa (1127–92; r. 1155–58), but rather one of his clients and later adversaries, Taira no Kiyomori (1118–81). Kiyomori's father and grandfather had long been clients of Retired Emperors and served as provincial governors. In 1156 and 1159, two skirmishes broke out between competing supporters of a Retired Emperor and Emperor, and in both cases, supporters of Go-Shirakawa, who was then the reigning Emperor, triumphed. Though these clashes involved only dozens of warriors, they were unprecedented, for buildings in the capital were destroyed, and prominent nobles and warriors were executed in the aftermath of the conflict. They were later immortalized as the Hōgen and Heiji Disturbances, and the subject of warrior tales and picture scrolls.

After the disturbances of 1156 and 1159, Kiyomori, who may have been actually fathered by the Retired Emperor Shirakawa, acted more as a powerful courtier than a provincial governor or warrior, sponsoring great Buddhist rites, overseeing trade with the continent, and advancing to the pinnacle of court society. He did not, however, establish particularly close ties with warriors in the provinces. Surviving documents reveal that Kiyomori, acting in typical fashion for nobles, granted the office of *gesu*, or manager, to an estate to his local supporters. But it was not a stable position and, as noted above, court officials could evict a *gesu* from the position at any time.

Ultimately, in 1179, Kiyomori staged a coup, placed Go-Shirakawa under house arrest, and forced the accession of Kiyomori's grandson Antoku (1178–85)—the product of a match between one of his daughters and the Emperor Takakura (1161–81; r. 1168–80)—to the throne, sparking the civil conflict that came to be known as the Genpei War. Though this civil war is often portrayed as a struggle between the Taira and Minamoto families, contemporary records reveal that it was in fact a much broader conflict waged between local warrior forces (both *zaichō kanjin* and *gesu*) against the agents of the central government, provincial governors, and their deputies.

Minamoto no Yoritomo and the Establishment of the Kamakura Shogunate (1185–1333)

During the 1180 outbreak of civil war, Minamoto no Yoritomo (1147–99), the exiled son of a man who had been defeated and killed in the Heiji Disturbance of 1159, established the completely new office of *jitō*, or land steward. He did so on an ad hoc basis, and remarkably—even though he had no authority to do so—he successfully attracted support through this new office and was able to defend these rights. This office of *jitō* was functionally the same as that of the *gesu*; but, unlike the *gesu*, the person appointed as the *jitō* could not be arbitrarily dismissed from the post by the court. Thus, Yoritomo, the rebel, attracted support by giving warriors in the province security of land possession through this office.

The Genpei War was fought between local warriors in opposition to the arbitrary policies of the court and its provincial governors. In the midst of this war, the court formally recognized Yoritomo's regime—an alliance created in 1183—as an organization charged with reestablishing order throughout the country. The greatest causality was Kiyomori and his descendants, who were thought to embody the excesses of the court. Kiyomori died in 1181, and almost all of Kiyomori's direct line, including his grandson Emperor Antoku, drowned at the Straits of Shimonoseki during the Battle of Dannoura in 1185.

The destruction caused by warfare did not bring peace. In the provinces, many warriors unilaterally declared themselves to be *jitō*, and Yoritomo spent much effort trying to adjudicate and vacate these claims. In 1189, Yoritomo destroyed the remains of the Six-District Army in the northeast, attacking them at a remarkable settlement of Hiraizumi, replete with a gold-covered temple, which had been founded by Fujiwara Kiyohira, Military Envoy (*ōryōshi*) of Mutsu Province. In his mobilization for this campaign, Yoritomo demanded that all *jitō* participate. The *ōryōshi* of Mutsu Province, and commanders of the Six-District Army from 1089–1189, were big men, generally over six feet tall, and the last of their line, Yasuhira, was killed in part because the small Japanese horses could not carry such large men.

In 1192, Yoritomo was invested with the same *Sei-i-tai shōgun* title Sakanoue no Tamuramaro had last received in 804. With this title, and later court appointments, he could open an administrative office (*mandokoro*) and govern the affairs of his *jitō*. This marks the official origin of the Kamakura Shogunate. Kamakura was the name of the town where the shogunate was located; it also describes this government, and the name Kamakura is given to the era of history lasting from 1185 until 1333.

Yoritomo served only briefly as *Sei-i-tai shōgun* and passed this post to his son, preferring instead to rely on a higher-ranking court office. Yoritomo died in 1199, and his sons succeeded to this post, but by 1219 both were dead. From 1219 until 1226, there was no *shōgun* in Kamakura.

Recognition of the office of *jitō* was the major innovation of Yoritomo's life. For over a century, scholars have asserted that this institution represents the advent of feudalism in Japan. According to this view, espoused most notably by Asakawa Kan'ichi (1873–1948), the position of *jitō* resembled that of a fief, which was recognized by Yoritomo and exchanged for service, thereby making these men "vassals." Certainly, in 1189 Yoritomo demanded that all *jitō* attack the Six-District Army in the north, but he was more concerned about the survival of his regime than demanding service from *jitō* who did not resemble vassals in the European context, although they have often been described by this term. Even during Yoritomo's lifetime, there seems no clear sense that his confirmation of *jitō* rights was contingent upon military service. Thus, the analogy of "feudalism" does not apply to him and his men; nor does its terminology of vassalage adequately characterize the warriors of Kamakura.

Another office, that of *shugo*, or protector, is also associated with Yoritomo's regime, but this position—a kind of quasi-judicial and policing office whereby holders created rosters of locals for guard duty and apprehended criminals and, if need be, rebels—appears only to have been formalized after Yoritomo's 1199 death.

The Rise of the Hōjō and the "Golden Age" of Kamakura Governance (1221–1333)

The Hōjō were related to Hōjō Masako (1157–1225), Yoritomo's wife. They staffed Yoritomo's executive office (*mandokoro*) and, after his death, consolidated their hold on this power by ruthlessly eliminating anyone they perceived as a threat.

Their position became imperiled after Yoritomo's final surviving son, Sanetomo (1192–1219, *shōgun* 1203–19), was assassinated in 1219. Sensing an opportunity, the Retired Emperor Go-Toba (1183–1239; r. 1183–98) declared war on the Hōjō, and argued that they were upstarts who had no rationale for any governing authority whatsoever. Go-Toba erred, however, in attempting to assert the authority to appoint and divest *jitō* of their cherished posts. A majority of these *jitō* joined the Hōjō, who had been preparing for a conflict, and may have even goaded Go-Toba into declaring war against them.

Although the Jōkyū War of 1221 lasted a mere six weeks, it proved decisive in a way that the earlier twelfth century conflicts had not. The Hōjō triumph allowed them to ensure that a shogunate would continue in Kamakura and, in the aftermath of the war, more *jitō* were appointed throughout Japan.

Kamakura's victory shocked many—warriors, courtiers, and monks alike—into rethinking the nature of imperial authority and the relationship of Buddhism and the state. The power of Retired Emperors, and their ability to meddle in provincial land rights, was thwarted. To the practical Hōjō, the war illustrated the relative ease with which they could consolidate their hold on political power as long as they had the support of provincial warriors.

After 1221, a series of Hōjō leaders established regulations and institutions of governance that helped usher in a period later recalled as a golden age. Their greatest governing accomplishment was a law code, the Jōei Formulary, promulgated in 1232. The laws provided guidelines for the transmission of *jitō* posts, giving the *jitō* freedom to determine who succeeded to their post. The Jōei Code, a foundational document, provided broader rights to a larger percentage of the population (both male and female), than did the English Magna Carta of 1215, to which it is sometimes compared.

After 1232, warrior status was linked to the prestigious office of *jitō*, the manager of an estate with local policing and judicial authority. This position guaranteed its holder revenue from the estate and authority over its inhabitants. Additionally, they exercised authority over all who lived in their house. *Jitō* rights could be bequeathed to offspring, or adopted heirs, which led to many inheritance disputes and the practice of dividing these lands among siblings. In some cases, the recipient of these *jitō* rights took the name of the lands they possessed. Both men and women could inherit lands, and brothers and sisters could adopt new surnames at will, often choosing to pick the name of where they resided as their new family name. These *jitō* became increasingly autonomous and were mostly concerned with the preservation of their household.

Scholars have characterized the period of 1221 to 1333 as consisting of a Dual Polity, where the court ruled alongside Kamakura. Sovereign affairs, state rites,

Introduction

and most taxes still went to the court, while Kamakura *shugo* provided stability in the provinces through their policing abilities and their ability to mobilize warriors for guard duty. The court was reorganized, with its laws and administration revitalized during the latter half of the thirteenth century.

Together, the court and Kamakura successfully defended Japan against the Mongol invasion attempts of 1274 and 1281. More than the damages suffered, which were limited to the Hakata region of northern Kyushu, the systemic need to maintain defense efforts, through guard duty or ongoing maledictions, led to concerted administrative reforms. Scholars have suggested that Kamakura lacked the lands and new *jitō* posts to reward its warriors and that this led to this later unrest. But much of the evidence suggests that Kamakura's new administrative policies caused the most turmoil.

Previously, Kamakura had promoted the notion of inalienable *jitō* rights. But in their quest to adjudicate cases more efficiently, they demanded that *jitō* appear in court by the third summons. Previously, some had avoided up to seventy of such commands. In the 1280s, Kamakura started enforcing this writ and confiscated the lands of those who failed to obey. Though these regulations made administrative sense, the *jitō* warriors felt that Kamakura was exceeding its mandate and encroaching on their own rights. They began to see Kamakura as being unjust. Some took to violence, openly defending their lands, and were described in the sources as being *akutō*, or brigands. Though Marxist historians have seen the *akutō* as being disgruntled marginal figures from below, they were predominantly local warriors upset with Kamakura's policies and willing to use violence to assert their local rights. Many *shugo* were in broad sympathy with them, so when commanded to find and apprehend *akutō*, they did so half-heartedly.

More than warriors, or the so-called *akutō*, it was the court that proved to be the most destabilizing presence. Many courtiers felt the events of 1221 had put Japan on the wrong path and agitated for a return of powerful emperors, whose powers had been reduced since the time of the Jōkyū War. Animosity was directed toward Kamakura because its officials would ultimately determine who, among several competing candidates to the throne, would be Emperor. One Retired Emperor (Kameyama 1249–1305; r. 1259–74) went so far as to employ a warrior in an attempt to assassinate the reigning emperor in 1290—an attempt that failed spectacularly (see Excerpt from "The Light and Shadows of the Day," *The Clear Mirror (Masukagami)* p. 100).

A new coalition—one comprised of ambitious nobles, an aggrieved Emperor, and dissatisfied *jitō*—arose and succeeded in overthrowing Kamakura and killing nearly all the Hōjō in 1333. These anti-Kamakura allies had remarkably divergent world views: Emperor Go-Daigo (1288–1339; r. 1318–31, 1333–36) expressed a desire to rule as a powerful autocrat; Ashikaga Takauji (1305–58), the most prominent warrior who survived the turmoil of 1333, saw himself as the natural successor to the post of *Sei-i-tai shōgun*; and the *jitō* believed removing Kamakura would enhance their rights. Unpleasantly surprised when the triumphant Go-Daigo asserted ultimate control over their rights, the *jitō* threw their support to Ashikaga Takauji. In 1335 Takauji rebelled against Go-Daigo, unleashing decades of civil war.

Ashikaga Takauji and the Wars of the Fourteenth Century

Immediately after the fall of Kamakura, Ashikaga Takauji acted as if he was a *Sei-i-tai shōgun*, even though he initially had no such appointment. Go-Daigo undermined Takauji's support by dispatching imperial princes loyal to him throughout Japan. He also revitalized the office of the Pacification General (Chinjufu *shōgun*) and appointed the young Minamoto court official Kitabatake Akiie (1318–38) to this position. From 1335 through 1338 wars raged, with no clear outcome in sight, until the Chinjufu *shōgun* Kitabatake Akiie was killed in battle in 1338 along with another general named Nitta Yoshisada (1301–38). That year Takauji was appointed to the office of *Sei-i-tai shōgun*, a position his descendants would hold through 1573. The defeated Go-Daigo fled to Yoshino in 1336 and founded what is known to posterity as the Southern Court. Though Go-Daigo died in 1339, his supporters continued to resist for decades.

The warriors of this period of turmoil did not feel that they were obligated to serve a lord. To the contrary, they believed that lords were required to compensate warriors for their service, and so an elaborate system for recording and verifying battle service was created in order that battle service could be verified and compensated.

Although loyalty to a lord would become a hallmark of how warriors were remembered, the notion of loyalty was valued more highly at the court than it was among warriors. Warriors with lands prized their autonomy. Although they expected obedience from landless members of their own households, they were loath to follow a lord. Nevertheless, the expenses of warfare proved prohibitive and, when paying for their armor and provisions for campaigns lasting many years, warriors had to sell their houses or borrow horses and other accoutrements from either the commoners (*hyakushō*) residing on their estates or sympathetic generals.

To help diminish the burden of war, which had been exacerbated by the turmoil of the 1350s, Takauji delegated great powers of taxation to holders of the post of *shugo*. That position had existed for centuries, but it was more of a policing office. After Takauji allowed its holder to levy taxes on half of a province's revenues, *shugo* used this authority to maintain durable armies and to embark upon the path of becoming regional warlords. The *shugo* had the resources to wage wars indefinitely; the old *jitō*, who found the campaigns prohibitively expensive, did not. The wars of the fourteenth century petered out, and the Southern Court finally surrendered in 1392, thereby ending this period of disunion.

The Ashikaga Heyday (1368–1441)

In 1350, the provincial constables known as *shugo* were given the right to use half of a province's revenues for military provisions. This was known as the "half-tax" (*hanzei*). As a result, over the course of the next century, these *shugo* became incipient provincial magnates. The previously autonomous *jitō* were no longer able to fight in war; they gradually became subsumed into these regional armies, whose leaders were increasingly known as *daimyō*.

Even though Takauji's half-tax, or *hanzei*, was an extraordinary levy initially allowed only in a time of warfare, *shugo* did not give up this authority. They instead maintained these revenues, sometimes confiscating the holdings of delinquent landholders, including some *jitō*. As had been the case before the *hanzei*, the court and the Ashikaga had access to half of the revenue, although Ashikaga leaders did also assess innovative taxes on trade.

Despite the limitations imposed on central power by the *hanzei*, three Ashikaga leaders—Yoshimitsu (1358–1408), Yoshimochi (1386–1428), and Yoshinori (1394–1441)—continued to exercise great authority through 1441. Symbolizing their rule was a new imperial residence on Muromachi Street in Kyoto, which has given its name to the age. Though the court remained, imperial power was undermined by Yoshimitsu, the third Ashikaga *shōgun*.

In 1392, having defeated the Southern Court, Ashikaga Yoshimitsu abdicated the post in favor of his son Yoshimochi. He did not govern as a *shōgun*, but instead acted first as a high-ranking courtier, then by assuming the prerogatives of the sovereign. Yoshimitsu was thus able to overawe *shugo* and force them to use their newfound wealth for his projects. In one case, he had them level a mountain in order to expand a pond in his garden. Yoshimitsu did isolate, attack, and militarily defeat the most powerful *shugo*, the Yamana, in 1391 and the Ōuchi in 1399. In 1402, the Chinese Ming Emperor recognized Yoshimitsu as the King of Japan; Yoshimitsu was then able to use his political ties to control lucrative trade with China. With his wealth, he built a lavish

Golden Pavilion (Kinkakuji), with a nine-story pagoda located nearby, in the region known as Kitayama to the immediate northwest of Kyoto. He named one of his sons an imperial Crown Prince, but his plans for this son's enthronement as Emperor came to naught when Yoshimitsu died suddenly in 1408.

Yoshimitsu's son Yoshimochi adopted a dramatically different pattern of rule, preferring to act as more of a warrior than a courtier or sovereign. During the period of his rule as *shōgun*—from 1408 through 1429—Yoshimochi governed through consultations with *shugo*. He did not overawe them, although he could effectively manipulate the *shugo*. He abandoned Kitayama, his title of "King of Japan," and even the Muromachi mansion. Of the *shugo*, he most favored the Ōuchi. They helped the Ashikaga govern in the west and took a leading role in trade with the continent. As they controlled mines in the west, they profited immensely from trade and were able to loan funds to the Ashikaga in the 1460s.

After Yoshimochi's death, his brother Yoshinori became *shōgun*. Yoshinori attempted to rule as an autocrat, going so far as to execute cooks for mistakes, or force courtiers into starvation as punishment. Yoshinori also poisoned some *shugo* and meddled in their succession until Mitsusuke (1381–1441), the leader of the trusted Akamatsu *shugo* family, assassinated him.

Although Ashikaga would hold this post of *Sei-i-tai shōgun* until 1573, they only governed Japan in a meaningful way from the late fourteenth century through 1441. Their regime had no such authority during the long century of its decline.

In the resulting turmoil, and the decline of Ashikaga authority, many *shugo* gained influence. The office of *shugo* proved powerful, for it allowed magnates to mobilize and command armies, but it was also destabilizing, as tensions over succession often led to political and military skirmishes. Because the *hanzei* gave *shugo* direct access to provincial tax revenue, *shugo* could mobilize and maintain what amounted to standing armies. *Shugo* logistical prowess led to improvements in military organization, as they could create massed formations of infantry capable of occupying territory. This happened in the 1450s, and the Hatakeyama were forerunners in this innovation.

The Rise of the Ōuchi and the Ōnin War (1441–1551)

The rise of the inept eighth *shōgun*, Yoshimasa (1436–90), led to an intense civil war. Though Yoshimasa tried to be a powerful *shōgun* like Yoshinori, he simultaneously antagonized multiple *shugo* houses, most prominently the Ōuchi. Yoshimasa's misguided attempt to confiscate their harbors, an action unacceptable to Ōuchi

Introduction

Masahiro (1446–95), led him to fight openly against the Ashikaga in 1465. In 1467, Masahiro led an armada to Kyoto. There, a conflict was waged for over a decade. It is named the Ōnin War after the era when fierce battles were fought in Kyoto. Masahiro, allied with Yamana Sōzen, established a "Western Army," and fought Ashikaga Yoshimasa, whose forces, known as the "Eastern Army," were directed by Shogunal Chancellor (*kanrei*) Hosokawa Katsumoto. Although the war is commonly thought to have occurred from 1467 through 1477, analysis of the Ōuchi's role in it indicates that it lasted from 1465 to 1478.

At the end of the Ōnin War, Ōuchi Masahiro returned to Yamaguchi. This city became a thriving and stable urban center. Ōuchi laws reveal the peace and stability in their western territories: curfews in Yamaguchi were enforced, its streets were swept, and the Ōuchi lords complained of people gawking at their gardens. By contrast, in this same period Kyoto experienced decay and ruin in the aftermath of the devastating war fought there because Yoshimasa was incapable of effective governance. Ashikaga Yoshimasa nevertheless began construction on a retirement villa known as the Silver Pavilion, which, in fact, was a building coated in black lacquer.

After Yoshimasa's death, the forces of the *kanrei* Hosokawa Masamoto (1466–1507) ousted the *Shōgun* Yoshitane (1466–1523) in a coup. Yoshitane escaped and ultimately fled to Yamaguchi. After Masamoto was killed by one of his disgruntled retainers, Yoshioki (1477–1529), the next Ōuchi lord, again led an army to Kyoto. Allying himself with Hosokawa Takakuni (1484–1531), head of a branch line of the Hosokawa, Yoshioki decisively defeated the main line of the Hosokawa at the battle of Funaoka. From 1508 until 1518, Yoshioki occupied the capital, eventually returning to Yamaguchi. The powerless Ashikaga remained in Kyoto. Having confiscated their King of Japan seals, Yoshioki was able to monopolize trade with the continent. This continued with his son Ōuchi Yoshitaka (1507–51), who oversaw the export of tons of Japanese silver to Korea and China.

While the west enjoyed relative peace and prosperity, eastern Japan experienced more turmoil. The Date codes of 1536 reveal a much-impoverished domain. The region continued to rely on the *jitō* for governance, even though the position had been largely eliminated elsewhere in the country. Eastern landholders exhibited considerable local authority, a level of autonomy unthinkable in the Ōuchi domains. The western peace lasted until 1551. Ōuchi Yoshitaka was felled by a coup as he was preparing to move his capital to Kyoto. By 1557, his entire lineage lost power, western Japan descended into turmoil, and Japan was convulsed by war from 1551 through 1573.

Introduction

The Arrival of the Europeans

When, in 1543, the Portuguese landed at Tanegashima, to the south of Kyushu, they brought with them guns and cannon, and these new weapons had a profound impact on the Japanese way of war. Initially, the Japanese, unfamiliar with Europe, assumed the Portuguese were Buddhist monks from India. Gradually, of course, they learned a great deal about Europe from the newly arrived Portuguese.

In military terms, gunpowder mattered as much, if not more, than the guns themselves, and one recipe for it was transmitted from Ōtomo Sōrin (1530–87), a Kyushu lord, to Uesugi Kenshin (1530–78) in the east (see the Portuguese Recipe for Gunpowder, p. 231). Several documents composed by Ōtomo Sōrin in 1580 are translated here and reproduced along with images of his saddle, which bore the monogram FRCO for "Francisco," the new name he adopted upon his conversion to Christianity sometime between 1578 and 1580 (see Photo of Ōtomo Francisco [Sōrin] Saddle, p. 226, and Images 13–15). A cannon he received, also bearing the FRCO monogram, is depicted here as well (Images 14–16). (This cannon ended up in St. Petersburg, after being captured by Russian forces in the nineteenth century when, having taken control of Siberia, they probed Japanese defenses of their northern islands.)

The warlord Oda Nobunaga (1534–82), who expelled Yoshiaki, the last Ashikaga *shōgun* in 1573, effectively used guns in battle during the 1575 battle of Nagashino (see Ōta Gyūichi, *The Chronicle of Lord Nobunaga*, p. 235), when he defeated the Takeda, a rival. Nobunaga subjugated many rivals but was killed by Akechi Mitsuhide (1528–82), one of his own generals, in 1582. Toyotomi Hideyoshi (?–1598), another one of Nobunaga's generals, then gained power. Hideyoshi, through a series of profound transformations, created the *samurai* order. The term *samurai* means "one who serves"; in this case, the now-landless warriors were obligated to serve and reside near a *daimyō* lord. Their status, and its constituent income, depended on ties to a lord. Those *samurai* who did not have direct investiture or a lord became known as *rōnin*, "masterless" *samurai*, or "wave men."

Hideyoshi forced warriors either to live on their lands and become "peasants" (*hyakushō*), a term which previously meant all commoners in general, or to leave the lands and become *samurai* (see Toyotomi Hideyoshi's Edict Concerning the Collection of Swords, p. 242; and Toyotomi Hideyoshi's Edict Regarding the Separation of Status, p. 243). Divorced from the countryside, *samurai* became urban dwellers in the newly established castle towns.

Hideyoshi based his concept of social status on revenue—in particular, the amount of rice a single person required in a year; this measurement was known as a *koku*. To be considered a *daimyō*, or great lord, a man had to have 10,000 *koku* or more at his disposal. He also initiated an ill-conceived attempt to conquer Ming China, which led to two invasions of Korea, in 1592 and 1597. Hideyoshi's armies never made it to China as Ming troops pushed his forces back, until they withdrew after his death.

The Samurai of the Tokugawa Era (1603–1867)

Shortly after Hideyoshi's death in 1598, Tokugawa Ieyasu (1543–1616)—a rival warlord and follower of Oda Nobunaga—took up arms against the Toyotomi supporters, winning the battle of Sekigahara against them in 1600. He put many Hideyoshi supporters to death or confiscated their properties; some of Tokugawa's enemies, such as the Uesugi and the Mōri, survived in much reduced circumstances, while only a few, such as the Shimazu, maintained their earlier power. In 1603, Tokugawa Ieyasu was appointed as *Sei-i-tai shōgun* and his descendants could justify their rule by governing through this this office through 1867. In 1615, Ieyasu destroyed the forces of Toyotomi Hideyoshi's wife and son and immediately thereafter codified his rule in the *buke shohatto* (see The *Buke Shohatto* of 1615, p. 264). These warrior codes were revised by Tokugawa Ieyasu's grandson Iemitsu (1604–51) in 1635 (see The Revised *Buke Shohatto* of 1635, p. 265).

The warrior codes of conduct established in the *buke shohatto* prohibited *daimyō* from having interactions with the imperial court. These *daimyō* could only have a single castle in their domains, and had to travel to the Tokugawa headquarters, a new city called Edo, located in eastern Japan, where their families were required to reside. Edo's population grew to over a million over the course of the eighteenth century. Yet the Japanese worldview seemed to narrow even as the urban center of Edo continued to grow: Japanese people were forbidden from traveling abroad and even required permission to travel within Japan. The faith of Christianity was banned, along with some sects of Nichiren Buddhism which did not acknowledge the primacy of Tokugawa authority.

As Japan experienced a certain level of peace and prosperity in the Tokugawa era, the need for fighting *samurai* waned, and these warriors slowly took on the roles of administrators, or local officials. Former *samurai* tended to look back nostalgically at their fiercer fighting days. Some wrote treatises explaining arms and armor; others studied Confucianism; still others studied marital arts. Some intellectuals, such as Kumazawa Banzan (1619–91) (see Kumazawa Banzan, "Abolition of the Separate Soldier Class," p. 267), argued that the removal of *samurai* from the land had enervated their military prowess. He referred to their lackluster attempts to quell a Christian uprising at Shimabara in 1637, during which the Christian rebels were able to kill a commanding Tokugawa general with a good shot from one of their cannons. Though they were defeated and slaughtered in the end, Kumazawa Banzan's critiques of policy of separating the *samurai* from the land had merit. Some *samurai* wrote in their diaries how they fainted at the sight of blood. Other *samurai* used their status and authority to become tax collectors even when they had no right to do so (see *Musui's Story: The Autobiography of a Tokugawa Samurai*, p. 280).

During the seventeenth century, the old bonds of warriors to their lands were sometimes recalled, however, such as when one murderous *samurai*, who became a serial killer, fled to his ancestral lands, where he was protected by his peasants (see Arai Hakuseki's *Autobiography*, p. 272). In general, though, *samurai* became urban dwellers, removed from villages, save for times when they traveled to extort extra taxes from these regions. Yet again, experiences differ, as some villages were hostile to their lords and remote from them (most notably Goganzuka village; see *Musui's Story*), while in other cases, villagers like Jinmori Heizō fought valiantly for their lord and supported the well-being of their domain as a whole (see *The Testament of Shiba Gorō*, p. 292).

The Collapse of the Tokugawa and the End of the Samurai (1867–77)

As the Tokugawa regime buckled under foreign pressure to engage in diplomatic relations with America and other nations, it also loosened the strictures imposed on *samurai* by the *buke shohatto*. Some domains immediately established ties with the imperial court and bought weapons, two developments which led directly to the wars that brought down the Tokugawa. The Tokugawa surrendered in 1867, but battles continued between *daimyō* forces of the west (Chōshū and Satsuma) and the northeast (Aizu Wakamatsu), who were allied with different factions. The *samurai* of Aizu Wakamatsu, in the northeast, were badly outmaneuvered and defeated, suffering casualties among men, women, and children (see *The Testament of Shiba Gorō*, p. 292, and Two Petitions for Reward [*gunchūjō*] Submitted in 1869, p. 297).

A new imperial government, known by the new era name of Meiji, or Enlightened Rule, took power in 1868. Forces from western Japan—in particular, the domains of Chōshū and Satsuma, nominally ruled by the Mōri and Shimazu families, respectively—dominated this new regime. Among the other reforms instituted by the Meiji government was the reestablishment of a conscription army.

Introduction

The *samurai* right to bear arms was formally abolished in 1876 (see *The Japan Mail: Abolishing of the Samurai Right to Wear Swords*, p. 300), but that year and the following year of 1877, witnessed massive rebellions in the west. The most famous of these uprisings was led by Saigō Takamori (1828–77) (see *The Diary of Kidō Takayoshi*, p. 302), an ex-Meiji leader from Satsuma. Saigō captured a local armory and tried to capture the castle of Kumamoto but was outgunned by the newly conscripted army and defeated. The *samurai* order was then dissolved, although it would linger in Okinawa until 1914.

In later centuries, however, the idea of the "Way of the Warrior," which had been debated in the Tokugawa era, became idealized as an ethical system, that of *Bushidō*, which had little to do with actual warrior behavior. Idealizations of the Japanese warriors and their imagined ethical system, if not the warriors themselves, live on in popular culture as an ideal which had passed beyond the boundaries of Japan to become a trope of the human condition and world culture.

A Note on Dates: The sources translated in this text rely on the Japanese lunar calendar, which does not correspond to the Julian or Gregorian calendars. Hence, months will be referred to numerically throughout the text.

A Note on Names: Full names of Japanese men will contain the genitive *no* particle only for sources dating from early times through the twelfth century. As this practice was eventually abandoned, names from the thirteenth century onward will not include this particle.

SECTION I

The Story of Swords: Understanding the Warriors of Ancient Japan (471–900)

From the earliest times, swords were prized objects in Japan. The inscriptions found on swords provide some of the most extensive examples of early writing in the archipelago. These inscriptions also provide the best evidence about the earliest warriors and the ways in which swords were used as gifts and symbols of allegiance.

This section tells the story of ancient Japanese warriors through five swords created between 471 and 811. The oldest sword was discovered at the Inariyama tomb in Saitama, and the second oldest at Eta Funayama, hundreds of miles to the west in Kyushu. The inscriptions on these swords are among the earliest known examples of writing in Japan.

1. An Inscription on the Sakitama-Inariyama Sword[1]

The Sakitama-Inariyama sword was discovered in a mounded tomb in Saitama, in eastern Japan, in 1978.[2] The inscription on this sword mentions the Great King Wakatakeru, or Emperor Yūryaku, who reigned from 456 until 479. "Shingai" is the name of a year in a cyclical sixty-year Chinese cycle. Though the word shingai was used to refer to the years 471 and 531, other evidence from the sword indicates it was forged in 471. Yūryaku was apparently discredited after his death, and this once-valued sword became the possession of a less prominent relative.

---

1. Translated by Thomas Conlan with Yoshikawa Shinji.
2. For more on this sword in English, see Anzawa and Jun'ichi, "Two Inscribed Swords from Japanese Tumuli," 380. For an alternate translation of this sword, and further analysis, see Lurie, *Realms of Literacy*, 94.

Remarkably, this sword was found in a small coffin buried in a mounded tomb. The person buried there was a later descendant of the figure for whom the tomb was made and lacked the authority to have his own tomb; instead, he was buried humbly in his ancestors' tomb. The tomb itself predates Yūryaku, but the coffin was dated from well after Yūryaku's time.

[This inscription was] recorded in the seventh month in the year of *shingai* (471). Wowake-no-*Ōmi*'s forefather's name was Ōhiko. His son was Takari-no-*sukune*. His son was Teyokari-*wake* by name. His son was Takahishi-*wake* by name. His son was Tasaki-*wake* by name. His son was Hatehi by name. His son was Kasahaya by name. His son was Wowake-no-*Ōmi* by name. From generation to generation, we have served as the heads of the Sword Bearers [and continue to do so] to this day. When the Great King Wakatakeru [Yūryaku] was in the Palace of Shiki, I helped [him] rule over the nation. Let [the swordsmith] make this hundred-times wrought sharp sword, recording the origins of my service.[3]

---

3. The differing titles, or *kabane* of the sword, indicate differences in rank. Those without titles, such as Hatehi or Kasahaya, were not influential. The most remarkable individual mentioned in the sword, Ōhiko, corresponds with Ōhiko-no-mikoto in the *Kojiki* (the oldest written account dating from 712 [Ōpo-biko-no-mikoto in the Philippi translation]) and Ōho-hiko in the *Nihon shoki*, the second history of Japan, written in 720.

The Sakitama-Inariyama sword of 471. The inscription on the blade represents one of the earliest known instances of written Japanese and the use of the Chinese cyclical calendar.

2. A Fifth-Century Sword from the Eta Funayama Tomb[4]

Three groups of people were buried in the tomb, with the sword bearer among the second, or middle, group. As in the case of the sword discussed above, the placement of this sword owner's body suggests he was a person of less than exalted status buried in an older tomb. Eta Funayama, where this sword was found, is in Kyushu, near the Iwai region and a source of silver. The author of the inscription, Chang An, most likely came to Japan from either China or the Korean peninsula.

During the Reign of the Great King Wakatakeru (Wakatakeru-no-Ōkimi), I served as a transmitter of records (*tensō ni tsukae matsuru hito*). My name is Murite. In the middle of the eighth month, I received a great iron cauldron and a four-foot-long sword (*teitō*), the metal of which had been folded over eighty or ninety times. The sword blade is three inches long[5] and of high quality. Those who shall bear this

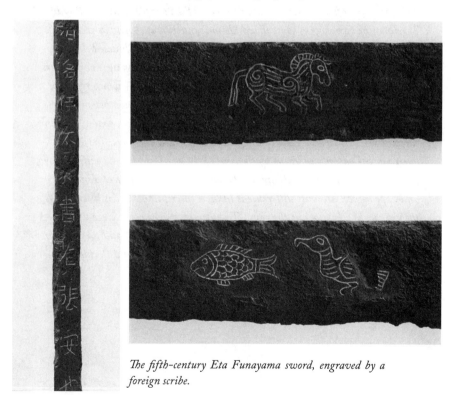

The fifth-century Eta Funayama sword, engraved by a foreign scribe.

---

4. Translated by Thomas Conlan with Yoshikawa Shinji.
5. This is a mistake and should read "three feet long." The scribe made an error.

sword shall live long, and their descendants will prosper and will receive rewards (*on*). They must also not lose possessions that they control. He who made this sword is named Itawa. He who wrote these words is named Chang An.

3. Bright (*yang*) Sword and Shadow (*yin*) Sword[6]

In the seventh century, Japan became a powerful polity, one capable of conducting a census, creating a system of conscription, and establishing a large capital and administrative centers. In response to political turmoil and illnesses such as smallpox, which ravaged the land, one Emperor, Shōmu, decided to build a temple dedicated to Rushana (*Sanskrit* Vairocana), *the Cosmic Buddha. It was the largest wooden structure in the world at the time, and people from India, China, and elsewhere attended the eye-opening ceremonies in 752. In 2010, two swords were discovered at the base of the temple's statue of Buddha. Together, the two swords symbolized Shōmu's martial authority as well as the importance of complementary* yin-yang *ideals. In ancient Chinese belief, the Great Ultimate was made up of two complementary forces:* yang, *which refers to brightness, heaven, activity, light, and maleness, and* yin, *which refers to darkness, passivity, absorption, and femaleness. The interaction between these two forces was thought to create the five phases of metal, wood, water, fire, and earth. These two swords were catalogued as important offerings. They were buried at the base of the statue by the time of the death of Shōmu's wife, Kōmyō, in the year 760. Both swords are nearly identical in length (2 feet 6 inches) and appearance. The only difference is in their inscriptions: one is inscribed as the* yin *sword, the other as the* yang. *Together, the two swords were used to symbolize the importance of complementary* yin-yang *ideals, and presumably, the complementary role of the state in protecting Buddhism and Buddhism protecting the state.*

---

6. Translated by Thomas Conlan.

3. Bright (yang) Sword and Shadow (yin) Sword

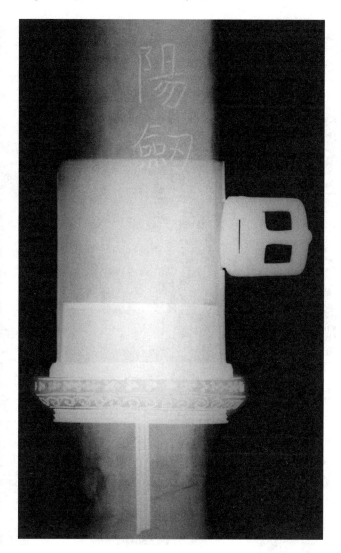

A photo and X-ray of Bright Sword (yang). This sword was buried at the base of Tōdaiji temple and symbolized the protection of the realm. The name "Bright" is visible only in the X-ray image.

Section I • The Story of Swords: Understanding the Warriors of Ancient Japan

A photo and X-ray of Shadow (yin) Sword. Together, this sword and Bright Sword (yang) represent the traditional Chinese belief that "bright" and "shadow" are complementary cosmological forces.

4. Sword of Sakanoue no Tamuramaro

In the year 749 gold was discovered in northern Japan. The region proved very productive: approximately two hundred pounds of gold a year were mined. Initially, the gold was intended solely for use in the Rushana statue of Tōdaiji, but it soon became the basis for Japanese continental trade. In 774, the emishi, *or "barbarians" of the northern reaches of Honshu, launched a rebellion, and in 780 they conquered or destroyed several major Japanese forts and administrative structures, such as Fort Taga in the north. This barbarian incursion initiated a thirty-eight-year war for control of the north.*

In 797 and 804, Sakanoue no Tamuramaro was granted the authority to wage war as he saw fit in the north with his appointment as Sei-i-tai shōgun *(or "Barbarian-Subduing General"). He pacified the* emishi *and expanded the Japanese state's control farther north, bringing an end to the conflict. After his success, his appointment to this office ended, and he returned to Kyoto, where, after his death, he was buried with his trusty sword. This sword, which has no inscription, was first discovered in 1919. In 2007, Professor Yoshikawa Shinji of Kyoto University identified this grave as belonging to Sakanoue no Tamuramaro. Its style is consistent with ninth-century blades and, as a sign of the prestige of its bearer, it most unusually has gold fittings attached. After Tamuramaro's passing, order would be maintained by the Chinjufu* shōgun *who exercised authority over the Six Districts of Mutsu Province in the north through 1083. This Six-District Army would remain as a viable institution until it was destroyed by Minamoto no Yoritomo in 1189.*

The sword of Sakanoue no Tamuramaro, appointed as Japan's first "Barbarian-Subduing General," in 797 and 804.

SECTION II
Warriors and the Court (900–1150)

The Tale of Genji, written by Murasaki Shikibu, the daughter of a provincial governor, provides a unique portrait of the warriors of her age. Born around the year 973, she accompanied her father, Fujiwara no Tametoki, to the province of Echizen, where he served as a provincial governor in the year 996. She was in her early twenties at the time and would have undoubtedly attracted many suitors there. Shikibu later returned to the capital and served the Empress Shōshi at the court. She wrote her famous novel around the year 1007 or 1008.

The complex world of the Heian warrior is vividly evoked in the passage reproduced below. This episode reveals that Shikibu was sensitive to the importance her audience—members of the court and the sons and daughters of provincial governors—placed on proper language and skill in poetry. It also reveals that warriors in the provinces, even powerful ones, were beholden to and enamored of courtiers.

Here, one doughty warrior, known by his title "the Commissioner," tries to marry Tamakazura, whose mother had died and who was looked after by her mother's nurse. The nurse pretended that the girl was the granddaughter of the Dazai Assistant. The Dazai Assistant had been appointed to an important diplomatic and administrative post in Kyushu, four hundred miles west from the capital, but his sudden death put his "granddaughter" in a precarious position. Members of his household moved to Hizen Province in Kyushu. Tamakazura's "grandmother" (actually her mother's nurse) had to deal with her "granddaughter's" many suitors, including the Commissioner (who was more attracted to the girl for her status than appearance) from the neighboring province of Higo. Although the Commissioner offered to serve her half-brothers as a retainer and to treat Tamakazura as his "empress," one can also detect his lingering resentment about the capital. Although he is mocked for his poor poetic skills, poor manners, and uncouth language, Shikibu's narrative professes grudging admiration of his health and strength. His offer to treat the young girl well, however gallant, carries undertones of menace.

The following, contrasting passage from a court diary offers insights to a courtier's life; the author of this text practiced martial arts, threw rocks at neighbors, and successfully established networks of patronage with provincial warriors. Nevertheless, revolts and uprisings did occur, and short accounts of two major events, the failed uprising (935–40) of Taira no Masakado and the *Tale of Mutsu*, whereby warriors struggled for control over a northern army in the mid-eleventh century, are here reproduced.

1. Excerpt from "Tamakazura," The Tale of Genji

Command of the Six-District Army of the North—whose commanders exhibited great autonomy and, simply by virtue of their location, controlled access to great wealth in the gold-rich north—was hotly contested throughout the eleventh century. Abe no Yoritoki (?–1057) was the commander of this army. But in 1051 Minamoto no Yoriyoshi (988?–1082?), a provincial governor from Mutsu, attempted to seize control of it. Yoriyoshi and his son Yoshiie (1039–1106) would eventually be remembered as important warrior leaders. From 1051 through 1063 they fought the Abe, first Yoritoki and then his son Sadatō (1019–62), in a conflict known as the "Former Nine Year's War." Though Yoriyoshi won the war and killed Abe no Sadatō, court officials believed that Yoriyoshi had exceeded his authority and recalled him to the capital, to which he returned yet was unrewarded for his victories. He did, however, found a shrine dedicated to Hachiman, a god of war, in what would later be the city of Kamakura. After the death of the Abe, a new family, the Kiyohara, gained control of the Six-District Army.

Yoriyoshi's son Yoshiie was again appointed governor of Mutsu in 1083, and he fought the "Latter Three Years War," which lasted until 1087. He successfully ousted the Kiyohara, but, like his father Yoriyoshi, he was recalled, and a new group, the Fujiwara of the north, took control of the army, albeit through the office of Military Envoy of Mutsu Province (*ōryōshi*). These Fujiwara founded a remarkable settlement at a place called Hiraizumi, where they built grand temples, including one coated in gold. They ruled this area for over three generations until they were destroyed by the forces of Minamoto no Yoritomo (1147–99) in 1189.

---

1. Excerpt from "Tamakazura," *The Tale of Genji*[1]

Murasaki Shikibu's father was a provincial governor, and she undoubtedly knew powerful provincial warriors. Her portrait here of the Commissioner is quite remarkable, as it shows how fawning he was in an attempt to intermarry with nobles, whom provincial warriors saw as their superiors. The Commissioner even tried to master poetry, albeit with poor effect. When he failed in his wooing of a court lady, he ominously criticizes courtiers for their arrogance.

They lived in the province of Hizen. All men of some quality living in the area desired the granddaughter of the Secretary of the Assistant Deputy of the Dazaifu

---

1. Translated by Thomas Conlan.

and pursued her unceasingly. It was a nuisance. One of these men, the Commissioner (*Taifu no gen*), had many relatives throughout the province of Higo. He was popular and ambitious and led a strong band of warriors. Though fierce, he was a womanizer as well, and liked to collect pretty young girls. He said about her, "Even if she is gruesome, I will ignore it and look after her." His persistence upset the nurse, who said, "This is impossible. She cannot listen to this as she is about to become a nun." Hearing this stirred him to action and he arrived in their province. There he told her half-brothers that if they let him have his heart's wish, he would abide by their command, and accordingly two of them decided to help him. . . .

Not knowing the opposition of some in her household to the match, the Commissioner, who saw himself as being cultured, sent her many letters, written on colorful, richly perfumed Chinese paper. His handwriting was not bad at all, although he had a provincial accent. He then convinced the second eldest half-brother to escort him to her house.

He was about thirty years old and was a towering figure (*jō takaku*), powerfully built, and not at all ugly, but rough and intimidating. Although he was of ruddy health, his voice rasped like withered leaves, and he spoke in some impossible-to-understand dialect. . . .

Not wishing to offend him, the lady's "grandmother"[2] came out to meet him.

He spoke most fervently. "The late Secretary of the Assistant Deputy of the Dazaifu was compassionate—a shining man—and I had long looked forward to the opportunity to talk with him. I am sad that he passed before I could tell him of my wish. I would like to serve you in place of him. I feel this so strongly that I have come here today. This young princess, of exceptional lineage, is too good for me, and it pains me to make this request. I intend to make her my liege and will treat her with the greatest care. I know that this request must pain you, and, yes, I am sure that you must have heard that I have a number of unworthy women. But rest assured—they cannot ever be compared to her. She, my liege, will be like an empress to me."

"You speak most marvelously, but how can you say such things?" the nurse replied. "She suffers because of some wrong in her past life. You should stay away from her. I find it sorrowful to see her in such despair, as she knows that because of her condition she can't be seen by others."

"Don't worry about it! Even if she is totally blind, or broken legged, I will not stop serving her. I have a special connection with the Gods and Buddhas of the land. She will be healed," he boasted. He then demanded that they set the

---

2. Actually, her nurse, but the nurse pretended to be the young lady's grandmother.

wedding day. This month is the end of the season, she said, appealing to rural customs.[3]

He thought that a parting poem was called for and waited for some time in thought.

For her, my lord, if I am untrue
May the Mirror God of Matsura
Reflect my pledge

"I think that poem will do!" he said, smiling to himself. He was not used to poetry.[4]

The nurse was at a loss, and felt quite light-headed, and her daughters, when pressed to reply in her stead, felt even more unsettled than she. Time passed; it seemed like an eternity. Finally, she responded with trembling voice:

For many years, I have prayed
And this is what I get?
I hate the Mirror God

"Wait. What was that you said?" He approached her ominously, and she blanched in fear.

One of her daughters burst out in laughter. "She's really different, you know. Of course, it would be too bad if things don't work out. Grandmother is doddering and really can't come up with a good poem about gods and mirrors."

"Oh, I get it," he said. "What a funny way of expressing yourself. We may be described as being country bumpkins, but there is more to us than that. We are not just 'the people' (*tami*). What is it that is so wonderful about you people of the capital? I've got this all figured out. Don't look down on us." He thought about reciting another poem, but then decided against it and went on his way.

2. Excerpt from *Chūyūki*, the Courtier Journal of Fujiwara no Munetada, 5.20.1108[5]

This 5.20.1108 (Kashō 3) passage from the Chūyūki, *the courtier journal of Fujiwara no Munetada (1062–1141), recounts a dispute involving Fujiwara no Tsunezane and his neighbor. Tsunezane, no model of decorum, threw rocks*

---

3. The end of the season was unsuitable for matches, according to local customs. This allowed the nurse to delay the date of the wedding.
4. Emphasizing that a god would reflect a broken pledge is an inauspicious poem.
5. Translated by Thomas Conlan. Japanese lunar months differ from Julian or Gregorian named months, and will be expressed numerically.

11

at his neighbor's house. One can imagine the boisterous Tsunezane inviting his house warriors who would have resembled the Commissioner of the Tamakazura chapter of The Tale of Genji.

Cloudy, later rain. At the hour of the horse [11 a.m.–1 p.m.] the provisional controller Tametaka dispatched a messenger whose document read as follows: "Over the last seven or eight evenings, rocks (*tsubute*) have been thrown into our house. We inspected the strange circumstances and discovered that the Grand Minister Fujiwara no Tsunezane, who lived in the house to our immediate west, was responsible." This is most unseemly! They were surprised and decided to notify me. I responded as follows: "I don't know why Tsunezane is doing this. But it would be best to avoid your Shichijō residence. Muneyoshi, the captain of the fourth rank is a companion. Could you exchange your house with another place of his?"

That noble Tsunezane is not a first-rate person. He has absolutely no talent, but is a glutton for drink, and invites brave warriors from throughout the realm, and every day and every night they get drunk and unsheathe their swords. They cannot read even a single character. On days of public court affairs, Tsunezane claims to be ill and does not attend; and even though he had no particular reason for doing so, he throws rocks in all four directions. I have heard of these rumors, but there is no cause for enmity. It is best to avoid living near such an evil person.

3. "How Taira no Masakado Raised a Rebellion and Was Killed" and "How the Noble Minamoto no Yoriyoshi Chastised Abe no Sadatō and His Followers," from *Konjaku Monogatari*[6]

The Konjaku Monogatari *is a compilation of tales from China, India, and Japan. This text dates from the eleventh century, and although it was written by someone with ties to the court, it appeared in an accessible style and garnered wide popularity and influence. Accounts of the tenth-century rebellion by Taira no Masakado, as well as the eleventh-century "Tale of Mutsu," are summarized and distilled here. Unlike* The Tale of Genji, *which mostly recounted*

---

6. Excerpts from Wilson, "The Way of the Bow and Arrow," "I. How Taira no Masakado Raised a Rebellion and Was Killed," 190–95, and "XIII. How the Noble Minamoto no Yoriyoshi Chastised Abe no Sadatō and His Followers," 222–31.

3. "How Taira no Masakado Raised a Rebellion and Was Killed"

the view from the court, these tales treat warriors as protagonists in their own right. These passages are abbreviated versions of longer tales, which have been translated elsewhere.

How Taira no Masakado Raised a Rebellion and Was Killed

It is now a long time ago, in the reign of Shujaku no In,[7] that there was a warrior called Taira no Masakado in the Eastern Provinces. He was the son of a man called the *Chinjufu Shōgun* Yoshimochi, who was the son of the Imperial Prince Takamochi, the grandson of the Kashiwabara Emperor. Masakado lived in Hitachi and Shimōsa, and he made weapons the embellishment of his person. Gathering many fierce warriors and making them his companions, he made battle his way of life.

Now at the beginning there was a man called the Vice-Governor of Shimōsa, Yoshikane, the younger brother of Masakado's father, Yoshimochi. After Masakado's father died, he had rather an unfortunate incident with his uncle Yoshikane and fell out with him. Then a dispute about rice lands and fields belonging to the late Yoshimochi finally reached the point of battle, but Yoshikane, being preoccupied with religion and devoted to worship of the Buddhist Law, did not particularly want to fight.

After this Masakado, along with his boon companions, invariably dealt with any matter by having recourse to battle. He burned down many men's houses and he took many men's lives. Because in this way he added only evil deeds to his karma, most of the people of the neighboring lands gave no heed to the cultivation of their rice lands and fields, nor was there time left for them to fulfil their taxes to the government. Thus the people of the provinces were in distress and lamented this state of affairs, and the local authorities sent a letter reporting the matter to the central government in the capital. The central government viewed this with concern and forthwith sent down a decree summoning Masakado to be examined about the matter. Masakado went up to the capital in response to the summons, and on his showing that he was without fault, it was ruled after much deliberation that he had done no wrong. After a few days he was excused and returned to his home country.

But before very long Masakado was once more making battle his main occupation and was incessantly fighting against his uncles Yoshikane and Yoshimasa, as well as against Minamoto no Mamoru and Tasuku. In addition, Taira no Sadamori, who had been in the capital serving in the central government and was a third-class

---

7. Emperor Suzaku (921–52), who reigned from 930–946. Wilson notes that Masakado's rebellion began in 937, and Masakado was killed in 940. [TDC]

official in the Left Horse Bureau, planned to revenge his house because his father Kunika had been struck down by Masakado. Putting aside his duties of office, he hurried down from the capital, but since he could not cope with Masakado's prestige and force he remained hidden in the country unable to carry out his plan.

While the incessant fighting was going on like this, a man called the Acting Governor of Musashi, Prince Okiyo, was of one mind with Masakado. He was not the legitimate provincial governor but had taken the office by force. There was a district governor in that province, but, although he said that there was no precedent for such an action, Prince Okiyo took no heed and rose up against him. Accordingly the district governor hid himself. At this juncture Minamoto no Tsunemoto, the vice-governor of that province, observed the situation and secretly rode up to the capital. He reported the matter to the central government, stating, "Masakado is already concerting with Prince Okiyo, Acting Governor of Musashi, and they mean to make a rebellion." On hearing this the central authorities were concerned, but when enquiry was made as to the truth or falsehood of this charge, Masakado denied that there was any truth in it and produced official letters to this effect from the governments of the five provinces, Hitachi, Shimōsa, Shimotsuke, Musashi and Kazusa. The central government recognized these as correct, and Masakado, far from being blamed, received Imperial approbation.

Now there was a man called Fujiwara no Haruakira from the province of Hitachi. The governor of that province was Fujiwara no Korechika, and Haruakira was insubordinate to him and failed to forward the rice and produce taxes due to the provincial governor. The governor was incensed and tried to take him to task, but he boldly failed to comply. So Haruakira followed the lead of Masakado, joined forces with him, and drove the provincial governor out of his official mansion. Thereupon the provincial governor hid himself and disappeared.

At this time Prince Okiyo held a conference with Masakado and said, "You have certainly managed to take one province; now try taking over the whole country east of the barrier in the same way and see how it goes."

Masakado replied, "This is my plan. I am thinking that, beginning with the Eight Eastern Provinces, I will rule over the capital itself. Indeed, I, Masakado, am the descendant in the fifth generation of the Kashiwabara Emperor. I will first seize the seals and keys of office of the various provinces and drive the provincial governors back to the capital."

Having thus announced his plan, Masakado crossed over to the province of Shimotsuke at the head of a great army. After he had quickly arrived at the provincial headquarters, he put on a ceremonial show. At that time the provincial governor, Fujiwara no Hiromasa, the former governor Onakatomi no Muneyuki and others were in the official mansion and saw that Masakado was about to seize the province. So they first made obeisance to him and then, kneeling on the ground, they offered up the seals and keys and invested him in office. After that they fled away. Masakado then moved over to the province of Kōzuke; he seized the seals and keys of office of the Vice-Governor, Fujiwara no Takanori, gave him a message and drove him back to the capital. After this Masakado held the provincial capitals and occupied the offices; he threw up fortifications and held appointment ceremonies in the various provinces. At this time there was a man who spoke in a trance, and declaring that he had a message from Hachiman Daibosatsu, he pronounced this oracle, "We confer Our Imperial Rank on Our Favored Child, Taira no Masakado. Quickly welcome him reverently with music." On hearing this, Masakado made a double reverence, and his several war-bands all joined in greatly rejoicing. Thereupon Masakado himself made out the official memorial, naming himself New Emperor. An announcement to this effect was then made to the Noble Houses.

At that time a man called Masahira, the younger brother of the New Emperor, said to him, "To reach the position of Emperor is something conferred by Heaven. You had better meditate well on this." The New Emperor replied, "The Way of the Bow and Arrow is enough for me. In these times one is sovereign because one overcomes. Why should I hold back?"

With these words he rejected Masahira's advice and with no further ado he set about assigning the governorships of the several provinces. His younger brother Masayori was appointed governor of Shimotsuke; Taji no Tsuneaki, governor of Kōzuke; Fujiwara no Harumochi, vice-governor of Hitachi; Prince Okiyo, vice-governor of Kazusa; Fun'ya no Yoshitatsu, governor of Awa; Taira no Masafumi, vice-governor of Sagami; Taira no Masatake, governor of Izu; and Taira no Masanari, governor of Shimōsa.

He also made a plan to build a capital at Minami no Tei in Shimōsa. He considered the bridge of Ukitsu as the bridge of Yamazaki at the capital, and he looked upon Ōi no Tsu in Soma District as Ōtsu of the capital. In addition to this he decided who was to be the Great Ministers of Left and Right, the Counsellors, Consultants, the Hundred Officials, the Six Controllers and the Eight Scribes. He fixed the measurements in which the seals of the Emperor and the Great Council of State should be cast, and the standard style of Chinese characters. Yet perhaps his power did not extend to Doctors of the Calendar.

In these circumstances the imperially appointed governors of the several provinces heard of these matters as they leaked out and they all hurried back to the capital. The New Emperor went everywhere around Musashi, Sagami, and the other provinces. He took possession of the seals and keys in all of them and commanded the caretaker District Governors and others to pay him the tributary obligations of government. He also announced to the Great Council of State that he was going to possess the Imperial Position. Everybody, beginning with the central government, was alarmed, and there was no end to the uproar within the Imperial Palace. The government thought it necessary to call on the power of the Buddha and obtain the help of the Gods, and many prayers in both exoteric and esoteric teachings were offered on mountains and in temples everywhere, not to mention in all the shrines.

While all this was going on, the New Emperor returned to Shimōsa from the country of Sagami, and without resting the hooves of the horses he set out for Hitachi to root out and destroy his enemies wherever they were left. Members of the Fujiwara clan there prepared a marvelous banquet at the border and offered it to the New Emperor. The New Emperor asked them where Taira no Sadamori and his men were. They replied, "Their lives, we hear, are like floating clouds, they do not fix the place where they are."

They succeeded in capturing the wives of Sadamori, Mamoru, Tasuku and others. When he heard this, the New Emperor ordered that the women should be respected, but before his instructions were received the women were violated by warriors. Although this had happened, the New Emperor released the women and sent them all back. At this juncture he had not heard where his enemies were, although time had passed. So he sent back all the warriors of the several provinces and he was left with less than a mere thousand men. At this point Sadamori, the Sheriff Fujiwara no Hidesato and those with them heard about this and reasoned among themselves, "We should rescue the Noble Houses from shame; we should fight him without regard for our lives." As Hidesato and his party set out against him with many warriors, the New Emperor was greatly surprised and led his soldiers to face them. Soon he came up against Hidesato's battle line. Hidesato was wise in strategy and broke the onslaught of the New Emperor's troops. Sadamori, Hidesato and their men clung to their rear, and the longer they pursued the more they caught up with them. The New Emperor wanted to stand up to them and fight, but he retreated because his warriors were far inferior in number. While the New Emperor was lying in hiding north of Sashima thinking to deceive his enemies, Sadamori, beginning with the dwelling of the New Emperor, burned down all the houses of his dependents and followers one by one.

The New Emperor then had only some four hundred warriors because the more than eight thousand soldiers who always followed him were not yet mustered. So he prepared a position on the North Mountain of Sashima and awaited the enemy. Sadamori, Hidesato and their men came in pursuit and engaged in battle. At first the New Emperor had the advantage and threw back the warriors of Sadamori, Hidesato and their party, but later these men in their turn won the advantage. They fought together without begrudging their lives. When the New Emperor himself

3. *"How Taira no Masakado Raised a Rebellion and Was Killed"*

engaged in battle and sped on his swift horse, the Punishment of Heaven was openly revealed; his horse no longer ran, his hand lost its skill, and finally, struck by an arrow, he died in the midst of the plain. Sadamori, Hidesato, and their group rejoiced at this and ordered a fierce warrior to cut off his head. They sent it up to the capital accompanied by an official letter from the province of Shimotsuke. The scheming of Prince Okiyo and his party had been fulfilled for the New Emperor in the loss of his name and his life.

The Court expressed approval and rejoiced at these events, and an Edict of Council was sent to the provinces of the East Sea and East Mountain Circuits ordering that all the brothers, dependents and followers of Masakado should be hunted down and arrested; it also offered rewards to those who killed these dependents and followers. The Generalissimo Consultant and Director of Palace Repairs, Colonel of Right Guards Fujiwara no Tadafumi was commissioned and dispatched to the Eight Provinces, accompanied by Senior Assistant Minister of Justice Fujiwara no Tadanobu and others, and they killed Masakado's older brother, Masatoshi, Harumochi and others in Sagami province. Prince Okiyo was killed in Kazusa; Sakanoue no Katsutaka, Fujiwara no Haruakira and others were cut down in Hitachi. Also, while they were searching out and destroying the rebels, Masakado's seven or eight younger brothers either took the tonsure and went deep in the mountains, or left their families and roamed the wilderness. And so reward was bestowed on Tsunemoto, Sadamori, Hidesato and others. Tsunemoto was promoted to Junior Fifth Rank, Lower Grade; Hidesato, to Junior Fourth Rank, Lower Grade; Sadamori, to Junior Fifth Rank, Upper Grade. It has been related and handed down that Masakado afterward appeared in the dream of a certain man and uttered this oracle, "While I was living, I did evil and not one single good deed; it is impossible to bear alone the suffering for this karma I have made."

How the Noble Minamoto no Yoriyoshi Chastised Abe no Sadatō and His Followers

Now, a long time ago, in the reign of Go-Reizei no In (1048–68), there was a man called Abe no Yoriyoshi living in the Six Districts of the Deep North. His father was called Tadayoshi, and he was Chief of District Chiefs, succeeding him in his generation from his grandfather. His power and prestige were so great that there was no one who did not submit to him. His relatives and friends were spread all over the country, even as far as beyond Koromogawa. They did not fulfil their tax and other dues to the Central Government and provincial governors, one after another in turn, were unable to bring them under control.

And so in the Eishō era (1046–53) the provincial governor, a man named Fujiwara no Naritō, called up many warriors and tried to bring pressure to bear on these people. But Yoriyoshi, along with his subordinate chiefs, held back the governor's troops, fought them and threw them back, and there were many who perished. When the Central Administration heard this, it forthwith sent down a decree to wipe out Yoriyoshi. The decree was addressed to the Noble Minamoto no Yoriyoshi and commissioned him to undertake this task. Having been appointed General of Pacification Headquarters, Yoriyoshi, accompanied by his eldest son Yoshiie, his second son Yoshitsuna, and many warriors, immediately went down to the province of Mutsu in order to destroy Abe no Yoriyoshi.

But a General Amnesty was suddenly issued and so Abe no Yoriyoshi was pardoned; he was greatly delighted and changed his name to Yoritoki. Another reason for this change was the taboo against having the same name as the governor. And so as Yoritoki submitted to the governor, there were no incidents during one term of office. In the final year of his term of office the governor entered the Pacification Headquarters to deal with various matters, and for a month or so there was no end to Yoritoki's bowing his head and obsequiously performing services to him; he also gave him gold and other precious gifts, as well as a fast horse.

But on his way back to his official mansion, while his men were encamped on the road near the Akurigawa, someone fired arrows into the camp of Mitsusada and Motosada, the sons of the Deputy Governor Fujiwara no Tokisada, and some men and horses were killed. No one knew who was responsible for this. When it became light, the governor heard about the matter and summoned Mitsusada and questioned him about suspects. Mitsusada answered, "Last year Yoritoki's son Sadatō said he would like to take my younger sister as his wife. But we didn't accept this as his house is inferior. Sadatō deeply felt that this was a disgrace. You can draw your conclusions from this—the shooting was certainly Sadatō's doing. Apart from him, there is no other enemy."

The governor was greatly incensed at this and said, "This was not shooting at Mitsusada—it was shooting at me." And so he summoned Sadatō and intended to accuse him of the incident. But Yoritoki spoke to Sadatō on this matter and told him, "The concerns of a man in this world are all for his wife and children. You are my son and it is impossible for me to abandon you. I could not see you killed and remain in this world. So it is better to close and guard the gates rather than hear what the governor has to say. And furthermore, he has already fulfilled his term of office and the day of his return to the capital is near. Even though he feels angry, he cannot come himself to call us to account. In any case we are strong enough to beat them back. You need not feel anxious."

3. "How Taira no Masakado Raised a Rebellion and Was Killed"

He then fortified and garrisoned the Koromogawa barrier, closed the road and let no one pass. The governor was even more angry when this happened, and he called up many warriors and came to attack. Everything was in tumult within the province and there was not a single case of [anyone][8] opposing the governor. Yoritoki's sons-in-law, *San'i* Fujiwara no Tsunekiyo and Taira no Nagahira, and their followers all turned against their father-in-law and adhered to the governor. Nagahira, clad in silver armor, served in the ranks of the army, but a certain man reported to the governor, "As Nagahira is Yoritoki's son-in-law, he is loyal on the outside, but on the inside he has treacherous intentions. It is certain that he will try to send a messenger secretly through the lines and report the situation of our army. Also, the armor he's wearing is not the same as his companions. This must be to mark him out in battle." When the governor heard this, he seized Nagahira and four of his male relatives, and cut their heads off.

At this Tsunekiyo was intimidated and greatly afraid, and he secretly said to someone who was on friendly terms with him, "I also will be put to death before long." The man replied, "Even though you serve the governor with all your might, there are bound to be slanders against you. Without a doubt you will be killed. So quickly make your escape and attach yourself to the Fifth Rank Abe [Yoritoki]." Tsunekiyo believed this and decided to leave. And so he addressed these false words to the troops of the army, "Yoritoki's army has come out by a shortcut, attacked the provincial capital and is about to take the governor's northern flank." When they heard this, the troops of the governor's army rose in confusion. Taking advantage of this disorder, Tsunekiyo, accompanied by more than eight hundred of his own warriors, turned himself over to Yoritoki.

Meanwhile, Yoriyoshi had finished his term of office and a new governor, Takashina no Tsuneshige, had been appointed. But when the latter heard reports of war, he resigned his office and did not go down to the province. As a result of this, Yoriyoshi was appointed again for the purpose of having him destroy Yoritoki. Yoriyoshi therefore sent an official letter from the province and made this proposal. "We should, through Kogane no Tametoki and Okishige, the governor of Shimotsuke, and their party, persuade the chiefs of the Mutsu area and bring them to our side, and then destroy Yoritoki." Thereupon the Central Government sent down a decree to this effect, and the chiefs of the three districts of Kanaya, Nitoroshi and Usori made Abe no Tomitada their leader and attacked Yoritoki with many warriors. Mustering his strength, Yoritoki fought and held them in check for two days, but finally, hit by a stray arrow, he died at the Tori no Umi palisade.

---

8. Missing word added to text. [TDC]

Accompanied by an army of about thirty-one hundred men, the governor then tried to destroy Sadatō and his group. But Sadatō, with more than four thousand troops, held them in check and the governor's army was broken, and many men were killed. Now the governor's son Yoshiie excelled other men in feats of daring. No arrow that he fired was wasted, but enemy arrows fired against him were all to no avail. The barbarians yielded and ran before him, and there was none bold enough to face him. They called him Hachiman Tarō.

Meanwhile the governor's troops either ran away or were killed, and he had only six mounted warriors left. These were his son Yoshiie, Shuri no Shōjō, Fujiwara no Kagemichi, Ōyake no Mitsutō, Kiyowara no Sadayasu, Fujiwara no Norisue and Noriaki of the same family name. The enemy numbered more than two hundred mounted men. They surrounded them and pressed in on left and right, and the flying arrows were like rain. The horse ridden by the governor was hit by an arrow and toppled over. Kagemichi got another horse and gave it to him. Yoshiie's horse also was hit by an arrow and died. Noriaki took a horse by force from one of the enemy and had Yoshiie mount it. As things were going like this, it was almost impossible to escape. But Yoshiie again and again shot enemy warriors to death while Mitsutō and the others also fought with the strength of a death-resolve. At length the enemy pulled back and withdrew.

Now at that time the governor had a follower, *San'i* Saeki no Tsunenori, a man of Sagami province, on whom he relied completely. When the army was broken, Tsunenori was not surrounded and barely managed to get away. He did not know where the governor had gone, and when he enquired from the scattered men, they answered, "The governor has been surrounded by the enemy and hasn't got many warriors with him. In such a situation it will certainly be hard for him to get away." Tsunenori then said, "This year I have at last reached my old age in the service of the governor. The governor also is not all that young. Now that I have reached the end of my time, why shouldn't I die with him?" His two or three retainers also said, "Lord, you are about to enter the enemy lines to die with the governor. How could we live on alone?" With this they entered the enemy lines together and fought. They shot and killed more than ten men before they themselves were shot and killed before the enemy.

Fujiwara no Kagesue, the son of Kagemichi, some twenty years old, also galloped into the enemy lines seven or eight times, shooting enemies to death before returning. But finally his horse fell over in the enemy lines. Having noted Kagesue's prowess and valor, the enemy admired him, but as he was a warrior cherished by the governor, they killed him. Performing in this manner, the followers close to the governor all fought their utmost, but many indeed were killed by the enemy.

Fujiwara no Shigeyori was a man who was on close terms with the governor. After the army was broken, for several days he did not know where the governor had gone. Thinking that he had been struck down by the enemy, he wept continuously and said, "I will search out his corpse and perform the obsequies. But it will be impossible to enter among the enemy without being a monk," and so he forthwith shaved his head and became a monk. When he met the governor as he travelled along the road toward the area of the fighting, he rejoiced and sorrowed by turns, and then went back with the governor.

Meanwhile Sadatō and his followers made their power felt more and more, going to various districts and placing levies on the common people. Accompanied by many warriors, Tsunekiyo came out at the Koromogawa barrier and sent emissaries to the districts to collect the rice and produce taxes due to the government. They announced, "White collection tallies are to be used; red tallies are not acceptable." Now the white tallies were Tsunekiyo's private tax-collection tallies and were called white because they did not bear the impression of a seal; the so-called red tallies were those of the provincial governor, and they were called red because they bore the provincial seal. The governor was unable to control or stop this.

Thus the governor was always proposing to Kiyowara no Mitsuyori, the master of the Ainu to the north of the mountains of Dewa province, and to his younger brother Takenori, that they should join forces. While Mitsuyori and his group were pondering on the pros and cons of this proposal, the governor repeatedly sent them precious and attractive gifts. He continued to persuade them with all courtesy, and finally Mitsuyori and Takenori and their group made up their minds and agreed to join forces with the governor. After that the governor repeatedly appealed to Mitsuyori and Takenori for troops. And so, calling up his sons and younger brothers and more than ten thousand warriors, Takenori came crossing into Mutsu province and sent ahead word of his coming. The governor was greatly pleased and went to meet them with more than three thousand warriors. The governor met Takenori at Tamurooka in Kurihara district and they discussed their plans. Next they fixed upon the commanders of the various battle positions; each was a son or relative of Takenori.

Takenori bowed to the distant capital and took an oath, saying, "I have already called up my sons, younger brothers, relatives, and companions, and I submit to the orders of the shogun. The thought of death does not worry us. We earnestly beg the gods enshrined as The Three Aspects of Hachiman to look with favor upon our sincerity. I do not hold my life precious beyond this." On hearing these words, his many warriors were all at once inspired to follow his example. At the same time doves flew over the army, and the governor and all his subordinates together bowed low.

Thereupon they set out on the Matsuyama road and camped at Ōkazesawa by Nakayama in Iwai district. Next day they reached Hagi no Baba in the same district. This place was more than six hundred yards from the Komatsu palisade of

Muneto's uncle, the monk Yoshiteru, but as the day was inauspicious and it was getting on toward evening, they did not press an attack. As Takenori's sons went up close to spy out the strength of the forces on the other side, foot-soldiers burned down the shelters outside the palisade. Just then there was the sound of shouting from within the citadel and the soldiers were bombarded with stones. Thereupon the governor said to Takenori, "I planned the battle for tomorrow, but this disorder has broken out of its own accord. So we can't pick the day." Takenori agreed.

Thereupon two men called Fukae no Korenori and Ōtomo no Kazuhide, at the head of some twenty fierce warriors, dug away the river bank with their swords and, using their spears as climbing staffs, they scaled the rocks. Cutting and breaking away the bottom of the palisade, they suddenly burst into the citadel, and crossed swords and exchanged blows with the defenders. Within the citadel all was in confusion and everyone was bewildered. Munetō, leading more than eight hundred mounted warriors, fought outside the citadel, but the governor, together with many fierce warriors sent as reinforcements, set upon him and broke up his forces. So Munetō's army abandoned the citadel and fled, whereupon the governor's troops burned down the palisade.

The governor wanted to rest his men and so did not press on to attack. In this way they passed eighteen long rainy days, and during this time their provisions ran out and there was nothing to eat. So the governor despatched many warriors to various places with orders to forage for food. Sadatō and his group heard rumors about this and awaited their opportunity. Then, at the head of many warriors, Sadatō led an attack, whereupon the governor, Yoshiie, Yoshitsuna, Takenori, and the others mobilised their men and advanced with a great army. They fought without regard for their lives and the Sadatō group finally gave up and fled. The governor and Takenori pressed on in pursuit until they caught up with them and fought at Sadatō's Takanashi camp and the Ishizaka palisade. Sadatō's army was again broken there, and abandoning their palisades, they fell back and entered at the Koromogawa barrier. Thereupon, the governor's troops pressed in upon the Koromogawa. Now the barrier passage was naturally very steep, and moreover trees increasingly blocked the road. Dividing his forces under three commanders, the governor pressed on the attack.

Takenori dismounted and went around to observe the vicinity of the riverbanks. Then he summoned a warrior called Hisakiyo and said to him, "There are trees bent over on both banks, and their branches cover the surface of the river. You are light on your feet and like to jump over things. Cross over to the other bank and pass secretly through the enemy lines and set fire to the base of their palisade. They will be terrified by the fire, and then I will break the barrier without fail."

In accordance with these orders Hisakiyo reached the bent trees on the other bank like a monkey, fastened a rope, and then by means of this some thirty warriors crossed over. They stealthily crept up to the palisade of Fujiwara no Narimichi, set it afire and burned it down. When they saw this, Sadatō's troops were greatly surprised and confused, and pulling out and fleeing without fighting, they retired to the palisade of Tori no Umi.

After reducing Narimichi's palisade, the governor and Takenori and his forces invested the palisade of Tori no Umi. Munetō, Tsunekiyo and their followers abandoned the citadel and fled before the army came up, and retired to the palisade of Kuriyagawa. The governor entered the palisade of Tori no Umi and while he was resting his troops a great deal of *sake* was found in one of the buildings. The foot soldiers were delighted to see this and hurried up and were about to drink it. But the governor restrained them, saying, "This is surely poisoned *sake*. It is not to be drunk." However, when one or two among the menials drank it, they suffered no harm, and so everybody in the army without exception drank it.

Then Takenori reduced Masatō's Kurosawajiri palisade in the same way, as well as those of Tsuruhagi and Hiyodori. Then having next reached and surrounded the palisades of Kuriyagawa and Nato, he set up battle positions and maintained a guard throughout the night. From five in the following morning they fought all day and all the next night.

Thereupon the governor dismounted and bowed to the distant capital; taking up a burning brand, he swore to the gods and said, "This is the fire of the gods," and threw the brand. Just at that moment some doves appeared and soared above the battle positions; when the governor saw them, he was moved to tears and bowed toward them. Then a violent wind arose and buildings within the citadel all at once burst into flame. There were several thousand men and women in the citadel and they raised their voices together, wailing and shouting, while the soldiers either threw themselves in the river or crouched down facing the attack. The governor's army crossed over the water and pressed in to attack; they surrounded the citadel and fought the enemy. The defending troops gave up hope, and swinging their swords they tried to break out of the encirclement. Takenori then issued orders to his warriors, "Open a road and let the enemy out." They therefore opened the encirclement and the enemy escaped without fighting. The governor's army then pursued them and killed them all.

Tsunekiyo was captured and was brought before the governor, who said, "You are a hereditary retainer of mine. But you have recently treated me with contempt and made light of the Imperial prestige and authority, and so your offense is most grave. I wonder whether your white tallies will be accepted today." Tsunekiyo hung his head and had nothing to say. The governor, using a blunt sword, finally managed to cut off his head.

Sadatō drew his sword and cut at the troops, but they stabbed him with their spears. Then they put him on a big shield and six men carried him into the presence of the governor. Sadatō's height was more than six feet and he was seven feet five inches around the waist; he was imposing in figure and white of skin. He was forty-four years of age. The governor looked at him and was well pleased, and cut off his head. He also cut off the head of his younger brother Shigetō. But Munetō fell into deep mud, fled and escaped. Sadatō had a thirteen-year-old son called Chiyo Dōji, a handsome boy; coming out of the palisade, he had fought well. The governor took pity on him and thought to spare him, but Takenori put a stop to this and had his head cut off. At the time the palisade fell, Sadatō's wife, holding a three-year-old child, said to her husband, "My lord, you are about to be killed. I cannot live alone, and so I will die while you watch." At this she threw herself into the deep river while still holding the child, and so she died.

After that, Sadatō's uncle, Abe no Tamemoto, and his younger brother Ietō soon came out and surrendered. Then, after a few days, Munetō and some others, nine men in all, came in and surrendered. They then sent an official provincial letter to the capital, reporting the persons who had given up and surrendered.

The following year they presented the three heads of Sadatō, Tsunekiyo and Shigetō to the Central Authority. On the day they entered the capital there was no end to the people, high, middle and low, who came to look at the heads and noisily chatter. While they were on their way to the capital, the Imperial Emissary had the boxes opened in Kōga district of Ōmi province, the heads were taken out and their topknots washed. Now the coolies carrying the boxes were retainers of Sadatō, men who had surrendered, and they said that there were no combs. The Emissary replied, "Then you'll have to comb their hair with your own combs." They therefore combed them with their own combs, weeping as they did so. On the day they brought them in, the Central Authority dispatched Imperial Police to the riverbed and took them in charge.

An Appointment Ceremony was later held, and on that occasion the merit achieved in these events was duly rewarded. The Noble Yoriyoshi was promoted to Senior Fourth Rank, Lower Grade, and appointed governor of Dewa. Jirō no Yoshitsuna was appointed Lieutenant of Left Gate Guards. Takenori was promoted to Junior Fifth Rank, Lower Grade, and appointed General of Pacification Headquarters. The Emissary who brought the heads, Fujiwara no Hidetoshi, was appointed Third Class Official of the Left Horse Bureau, while Mononobe no Nagayori was appointed Fourth Class Official of Mutsu province.

It has been related and handed down that when the people of that time observed the novelty of the rewards thus bestowed, all of them were indeed delighted and full of admiration.

SECTION III

The Wars of the Twelfth Century (1150–89) and the Creation of a Warrior Government

Japan in the eleventh century also witnessed a political transformation with the rise of Retired Emperors. These men took the tonsure but did not renounce the affairs of the world. To the contrary, they engaged in direct administration and oversaw rituals which were thought to be the essence of court governance. The first of these Retired Emperors was Go-Sanjō (1032–73; r. 1068–73). But the position was solidified by Shirakawa (1053–1129), who reigned as emperor from 1073–87 but then continued to govern and oversee rites which demonstrated that he, rather than the nominally reigning Emperor, was sovereign. He became known as the *chiten no kimi*, or the "lord who rules" and continued to exercise sovereign authority. Thus, even though others served as emperor after his retirement, Shirakawa continued to wield power until his death in 1129. As we shall see, three political factions, all with close ties to Shirakawa, would eventually jockey for power, and their battles would have a profoundly destabilizing effect on Japanese society. Some of these political actors were Minamoto no Yoshiie (1039–1106), who owed his success to his close ties with Shirakawa and briefly served as the Pacification General (Chinjufu *shōgun*) of the north; the Military Envoys (*ōryōshi*) of Mutsu Province (1089-1189), otherwise known as the Fujiwara of the north, who also had close ties to the Fujiwara Regents of the capital; and the Taira family from Ise Province.

This rule by Retired Emperors proved profoundly destabilizing for several reasons. While succession to the throne had long been governed according to standard procedures and precedents, once multiple emperors retired, the dominant retired or reigning emperor could only be determined through ritual actions, administrative policies, or, at times, through force of arms, as evident particularly with the skirmishes of 1156 and 1159. In addition, the Retired Emperors created portfolios of estates through administrative fiat, dispossessing powerful provincials (*zaichō kanjin*) in the process. Some of their clients, such as the Taira, ruled as nobles and only gave their followers weak managerial rights (*gesu*), while in other cases, warriors staged insurrections and promised their followers more durable rights.

Section III • The Wars of the Twelfth Century and the Creation of a Warrior Government

1. Excerpts from "The Heiji Rebellion" in Jien's Thirteenth-Century History *The Gukanshō*[1]

Jien (1155–1225), a Protector Priest (gojisō) *for Go-Toba, wrote a remarkable history of Japan in the 1220s. The selection below includes an account of the Heiji Disturbance of 1159, during which Minamoto no Yoshitomo and Fujiwara no Nobuyori's forces attacked the palace where Go-Shirakawa—a Retired Emperor and Japan's* de facto *sovereign—resided. The attack failed when Taira no Kiyomori returned from a pilgrimage to the capital and defeated Yoshitomo and Nobuyori in battle.*[2]

On the night of the ninth day of the twelfth month of the first year of Heiji [1159], the palace at Karasuma and Sanjō, where the Go-Shirakawa[3] lived, served by Shinzei and his sons, was surrounded in an attempt[4] to trap everyone in the palace and burn them to death. . . .

Taira no Kiyomori, Deputy Governor General of Dazaifu (*Dazai Daini*), was on his way to the Kumano shrines on a pilgrimage when he heard of this. Kiyomori had not yet arrived at the shrines, but was staying at what was then called Futagawa, otherwise known as the Tanobe station. A messenger reported what had happened in the capital. Kiyomori, who was with his sons Motomori, Governor of Echizen, and the thirteen-year-old Munemori, Governor of Awaji, wondered what to do. He had only fifteen *samurai*.[5] He thought his only option was to flee to Kyushu (Tsukushi) and wait there for reinforcements. But then Yuasa Muneshige, a Kii Province warrior (*musha*) known as the Acting Governor, arrived with exactly thirty-seven horse riders, a good-sized force for that time. Muneshige told Kiyomori he should quickly attack the capital. Though Tankai of Kumano was not one of Kiyomori's *samurai*, he gave seven suits of armor and all his gear, including bows and arrows, to Kiyomori without hesitation. Muneshige's thirteen-year-old son gave his own small suit of *haramaki* armor, of leather dyed purple, to Munemori, Kiyomori's thirteen-year-old son, who put it on.[6]

---

1. Translated by Thomas Conlan.
2. Okami Masao, comp, *Gukanshō* (Iwanami shoten, 1967), 227–36. Brown's translation in *The Future and the Past*, 108–15, was also consulted.
3. The Retired Emperor Go-Shirakawa. He is referred to here as the In.
4. The attackers were Minamoto Yoshitomo and Fujiwara Nobuyori.
5. This refers to low-ranking followers.
6. *Haramaki* constituted a simplified suit of armor which closed on the side. This boy, the text explains later, became a monk and supporter of the famous Buddhist figure Mongaku (1139–1203).

1. Excerpts from "The Heiji Rebellion" in Jien's Thirteenth-Century History The Gukanshō

Kiyomori dispatched a representative (*daikan*) to Kumano in his stead, finally arriving in the capital on the seventeenth day of the twelfth month [of 1159]. [Minamoto] Yoshitomo should have attacked him at that time but did not, most likely because his reinforcements had not yet arrived from the east. . . . Kiyomori uneventfully took up residence at Rokuhara. . . .

> *The omitted passages recount how Kiyomori cleverly managed to move the retired and reigning emperors to his mansion at Rokuhara, making it the new palace. The narrative resumes with a description of Minamoto no Yoshitomo's desperate attack on that compound.*

Eventually Yoshitomo tied the strings of his helmet and set forth, whipping his horse along the narrow streets of Kyoto [so fast that] he left his *samurai* behind in the narrow streets of the capital. The [Taira] forces of Rokuhara approached the palace. Yoshitomo called out: "I hope to fight and die at Rokuhara!" and advanced. On the Taira side, *Saemon no suke* Shigemori, Kiyomori's eldest son, and the Governor of Mikawa Yorimori, Kiyomori's younger brother, fought like real great generals. Shigemori was most magnificent—when his horse was shot out from under him, he used his bow to catapult himself, from lumber piled on the bank of Horikawa, onto a new horse. With broken arrows protruding from their armor, both men returned to Rokuhara. Their victory eased the minds of all who had watched the battle.

Yoshitomo advanced as far as Rokuhara's boarded barricades. In the ensuing turmoil, the great general Kiyomori, wearing black armor of black weave over dark indigo robes (*hitatare*) and carrying lacquered black arrows, rode forth from the central gate of the [Rokuhara] palace on a black horse. Tying his general's helmet, with its protruding crest (*kuwagata*), fast to his head, he rushed forward. Twenty or thirty *samurai*, mounted and on foot, ran with him. "What is causing the ruckus? Let's take a look here," he said as he and his men confidently sped forth.

Yoshitomo, who had only ten followers (*rōtō*) remaining, could not continue the fight and was forced to retreat to the lands of the east. . . . At that moment, Jūyu, the Protector Priest of the palace who came from Mt. Hiei, dressed in pale reddish yellow robes, turned to the northeast[7] and repeatedly prostrated himself, chanting "Hail the Three Treasures of Mt. Hiei." At such times, a person like this should always appear.

---

7. *Kimon*, an unlucky direction (northeast), where evil spirits would need to be quelled, and also the location of Mt. Hiei.

2. An Order (*kudashibumi*) Issued by Taira no Kiyomori[8]

Taira no Kiyomori (1118–81) fought prominently in the Hōgen Disturbance of 1156 and the Heiji Disturbance of 1159. As a result of his success, he was promoted and became a prominent courtier. Having achieved the office of Provisional Middle Councilor, Kiyomori ensured that his follower Taira no Ietsuna would receive managerial rights of Shidō estate. Ietsuna, who appears in the Tale of Heiji, was one of Kiyomori's most trusted followers. He apparently was the original lord of these lands, but they were commended to Itsukushima Shrine in Aki Province. The office of gesu, or manager, was not a particularly durable right as the proprietor of an estate could easily divest a gesu from office. By contrast, Taira no Kiyomori's rival Minamoto no Yoritomo would devise a much more durable managerial right, that of jitō, in 1180. The utter destruction of the Taira in 1185 meant that nearly all their documents were lost, but this one survived because of the ongoing importance of Itsukushima Shrine, the proprietor of these lands.

Issued from the office (*mandokoro*) of the house of the Provisional Middle Councilor [Taira no Kiyomori] to Kagehiro, Deputy of the Custodian Bureau (*Kamon no suke*).

Ietsuna shall immediately assume the managerial office (*gesu shiki*) of Shidō estate, in Yamagata district (*gun*) [Aki Province]. Ietsuna is the lord of these lands (*jinushi*), which have been donated to your holdings. It is so ordered that he shall be given managerial office (*gesu shiki*). Please take note. Appoint this person as stated thus. Therefore, this order.

The sixth month of the second year of Chōkan (1164).

[Names omitted]

3. Civil War in the 1180s

Prince Mochihito, passed over for succession, rebelled shortly after the Taira placed his father, Go-Shirawaka, under house arrest in 1179. The edict Mochihito issued in response—which does not exist in a reliable copy—sparked the "Genpei War" (1180–85). Although the war was retrospectively remembered as a conflict

---

8. Takeuchi Rizō, comp., *Heian ibun*, vol. 7, doc. 3285, 6.1164 (Chōkan 2) *Gon Chūnagon* (Taira no Kiyomori) *ke mandokoro kudashibumi*, p. 2609. Translated by Thomas Conlan.

between the Minamoto (Gen) and the Taira (Hei) these lineages did not determine political allegiances at the time. To the contrary, the wars were fought by local warriors against central authorities. This rebellion could be justified through Prince Mochihito's edict. Mochihito's edict gave Minamoto no Yoritomo the excuse to launch an attack on the forces of a provincial governor. Mochihito was eventually hunted down and killed by the forces of Taira no Kiyomori.

Yoritomo unilaterally asserted his authority to commend lands—a radical step. The following document, the earliest surviving record we have of him, provides a better picture of his actions. Though long assumed to be a forgery, this document was in fact a copy, made by Yoritomo himself later in life, of one of his earliest documents.[9] *Both early documents survive at Mishima Shrine, where he initially staged his rebellion.*

An Order (*kudashibumi*) of Minamoto no Yoritomo I[10]

(Monogram of Yoritomo)

Ordered: To the Provincial Headquarters (*rusu dokoro*) and to resident provincial officials (*zaichō*)[11]

The appointment of the office (*shiki*) having authority over Mizono and Kawaragaya districts, is granted to: Miya Morikata[12]

Concerning the above, these districts have been commended to the Mishima Deity (*Daimyōjin*). The districts' residents shall obey. Do not be remiss. Wherefore this order.

The fourth year of Jishō [1180], eighth month, nineteenth day

---

9. Hayashi Yuzuru, "Yoritomo no kao ni tsuite—sono keitai henka to Jishō Jūei nengo no shiyō o megutte."
10. *Shizuoka kenshi shiryōhen* vol. 5, *Chūsei* 1, doc. 7, p. 15. Translated by Thomas Conlan.
11. Another name for the most powerful warriors of a province.
12. Miya Morikata was the head (*kannushi*) of Mishima Shrine.

An Order (*kudashibumi*) of Minamoto no Yoritomo 2[13]

Ordered: To the officials (*satanin*) of Izu Province, Kawaragaya district

The Hata shall immediately have authority within this district.[14]

As for the above, this area has customarily been part of Kawaragaya district. These lands shall immediately become the lands of the Mishima Deity. Let there be no disturbances. Thus this matter is decided.

The fifth year of Jishō [1181] seventh month, twenty-ninth day

Minamoto ason (Monogram of Yoritomo)

Azuma Kagami, 4.27 Jishō 4 [1180] [15]

Compare the surviving documents of Yoritomo with how his actions were later retrospectively characterized in the Azuma Kagami *(Chronicle of the East), which describes how Yoritomo received an edict from Prince Mochihito. This chronicle, which was compiled in the 1260s, is an important source for early Kamakura history, as much of its evidence does not appear elsewhere. But at times its narrative is anachronistic, particularly when describing the actions and achievements of Minamoto no Yoritomo. In particular, it papers over the ad hoc nature of Yoritomo's rebellion, in favor of portraying him as a perspicacious leader. Likewise, the* Azuma Kagami *portrays the provincial officer of shugo, or protector, as being created by Yoritomo in 1180 as well, but the notion of a protector was initially ad hoc, and this office only became formalized after his death in 1199.*

Twenty-seventh day. Today the edict (*ryōji*) issued by Takakura no Miya (Mochihito) was delivered to the former chief of the Palace Guards (*saki no buei*) (Minamoto no Yoritomo) at the Hōjō Residence in Izu Province. It was brought by Minamoto no Yukiie. The chief of the Palace Guards (Yoritomo), wearing ceremonial robes and bowing respectfully toward distant Otokoyama, gave instructions

---

13. *Shizuoka kenshi shiryōhen* vol. 5, *Chūsei* 1, doc. 88, p. 92. Translated by Thomas Conlan.
14. This phrase remains difficult to decipher. It could also refer to field for *kibi*, a type of rice used for brewing *sake*. In which case, it should be translated as "Authority over the brewing rice fields in the district shall immediately [belong to the shrine]." I believe, however, the characters represent a corruption for the name Hatano, a prominent local family.
15. The *Azuma Kagami* has been translated by Shinoda, *The Founding of the Kamakura Bakufu*, 157–62. Documents 5–8 are available in multiple editions. All have been translated by Thomas Conlan.

to have the pronouncement opened and read. Meanwhile, Yukiie set out for Kai and Shinano provinces to convey the prince's intentions to Minamoto warriors there.

Azuma Kagami, 8.17 Jishō 4 [1180]

This passage from the Azuma Kagami *describes Yoritomo's initial rebellion and suggests that he had a coherent vision of his future authority. It obscures the ad hoc nature of his initial actions.*

Minamoto no Yoritomo began his rebellion by attacking Taira (Yamaki) Kanetaka on the festival day for Mishima Shrine, on 8.17.1180. Two days later, he issued the following order concerning the Kamaya Shrine lands (*mikuriya*) controlled by Yamaki Kanetaka's uncle Tomochika.

Ordered: To the residents (*jūnin*) of the Kamaya Shrine lands (*mikuriya*)

Immediately, the Scribal Secretariat (*shi no taifu*)[16] [Nakahara] Tomochika's administration is nullified.

As for the above, the Prince's edict is clear: all of the public and private lands in the east shall all be under my authority. Hence, the residents shall be made known of this, and [take steps to have their properties] confirmed. Thus it is commanded. Wherefore this order.

The fourth year of Jishō [1180], eighth month, nineteenth day

4. The Difficulty of Estimating Army Size

As Taira forces were desperately clinging to the capital, Regent Kujō Kanezane— author of the chronicle Gyokuyō—*had his servants count the size of a single Taira army and discovered that its strength had been exaggerated by a factor of seven to ten. This Taira army, led by Taira no Sukemori, headed toward Uji in the south before turning toward the east in an attempt to thwart the forces of Minamoto no Yoshinaka. In another chronicle of the same period, Yoshida Tsunefusa (the* Kikki) *recounts how, after spying on this Taira army of*

---

16. This represents an office of scribe within the Office of Records (*shokikan*).

roughly a thousand men, the Retired Emperor Go-Shirakawa secretly viewed these forces, believed it to be made up of three thousand. Both entries date from 7.21 of the second year of Jūei [1183].

Kujō Kanezane, *Gyokuyō* 7.21 Jūei 2 [1183]

At the hour of the horse [11 a.m.–1 p.m.], the Envoy to Pursue and Punish (*tsuitōshi*) departed. The Captain recently appointed to the third rank, Sukemori, was the General, and Sadayoshi, the governor of Higo, accompanied him as they set off for Tahara.[17] They passed by a narrow road to the east of my house. My servants secretly observed them and said that their force comprised 1,080 horse. Recently, rumors circulated that these forces consisted of seven to eight thousand men, or even ten thousand. But the force as it is seen now is only a thousand. A rumor without foundation.

Yoshida Tsunefusa, *Kikki* 7.21 Jūei 2 [1183]

Today, the Captain recently appointed to the third rank, Lord Sukemori, and his brother, Governor of Bitchū Moromori, also with the Governor of Chikuzen Sadatoshi, led their men. Lord Sukemori had the edict of his promotion hanging from his neck. Sadayoshi, the Governor of Higo, also followed, and at noon he departed. I would estimate a force of three thousand horse. The Retired Emperor [Go-Shirakawa] secretly watched. After passing the road to Uji, they turned toward Ōmi Province.

---

17. This region is more famously known as Uji and was the site of a strategic crossing, which led to the capital from the south.

SECTION IV
The Age of Kamakura Ascendancy (1221–1333)

Minamoto no Yoritomo successfully established the right of *jitō*, and a modicum of recognition of his position as a leader in the east, but his regime remained precarious. Yoritomo died in 1199, and both of his sons were killed by 1219, leaving Kamakura without anyone being invested with the office of Sei-i-tai *shōgun*. This meant that precious little rationale remained for this regime to exist. The Retired Emperor Go-Toba decided that it was high time to assert control over the office of *jitō* and destroy Kamakura (see Go-Toba's Order to Chastise Hōjō Yoshitoki, p. 34). The Hōjō, by contrast, being veterans of the wars of the 1180s, realized that decisive action mattered more than elaborate justification (see Hōjō Yoshitoki's Letter to the Shimazu of Satsuma Province, p. 36; and A Directive from Hōjō Yoshitoki to Ichikawa Rokurō, p. 36). They moved their armies quickly and defeated Go-Toba within six weeks of his declaration of war. Just as he surrendered, some warriors belatedly joined his cause, showing the precariousness of the Hōjō position and their realization that their survival depended upon a quick and decisive war.

This section begins with sources related to the Jōkyū War of 1221. These are followed by Kamakura's 1232 laws, translated here in their entirety for the first time since 1906 (see The Formulary of Adjudication, p. 42), as well as amendments to the code concerning marriage and letters and precepts written by Hōjō leaders (see Letter from Hōjō Yasutoki Concerning the Formulary, p. 60; Kamakura Amendments, p. 61; and Hōjō Shigetoki's Letter to His Son Nagatoki, p. 69).

The next series of sources focus on Japan's defenses when the Mongols attempted to invade Japan in 1274 and 1281 (see Suenaga's Audience with Adachi Yasumori, p. 85; Tōgan Ean's Statement of Opinion, p. 87; Summons of the Chinzei Eastern Administrator, p. 88; Kamakura's Attempt to Dispatch Forces to Korea, p. 88; Petition for Reward by Shami Shukumyō Ōkami Korechika, p. 91; and Letter by Shōni Kagesuke, p. 92). Later law codes, amended in 1285 (see The New Laws of Adachi Yasumori, p. 93), and a remarkable assassination attempt by a flamboyant warrior named Asahara Tameyori reveal the increasing turmoil (see "The Light and Shadows of the Day," *The Clear Mirror*, p. 100; and Kamakura's

Response to the Asahara Assassination Attempt, p. 102). This incident in particular reveals the intensity of the political struggles at the court, which would destabilize Japan. A passage from a visiting court lady describes Kamakura as a small, densely packed outpost, and recounts when the Hōjō ousted their *shōgun* and sent him back to the capital (see *The Confessions of Lady Nijō*, p. 96). Local histories reveal the resistance to Kamakura rule and increasing turmoil in the provinces (see *Mine'aiki*, p. 103). Finally, an edict by Prince Moriyoshi (1308–35) indicates that court officials did not forgive the Hōjō for their role in defeating the court in 1221 (see Command of Prince Moriyoshi, p. 112).

1. Go-Toba's Order to Chastise Hōjō Yoshitoki[1]

Go-Toba declared war on Kamakura in 1221. At this time, Kamakura was vulnerable—it had no Sei-i-tai shōgun *and as its administrative offices were derivative of this post the regime technically had no reason to exist. Go-Toba criticized the Hōjō for their arrogance because they, as shogunal administrators, continued to govern even without a* shōgun. *He also asserted control over the posts of* jitō *and* shugo. *Go-Toba succeeded in attracting some support, but he required time to cobble his supporters into an army drawn from the Capital Police* (kebiishi) *as well as the* jitō *and* shugo *who joined his cause.*

From the Ministry of the Right: Ordered to the Various Provinces of the Five Circuits—
Tōkai, Tōzan, Hokuriku, San'in, Sanyō, as well as Nanyō and Dazaifu
To the protectors (*shugonin*) of the estates of various provinces and *jitō*, respond with haste to this Imperial Summons. Report to the Office of the Retired Emperor (*In no chō*) and chastise Taira Yoshitoki, the Governor of Mutsu.
An imperial edict (*choku*) has been received and conveyed by the Controller of the Palace Minister (Koga Michimitsu). It states: "Recently the judgments of Kamakura (literally Kantō, 'the eight provinces of the east') have disturbed the governance of the realm. Although they claim to be acting in the name of the *Shōgun*, he is but an infant. Nevertheless, this Yoshitoki treats [the young *Shōgun*'s pronouncements] as if they are an Imperial Prince's edict (*kyōmei ni kari*) and makes judgments in the affairs of both the capital and the provinces. His authority

---

1. Takeuchi Rizō, comp., *Kamakura ibun*, vol. 5, doc. 2746, 5.15.1221 (Jōkyū 3) *Kansenji an*, 14–15. Translated by Thomas Conlan.

increases and he has apparently forgotten the nature of imperial rule. Those who speak of his 'governance' are advocating treason! All residing in the Five Circuits and Seven Roads and various provinces should immediately chastise him. In addition, if the various protectors (*shugonin*) and *jitō* of the provinces have disputes, they should appear before the Office of the Retired Emperor (*In no chō*) for judgment. Provincial Governors and Court Proprietors (*ryōke*) must not use this edict to create troubles. Nothing is to be at variance with this command." All of the various provinces shall abide by this order. This edict is thus.

Third year of Jōkyū [1221] fifth month, fifteenth day

Daishi Miyoshi *ason*[2]

The Controller (*daiben*) Fujiwara *ason*

2. The Will (*yuzurijō*) of Nejime Kiyoshige[3]

One reason why Kamakura defeated Go-Toba so quickly in a stunning six-week campaign was because they had long trained for war. Rumors of a rebellion in Ōmi Province, near the capital, appear in the Azuma Kagami, *as well as a reference to a brief uprising in Suruga in 1220.*[4] *The following document provides some more information about the situation in Ōmi and shows that Kamakura armies were mobilized just to the east of the capital in 1220.*

The head of Nejime-in[5] and novice (*nyūdō*) Kiyoshige renounces his rights and bestows to Kenbu Bōmaru this *inshi* and *jitō* office. Hereditarily transmitted documents are appended.

The above offices belong to Kiyoshige. Nevertheless, they had been encroached upon by others and fell into abeyance. When Kiyoshige appealed to the *Shōgun* regarding this, he was reappointed because our rights are manifest in our records.

---

2. The term *ason* was originally an inherited noble title, but by the time of this document, merely refers to its recipient as having social status.

3. *Kamakura ibun*, vol. 5, document 2731, 3.23.1221 (Jōkyū 3) Nejime Kiyoshige *yuzurijō*, 10–11. Translated by Thomas Conlan.

4. See Mass, *The Development of Kamakura Rule*, 15.

5. The old district name of Nejime, in Ōsumi Province, was later identified by temple names. Hence, it came to be referred to as Nejime-in, and the title of *inshi* denoted that one was the head of one of three plots of land. In the case of the Nejime, this title fused with a *jitō* post.

Nevertheless, because the world is in disorder, these documents were entrusted to Kenbu Kiyotada. He had these records in his possession, but on the sixth day of the eleventh month of Jōkyū 2 (1220), when Kantō[6] forces neared the capital, enemies at Ōmi killed him in a night attack. Nevertheless, as Kenbu Bōmaru is his heir (*chakushi*), I Kiyoshige bestow the office of Nejime (*inshi*) and the *jitō* rights (*shiki*) to him. Thus, for future reference, this testament is thus.

Third year of Jōkyū [1221], third month, twenty-third day

The *inshi* of Nejime (monogram)

3. Hōjō Yoshitoki's Letter to the Shimazu of Satsuma Province[7]

This document suggests that Kamakura had almost immediately decided to attack the capital. However, this document is a copy of an original and it is possible the copyist misread the date.

I understand that the Honorable Saburō *hyōe*[8] will travel with the Musashi Governor[9] to the capital. This is most wonderful. Respectfully.

(Monogram copy) (*arihan*)[10]

(Third year of Jōkyū [1221]) fifth month, nineteenth day

4. A Directive (*mikyōjo*) from Hōjō Yoshitoki to Ichikawa Rokurō[11]

Ichikawa Rokurō was a member of a gokenin *family from Shinano Province. The term* gokenin *refers to warrior householders who received recognition as having a status (or "house") and were responsible for helping* shugo *apprehend*

---

6. A synonym for the Kamakura *Bakufu*.
7. *Kamakura ibun*, vol. 5, doc. 2747, 5.19 Hōjō Yoshitoki *shojō an*, 15. Translated by Thomas Conlan.
8. Shimazu Tadatoki.
9. Hōjō Yasutoki, the Governor of Musashi and Yoshitoki's son and heir.
10. This means "a copy." Yoshitoki's monogram would have been located here in the original document.
11. *Kamakura ibun*, vol. 5, doc. 2753, 6. 6 [1221] Hōjō Yoshitoki *sodehan mikyōjo*, 16–17. Translated by Thomas Conlan.

4. A Directive (mikyōjo) from Hōjō Yoshitoki to Ichikawa Rokurō

criminals and providing order in the provinces, but they did not necessarily possess the coveted office of jitō. At times this term is translated as "vassal," but such a characterization is misleading. In writing to him, Yoshitoki recounted the difficulties encountered by the northernmost of Kamakura's three armies, led by Hōjō Tomotoki. Tomotoki's army defeated the enemy forces allied to Go-Toba at Noto on 6.8.1221, but Yoshitoki remained unaware of this victory. To the contrary, he encouraged Shinano warriors to join Tomotoki, who was delayed when passing through narrow passes. This informative document reveals much about this brief conflict while it was being fought, but it has been ignored because Tomotoki's forces did not significantly affect the outcome. They arrived in Kyoto on 6.20.1221, six days after Go-Toba's decisive defeat by the forces of Hōjō Yasutoki.

(Monogram)[12]

Your letter, written at the hour of the dog [7–9 p.m.] on the thirtieth day of the fifth month arrived today, the sixth of the sixth month at the hour of the monkey [3–5 p.m.]. On the last day of the fifth month our forces attacked and defeated Kanbara.[13] On the same day, at the hour of the monkey, I heard a report that our forces had taken Miyazaki.

Numerous reports stated the attack began before *Shikibu no jō*[14] arrived. Even though Shinano Jirō set off with a force of three hundred horse, what can he do? Help the Honorable *Shikibu* [Hōjō Tomotoki] hurry along. I have heard that the forces of Miyazaki *no saemon*, Nishina no Jirō [Moritō], Kasaya no Arihisa *saemon*, Kuwasa *no in tō* Tōsaemon, and one more—a Genji from Shinano—approached [Tomotoki] on the Hokuroku highway.[15]

We must ensure that we can prevent even a single enemy from escaping. If we force the enemy into the mountains, where they will be forced to wander aimlessly, then we should be able to capture them. If we force the enemy into the mountains, then nearly all of the warriors (*mono*) from the provinces of Echū, Kaga, Noto, and Echizen will ally with us. If we can secure local support, we will gain local knowledge of the nearby mountains [and passes], which will allow us to capture the

---

12. Hōjō Yoshitoki.
13. Name of a warrior from Suruga province, located midway between Kamakura and Kyoto. Other members of the Kanbara fought for Kamakura.
14. Hōjō Tomotoki, who led one of Kamakura's armies.
15. The Hokurokutō, the "northern road," one of the seven major roads of Japan created in the seventh-eighth century linking the provinces of Wakasa, Echizen, Kaga, Noto, Echū, Echigo, and Sado.

enemy. Don't pursue the defeated enemy in haste, abandon our positions, or rush to the capital unnecessarily.

I know of many cases where *gokenin* have fought and defeated the enemy, performing outstanding service and being recommended for rewards. I repeatedly heard that Shintaka's younger brother, Shirō *saemon*, and you, Rokurō, together performed exhaustive military service. In addition, all the *gokenin* who fought most devotedly (*kokoro mo irete*), traipsed through the mountains, and tried to smite the enemy shall be witnessed and rewarded. This should be made known. Respectfully.

Sixth month, sixth day at the time of the monkey   Fujiwara Kanesuke, humbly received[16]

A reply to the Honorable Ichikawa Rokurō *gyōbu*

5. A Rokuhara Order (*gechijō*)[17]

On the fourteenth day of the sixth month of 1221, Hōjō Yasutoki's army won a decisive battle against Go-Toba and entered the capital (Kyoto) the following day. Yasutoki's victory was so swift that warriors late to the battle, such as Kōno Michinobu, joined Go-Toba's opposing forces only after Go-Toba had been decisively defeated.

Claiming that he carries a Retired Emperor's edict (*inzen*), Kōno Shirō Michinobu of Iyo Province, led his family, along with brave warriors from that province, in fighting battles [against Kamakura forces]. Since Kōno Shirō Michinobu is the ringleader of these forces, you must quickly unite your forces and perform battle service against him, advancing without delay. Military forces will be dispatched to put down those traitorous rebels (*kyōto*). Thus, it is decreed by the Kamakura lord.

Third year of Jōkyū [1221], sixth month, twenty-eighth day

Musashi *no kami* (copy of seal)

[To: Kōno Michihisa]

---

16. He was the scribe who recorded the spoken words of Yoshitoki.
17. *Kamakura ibun*, vol. 5, document 2762, 6.28.1221 (Jōkyū 3) Rokuhara *gechijō*, 20. Translated by Thomas Conlan. For more on Kōno Michinobu and Michihisa, see Mass, *The Development of Kamakura Rule*, 20–21, and Conlan, "Warfare in Japan 1200–1550," 528. This document was translated by Mass, *The Development of Kamakura Rule*, 183–84.

6. A Kantō Order (*gechijō*)[18]

Few documentary descriptions of the battles of 1221 are extant. But we do have Kamakura's rosters of participants. In addition, confirmations of the holdings of Gotō Motoshige's widow reveal that her husband perished in the conflict and that Kamakura then gave her his lands.

Gotō Rokurō *hyōe no jō* Motoshige fought for our forces at the Battle of Uji River. It has been reported that his widow now lives in Yasuda Estate, Harima Province. She should be confirmed [in these holdings]. It is so decreed.

Third year of Jōkyū [1221], seventh month, twenty-fourth day

Musashi *no kami* Taira (monogram)

Sagami *no kami* Taira (monogram)

7. Excerpt from *The Chronicle of Jōkyū*[19]

The Chronicle of Jōkyū reveals that authority over the post of jitō, *or land steward, served as a crucial source of contention. Go-Toba attempted to assert the authority over this office. Although he most likely bestowed the office on members of the imperial guards, he was portrayed in this chronicle as giving it to his favorite dancing girl* (shirabyoshi) *"Chrysanthemum Turtle"* (Kamegiku).

The world did not generally approve of Go-Toba's ways. From morning to evening he devoted himself not only to hunting small birds or racing horses, but also to swimming, acrobatics, sumō wrestling, archery, and, above all, to practicing the arts of war. He spent his time day and night readying weapons and planning an armed uprising. Irascible as he was, he visited instant, arbitrary punishment on anyone who crossed him. Whenever he liked a minister's or a senior noble's home, or villa, he had the place designated an imperial residence. There were six

---

18. *Kamakura ibun*, vol. 5, doc. 2782, 7.24.1221 (Jōkyū 3) Kantō *gechijō*, 27. Translated by Thomas Conlan. This same document has been translated sligtly differently in Mass, *The Development of Kamakura Rule*, 173–74.
19. The following translation is excerpted from Tyler, *Before Heike and After*, 211–13.

such establishments in the capital and many more in the countryside. Such was the scope of his amusements that he summoned *shirabyōshi* dancers from hither and yon, and favored them one after another. The way he invited them up into the headquarters of the Eight Bureaus, there to trample and soil the brocade cushions spread on the floor, suggested, to the observer's horror, the imminent collapse of the Sovereign's Way and of all imperial authority. He readily took over the hereditary property of senior nobles and privy gentlemen, appropriated shrine and temple paddy fields, merged ten holdings into five, and gave everything away to his *shirabyōshi* favorites. Perhaps it was the mounting distress of venerable shrine and temple priests, who had seen their institutional lands confiscated, that finally provoked Go-Toba to initiate an armed disturbance that led to his banishment. This was a terrible thing.

How did it all start? Apparently with a dancer named Kamegiku, who lived at Sameushi and Nishi-no-tōin. Go-Toba was so mad about her that he appointed her father to a post in the Bureau of Justice. Finding the compensation for the post insufficient, he then issued a decree granting Kamegiku, for as long as he himself should live, the more than three hundred *chō* of the Nagae estate in Settsu. Kamegiku's father received this document, pressed it reverently to his forehead, and rushed down to the estate, where he announced that he was now in charge.

The Kamakura-appointed steward ignored him. "Lord Yoshitoki was granted this estate by the late Lord Yoritomo," he said, "and imperial decree or not, I will not have you claim it without a formal order ceding it to you and bearing Yoshitoki's seal." He sent the man packing.

Kamegiku's father complained to Go-Toba, who was not at all pleased. He summoned Fujiwara no Yoshimochi. "Go down to the Nagae estate," he commanded, "get rid of that steward, and deliver him to me. Yoshimochi hastened there and ordered the steward out, but the steward ignored him, too.

Yoshimochi returned to the capital and reported the outcome to Go-Toba. "If that is the way even the lowest of the low are talking," Go-Toba declared, "then naturally Yoshitoki would have only contempt for a retired emperor's decree."

When Go-Toba heard what Yoshitoki himself had to say on the subject, he issued another decree. It said, "Yoshitoki may well own a hundred or a thousand other estates, and if so, he is welcome to them all. However, he is to give up the Nagae estate in Settsu."

Yoshitoki read it. "How can the retired emperor possibly issue such a decree?" he said. "Let him claim, if he wishes, a hundred or a thousand other estates. Nagae, however, was granted me in recognition of my services by the late Lord Yoritomo. He will have to execute me to get it." So it was that for a third time he rejected Go-Toba's decree.

8. Excerpt from the *Baishōron* Account of the Jōkyū War[20]

Japanese Emperors, known as the Lord of the Ten Good Acts, were thought to rule through moral suasion. The conversation between Hōjō Yoshitoki and Yasutoki is at variance with the sentiments expressed by Yoshitoki in his 1221 directive (see A Directive from Hōjō Yoshitoki to Ichikawa Rokurō, p. 36), but it reflects a later concern with how warriors could take up arms against the emperor.

Meanwhile Yasutoki and his deputy, Tokifusa, conducted affairs of state. In the summer of Jōkyū 3 [1221], Retired Emperor Go-Toba decided to destroy the Kantō Bakufu. First, he had Miura Heikurō Taneyoshi, and Sasaki Yatarō Takashige and his son Tsunetaka, and others,[21] executed by Iga Tarō Mitsusue and others. On the nineteenth of the fifth month, Kamakura learned that an imperial army was to set out immediately for the Kantō.

Accordingly the nun Lady Masako summoned her younger brother and the shogun's retainers. Weeping, she said, "I would be very sorry to live to see the graves of the three Shoguns trampled by the horses of western warriors. There is no reason for me to go on living. Kill me first, then go to join the Emperor."[22]

The retainers replied: "We are all deeply indebted to the Shoguns. Must we not treasure their remains? We will die in the west."

On the twenty-first of the same month—even though the day was so unlucky that the odds against survival were ten to one—Yasutoki and Tokifusa therefore left Kamakura at the head of an army.[23]

However, before his departure, Yasutoki told his father Yoshitoki: "The whole country has always been the imperial domain. Therefore, both in ancient times and in our own day, in this land and in China, no one who defied an imperial command has ever escaped retribution. For example, the former prime minister and lay priest Taira no Kiyomori harassed Retired Emperor Go-Shirakawa. As

---

20. Tyler and Uyenaka, *Fourteenth-Century Voices II*, 32–34.
21. Neither Takashige nor Tsunetaka appears in the *Jōkyūki* account of Mitsusue's death. Takashige figures only in a list of warriors summoned to the trap prepared for Mitsusue at the palace. *Jōkyūki* does not mention Tsunetaka.
22. The opposite of Masako's defiant and much longer speech in *Jōkyūki*. This change probably reflects a growing tendency during the fourteenth century to glorify imperial power.
23. According to the almanac, an extremely unlucky day to start a military campaign. *Jōkyūki*, to the contrary, has Yasutoki exclaim, "Gentlemen, set out with all speed along the Tōkaidō behind your commander, Tokifusa, as soon as I have selected an auspicious day. Yes, the twenty-first of the fifth month is a day to begin a great undertaking. Go then, go!"

a result, the late Shogun Yoritomo secretly received an imperial order, initiated a punitive expedition against the Heike, and was fully rewarded for his service with offices and lands. And of course there is our house, beginning with my grandfather Tokimasa, whose rewards were greatest of all. This is why it would be all the more regrettable if I were subjected now to imperial censure. However, it is impossible to escape Heaven's decree, and we should therefore give up the idea of fighting and surrender."

After a short while, Yoshitoki replied to Yasutoki's earnest appeal. "You have spoken admirably," he said. "However, your words apply only when the ruler's government is righteous. When I look at what has been done in the country in recent years, I see that imperial governance has lost its substance and is no longer what it was in ancient times. For example, an imperial ordinance will be issued in the morning and repealed in the evening, and there is unrest everywhere because the imperial government appoints more than one governor to a province. The places that are still free from misfortune may owe their condition to being under Bakufu administration. Order and disorder are as incompatible as fire and water. Because things have come to such a pass, and because, after all, we would be acting to restore peace in the land, we should fight and put our trust in Heaven. If we eastern warriors gain victory, the rebellious subjects who influenced the Retired Emperor will be in our hands, and we should punish them severely. As for the throne, one of the Retired Emperor's descendants should be appointed Emperor. If he himself resists, then doff your helmet, unstring your bow, bow your head, and surrender. This point of view also has something to be said for it."

9. The Formulary of Adjudication/Jōei Code (*Goseibai shikimoku*) (1232)[24]

These edicts were crafted in the aftermath of Jōkyū and attempted to establish how the post of jitō *could be inherited, and what constituted the bounds of individual responsibility. Great freedom was given to* jitō *in passing the lands*

---

24. This translation is indebted to, and extensively revised from John Cary Hall, "Japanese Feudal Law: The Institutes of Judicature: being a translation of 'Go Seibai Shikimoku'; the Magisterial Code of the Hojo Power-Holder." Text was also drawn from Satō Shin'ichi and Ikeuchi Yoshisuke, comp., *Chūsei hōsei shiryōshū* vol. 1. Translated by Thomas Conlan with great help from Horikawa Yasufumi.

9. The Formulary of Adjudication/Jōei Code (Goseibai shikimoku)

to whomever they saw fit, and women enjoyed strong rights to the lands. This document established strong rights to the lands and led to the rise of a transcendent notion of right.

Fifty-one clauses.

Eighth month of the first year of Jōei (1232)

Item (1). Shrines must be kept in repair; and their worship performed with the greatest attention.

The majesty of the gods is augmented by the veneration of men, and the fortunes of men are fulfilled by the virtue of the gods. Established rituals to them must therefore not be allowed to deteriorate; and one must not be remiss in honoring them as if (*nyozai*) they are present.[25] Accordingly, throughout the provinces of the east (Kantō) and likewise on estates (*shōen*), *jitō* managers, shrine attendants (*kannushi*) must bear this in mind and carry out their duties. Moreover, in the case of shrines endowed with households (*ufu*) from ancient times, in accordance with deeds granted to them for generations, minor repairs are to be executed from time to time as prescribed therein. If a shrine should suffer serious damage, a full report of the circumstances is to be made, and directions will be given as the exigencies of the case may require.

Item (2). Temples and pagodas must be kept in repair; and Buddhist services diligently celebrated.

Although temples are different from shrines, both are alike as regards to worship and veneration. The merit of maintaining them both in good order and the duty of keeping up the established services is thus the same in both cases. Let no one bring trouble on himself through negligence herein. In cases where the incumbent does what he pleases with the income of the temple benefice or covetously misappropriates it, or if the duties of the clergy are not diligently fulfilled, the offender shall be promptly dismissed and another incumbent appointed.

Item (3). On the responsibilities of protectors (*shugo*) in the various provinces.

During the time of Yoritomo, the Great Captain of the Right (*utaishō*)[26] it was settled that those duties should be the mobilizing and dispatching of guards for service at the capital; the suppression of conspiracies and rebellion; and the punishment of murder and violence, which include night attacks, robbery, banditry,

---

25. Famously, Confucius purportedly stated that when attending ceremonies, one should behave as if the spirits are present. For more on this term in Japan, see Conlan, *From Sovereign to Symbol*, 15–16.

26. The office that Yoritomo held for a month in 1190. He coveted this more than that of *Sei-i-tai shōgun*. This phrasing is a more general reference to Yoritomo rather than that single month of his life.

and piracy. In recent years, however, delegated representatives (*daikan*) have been appointed over the districts (*gun*) and counties (*kōri*), and they have been imposing taxes on public and private (estate) lands. Not being governors of the provinces, they yet hinder the affairs of the province: not being *jitō* they are yet greedy of the profits of the land. Such proceedings and schemes are utterly unprincipled. Even members of a family known to be householders (*gokenin*) for generations cannot be mobilized for guard duty if they have no current possessions. On the other hand, it has been reported that various estate managers (*shōkan*) and officials (*gesu*) make use of the name "*gokenin*" as a pretext for ignoring the orders of provincial governors (*kokushi*) or estate proprietors (*ryōke*).[27] Such persons, even if they desire to be taken into the service of a *shugo*, must not under any circumstances be enrolled for service on guard duty.[28] In short, conforming to the precedents of the time of Yoritomo, the *shugo* must cease all actions save for mobilizing *gokenin* for guard duty, and the suppression of plots, rebellion, murder, and violence. In the event of a *shugo* disobeying this article and meddling in affairs other than those herein named, if a complaint is instituted against him by a provincial governor or an estate (*shōen*) proprietor (*ryōke*), or if the *jitō* or people of the land (*domin*) petition for redress, this lawlessness being thus brought to light, he shall be divested of his office and a person of good character appointed in his stead. As regards to deputy (*daikan*), only one is to be appointed by a *shugo*.

Item (4). On *shugo* failing to report crimes and confiscating land holdings.

When persons are found committing serious offenses, the *shugo* should make a detailed report of the case and follow such directions as may be given them in relation thereto; yet there are some who, without ascertaining the truth of falsehood of an accusation, or investigating whether the offense committed was serious or trifling, arbitrarily pronounce the escheat of the criminal's hereditary lands and selfishly cause them to be confiscated. Such unjust judgments represent willful artifice and evil scheming. Let a report be promptly made to us of the circumstances of each case and our decision upon the matter be respectfully asked for, any further persistence in transgressions of this kind will be dealt with criminally. Next, with regard to a culprit's paddies and fields, his dwelling (*zaike*), his wife and children, and other articles of property. In serious cases, the offenders are to be handed over to the *shugo*'s office; but it is not necessary to take in charge their fields, houses, wives, children, and miscellaneous gear along with them. Furthermore, even if the criminal should in his statement implicate others as being accomplices

---

27. *Ryōke* were proprietors of *shōen*. Their rights (*shiki*) were status-based and, until the onset of the fourteenth century, were confined to court nobles.

28. For this would ipso facto make them *gokenin*.

9. The Formulary of Adjudication/Jōei Code (Goseibai shikimoku)

or accessories, such are not to be included in the scope of the *shugo*'s judgment, unless they are found in possession of stolen goods.

Item (5). Of *jitō* in the provinces detaining a portion of assessed taxes (*nengu*).

If an estate proprietor (*ryōke*) instigates a complaint alleging that a *jitō* is withholding the land-tax payable to him, the *jitō* should pay it at once (*kechige*) and have his payment audited (*kanjō*). If the *jitō* were judged to be in default, and has no valid plea to urge in justification, he will be required to make compensation in full. If the amount is small, judgment will be given for immediate payment. If the amount be greater than the *jitō* is able to pay at once, he will be allowed three years within which to completely discharge his liability. Any *jitō* who, after such delay was granted, shall make further delays and difficulties contrary to the intention of this article shall be deprived of his post.

Item (6). Provincial governors and *shōen* proprietors (*ryōke*) exercise their authority without referring to the intercession of Kamakura.[29]

In cases where provincial governors, *shōen* proprietors, shrines, or Buddhist temples exercised jurisdiction as a proprietor (*honjo*), we shall not intervene. Even if they wish to bring a suit before us, they are not permitted to do so. Next, as regards to direct appeals, the proper procedure in bringing a suit is for the parties to come provided with letters of recommendation from their own administrative offices, whether it be that of a provincial governor, a *shōen* proprietor, a shrine, or a Buddhist temple. Hence, persons who come without such letters have already committed a breach of principle (*ri*) and henceforth their suits will not be received.

Item (7). Whether the land holdings (*shoryō*) which have been granted since the time of Yoritomo by the successive Shoguns and by Her Ladyship of the Second Rank (Masako) are to be revoked in consequence of suits being brought by the original owners (*honshu*).[30]

Such lands having been granted as rewards for distinguished merit in the field, or for valuable services in official employment, have not been acquired without reason. And if judgment were to be given in favor of one who alleged that such lands were the original holdings (*honryō*) of his ancestors, his face would beam with joy, but other comrades (*bōhai*) could assuredly feel no sense of security. Such spurious suits

---

29. Literally the Kantō, a term describing the eight provinces of the east and the Kamakura regime itself. This term will be hereafter translated as Kamakura.

30. The three successive *shōgun*s of the Minamoto line were Yoritomo (1192–99), and his two sons Yoriie (1199–1203) and Sanetomo (1204–19). Yoriie was deposed and soon after killed. Sanetomo was assassinated by his nephew, a son of Yoriie, and Fujiwara Yoritsune became the *shōgun* after a gap of seven years (1226). Masako was the wife of Yoritomo and mother of Yoriie and Sanetomo. She achieved the second rank.

(*ranso*) must be prohibited. In case, however, one of the current grantees (*kyūnin*) should commit a crime, the dispossessed original owner (*honshu*), taking advantage of this opportunity, cannot well be prohibited from bringing a suit for recovery.

Next, it is a serious offense for persons to scheme after an interval of years has elapsed to cause a disturbance by scheming falsely, having already found lacking in principle after repeated judgments have been issued. Henceforth, should anyone disregard previous adjudications and wantonly institute spurious suits, the claim shall invariably be judged as being invalid, and this shall be recorded at length of the title and deeds in the possession of the plaintiff.

Item (8). Of land holdings (*ryōsho*) that have not been held (*chigyō*) for several years, even though deeds of investiture exist.

With respect to the above, if possession (*chigyō*) has continued after more than twenty years have elapsed, the rights are not to be inquired into and no change can be made. This follows the precedent of Yoritomo's time. And if anyone falsely lays claim to possession (*chigyō*) and deceitfully obtains an investiture (*onkudashibumi*), this document, even if it is in his possession, will not be recognized as having validity.

Item (9). On plotters of treason (*muhonnin*).

The provisions of the formulary relating to such persons cannot well be determined beforehand.

In some cases, precedent is to be followed; in others, such action should be taken as the particular circumstances may require.

Item (10). On the crimes of killing, maiming, and wounding: furthermore, whether parents and children are to be held mutually responsible for each other's guilt.

One who is guilty of killing accidentally, as in a chance altercation or in the intoxication of a festive party, shall be punished by death or else by banishment or by confiscation of his investiture; but his father, or his son, unless they have actually been accomplices, shall not be held responsible. Next, the offense of cutting or wounding must be dealt with in the same way, the culprit alone being responsible. Next, in case a son or a grandson slays the enemy of his father or grandfather, the father or grandfather, even if they were not privy to the offense, are nevertheless to be punished for it. The reason is that the gratification of the father's or grandfather's rage incited this deed. Next, in the case of a son who attempts to kill another for the purpose of appropriating that other's post or seizing his property or valuables, if the fact of the father's innocence is clearly proven by the evidence, he is not to be held responsible.

Item (11). Whether or not the estate of the wife is to be confiscated because of a husband's crime.

9. The Formulary of Adjudication/Jōei Code (Goseibai shikimoku)

In cases of serious crimes, such as treason, murder, banditry (*sanzoku*), piracy (*kaizoku*), night attacks, robbery, and the like, the guilt of the husband also extends to his wife. Nevertheless, in cases of murder, cutting, or wounding that arise out of sudden disputes, she is not to be held responsible.

Item (12). On abusive language.

Abusive and insulting language causes quarrels and murders. In grave cases the offender shall be sent into banishment, in minor cases, ordered into confinement. If during the course of a judicial hearing one of the parties gives vent to abuse or insults, the lands in dispute shall be granted to the other party. However, in cases where the confiscation of land holdings of the offender in dispute is inappropriate (*ri*), some other land holdings of the offender shall be confiscated. Those with no land holdings (*shoryō*) shall be punished by banishment.

Item (13). On the offense of beating a person.

In such cases the person who receives the beating is sure to want to kill or maim the other in order to wipe out the insult so the offense of beating a person is by no means a trivial one. Accordingly, if the offender is a *samurai*, his lands (*shoryō*) shall be confiscated; one with no land holdings shall be sent into banishment: retainers (*rōjū*) and persons of lower rank shall be placed in confinement.

Item (14). Whether or not a lord (*shujin*) is responsible for crimes or offenses caused by his deputy (*daikan*).

When a deputy is guilty of murder or any lesser serious crime, his lord (*shujin*) shall not be held responsible if he arrests him and sends him to trial. But if the lord defends his deputy, stating that he is not to blame, and incriminating evidence is later uncovered, the lord cannot escape responsibility and accordingly his land holdings (*shoryō*) shall be confiscated. In such cases the deputy shall be imprisoned. If a deputy withholds a portion of the tax to a proprietor (*honjo*), or contravenes precedents regarding assessed taxes, his lord shall nevertheless be held responsible, even though this action was committed by the representative alone. Moreover, whenever a representative receives a summons from Kamakura (the Kantō) or is sent for from Rokuhara regarding a suit instigated by a proprietor (*honjo*), or in connection with matters of fact alleged in a plaintiff's petition, if he does not appear in court and continues to be disobedient (*chōgyō*), his lord's investiture shall be revoked. Extenuating circumstances may, however, be taken into consideration.

Item (15). On the crime of forgery.

If a *samurai* commits the above, his land holdings shall be confiscated; if he has no investiture, he shall be sent into exile. If one of the base (*bonge*) commits it, he shall be branded on the face.³¹ The scribe shall receive the same punishment. Next, if it is persistently alleged in suits that the document in the defendant's possession is a forgery, and when the document is opened and inspected, and is found to be indeed a forgery, then the punishment shall be as stated above; but if it be found to be without flaw, then the false accuser shall be required to repair shrines and temples. Those lacking the means to do so shall be cast out (*tsuihō*).

Item (16). Of the lands that were confiscated at the time of the Jōkyū Disturbance (1221).

Regarding those who had their lands confiscated as a result of reports that they fought for Capital forces but now claim that they were innocent of such wrongdoing.³² Where the proof is full and clear, other lands will be assigned to the current grantees of the confiscated estates, which will be restored to the original holders (*honshu*). The reason for taking such measures is that the current grantees have performed meritorious services and shown merit in war. Next, there were some who, although they received rewards from Kamakura (the Kantō), later fought for the capital. Their crime is especially severe. Accordingly, they were themselves put to death and their holdings were confiscated. Of late years, however, it has come to our knowledge that some have, through force of circumstances, had the luck to escape punishment. Seeing that the time for severity has now passed, in their case the utmost generosity will be exercised, and a slice of their land holdings, amounting to one-fifth, is to be confiscated. However, for those estate officials (*gesu* and *shōkan*), save from those who are otherwise *gokenin*, it is to be understood that it is not now practicable to call them to account, even if it should come to be found out that they were guilty of siding with the capital. The case of these men was discussed in the Council last year and settled in this sense. No one contested this decision.

Next as to whether suits may be brought by those claiming to be original owners of confiscated lands. It was in consequence of the guilt of the then holders that those lands were confiscated and assigned to those who rendered meritorious service. We hear that there are many who now petition and request that those who held lands then (at the time of the Jōkyū Disturbance) were unworthy holders, so, in accordance with the principle of heredity, the lands may be allowed to revert to

---

31. *Bonge* consists of a low status that had specific legal meaning. Such individuals did not possess surnames and were incapable of autonomy. If granted a surname, they could be considered *samurai*. *Samurai* in this context refers to warriors with surnames, but they remained dependent followers of *gokenin* or *myōshu*.

32. Capital forces refers to the army of Go-Toba, the sovereign who fought against Kamakura and was defeated in a brief war.

9. The Formulary of Adjudication/Jōei Code (Goseibai shikimoku)

them. All lands that were confiscated were based on ownership in 1221 (whether legitimate or not). Is it possible for us to put aside the present holders and inquire into historical claims to the land? Henceforth a stop must be put to these disorderly expectations.

Item (17). A distinction is to be made between fathers and sons regarding the guilt of those who fought at the same time in battle.

Regarding cases whereby the father took the side of the capital and the son nevertheless fought with Kamakura (the Kantō) and likewise those in which although the son took the side of the capital the father fought with Kamakura (the Kantō), rewards and punishment have been decided already by the difference in their treatment. Why should one generation be confused with the other regarding guilt? As regards cases of this kind occurring among residents (*jūnin*) in the western provinces, if one went to the capital, whether he was the father or the son, then the son or the father who remained at home cannot be held blameless. Although he may not have accompanied his guilty kinsman, he was his accomplice. Nevertheless, in cases where owing to their being separated by long distances or boundaries it was impossible for them to have had communication with one another or to be cognizant of the circumstances, they are not to be regarded as being reciprocally guilty.

Item (18). Whether, after transferring land holdings to a daughter, parents may revoke the transfer on account of a subsequent estrangement.[33]

Although men and women are distinct, there is no difference between them as regards parental benefactions. That is a saying (*rin*) of experts of law (*hōke*).[34] If, however, the deed of assignment to a daughter were held to be irrevocable, she would be able to depend upon it and would not refrain from unfilial (*fukō*), reprehensive (*zaigyō*) deeds.

And fathers and mothers, on the other hand, aware of the possibility of conflicts arising, must beware of assigning landholdings to a daughter. Once the relation of parent and child begins to sever, the foundation for a violation of the law is laid. In case a daughter shows any unsteadiness of behavior, the parents ought to be able to exercise their own discretion accordingly. When the question is understood to rest on this foundation, the daughter, induced by the hope of a bequest, will be on her best behavior and punctilious in the discharge of her filial duty; and the parents, impelled by the desire of completing their fostering care, will find the course of their affection uniform and even throughout.

---

33. For an alternate recent translation of this clause, see Adolphson, "Weighing in on Evidence," 311.
34. The implication here is that a grant to a daughter would be as irrevocable as that to a son.

Item (19). When those under obligation, whether intimate or estranged, who having been reared and supported, afterward ignore the descendants of their original lords (*honshu*).

Of persons who were dependent for their upbringing, some were treated on a footing of affectionate intimacy as if they were children; otherwise, they were just retainers. When such persons rendered some service to their lords, the latter, in their great appreciation, have in some cases handed them an allocation note and in other cases have willed them lands. Nevertheless, those who had been dependent disobey to the descendants of the original lords by inappropriately insisting that the lands were given to them as gifts (*wayo*)[35] (and were not an inheritance). For a while these persons will act deceitfully, behaving as if they were sons or acting as (if they were) retainers and then, after disobeying, they either claim to be nonrelatives (*tanin no gō*), or to feel enmity and so forget the previous rewards of their lord, and in doing so, disobey his descendants. In such cases, the land holdings that were so assigned to them are to be confiscated and transferred to descendants of the original lord.

Item (20). On the land holdings granted to children who, after succeeding to them, predecease their parents.

Even when the child is alive, what is to hinder the parents from revoking the assignment? How much more, then, are they free to dispose of the land holdings after the child has died; the thing must be left entirely to the discretion of the father or the grandfather.

Item (21). Whether a wife or consort who has received an inheritance from her husband can retain her tenure of land holdings (*ryōchi*) separating from her husband.

If the wife in question has been repudiated in consequence of having committed some serious transgression, even if she holds a written promise, it is difficult for her to possess (*chigyō*) the land holdings (*shoryō*) of her former husband. On the other hand, if the wife in question has merit and was innocent of any fault, abandoned by reason of the husband's preference for novelty, her land holdings cannot be revoked.

Item (22). Regarding adult heirs who have not been disowned, but who have not been willed any holdings by their parents.

When a son who has been raised by their parents to be diligent and deserving, but through a stepmother's slanders or through favoritism of a later-born child, is left with no inheritance for no good reason, represents the epitome of arbitrariness.

---

35. Originally *wayo* meant to give something as a gift and not a compromise, which later became a common meaning of the term. The act of such a gift to nonrelatives was thought to be irrevocable because they were outside the scope of rights based on heredity.

9. The Formulary of Adjudication/Jōei Code (Goseibai shikimoku)

Accordingly, one-fifth of the main heir's (*chakushi*) holdings are to be granted to any landless (*musoku*) elder brother. However small this grant may be, it should depend on the proofs given, regardless of whether the recipient is the son of a wife or of a consort. A son of a wife who has shown no particular service or who has been unfilial does not come within the scope of the rule.

Item (23). Of the adoption of heirs by women.

Although the laws of old do not allow of adoption by women, it has been customary for women who had no children of their own to adopt an heir and so transmit land holdings from the time of Yoritomo down to the present day. In addition, in the capital as well as in the provinces, this practice is exceedingly common and is hereby confirmed.

Item (24). Whether a widow who has inherited her husband's land holdings can continue to possess them after remarrying.

Widows who have inherited the land holdings of their deceased husband should give up all else and devote themselves to praying for their husband's afterlife. Those who disregard the formulary cannot be held blameless. Hence, if any should soon forget their conjugal constancy and remarry, the land holdings held by their late husband are to be granted to the husband's son. If the deceased husband had no son, the land holdings should be disposed of in some other way.

Item (25). Concerning Kamakura (Kantō) *gokenin* who marry their daughters to court nobles and assign land holdings to their sons-in-law causing public service to be diminished.

Such land holdings were assigned to daughters, so as to allow them some autonomy (*kakubetsu seshimuru*), nevertheless the assessment for public services must be imposed in accordance with the holders' rank and standing. When the father was alive, the service required based on these land holdings may have been, as a matter of favor, exempted, but after the father's death, service must be insisted upon. If, presuming on the authority of his position, the holders of such land holdings fail to perform service, they should resign their land holdings (*shoryō*). Even women (*nyobō*) who serve at the shogunal palace in Kamakura (the Kantō) should not ignore public services that are equally imposed. If anyone has difficulties with this, they are not to possess (*chigyō*) land holdings (*shoryō*).

Item (26). On revoking an inheritance that has been promised one son and already confirmed by an edict of confirmation (*ando no kudashibumi*) and granting these lands to another.

That matters of this kind are best left to the discretion of the parents has been already practically laid down in a preceding section. Hence, even a confirmation exists for an earlier testament; if the father changes his mind and decides to assign the land holdings to another child, it is the subsequent will that is to take effect and must be confirmed by adjudication.

Item (27). Concerning land holdings with no clearly designated successor.

These lands are to be distributed considering the circumstances and according to the degree of service rendered, and the varied abilities (of the claimants).

Item (28). On trumping up false statements and instigating slanderous suits.

Those who beguile with soothing words and artful innuendo prejudice their lord's mind in order to ruin innocent others. Such examples appear often in records of old. For the sake of all people, and the current age, they must be rebuked. If a slanderous accusation is made in order to procure lands, the slanderer must give his holdings to some third party. If the slanderer has no investiture, he must be banished. If, on the other hand, the slander has been concocted in order to mar another's career, the offender must be disqualified from ever holding office again.

Item (29). Concerning those who bypass a proper official and plot to take their appeal to another person.

In cases where one concocts an appeal and presents it to someone other than the proper magistrate, a clash of judgments is inevitable, even when nothing of the kind is intended. In such cases the plaintiff must therefore be debarred from bringing his action for some time, while intermediaries (*torimōsu hito*) must be prohibited. If a magistrate is neglectful when a suit is brought before him and allows twenty days to pass without taking any action in the matter, the parties may mention this directly to the Court of Appeals (*teichū*).

Item (30). Concerning parties of a pending suit who, instead of awaiting a judgment, send in a document from a person of powerful houses (*kenmon*).[36]

In such cases, the successful party exults in winning the case by the strength of his powerful connection, while the losing side grieves over the influence wielded by those high in office and position. Hence, one vaunts his obligation to his powerful patronage, while the other distrusts the judgments of the established legal tribunals. It is mainly in this way that the course of government administration is polluted. Accordingly, this practice must henceforth be peremptorily ended. Suitors must either have recourse to officials or the case must be referred directly to the Court of Appeals (*teichū*).

---

36. Often described as a "power bloc," this term designates an individual of the third rank or above, or other privileged institutions (e.g., temples) which, by having this high status, could open a chancellery (*mandokoro*) and issue edicts concerning the governance of their territories.

9. The Formulary of Adjudication/Jōei Code (Goseibai shikimoku)

Item (31). Concerning those who lack justice (*dōri*) and fail in their suits and then accuse officials of partiality.

It is extremely reckless and reprehensible for a person whose cause lacks justice and whose suit has been defeated to then trump up a charge of partiality. Henceforth, any such people who, after making false allegations, make up groundless accusations shall be punished by the confiscation of one-third of their land holdings. If the offender has no investiture, he or she is to be expelled from the locality. If, again, an official has been guilty of some mistake in the matter, he is to be disqualified from ever holding office again.

Item (32). Of harboring brigands and bands of evildoers (*akutō*) within one's lands.

It is clear that if rumors exist that such persons are being harbored but have not actually been discovered, it is impossible to punish the culprits, and those suspected of harboring them will not be rebuked. When men of the provinces (*kokujin*) point out the places of hiding of brigands and evildoers (*akutō*) and they are arrested and summoned to Kamakura, the province becomes peaceful; if they remain at large, then provinces (*enpen*) descend into a state of outrage (*rōzeki*) and suppressive measures must be taken accordingly. In addition, if *jitō* are found allowing gangs of brigands to find refuge, they will be held to be equally guilty. First of all, when the information received gives ground for suspicion, the *jitō* will be summoned to Kamakura and detained. This *jitō* is not allowed to return to his province so long as it remains disturbed. When such gangs of evil men (*akutō*) are found to reside within localities into which a *shugo*'s representative is prohibited from entering, these men must be arrested without delay and handed over to the *shugo*'s office. If the deputy *jitō* fails to hand over the miscreants, the *shugo*'s deputy will be authorized to enter into the domain to apprehend those so arrested, and the *jitō*'s deputy (*daikan*) must be replaced. If the *daikan* remains, the *jitō* will be dismissed, and the *shugo*'s representative will have the authority to enter the said lands.

Item (33). Concerning the two types of stealing: armed robbery, and theft, as well as arsonists. The punishment [of death] is already established through precedent. How could a reconsideration (*shingi*) of that point arise? Next, arsonists are to be treated as brigands, and they should be outlawed.

Item (34). On the crime of illicit intercourse with another's wife.

Whoever embraces another man's wife is to be deprived of half of his land holdings and to be forbidden from rendering further service, regardless of whether it was a case of rape or adultery. Those who have no investiture must be banished. Women who commit adultery shall likewise be deprived of their land holdings, and those with no holdings will suffer banishment. Next, for those who abduct (*tsujitori*) women on the roadways, if *gokenin* they will not serve for a hundred days, but if a retainer (*rōjū*) or those below, the custom that has been in place since the time of Yoritomo will be in effect and they will have half of their hair (*binpatsu*) shaved off. Nevertheless, if the culprit is a monk (*hōshi*) the punishment for the crime will be dealt with accordingly (*shinshaku*).

Item (35). The penalty for those who refused to obey repeated summons (*meshibumi*).

When a defendant has been thrice served with a summons to appear and plead in a case, but does not come and abide judgment, the plaintiff, he shall forthwith obtain judgment in his favor if his case has merit (*ri*); if he has not right (*ri*) on his side, the property in dispute shall be awarded to some third party. In cases where the object of dispute consists of items such as dependent persons, horses, cattle, or sundry items, they shall be restored exactly according to the inventory or description furnished. Otherwise, they shall be appropriated for the repair of the temples and shrines.

Item (36). Concerning those who alter old boundary markers and engender disputes.

Some people transgress the ancient boundaries of their lands and trump up some new pretext for a rival claim, while others disregard recent precedent and submit some old document and found a claim on it. The judiciary is overly burdened with unnecessary trouble because nefarious people (*mōaku no tomogara*) lightly concoct and instigate frivolous lawsuits that cause them no particular harm even if they are unsuccessful in their claims. In the future, when such suits are brought forward, a surveyor must be sent to the locality in question to investigate accurately the boundaries and proofs; and if the claim of the plaintiff is found to be baseless, the extent of the land that he wrongfully sought to obtain by his suit shall be measured, and a portion of like extent shall be subtracted from his land holdings and added to that of the defendant.

Item (37). Concerning Kamakura (Kantō) *gokenin* who, on the side, apply to Kyōto for lands (*shoryō*) in possession of comrades (*bōhai*), and higher management office than them (*jōshi*).[37]

This practice was strictly forbidden in the time of Yoritomo. Recently, however, some have followed the bent of their own ambitions and not only disregarded this prohibition but quarreled with others. Henceforth, those found indulging in such ambition will be punished with the confiscation of one of their land holdings.

---

37. In another reading, this passage could also refer to a person who would be responsible for the management of the estate, serving as its delegated representative (*azukari dokoro*) in the capital without residing there. The term *jōshi* can also be read as *uwazukasa*.

9. The Formulary of Adjudication/Jōei Code (Goseibai shikimoku)

Item (38). Concerning over-*jitō* (*sōjitō*) who encroach on the rights of lords of the land (*myōshu*) living within their land holdings.[38]

It is difficult for an over-*jitō* (*sōjitō*) who has encroached upon separate villages to escape punishment, particularly when he claims his authority over land holdings as the pretext for his actions. Regarding an edict (*onkudashibumi*) issued in the past: even if it regards the office (*shiki*) of a *myōshu*, if the over-*jitō* takes advantage of a difficult situation and tries to unlawfully absorb rights beyond those specifically allocated to him, a new edict will accordingly be issued to the *myōshu* empowering him to pay taxes directly and bypass the *sōjitō*. On the other hand, if a *myōshu* disregards established precedents in disobeying the *jitō*, his office will be revoked.

Item (39). Those wishing to obtain court office or rank must have a written recommendation from Kamakura (the Kantō).

It is an established custom that those who desire ranks and offices[39] should be recommended to the court by Kamakura. Consequently, there is no need to prescribe regulations about it. It is strictly prohibited for those who desire to advance (in another way), be they of high or low status, to apply to Kamakura for recommendations to the court. Nevertheless, those who desire to be invested with the office of the Capital Police (*kebiishi*) or provincial governor (*zuryō*) are permitted to do so without a letter of recommendation from Kamakura. If they are suited to receive the imperial permission, they may be directly appointed to office or rank. Those who are slated to be regularly promoted at the court or who are newly appointed to the junior fifth court rank, but then are due to be promoted to the post of provincial governor, are excluded from the above restriction.

Item (40). Concerning disputes by Buddhist priests in Kamakura regarding monastic positions and rank.

The practice of applying at will for advancement to high monastic rank is a source of disorder and furthermore entails an undue increase of the number of high-ranking ecclesiastical figures. Mature clerics of great learning are passed over for younger men of slight ability, and the ecclesiastical hierarchy is undermined, and the teachings of the sutras and contravened. Henceforth, if anyone should in the future apply for preferment without first having received our permission, if he be the incumbent of a temple or shrine, he shall be deprived of his benefice. Even

---

38. *Sōjitō* had broad authority over larger regions, but this did not preclude others, *myōshu*, from asserting that they were "lords of the land" over regions nominally within the purview of the *sōjitō*. The institution of *sōjitō* was confined to the island of Kyushu and led to tensions between them and smaller warriors who attempted to assert autonomy. For more on *myōshu*, see Conlan, *State of War*, 114–16.

39. *Jōgyō* here refers to the practice of paying for appointment to court office, particularly that of the junior fifth rank, the most prestigious court title available to warriors in the provinces.

if he is a specially favored member of the clergy, he shall nevertheless be dismissed. Should, however, one from a Zen sect make such an application, an influential member of the same sect will be directed to administer an admonition.

Item (41). Concerning slaves and miscellaneous persons.[40]

The precedent established by Yoritomo must be adhered to; that is to say, if more than ten years have elapsed without a lawsuit (regarding competing claims of ownership) there shall be no discussion as to the merits of the case and the possession of the present owner is not to be interfered with. Likewise, concerning children born from such people, the purport of the law is different, the precedent from the time of Yoritomo is clear: boys are to be with their father and girls with their mother.[41]

Item (42). Concerning damages inflicted under the pretext of punishing absconding (*nigekobochi*) commoners (*hyakushō*) when they run away.[42]

When people living in the provinces run away and escape, lords of the lands (*ryōshu*) and others, proclaiming that runaways must be punished, may detain their wives and children and confiscate their property. Such behavior is quite the reverse of benevolent government (*jinsei*). If it is found that the absconded commoner (*hyakushō*) is in arrears as regards payment of his land tax and levies, he shall be compelled to make good the deficiency. If he is found not to be in arrears, the property seized from him shall be forthwith restored. Nevertheless, it shall be entirely at the discretion of the *hyakushō* to decide whether to continue to live on certain lands or to go elsewhere.

Item (43). Concerning those who falsely pretend that another's land holdings are their own and who greedily appropriate the produce thereof.

To covertly gain possession of land holdings under false pretext is a crime that goes against the formulary (*shikijō no osu tokoro*); punishment cannot be avoided.[43] Those goods that have been wrongfully appropriated must be promptly accounted for and restored. If the perpetrator has lands, he shall have his holdings confiscated. If he has no lands, he must be banished. Next, as regards the practice of obtaining a confirmation edict (*ando no onkudashibumi*) for lands that the applicant actually holds, without there being any special ground for making such a request, it is open

---

40. The term *zōnin* refers to low-ranking persons.

41. The purport of the law referred to here would be the Yoro and earlier codes, where this clause is stipulated.

42. The term *hyakushō* best describes commoners, not peasants, some of whom had surnames and were capable of owning and riding horses.

43. This refers to item 3 of the formulary. See above.

9. The Formulary of Adjudication/Jōei Code (Goseibai shikimoku)

to the suspicion that some sinister motive underlies it. Henceforth, the practice must be stopped.

Item (44). Concerning competition over lands belonging to comrades (*bōhai*) under threat of forfeiture because they had been charged with a crime in a case that has not yet been decided.

It goes without saying that those who have piled up meritorious services should desire rewards. Nevertheless, it is not right for some to condemn one in question and request his lands when only a rumor exists of offense having been committed and before any degree of guilt has been ascertained. Those desiring such land holdings will slander that person, and their actions will not be just (*seigi ni arazu*). If their petitions are looked upon favorably, slander will become rampant and unceasing. However reasonable they may be, requests made before judgment (for contested lands) shall be ignored.[44]

Item (45). When a report is made of some offense having been committed, of relieving one of their post or possessions without investigating the matter.

If judicial action is taken in such cases without fully adjudicating the matter, regardless of whether or not the offense was committed, feelings of grievance and resentment will invariably arise. Consequently, a prompt and thorough investigation is required in such cases.

Item (46). Concerning the authority of the incoming and outgoing *jitō* during times of succession.

Concerning the annual tax (*nengu*), the new *jitō* should assess it. Nevertheless, he should not confiscate the private gear, retainers (*shojū*), horses, and cattle of the previous *jitō*. It goes without saying that any slights offered to the previous *jitō* shall be severely punished. Nevertheless, in cases where lands were confiscated (from the old *jitō*) on account of serious offenses, this provision shall not apply.

Item (47). Concerning the act of giving documents to another person, even though the said lands are not in actual possession. Furthermore, concerning the commendation of *myōshu shiki* to powerful houses (*kenmon*) without notifying the proprietor (*honjo*).

Henceforth, those who make such commendations shall be banished; those who receive them shall be required to repair temples and shrines. Next, those *myōshu* who commend their post without the knowledge of the proprietor shall of course

---

44. Literally, even if it is a case of claiming a redress of fortune (e.g., a suit of recovery). An indirect reference to item 7 of the Formulary. The term *riun no soshō* would refer to original owners or their relations recovering lands.

be divested of their post, and this will be added to the *jitō*'s lands. In places where there is no *jitō*, it shall be added to the proprietor's share.

Item (48). Concerning the buying and selling of land holdings (*shoryō*).

It is a set custom (*jōhō*) that those who have inherited a private estate from their ancestors may dispose of it by sale in times of need.[45] But as for those persons who either in consequence of accumulated merit or on account of their personal exertions have been granted rewards (*go'on*), then to buy and sell such lands at their own pleasure is a crime. Henceforth, it certainly must be stopped. If, nevertheless, anyone disregards this prohibition and disposes of such land holdings by sale, both the sellers and the buyers shall be equally dealt with as guilty.

Item (49). On holding a formal trial in a suit when it is quite clear from the documents that one of the parties has no case.

When the documents sent in by both sides disclose with perfect clearness the right or wrong of a claim, adjudication may be given at once without confronting the parties at a formal hearing.

Item (50). Concerning those who proceed to the scene of an affray without knowing the particulars when an outrage (*rōzeki*) occurs.

Regarding those who, in such cases, rush in to offer aid as partisans, it is needless to say that they should be punished. As regards the gravity of their offense, it is impossible to lay down a rule beforehand. The circumstances of each case must be taken into consideration. It is not necessary to regard as culpable those who are not privy to the cause, but who proceed to the scene of an affray in order to ascertain the facts.

Item (51). Of outrages (*rōzeki*) by those holding a decree of summons (*toijō*) in a suit.

It is established practice that when a complaint is instituted, a writ of summons should be issued. But if the writ causes outrages (*rōzeki*) or malicious plots (*kanran o kuwadatete*), culpability is obvious. If it is shown quite clearly that the claims are unreasonable or petty, the granting of summons will be altogether stopped.

The Seventh Month of Jōei 1 (1232)

Oath: Questions of right or wrong shall be decided at Council meetings.

An individual is liable to make mistakes through defect of judgment, even when the mind is unbiased. They can also, out of prejudice or partiality, reach an erroneous

---

45. According to Ishii Susumu and the other editors of *Chūsei seiji shakai shisō*, vol. 1, 439, the set law mentioned here refers to a Karoku 2 (1226) judgment (*ongechijō*) that was quoted in a 7.7 1250 (Kenchō 2) Kantō *gechijō an*, *Kamakura ibun*, vol. 10, doc. 7211, 166–67.

9. The Formulary of Adjudication/Jōei Code (Goseibai shikimoku)

decision while believing they are right. Furthermore, they can claim that proof exists, even in cases where there are no facts to be found. Or, even when being cognizant of the facts, they might be unwilling to expose another's shortcomings and therefore refrain from reporting the truth of the matter. When intention and facts are not aligned, catastrophe ensues. Therefore, at meetings of Council, whenever questions of right or wrong arise, there shall be no regard for ties of relationship. None shall give in to likes or dislikes, but rather all shall speak out in whatever direction reason pushes and the inmost thought of the mind leads, without regard for companions or fear of powerful houses (*kenmon*). Even when a decision given in a case is perfectly just, it shall be agreed upon by the whole Council in session. The entire Council shall be held accountable for misguided actions taken on the basis of faulty information. Council members will never say to litigants and their supporters, "Although I personally had the right understanding of the matter, so-and-so among my colleagues of the Council dissented, and caused confusion." Should such things be said, the solidarity of the Council would be fractured, and we would be ridiculed. Were an individual Council member to agree to support the appeal of a plaintiff who, because they do not have a legal leg to stand on, was denied a trial by the full Council, such an act would be tantamount to the single Council member declaring that all the others are wrong. Such are the reasons for these articles. If even in a single instance we swerve from them either to bend or to break them, may the gods—Bonten, Taishaku, the four great Kings of the Sky, and all the gods great and little, celestial and terrestrial of the sixty-odd provinces of Japan (Nihon), and especially the two avatars (*gongen*)[46] of Izu and Hakone, the Mishima *Daimyōjin*, Hachiman *Daibosatsu* and Temman Daijizai Tenjin—divinely punish us. So may it be, accordingly we swear a solemn oath as above.

The Seventh Month, Tenth Day of the First Year of Jōei (1232)[47]

Shami Jō'en

Sagami *no daijō* Fujiwara Naritoki

Genba no jō Miyoshi Yasutsura

Saemon *no shōi* Fujiwara *no ason* Mototsuna

Shami Gyōnen

San'i Miyoshi *no ason* Tomoshige

Kaga *no kami* Miyoshi *no ason* Yasunaga

---

46. *Gongen* were manifestations of buddhas as Japanese gods (*kami*).
47. Names as depicted in *Chūsei hōsei shiryōshū*, vol. 1, 30–31.

Shami Gyōsei

Saki no Dewa *no kami* Fujiwara *no ason* Ienaga

Saki no Suruga *no kami* Taira *no ason* Yoshimura

Settsu *no kami* Nakahara *no ason* Morokazu

Musashi *no kami* Taira *no ason* Yasutoki

Sagami *no kami* Taira *no ason* Tokifusa

10. Letter from Hōjō Yasutoki Concerning the Formulary[48]

The following letter from Hōjō Yasutoki (1183–1242) concerning the Formulary (shikimoku) *was often copied along with the codes themselves as they were transmitted and explains why he crafted this code.*

Eighth day of the Eight Month of the First Year of Jōei (1232)

Concerning the adjudication of various affairs, even over the same type of case (*onajiki tei*), the arguments of the strong are upheld and the weak overturned. However carefully we consider (the need for fairness in) cases, unjust decisions are invariably made based on the relative strength and weakness of parties, so in order to prevent this, we created this law, a copy of which is appended here.

Indeed, most important law codes need to be known, but in rural areas, it is likely that there is not one in a thousand, or perhaps ten thousand, who understand them.[49] The crimes of thieves or night robbers deserve to be punished instantly, but nevertheless, there are many who make such plots and hurt themselves. Even common acts done by those not knowing the details of the law are to be punished by that very law they do not know for their infraction. They are like deer who climb a mountain, unbeknownst to them full of pitfalls, and fall into them.

It was for this reason that Yoritomo did not base his judgments on the text of laws. The *shōgun*s since then also did not refer to them, and their precedent remains in effect.

---

48. *Kamakura ibun*, vol. 6, doc. 4357, 8.8.1232 (Jōei 1) Hōjō Yasutoki *shojō*, 391; *Chūsei seiji shakai shisō*, vol. 1, 39–40; and *Chūsei hōsei shiryōshū*, vol. 1, 56–57. Translated by Thomas Conlan with Horikawa Yasufumi.

49. The term for laws here, *hōrei*, designates both the ancient codes and court (*kuge*) law.

11. Kamakura Amendments (Tsuikahō)

In short, if retainers serve their lord faithfully; if children are filial to their parents, if wives obey their husbands, then we will be able to aid the honest and thwart the evil. I thought that I could put people at peace by proclaiming this Formulary. I hesitate to do so, however, because people in the capital could ridicule it, saying that it is just the haphazard writings of ignorant barbarians, which would be shameful. However, without a clear standard, unjust decisions based on the relative strength and weakness of parties could be made, so I proclaim this Formulary.

Have this code known, as people should know its core principles. Copy the regulations and distribute them to *jitō* and *shugo* offices, so that throughout the land, every single *jitō* and *gokenin* shall know them. If something escapes the codes, it should later be appended. Respectfully.

Eighth day of the eight month of the first year of Jōei (1232) Musashi *no kami (gohan)*[50]

To: Suruga *no kami*[51]

11. Kamakura Amendments (*Tsuikahō*)[52]

Kamakura's laws were frequently amended. Included here are three of its approximately 750 amendments concerning remarriage, showing how Kamakura honed its judgments and referred to the provisions of the earlier codes.

Item (121) Regarding remarriage (9.30.1239 [Enō 1])[53]

Whether a woman should manage (*seibai*) her landholdings (*shoryō*) or perform various household duties, if [the remarriage] becomes manifest, she should be definitely admonished (and her lands from the former husband confiscated). Nevertheless, secret acts committed in private, even if there are rumors, are not to be acted upon. Next, nuns who return to the laity and remarry are subject (to this law) but the Council has determined that (such punishments) will not be recorded.

---

50. Hōjō Yasutoki.
51. Hōjō Shigetoki.
52. Translated by Thomas Conlan with Horikawa Yasufumi.
53. The item numbers denote the numbering of these clauses in Satō Shin'ichi and Ikeuchi Yoshisuke, comp., *Chūsei hōsei shiryōshū* vol. 1.

Item (435). Whether divorced wives or concubines can possess (*chigyō*) landholdings (*shoryō*) of their previous husbands (12.26.1267 [Bun'ei 4])

If the wife or concubine has merit and was innocent of any fault, even if she has divorced from her husband, she should not be dispossessed of landholdings that she had received from her previous husband. It is so written in the Formulary (*shikimoku*). Nevertheless, after divorcing, if she marries another man, and possesses his landholdings, it is unjust. Henceforth, if a divorced woman remarries, then she will have landholdings that she had received (from the former husband) immediately confiscated.

Item (597). Concerning the remarriage of widows (7.25.1286 [Kōan 9])

Concerning secret acts committed in private, even if there are rumors, they are not to be acted upon. So states an Amendment to the Formulary (*shikimoku no tsuika*).[54] As a result of this, some claim that the (remarriage) is secret and (the laws) do not apply, even though these (remarriages) have become manifest. Henceforth, even if the woman does not manage (*seibai*) her landholdings (*shoryō*) or perform various household duties, rumors of impropriety will result in her punishment in accordance with the fundamental laws (*hon shikimoku*).

12. *Bakufu* Justice: A Case Study[55]

Kamakura's frequent amendments concerning marriage stemmed from the fact that it proved difficult to determine if remarriage had taken place, as no paperwork was generated with such matches, which were often duolocal and difficult to trace because couples did not commonly combine their assets. The following documents, introduced and curated by Jeffrey Mass, offer a remarkable case study, showing how widows could serve on guard duty and convey their deceased husband's possessions, even if doing so was in variance with this final testament. In his study, Mass translates gokenin, *or householder, as vassal, which is at variance with the practice of this book. Mass's introduction follows below.*

As we have seen, the Bakufu's eagerness to uncover the truth (or at least to provide equitable settlements) could sometimes reach extraordinary lengths.

---

54. See *Kamakura Amendments*, Item (121) above.
55. Mass, "Bakufu Justice." The numbering of these documents (138–44) follows Mass. Primary sources exclusive to this article will not be included in the bibliography.

12. Bakufu *Justice: A Case Study*

Often this led to productive results, though on other occasions the outcome was simply extravagance. Modern judicial systems are no different in this regard. In the case presented here, a competent judgment by Rokuhara was ignored by the unsuccessful plaintiff, who took her grievance to Kamakura in a slightly altered form. Thus commenced a laborious proceeding that yielded nothing at all in the way of new evidence. Along the way, however, we are afforded valuable insights into the Bakufu's thinking about different modes of proof. We are also introduced to several of the principles around which inheritance practices developed.

ROKUHARA ATTEMPTS TO RESOLVE AN INHERITANCE DISPUTE BETWEEN A WIDOW AND HER DISINHERITED DAUGHTER 1238, 1239[56]

138

Concerning the dispute between the daughter, named Minamoto,[57] and the widow, the nun Hō-Amidabutsu, of the late vassal Yamashiro Saburō Katashi of Hizen Province, over his property [*shoryō*] and other wealth.

On the occasion of a trial confrontation between the daughter and Hō-Amidabutsu's representative, Minamoto Hiroshi, the statements [*mōshijō-tō*] presented contained numerous details. In brief, however, the daughter did not dispute that Katashi's testament [*yuzurijō*], submitted by Hiroshi, was in his own hand. [By contrast,] Hiroshi argued that Katashi's private letter [*shojō*], submitted by the daughter, was not an actual will, was not in [Katashi's] hand, and bore an incorrect seal. Although the daughter rejoined that the seal was authentic, she acknowledged that [the letter] was not personally written [by Katashi]. Moreover, a private letter in the daughter's hand, submitted by Hiroshi, included a request that [the daughter's] disinheritance be overturned. Proof that this was ever done, however, is unclear. [Finally,] Hiroshi did not dispute that the daughter's son, Michihiro (original name, Daigūji[58]), had his coming of age ceremony [*shufuku*] at the house of his grandfather Katashi; nor

---

56. Doc. 138, *Yamashiro monjo* 1238/10/27 Rokuhara gechijō, *Matsuura tō shoke monjo*, 61–62, doc. 5 (*KI*, 7: 415, doc. 5,316). Doc. 139: *ibid.*, 1239/1/27 Rokuhara rensho shojō, *Matsuura tō shoke monjo*, 63–64, doc. 7 (Kl, 8: 18, doc. 5,375).

57. Literally, "Minamoto no uji." In testamentary matters women are invariably referred to by their clan names, presumably as a protection against the takeover of property by their husbands. In the present case the daughter's father, Yamashiro Saburō Katashi, was of Minamoto stock: see *Yamashiro monjo*, 1192/6/2 saki no utaishō ke mandokoro kudashibumi, *Matsuura tō shoke monjo*, p. 59, doc. 1 (*KI*, 2: 18, doc. 593).

58. I.e., his name as a child.

that Michihiro's younger brothers also came and went [freely] at Katashi's residence. However, is it not a regular practice for grandchildren to be supported, even when progeny [*shisoku*] have been disinherited? It therefore seems difficult to use this as proof that the daughter is not disinherited. Moreover, even if the daughter had never been disinherited, it is [still] the widow who possesses the testament, and this cannot be disputed. In consequence, the property and other wealth of Katashi shall be held by the widow, Hō-Amidabutsu. It is [commanded] thus.

Fourth year of Katei [1238], tenth month, twenty-seventh day

Echigo no kami, Taira (monogram)

Sagami no kami, Taira (monogram)

139

Concerning the dispute between the widow and daughter of the vassal Yamashiro Saburō Katashi of Hizen Province, over his property and wealth. This past year a trial confrontation took place, and a decree[59] was handed down in response to the spoken and written evidence and to an instruction [from Kamakura]. Nevertheless, when the widow was in the capital to take part in the palace guard service [*ōban'yaku*],[60] a summons was issued in response to a [renewed] suit by the daughter.[61] In consequence, the widow is proceeding [to Kamakura]. We beg that this be announced.

Respectfully.

Second year of Ryakunin [1239], first month, twenty-seventh day

Echigo no kami,

Tokimori (monogram)

Sagami no kami,

Shigetoki (monogram)

To: Saitō hyōe nyūdō dono[62]

---

59. I.e., Document 138.

60. This reference provides a valuable insight into the status of women during the Kamakura period. The *ōban'yaku* was incumbent on all Kamakura vassals.

61. Kamakura's readiness to accept a matter already adjudicated by Rokuhara is explained in Document 140. As we will see, the daughter had charged that her mother had remarried, thereby invalidating the original testament (see Goseibai shikimoku, art. 24).

62. A member of the *hyōjōshū* in Kamakura. This marks the document as a report to the Kantō.

12. Bakufu *Justice: A Case Study*

Kamakura Rejects a Suit Renewal Alleging a Widow's Remarriage, 1239[63]

140

That the false suit [*ransō*] of Minamoto *no uji*,[64] the daughter of Yamashiro Saburō Katashi, shall be terminated, and that, in accordance with Katashi's testament, Minamoto Hiroshi, Katashi's adopted son [*yūshi*], shall enjoy hereditary possession, after the life tenure of [Katashi's] widow, the nun [Hō-Amidabutsu].[65]

On the occasion of a trial confrontation regarding the above, the statements of the two sides were very detailed. In brief, however, of the four documents of Katashi submitted by Minamoto *no uji*-dated the twelfth month, seventh day, first year of Jōei [1232] affixed; the tenth month, eighth day; the tenth month, thirteenth day, second year of Jōei [1233] affixed; and the twelfth month, fifth day, second year of Katei [1236] affixed—three dealt with other matters.[66] The single [relevant] document contained many details, but said nothing about the disposal of land rights. [By contrast,] the testament of the late Katashi, dated the third year of Antei [1228], first month, twenty-fifth day,[67] submitted by the widow, is in Katashi's own hand. Even though the names of the holdings [*shōryō*] are recorded [in the daughter's document], we can hardly hesitate [in deciding] between a testament and a private letter. Nevertheless, because the suit lodged by Minamoto *no uji* claimed that the widow had remarried, a summons to trial was immediately issued. However, the arguments [*mondō*] of the two sides were contradictory, and thus an instruction was given for a sworn oath [*kishōmon*] to be recorded and submitted. As a result, the document offered by the widow revealed the [daughter's] lie. In consequence of this, the false suit of Minamoto *no uji* is terminated, and, in accordance with Katashi's testament, hereditary possession shall lie with Hiroshi after the life tenure of the nun-widow. By command of the Kamakura lord, it is so decreed.

---

63. SOURCE: *Yamashiro monjo*, 1239/5/25 Kantō gechijō, *Matsuura tō shake monjo*, pp. 64-65, doc. 8 (*KI*, 8: 46, doc. 5,434).

64. See n. 1, Document 138.

65. Here we learn for the first time that Hiroshi, the widow's representative in the Rokuhara phase of the dispute (Document 138) was heir-designate after her death. This explains the opposition of Minamoto *no uji*, who was the true daughter. Normally sons adopted under the designation *yūshi* were not entitled to inherit property; that privilege was limited to sons adopted as *yōshi*.

66. I.e., irrelevant matters. None of these documents is extant.

67. Not extant.

Section IV • *The Age of Kamakura Ascendancy*

First year of En'ō [1239], fifth month, twenty-fifth day

saki no Musashi no kami,

Taira (monogram)

shuri gon no daibu,

Taira (monogram)

THE BAKUFU DISPOSES OF A DISPUTE REGARDING MOVABLE WEALTH, 1239[68]

141

Concerning the movable wealth [*izai*] and private servants [*shojū*] of Yamashiro Saburō Katashi. A decree has already been issued that rights in land [*shoryō*] shall be hereditary with Hiroshi after the life tenure of the widow. In regard to movable property, although the daughter, Minamoto *no uji*, refers to this in her testimony, she possesses no actual will. Therefore, this matter cannot be taken up. By this command, it is so conveyed.

First year of En'ō [1239], fifth month, twenty-fifth day

saki no Musashi no kami

(monogram)

shuri gon no daibu (monogram)

[To:] the Yamashiro widow

142

Concerning the movable wealth and private servants of Yamashiro Saburō Katashi. We have taken note of a Kantō directive of the fifth month of this year, twenty-fifth day.[69] In accordance with this, let matters be so understood. It is [commanded] thus.

---

68. Sources: Document 141: *Yamashiro monjo*, 1239/5/25 Kantō migyōsho, *Matsuura tō shake monjo*, pp. 65, doc. 9 (*KI*, 8: 46, doc. 5,435). Document 142: *ibid.*, 1239/6/16 Rokuhara shigyōjō, *Matsuura tō shake monjo*, pp. 65-66, doc. 10 (*KI*, 8: 50, doc. 5,440). Document 143: *ibid.*, 12 39/6/18 Mikuriya-no-shō azukari dokoro kudashibumi, *Matsuura tō shake monjo*, p 66, doc. 11 (*KI*, 8:50, doc. 5,441).

69. This Rokuhara document, then, is in response to Kamakura's edict refusing to hear Minamoto *no uji*'s suit claiming her father's movable wealth and servants. Either Rokuhara's enforcement of the main settlement is not extant, or the deputyship failed to issue a *shigyōjō* for a matter it had previously settled.

First year of En'ō [1239], sixth month, sixteenth day

Echigo no kami (monogram)

Sagami no kami (monogram)

[To:] the Yamashiro widow

143

Ordered: to Mikuriya Estate.[70]

That the property rights of Yamashiro Saburō Minamoto Katashi shall be [held] in accordance with the Kantō order [*onkudashibumi*] and the Rokuhara edict [*ongechijō*].[71]

Details concerning the above appear in the Kantō order. Forthwith, Minamoto *no uji*'s false suit is terminated, and in accordance with the testament of Katashi, hereditary possession shall lie with Minamoto Hiroshi, the adopted son of Katashi, after the life tenure of the widow. It is [commanded] thus.

First year of En'ō [1239], sixth month, eighteenth day[72]

azukari dokoro (monogram)

The Bakufu Interrogates Witnesses in a Final Rehearing of a Remarriage Charge, 1244[73]

144

Concerning the dispute between the vassal Michihiro of Hizen Province, son of Masuda Rokurō *nyūdō*,[74] and the nun-widow of Yamashiro Saburō Katashi over [her alleged] remarriage.

---

70. The site of the Yamashiro family's homelands in Hizen Province.

71. I.e., Documents 140 and 138. (Note the apparent confusion here between *okudashibumi* and *gechijō*.) This endorsement was for the main suit, not the secondary matter, though the rationale for the present document (a custodian's confirmation) is not clear.

72. A further validation of the main suit was issued by the *dazaifu*: see *Yamashiro monjo*, 1239/9/20 dazaifu shugosho kudashibumi, *Matsuura tō shake monjo*, pp. 67–68, doc. 13 (*KI*, 8: 65–66, doc. 5,476).

73. Source: *Yamashiro monjo*, 1244/4/23 Kantō gechijō, *Matsuura tō shake monjo*, pp. 68–69, doc. 14 (*KI*, 9: 76–77, doc. 6,308).

74. Masuda Rokurō was the husband of Minamoto *no uji*, the loser in the 1239 litigation. Note that both the widow (Document 139) and her grandson Michihiro are listed as Kamakura vassals.

On the occasion of a trial confrontation regarding the above, many details were presented by both sides. In brief, however, Michihiro charged that Katashi's widow had remarried, citing as witnesses [*shōnin*] Fuku, a daughter of Izumi and the wife of the estate financial officer; Daigūji Suetoki; Fuji *daibu* Ietsugu . . . ;[75] Jibefusa Nagaari; Genzō Hiroshi; and Arita Saburō Kiwamu.[76] The nun-widow defended herself by arguing that this was not the first time that such a charge had been brought: previously a similar suit had been lodged and considered, and she had been awarded a settlement edict.[77] Therefore, there were no grounds for relying on [the present charge].

At this point, the persons listed by Michihiro were interrogated; and though Jibefusa Nagaari's deposition appeared to contain particulars, his earlier and later remarks were contradictory. Moreover, none of the other depositions contained any specific proof. Most importantly of all, when vassals from this province came to be queried,[78] two cosigned affidavits [*kishōmon*] were submitted for examination. The first of these, from the first year of Kangen [1243], fourth month, twenty-ninth day, bore the signatures of nine persons. Mine Saburō *nyūdō*, Mine Gentōji Tamotsu, Mine Yajirō Katsu, and *sakon no shōgen* Nami, a total of four persons, gave some acknowledgment [of the charge], citing the opinion of the estate's deputy [*mokudai*] Yoshihiro; but they admitted that they knew nothing specific. [In contrast,] Shigyō Meguri, Shisa Rokurō Sada, Shijiki *gūji* Ieyasu, Aikamiura Saburō Ietada . . . ,[79] and Osaza Tarō Shigetaka, a total of five persons, were aware of the rumor, but stated that they did not know whose opinion was accurate.

The [second] affidavit, of the fifth month, eleventh day, contained the signatures of five persons. Among these, Hata Genjirō *nyūdō* and Isshi Shijirō Kiramu had questioned certain personal servants [*ge'nin*],[80] but claimed that they did not know whose opinion might be correct. [The remaining three,] Sashi Genjirō Gyō, Chiga Yozō Takeru, and Yoshitomi *ukon* Tarō Sukenari, asserted that they had no knowledge owing to the long distances involved.[81]

---

75. The character "tsugu" is half-size, followed by a phrase meaning "character omitted." Thus, literally, "Ie-character for tsugu omitted." This construction occurs again in the document.

76. The transliteration of the personal names given here and later in the document is speculative. Moreover, the various printed transcriptions separate the characters differently.

77. I.e., Document 140.

78. Presumably at the *shugo* headquarters or by agents of the *shugo*. The Bakufu, as a final recourse, was evidently turning to its own vassals in hopes of establishing the truth in this matter.

79. The construction here is the same as that described in n. 87.

80. Are these the servants (*shojū*) referred to in Document 141 (i.e., those awarded to the widow)?

81. I.e., because they lived too far away.

In response to Michihiro's petition, numerous witnesses were interrogated, but not one possessed any proof. Therefore, the charge cannot be acted upon.[82] Forthwith, Michihiro's false suit is terminated. By this command, it is so decreed.

Second year of Kangen [1244], fourth month, twenty-third day[83]

Musashi no kami,

Taira ason (monogram)

13. Hōjō Shigetoki's Letter to His Son Nagatoki[84]

Hōjō Yasutoki's younger brother Shigetoki (1198–1261) wrote two letters to his son, which reveal attitudes regarding family, status, pride, the nature of good and evil, and how officials should behave. A comparison of his letters, one of which is reproduced here, with his brother's laws reveals the mindset of the Hōjō and much about the social and intellectual world of the warriors of thirteenth-century Japan. His second letter, "The Gokurakuji Letter," written by Shigetoki later in life, is not included here but has been published in Monumenta Nipponica.

Letter of Instruction from [the Lord of] Rokuhara and Governor of Sagami to his son—Penname (*gō*) "Gokurakuji Shigetoki."

[*Preamble*]

As the minds of men are so different, it is preposterous—and might invite ridicule—to tell others how they should behave and think. Yet, a son tends not to exceed his father, even when his father is dull (*otoru oya*). For this reason, I have here outlined for your benefit some observations I have made.

---

82. What remains puzzling is why an alleged remarriage could not have been confirmed or denied more easily. Why were the various local persons questioned not able to give a more definitive answer?
83. Enforcement edicts were subsequently issued by Rokuhara and by the *dazaifu*: see *Yamashiro monjo*, 1244/7/27 Rokuhara shigyōjō, *Matsuura tō shake monjo*, pp. 69–70, doc. 15 (*KI*, 9: 103, doc. 6,351); ibid., 1244/8/18 dazaifu shugosho kudashibumi, *Matsuura tō shake monjo*, pp. 70–72, doc. 16 (*KI*, 9: 107–8, doc. 6,363).
84. Steenstrup, "Letter to Nagatoki," in *Hōjō Shigetoki (1198–1261)*, 143–57. Primary sources exclusive to this article will not be included in the bibliography.

You had better not swerve from my teachings: for even if they were of a nature to make you behave badly, people would think, "Why blame the son, one had rather blame the father for not teaching him better!"

To impart my precepts by word of mouth would be inadequate; that is why I have put them in writing. Never show them to a stranger; but in your spare time you should get someone in whom you can have complete trust to read them aloud to you while you listen carefully to every detail.[85]

1

Fear the Buddhas, the Gods, your lord, and your father.[86] Being aware of the law of retribution (*inga no kotowari o shiri*) you should out of regard for your posterity be humane towards everybody and not even treat the incompetent harshly; you should be tolerant [toward others' faults], but strive to be praised [for your own conduct].

You should act with imperturbable courage, and you must never be considered a coward; you should constantly train in the bow and arrow.

On every occasion, try to be charming; when facing others, see to it that they come to think well of you; therefore, talk with all of them equally graciously; have pity on the poor; and towards your wife, children, and household members, too, you should always show a jovial and never an angry face.

When you employ knights,[87] labor soldiers, foot soldiers (*samurai, zōshiki, chūgen*) etc., you should never take on those who are querulous or obstreperous. Or you may lose instead, to your great disadvantage, many good servants.

2

Do not discuss important affairs with an unintelligent servant, even though he is faithful and his status (hereditary). Grave matters you should deliberate with those of your staff who have experience and wisdom. If the problem still baffles you, say to your advisors, "I'll lay the matter before my father in writing." If you rashly decide on important matters without taking advice, you will run into troubles afterwards.

3

However profitable an undertaking might be, desist from it, though the gain be huge, if your reputation is at stake; stick to your respectability.

---

85. How old Nagatoki was when Shigetoki told him this is a disputed question.

86. Steenstrup's uses the term *feudal lord* in his translation, but this may cause confusion and so *feudal* is omitted here. [TDC]

87. Steenstrup unorthodoxly translates *samurai* as knights. In this case, he is referring to dependent warrior followers. [TDC]

4

Never pass a death [sentence] in anger. When you feel that indignation is warping your judgment, remand the accused person to the custody of others; after you have calmed down completely, impose the appropriate punishment. Do not decide a case on the spot. If you pass sentence before your anger has subsided, you will afterwards regret what you have done. If you cannot suppress your emotions, close your eyes and concentrate upon calming down.

5

When otherwise well-behaving retainers or foot-soldiers commit some minor fault, calm down, and let them off with a scolding, but do not be so strict as to punish them. If you fall into the habit of getting angry with and punishing your men, those who hear about it will not want to become your close retainers. Avoid humiliating them if they already have a sense of shame.[88]

Similarly, towards ordinary servants, no matter how young or lowly they are; if they have a sense of shame, you can be gentle towards them. Remember that if you think, "They are mere serving-men," and speak scathingly to them, you may leave them (resentful). You should talk to them in such a way that they realize their own mistakes. When someone points out to them that you [deliberately spared them from punishment], they will feel deep gratitude towards you.

6

Never show men to their faces that you regard some of them with more sympathy than others. Speak in the same manner to all of them. Those who hear that you treat even the very incompetent just like the others will appreciate you [as a good leader]. Yet, for all that, you must never lose sight of the real differences between men's ability levels.

7

Never think big of yourself. You should always consider, "What do others think of the things I do?" Deliberately take a low posture. Be polite even to persons of no consequence.

8

At banquets, you should also talk to poor-looking guests, no matter whether they sit higher or lower [than you]; in the latter case, make a point of inviting them to move up.

---

88. To have a sense of shame defined the warrior.

You should not seat guests according to their exterior only. Of course you must pay proper respect to those who have high status. But you should also take good care of those who are poor but have fine characters. In short, you must not lose sight of the true qualities of other people. Thus you will win the appreciation of those who can judge character. [In cases of doubt, however,] status considerations must prevail.[89]

Besides observing the two criteria I have already outlined [—status and worth—] you will also be obliged to treat those whom you know well [with particular attention]. But do so in an inconspicuous way! For your behavior must not offend anybody.

9

When men who depend on you for their livelihood and men who only occasionally work for you (*waga on shitaran to sanjo no hito*) are together in your presence, you should show more attention to the latter. For the former, though they sometimes, within your household, grumble against you, are easy to manipulate (*nadameyasushi*). But when people outside your control [such as the latter] complains against you, it is only by chance that you may hear about it, and are able to do something [to win them back]. Therefore, you had better see to it that people outside your control get no reason to think ill of you.

10

When someone accuses another of a crime, you must never pass judgment on the spot after having heard only the accuser's story. No matter how abominably the accused person appears to have acted, you must first calm down; then consider that the accused person may, after all, have justice on his side; compare the statements of both parties; then pass judgment according to who is right and who is not. Never heed whether you know the party well or not. Let reason be your only guide (*tada dōri ni yorubeki nari*).

11

When you have received a letter—even when you think that you need no advice—you should discuss with someone[90] how to answer. Only when the letter comes from a man in your service or from a trusted friend is it correct for you to reply on your own. But when transacting business for the *bakufu*—even if it is a matter of

---

89. The status criterion is repeated in a way which makes it likely that it was meant as a guideline for decision in situations where "status" and "intrinsic worth" pointed to different solutions. But possibly the author simply left the dilemma for consideration. Ishii Susumu, in *Chūsei seiji shakai shisō*, 312n8, thinks that the repetition is due to scribal error.

90. That is, with experienced retainers. The Hōjō experimented with establishing deliberative councils.

no particular importance—you should always call in men who know precedents well and discuss thoroughly the case with them. So much the more if the case is an important one!

12

Never drink *sake*, even a single jar, alone. Whenever you have any *sake*, you should invite all friends of your own status who are able to attend, and have them drink the *sake* with you. To do so will create an attachment to you.

13

Never visit a woman in her home. If it is awkward to have her come to your house, ask her to meet you in the house of some young knight whom you can trust. With greater reason, never stay overnight in a woman's home.[91]

14

[When asked to show your] skill in the polite arts, even if it is something you can do easily, it is best to say that you cannot, because you lack such skill, and to comply only when they insist. Even then, never allow yourself to be puffed up by success, so that you come to angle for applause and expressions of personal popularity. You, a warrior, should, [on the contrary,] excel in the skillful handling of public affairs, in possessing sound judgment, and above all, in specializing and excelling in the way of the bow and arrow. What lies beyond these fields is of secondary importance.[92] Never immerse yourself unduly in the pursuit of polite accomplishments! Yet, when you are in a party with good friends, and they are in the mood for having some relaxed fun together, you should not refuse too steadfastly [their pleas that you, too, contribute to the common pleasure by performing], or they will come to dislike you as a stand-offish person. Remember that you must, on every occasion, strive to be well thought of by others!

15

When you are in the company of a group of friendly gentlemen, and there is even one among them whose attitude you do not know well, you must never say anything

---

91. Courtiers, too, often did what Shigetoki here advises; see Ivan Morris, *The World of the Shining Prince*, pp. 234 and 240–41.

92. The polite arts in which a warrior ought not to excel were such skills as dancing, singing, calligraphy, and verse-capping. The idea that a warrior ought to master the arts of culture in addition to those of war arose about 1250, and spread rapidly in the Kyoto-influenced shogunal court. But the idea did not become a commonly accepted part of warrior ideology until during the Ashikaga era, when the warrior government ruled from Kyoto.

critical of others. In general, you should not speak of other people's affairs. And you should forbid your young knights, too, to do so.

16

Morning and evening when you are at home, you should test out on the members of your household the behavior you intend to use towards people at large, with a view to finding out how the latter will respond; but you must never show even the young knights in your immediate surroundings what you really think. When you observe these two rules, people will say that you have good qualities, and thus you will be able to excel over them. Keep this enclosed within your heart, though you feel elated by success![93]

If someone sends a clumsy letter to you, you should make a point of observing the proper letter forms when answering. It is never out of place to be polite towards others. To answer impolitely, or, because you do not know the other person's circumstances well, to be overpolite: of these alternatives the latter one is always the safer! In letter writing as in all other matters, nothing is as useful as politeness.

17

If a person who is not in your service, but in mine, presents a gift to you, you should answer that you are very happy for the gift.[94] When you do so, the giver will feel attached to you. Whereas, if you give an indifferent answer, he will feel rejected. Further, if you let the giver know that for the time being it is inconvenient for you to receive him, he will suspect that he will get nothing for his trouble (*mashite tadaima wa bengi ashikute genzan ni irezu nando henji shitsureba kokoroezu omou nari*). He will think that you will not receive him, because you despise his gift, and he will feel resentment against you. Thinking that he has given in vain, he will say to himself, "To serve that lord (i.e., you) would surely be effort wasted"; and in secret, he will speak disparagingly about you.

18

You must never disregard what I say, no matter how unreasonable my words may appear to you. If you think of thwarting me, do not hope to become my

---

93. One may see in this precept a Machiavelian mastermind at work, or just a perceptive use of a given system of situational, outer-directed ethics; at any rate, the statement is remarkable for its undisguised utilitarianism. The second half of the Article deals with the unrelated subject of letter-writing, and was probably originally an independent Article.
94. The underlying idea of this Article seems to be: "Treat the members of my staff with consideration; one day when you take over the *tandai* office you will need their assistance."

heir![95] Show total obedience if you want to inherit. Do you think anyone who wants something from another dares disobey him? A hand wishing to grasp must keep its fingers intact!

19

If you receive a horse as a gift from your superior (*oyakata*), then you should step down from the house, take hold of the bit, and then ask some of your men to lead the animal away. You must not order some servant to lead it out of your courtyard; still less you should deal with the matter by answering from behind a bamboo blind. A person who does so is what I would call a yokel! You must, however, act according to the circumstances of the superior who gave you the horse. If he is young, has no particular prestige, and you stand in no previous obligation to him, and yet you behave with such great respect, the onlookers will think, "Why does he do that?"; the impression will be that you have fussed too much. In such a case you should have made some young knight of suitable rank take the bit of the horse, and not have it done yourself.

20

If someone has given you a horse, you must not immediately pass it on to somebody else for keeping. Even less should you [immediately] give it away to another person. At least for one day you must leave it standing in your own stables: on the second or the third day you may pass it on to someone else. When the giver, having returned to his own place, hears that the horse he gave you was put into your own stables, he will be very pleased. Further, you must not have a presented horse led away without looking at it. If your giver asks, "Was the lord pleased with the horse I gave him?" and gets the answer, "It was immediately given away to somebody," the giver will feel disappointed, and think, "This lord does not seem to feel any gratitude in respect of my gift": you have left the giver resentful.[96]

21

When you are on horseback, you should have a foot soldier or a labor soldier walk beside the horse. But if the occasion is not particularly important, and men

---

95. The succession laws of the period gave the father considerable freedom of testamentary disposition.

96. The notion is reminiscent of a modern Japanese family's "present-box" where courtesy gifts are stored until one can safely present these to someone else. The ritualization and formalization of gift-giving was an important part of what warriors learned from Kyoto.

of these classes are not available, it is all right if you take a stalwart servant of a young knight with you. Yet, if you are out at night, you *must* have a young knight with you; and you should not be out at night unless it is absolutely necessary. If you have to be out at night, and you think there is the slightest risk involved, the accompanying young knight should carry a sword and be adept at using it; under no circumstances whatever should you permit a [mere] foot-soldier to carry a sword.[97]

22

Let no person of discernment—not even a servant—ever see you with a loosened topknot or in underwear; nor should you sit on the *nageshi*[98] with your legs spread out. If you permit yourself such informal behavior, people will think ill of you. Should your topknot come loose of itself, put on your cap quickly. Remember that if you sometimes display slovenly behavior, people will notice for whom you dress up and for whom you don't; and they will go home and make comments about you to their wives and children.[99]

23

When you enter a room where many persons have already taken their seats, you should neither take a too prominent, nor a too lowly seat, but one according with your status. Do not seat yourself below people of low rank; they will make a commotion [trying to come to sit lower than you;] and you will feel very embarrassed.

24

You must under no circumstances seat yourself on the same level as your superior; you must sit in a lower seat. If a party develops into an informal drinking bout, you should still—even when invited to move up—ask your superior to sit higher than you, whereas you take for yourself the second place downwards from his seat.

---

97. The sword had more prestige than any other weapon, because a sword-fighter met his opponent in close combat. Even in Tokugawa times, swordsmen had higher rank and salary than the militarily more efficient musketeers. Strangely enough, nothing sneaky was seen in the use of the silent, long-distance weapon, the bow; but the *naginata* or halberd . . . met the warriors' opprobrium.

98. The frame timbers mentioned are the *nageshi*, that is visible, horizontal beams keeping wall and floor together, and likewise wall and ceiling, see s.v. *nageshi* in *Nihon kokugo daijiten* and in *Kogo jiten* (Tokyo: ōbunsha, 1972), p. 1270. The lower *nageshi* was a favorite, but improper seat.

99. Conjectural reading; the original text is very faded.

13. Hōjō Shigetoki's Letter to His Son Nagatoki

25

Do not in front of other people eat simple food such as wheat with a self-satisfied air.[100] Eat in a manner not inviting comment. However, in your close family circle you can do as you like.

26

Do not drink water in a room where many people are assembled.[101] If you want water, drink it where there are no others around. But when many others drink, or when whole groups drink together at a spring from a cup going round, then you, too, may drink a little. Even there, drink with moderation; or you will appear boorish.

27

When fish or fowl are set before you to eat, do not daintily divide the food up too small. On the other hand, you should not bite off the wings of fowl with your teeth, or lick or tear the food: it is ill-mannered. Try to find a proper medium.

28

It is foolish to wedge yourself into a throng of people attending a superior in a crowded room. It is quite another matter if there is plenty of space. When a room is overcrowded, unless you have something important to do there, stay out.

29

(When visiting somebody's house, do not roam about, eventually hitting upon some dirty spot: your host will be angry when you next time appear before him. Such behavior is foolish: yet, at drinking parties maybe nobody cares).[102]

30

You must not let your short sword get rusty. If your lord or your father should order you to draw it, and it is rusty, you will be despised. [Even less] should you, being a

---

100. The purpose is not to warn a warrior against flaunting his frugality; but that he should not invite guests to share, or otherwise show pride in food which he regards as delicacies, but which the courtiers consider as rustic fare. What we have here is advice for a warrior stationed in Kyoto; in Kamakura the utmost simplicity in matters of diet was part of the image which Hōjō leaders studiously cultivated.

101. He might slurp, and the courtiers would laugh; or they might feel that he spoiled the fun of the occasion, drinking water while they quaffed *sake*.

102. Conjectural reading. Original text partially illegible because of discoloring.

warrior, let the long sword get rusty. Always remember that you may be called upon to draw it when you do not expect it!

31

When others are present, and you want to spit, keep your mouth shut, turn away, and spit into a piece of tissue paper. Long-distance spitting is bad, because it shows disrespect of others. It is also utterly vulgar and will make others look down upon you. Avoid loud laughing, the habit of lounging with legs spread, and inconsiderate pranks, or you will create the impression of being an undisciplined person.[103] And those who know character well will consider you a nobody. Whereas, if you avoid such behavior you will be regarded as a "mature young man."

32

Before you go to see other people, look carefully into a mirror, make sure that your clothes sit well, straighten the front of your robe, and take the necessary time for these things. After having entered into the presence of others, you must not at all rearrange your figure, or your sitting posture, or pose relaxedly. If you do such things, people in general will think that you are a person of slight importance, and men of strict manners will deride and despise you. All forms of dressing-up should take place in your home, never when you are among other people.

33

When in service, (do not criticize others),[104] and do not (speak) lengthily on trivial matters.

34

While others are merrymaking together, it is wrong of a guest to think, "I am a serious person" and not join the fun. When people have come together to relax in each other's company, then a guest who stays aloof from the merriment will [simply] be thought of as a puffed-up person who disrupts the joviality of the party. On such an occasion you should make a point of being even more immersed in the merrymaking than the others. You should follow the trend of the situation, and behave in conformity with the others.

---

103. Conjectural reading. Original text badly faded.
104. Conjectural reading. Original text partly illegible because of discoloring.

35

Never at a party imprudently say something vulgar: others may hear it. In your elated frame of mind you may intend nothing serious, but people who can judge character may overhear you.

36

As for clothes, wear what people normally wear. If you wear unusual clothes, people will stare at you, and ask themselves, "Why does he do that?" Regard this situation as a bad one. Do not wear fancy clothes: they make people stare. It is bad, too, for a young man to wear clothes fit for older men, and vice versa. Do not wear the [ostentatious] clothes preferred by the pages and acolytes of Buddhist temples, and by foot soldiers. Wear only what is normal. Even men of rank ought not to wear [gorgeous colors like] dapple dyes, polychrome dyes, or cord-patterned dyes (*makizome*); however, as such clothes are [now] common, I will not forbid you to wear them. But beware of wearing clothes only fit for old men, such as long gowns in light-blue patterns, or in white; or clothes dyed auburn or brownish yellow (*kōzome*).[105]

37

(Do not wear a cap different from what is normal).[106] Neither its height, nor the quantity of material should be excessive. People will stare if your cap is too elegant, or too plain. Your cap should correspond to your status.

38

No matter how disorderly a party gets, you should not snatch *sake*, appetizers, etc. standing in front of other guests.

39

If your servants happen to meet other men's servants [on the street], you must be careful to prevent them from (quarreling, fighting, etc.).[107]

---

105. *Makizome*, i.e., a process of dyeing in which some parts, that are to be kept the color of the ground, are wound with cord and dyed in the skein. *Kōzome*, the word which I have, for lack of a better English term, translated as 'auburn' is the color of fabrics dyed in the red-yellow-brown juice of the clove tree. Clothes dyed thus made the wearer look like a monk. 'Brownish yellow' translates *kaki* or persimmon. The juice of its fruits dyes fabrics brownish-yellow; such fabrics were worn by old men.

106. Conjectural reading. Original text badly faded.

107. Warriors' servants were lusty rustic roughs from northern and eastern Japan, prone to quarrel and fight, e.g., over right of way, on the slightest occasion.

40

Do not without urgent reason visit the house of a knight who is not in your service. He will politely invite you in, but he may actually resent your visit (and say so to others). (When having to deal with such a man,) you should discuss the matter with experienced men and [send them] to deal with him [instead of going yourself].

41

When you are drunk, and your face is flushed, you should not walk the streets; go home when it gets dark, or call your carriage, except when the distance is very short.[108]

42

Do not practice archery on dogs (*inu-ou-mono*) which happen to be in front of any persons.[109]

43

Do not trample people's crops. It is against the law (*muhō*).[110]

[Copyist's note:]
On the sixth day of the ninth lunar month of the third year of the Jōwa era [1347], with the cyclical characters "Hinoto-i," in the monk's cottage *Chishunbō* belonging to Daigo temple, I finished copying the original. Its title read, "Excerpts of Precepts by the Lay Priest of Mutsu (Ōshū Zenmon *gikyōshō*)." From the general impression I got of the text I hit upon [an additional] title for it, "The Precepts of the Night Crane."

---

108. The warriors' attitude toward alcohol was ambivalent. On the one hand, alcohol provided escape, conviviality, and emotional outlets (see Articles 12, 14, 34). On the other hand, warriors were afraid of falling into the traps of alcoholic indulgence, and committing indiscretions, gaffes, or crimes of violence, the latter a particular danger because warriors went about armed; see Articles 24, 35, 38, and 42.

109. Target shooting on dogs from horsebacks (*inu-ou-mono*) was part of the warriors' archery practice routine. The arrows used in *inu-ou-mono* were blunt, but the impact of the longbow, particularly at short range, was considerable. The rule warns against such archery practice under the circumstances where others may be hit and quarrels ensue.

110. There were statutory legal provisions against such behavior by warriors; their horseback hunting parties damaged crops, and the hunt itself outraged Buddhist sentiment in the temple-studded Kyoto environment. The term which I translate as 'against the law' is *muhō*; it may refer to law, to Buddhist principles, or to Kyoto sentiment in general.

14. Excerpt from Takezaki Suenaga's *Scrolls of the Mongol Invasions*[111]

An account by Takezaki Suenaga (1246–?) recounting a warrior's attempt to be rewarded by official Adachi Yasumori (?–1285) for his performance in battle against the Mongols. Accompanying this translation is a later illustration of the Mongol invasion scrolls illustrating Suenaga's audience with the Hōjō administrators and Yasumori himself.

The following is an excerpt from Takezaki Suenaga's account of his arrival in Kamakura, where he had an audience with Adachi Yasumori, shugo of his province and a powerful figure within the Kamakura regime. In Suenaga's record of their meeting, one can see how legal thinking influenced the process of assessing military action and granting rewards. The official format of military affairs reports was being revised at this time, causing great confusion. Suenaga wanted to be rewarded for being the first mentioned in a roster of participants, while Yasumori wanted to reward only those who had performed noteworthy, verifiable deeds—such as being the first to charge into battle. In the end, Yasumori relented and awarded Suenaga a horse and lands. Suenaga would later praise Yasumori posthumously.

On the twelfth day of the eighth month, I arrived in Kamakura. In the spirit of my purification at Mishima Shrine, I bathed in the saltwater of Yuinohama, and then, even before stopping at the inn, I went to the Tsuruoka Hachiman Shrine and had an offering presented, praying with all my heart for success of the bow and arrow.

Afterward I visited any number of officials (*bugyō*) and told them my tale, but they ignored me because I appeared to be a petty warrior with only a single low-ranking follower (*chūgen*). Since no officials would see me, I realized that I could rely only upon the support of the gods (*shinmei no kago*). So once again I visited Hachiman and prayed with all of my heart. On the third day of the tenth month, I had the opportunity to speak at the Court of Appeals (*teichū*) that was administered at that time by Akita no *Jō no suke* Adachi Yasumori.

[There I said:] "I, Takezaki Gorō *hyōei* Suenaga, a *gokenin* of Higo Province, state my case. Last year on the twentieth day of the tenth month, during the battle with the Mongols, I set off toward the harbor of Hakozaki and heard reports the pirates (*zokuto*) were going to attack Hakata. As I left for Hakata, the general

---

[111]. Translated by Thomas Conlan. For the full translation of Takezaki Suenaga's scrolls, as well as sixty-seven documents pertaining to the Mongol Invasions, see Conlan, *In Little Need of Divine Intervention*. For visual depictions of the scrolls and an animated map, see http://digital.princeton.edu/mongol-invasions/; for an annotated version, see http://digital.princeton.edu/annotatedscrolls/.

(*taishō*) of the day, Dazai no Shōni Saburō *saemon* Kagesuke, who had fortified his encampment at Hakata's Okinohama, said that [we should] fight together. Because of this, most of the members of my clan remained behind in camp. I went before Kagesuke, faced him, and explained: "Because my dispute (*honso*) [with my relatives] has not been settled, I have only five mounted warriors. Therefore, I have no choice but to fight against the enemy. I have nothing to live for save for advancing and having my deeds known. I want to lead the charge and have this reported to the lord." Kagesuke replied: "I don't expect to survive tomorrow's battle but if I do, I will speak of your deeds." After that I set off from the Hakata encampment and made my way to Shiohikata of Torikai, where I led the charge. My horse and my bannerman's horse were shot and killed and I, Suenaga, Mii Saburō, and one other mounted retainer (*wakatō*) were wounded. Shiroishi Rokurō Michiyasu, a houseman (*gokenin*) of Hizen Province, stood as my witness. Kagesuke recorded me as being the first. I then asked Tsunesuke to note in his document (*kakikudashi*) that [my deeds] should appear in a battle report (*onchūshin*), and he wrote 'If you have any questions regarding the first, then I will explain the particulars,' and left it at that.[112] If these documents are not shown to the lord, then I lose the honor of the bow and arrow."

Lord Adachi *Jō no suke* said: "You have spoken of Tsunesuke's report. Do you know your deeds are not worthy of mention in a battle report (*onchūshin no bun*)?"

"How could I possibly know?"

"Then tell me precisely what you do know. If you don't know [everything], then how can you possibly say that Kamakura's response has been insufficient?"

"Tsunesuke wrote that if you have any questions regarding the first then he would fully examine the particulars if so ordered. I thought what he wrote in his document (*kakikudashi*) was worthy of being recorded in a battle report (*onchūshin no bun*), but my being first [in battle] is omitted from the report (*onchūshin*)." As I spoke, I took Tsunesuke's document (*kakikudashi*) and looked at it.

"Did you take any enemy heads? Were any of your men killed?" Yasumori asked.

"No heads taken. None were killed," I replied.

"If that's the case, then you have not performed sufficient battle service (*kassen no chū*). Other than being wounded, you did nothing at all. How can our response be insufficient?" Yasumori countered.

"So I can't have an audience with the lord because my being first in battle was not recorded in the battle report? But if you have any doubts about my truthfulness

---

112. Suenaga thinks it is significant that he was mentioned first in the document, but Adachi Yasumori was more concerned with Suenaga's actions on the battlefield as opposed to when he was mentioned in the battle report.

14. Excerpt from Takezaki Suenaga's Scrolls of the Mongol Invasions

and need proof, why don't you dispatch a directive (*mikyōjo*) to Kagesuke and ask him about it? If he writes an oath (*kishōmon*) declaring that my statements are false, then not only can you ignore my military deeds, you can also take my head!"

"There is no precedent (*hikake*) for issuing an edict questioning Kagesuke. There is nothing I can do."

"I don't think that precedent matters here, for there is something that you have not considered."

"What is it? Tell me what it is I haven't considered," [replied Yasumori].

"If this concerned disputes over land rights (*shomu sōron*) or if it were a battle involving only Japan (*honchō*), I know that I could not make such an unprecedented request. But this is a battle involving a foreign court (*ichō*). Precedent does not apply. It seems that I can't be questioned or have [my reports] viewed by the lord for lack of precedent! How then can I maintain my martial valor?"

"What you say is true, but the law (*onsata no hō*) is perfectly clear. Without precedent, nothing can be done."

"With apologies for my rudeness, let me make myself perfectly clear. This is not a legal dispute. I want to receive rewards. And, as I said before, if my assertion of being first to charge turns out to be false, then I revoke my claims for rewards and ask you to take my head. If what I say is true, then show [my battle report] to the lord in order to prove my valor in battle. If you ignore my request, it is as bad as [ignoring] a lament from a past life. What could exceed that?"

When I countered Yasumori for the third time, he relented. "Very well. I acknowledge your deeds in battle. I will state that your deeds should be seen [by higher authorities] and am sure that rewards shall be directly granted as you wish. Return now to your province at once and prepare to perform military service once again."

"As you will show [my report] to the lord, I will abide by your command. Nevertheless, since a judgment has not been reached regarding my disputed holdings, I am landless (*musoku no mi*). I don't know where to go to live. I know many men well enough to enter their service as a retainer, but I want to plant my own little flag [and do things my way]. There is no one to help me (*fuchi suru*), so I don't know where to go or what to do while waiting for the next great event."

"Your situation," Yasumori reflected, "is most difficult indeed. I now must immediately report to the Yamanouchi lord. He will hear of your battle deeds."

On the fourth day of the same month, as I was reporting to Yasumori's Amanawa residence, the servant (*kogirimono*) Noto Jirō, a *gokenin* of Hizen Province came up to me and asked: "What happened yesterday at Yasumori's Court of Appeals (*teichū*)?"

"I repeatedly explained the situation to the administrators (*onbugyō*) but they would not take up my case so I appealed directly [to Yasumori]."

"Yasumori told the high-ranking followers (*miuchi*) of the Hōjō that a warrior of unusual strength of will appeared in his Court of Appeals. This man declared that his rewards should be confiscated, and his head should be chopped off if, after being questioned, Saburō *saemon* were to say his account was false. In a time of crisis, remember this man, Yasumori told Tamamura, [adding that] he liked men from Tsukushi (Kyushu) because they speak of honor (*onmenboku*) even though [their documents] have not yet been reviewed. He recommended that this man [Suenaga] should be granted rewards." So Noto Jirō informed me. From then on, we spoke as usual.

On the first day of the eleventh month, at the hour of the sheep [1–3 p.m.], I, Suenaga was worshiping at Hachiman Shrine when Tamamura *Uma no* Tarō Yasukiyo came up and summoned me alone to an audience hall.

"This edict (*onkudashibumi*) confirming your land holdings has been granted from above as a reward for your battle service. Here."

Responding to his summons, I left the chamber (*ima futama*) and approached Yasukiyo. [Bowing deeply, I] respectfully looked to Yasukiyo and received the document. As I was taking the document, Yasukiyo also said, "Yasumori personally requested that you be directly rewarded. Here." Again I respectfully received Yasumori's edict (*onkudashibumi*).

"Now will you finally leave?"

Believing that Yasukiyo thought that I had spoken as I had done solely to receive more rewards, I said: "As I said before, if I gain recognition from the Kamakura lord and am granted rewards then I will go back [to Kyushu] the following day and will wait for the next crisis. If that is not the case, then notify Kagesuke immediately [and have him punish me]."

"As a result of your complaint you have personally received your own edict (*onkudashibumi*). Now, one hundred and twenty others have been rewarded by Dazaifu. Since you have had an audience, go back and be prepared to perform military service again. Here is a fully equipped horse. How about returning now?"

I was speechless at having been so honored. Respectfully I received a chestnut horse with a saddle decorated with a small, comma-shaped heraldic device (*kotomoe*). Saeda Gorō, master of the stables, provided the horse's bridle and other well-made accoutrements. It was the first day of the eleventh month, at the hour of the sheep [1–3 p.m.].

Of Adachi Yasumori.

I speak of how I feel toward him. . . . Well over one hundred [and twenty] men received praise but only I received an edict (*onkudashibumi*) and a horse. What could exceed my honor of the bow and arrow? [During the Bun'ei battles . . .]. How could I ever [repay] this? You shall be filial sons if [you] are always first in leading the charge during times of great importance for the lord.

The first year of Einin [1293], ninth day, second month[113]
When I went to the Kantō, I had a dream (*gomusō*) . . . [text missing]. On 5.23 [1275], the deity of the Kōsa Shrine appeared, flew over the shrine, and settled in a cherry tree to the east. I went to the Eastern Barrier (Kantō) and thus received the lands of Eastern Sea (Kaitō)—these are the same characters as those of the shrine where I worshipped . . . [text missing]. It was the . . . virtue of the deity that allowed Suenaga's honor of the bow and arrow to flourish once I entered the Kaitō. This can be known, for I saw the deity in a cherry tree. Because of that, I received an edict (*onkudashibumi*) on the first day of the eleventh month of the same year, returned to Takezaki on the fourth day of the first month of the new year, and entered my Kaitō lands on the sixth day of the same month. Reflecting upon this, I knew that I had to praise the deity. Thus it is recorded.

15. Legal Amendment (*Tsuikahō*) Concerning Rewards[114]

In 1281, Kamakura prohibited warriors like Takezaki Suenaga from traveling long distances to the capital, instead ordering them to remain in Kyushu.

Item (486). Concerning pirate ships (*zokusen*) (9.16.1281 [Kōan 4])

While it is true that they should be defeated and dispersed, one should not, of one's will, travel to the capital or commence long journeys. If there is special need, state the particulars and abide by instructions.

16. Suenaga's Audience with Adachi Yasumori

A scene depicting Takezaki Suenaga's audience with Adachi Yasumori. This image comes from a nineteenth-century copy of Suenaga's scrolls. Particularly noteworthy, one can see a Hōjō official with their triangular crest embossed on their robes.

---

113. The era name did not change for Einin until the eighth month. Suenaga wrote this document after 1293 but predated it to the time when Yasumori's murderer, Taira Yoritsuna, lived. In fact, he wrote it sometime after Yoritsuna's death. For more on Yoritsuna, see *The Confessions of Lady Nijō*, p. 96.
114. Text from *Chūsei hōsei shiryōshū*, vol. 1. Translated by Thomas Conlan.

Section IV • *The Age of Kamakura Ascendancy*

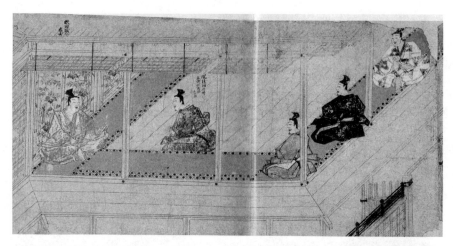

A scene from the Mongol Invasion Scrolls depicting Takezaki Suenaga's audience with Adachi Yasumori. To the left of the upper panel, Suenaga (center) faces Adachi Yasumori (to the far left), while a Kamakura official with the triangular familial crest of the Hōjō appears on the far right.

The lower panel, a continuation of the scene, shows one named official, Ashina no hangan, and guards, who are described as samurai.

17. Excerpts from Tōgan Ean's Statement of Opinion (*ikenjō*)[115]

Japan struggled to mobilize their warriors and organize their forces in response to the Mongol invasions. The Mongols' appreciation for the Japanese warriors' skills is evident in the first document below (Tōgan Ean's Statement of Opinion). The next document (Summons of the Chinzei Eastern Administrator, p. 88) illustrates the ways in which Kamakura tried to verify warriors' services in battle. Other documents in this section show how the Japanese attempted to "liberate" Korea from Mongol rule. Though this campaign came to naught, these documents reveal how Kamakura tried to mobilize an army and prepare for an amphibious attack. Finally, two documents (Petition for Reward by Shami Shukumyō Ōkami Korechika, p. 91; and Letter by Shōni Kagesuke, p. 92) recount the invasions of 1281 and reflect the formalization of the format used for recording battle service.[116]

An excerpt from a letter written in 1270 by the Zen monk Tōgan Ean, who believed that the Mongols desired to incorporate Japanese warriors into their armies because of their martial prowess.

Because Japan's military skills (*Nihon koku no bugei*) supersede those of all other nations, because our bows and arrows [are used with] peerless skill, and because our armor makes even the gods tremble, . . . the Mongols desire to conquer Japan. Once Japan's warriors are under their control, they will be able to conquer China (*Karado*) and India (*Tenjiku*). The country of the Mongols would direct strategy while Japan would fight in the field for their victory. With the strength [of Japan and the Mongols] combined, no country could resist. That is why the Mongols now desire to subjugate Japan.

---

115. *Kamakura ibun*, vol. 14, doc. 10559, Tōgan Ean *ikenjō*, 112–13. Translated by Thomas Conlan. See also Conlan, *In Little Need of Divine Intervention*, document 1, p. 201.

116. Copy of a Kantō Directive (*mikyōjo an*), Copy of a Document (*kakikudashi*) of Shimazu Hisatoki, and Kamakura's Attempt to Dispatch Forces to Korea are translated here for the first time. All other documents pertaining to the Mongol invasions appear in Conlan, *In Little Need of Divine Intervention*, although some (particularly Copy of a Letter by Shōni Kagesuke) have been revised.

18. Summons (*meshibumi*) of the Chinzei Eastern Administrator[117]

A summons written by Odawara Kageyasu, one of Ōtomo Yoriyasu's retainers, requesting that three warriors report to Yoriyasu so that he could question them, write a report, and forward it to Kamakura. Such an investigation was required to satisfy the Kamakura's lingering doubts about their military service.

There has been a further inquiry [from Kamakura] regarding the battle service (*kunkō*) of those who fought against the Mongols. [In order for the *shugo* Ōtomo Yoriyasu to create] a report (*onchūshin*), you shall dispatch a representative (*ondaikan*) prior to the tenth of this month. By [Yoriyasu's] authority (*onsata*). Respectfully.

(The first year of Kenji [1275]), sixth day, eleventh month

[Odawara] Kageyasu (monogram)

[To:] The Honorable Matama Matajirō

The Honorable Imi *Hyōe* Jirō

The Honorable Togō *Saemon* Gorō

19. Kamakura's Attempt to Dispatch Forces to Korea

These documents, issued by the Kamakura Shogunate, represent an attempt to shore up the authority of Shōni Tsunesuke and to mobilize more sailors and oarsmen for the invasion of Korea. Plans for an invasion had progressed to the point that a provisional date for launching an attack, the third month of 1276, had been determined.

Copy of a Kantō Directive (*mikyōjo an*)[118]

The subjugation of foreign countries (*ikoku*) is planned for the third month of the next year. If oarsmen and sailors from Kyushu (Chinzei) are insufficient, Dazai Shōni Tsunesuke has ordered the mobilization of men from the San'in, San'yō, and

---

117. *Kamakura ibun*, vol. 16, doc. 12107, Chinzei higashikata bugyō *meshibumi*, 154. Translated by Thomas Conlan. See also Conlan, *In Little Need of Divine Intervention*, document 9, p. 208.

118. *Kamakura ibun*, vol. 16, doc. 12170, 12.8.1275 (Kenji 1) Kantō *mikyōjo an*, 171. Translated by Thomas Conlan.

19. Kamakura's Attempt to Dispatch Forces to Korea

Nankai districts. Those *jitō gokenin* and men with complete administrative authority over lands in Aki Province must mobilize sailors and oarsmen. Please report the allotted numbers [of men and boats] and dispatch them to Hakata. Thus it is ordered and conveyed.

The first year of Kenji [1275], eighth day, twelfth month

Musashi *no kami* [Hōjō Yoshimasa] (*arihan*)

Sagami *no kami* [Hōjō Tokimune] (*arihan*)

To: The Honorable Takeda Gorōjirō [Nobutoki]

COPY OF A DOCUMENT (*KAKIKUDASHI*) OF SHIMAZU HISATOKI[119]

In order to conquer Koryŏ [Korea], warriors have been dispatched. It has been ordered that you are to cross over [the ocean]. Respectfully

[Shimazu] Hisatoki (seal)

The second year of Kenji [1276], fifth day, later third month

[To:] The Honorable Ōsumi Gorō

AN ACKNOWLEDGMENT (*UKEBUMI*) BY JŌYŪ, A PRIEST AND ESTATE MANAGER[120]

Here, Jōyū, the manager (azukari dokoro) *of Kubota estate in Higo Province, has recorded the men, equipment, and horses he could muster for the invasions of Korea. The defensive tone of Jōyū's reply suggests that a response was expected prior to the tenth day of the third month of 1276.*

Hashiuragaki: A reply from the Kubota *azukari dokoro*. An acknowledgment of orders (*ukebumi*) by the priest and *azukari dokoro* of Kubota estate in Higo Province, Jōyū.

On the twenty-ninth day of this month, an order, written on the twenty-fifth, was received [stating that] in order to conquer foreign lands, we should submit a list of forces, weapons, and horses.

---

119. *Kamakura ibun*, vol. 16, doc. 12293, *urū* 3.5.1276 (Kenji 2) Shimazu Hisatoki *kakikudashi an*, 238. Translated by Thomas Conlan.
120. *Kamakura ibun*, vol. 16, doc. 12271, 3.30.1276 (Kenji 2) Higo Kubota *no shō* Sō Jōyū *ukebumi*, 227. Translated by Thomas Conlan. See also Conlan, *In Little Need of Divine Intervention*, document 17, 215–16.

In accordance with previous orders, I had already counted the number of troops and weapons in my own forces (*gushinsei*) and reported them to the military envoy (*ōryōshi*) Kawajiri *hyōe no jō*, on the past tenth day. Since I received a second notification, I personally have recorded this again. This purport should be made known. Respectfully, Jōyū.

The second year of Kenji [1276], thirtieth day, third month

The priest and *azukari dokoro* of Kubota estate Jōyū

Jōyū's List of Followers, Weapons, and Horses[121]

The followers, weapons, and horses of the priest and *azukari dokoro* of Kubota estate in Higo Province.
1. Myself, age thirty-five.
One retainer (*rōjū*), three followers (*shojū*), and one horse.
2. Weapons:
One suit of full armor (*yoroi*), one suit of simplified armor (*haramaki*), two bows, two quivers of war arrows (*ōya*), and one sword (*tachi*).
Thus it is recorded in accordance with the command.

The second year of Kenji [1276], thirtieth day, third month

The priest and *azukari dokoro* of Kubota estate Jōyū

A Document (*KAKIKUDASHI*) of Ōtomo Yoriyasu[122]

> *Ōtomo Yoriyasu dispatched the following document to his representative, the Bungo gokenin Nokami Sukenao. Each gokenin was responsible for overseeing the mobilization of troops and sailors from within his domains for the invasion of Korea and for reporting the composition of these forces to the shugo. These efforts came to naught, and no force was ever dispatched to Korea.*

Preparations for the advance into foreign countries:
—Submit a list of large and small boats within your holdings and the names and ages of sailors and oarsmen. You shall make preparations to dispatch these men to Hakata by the middle of next month.

---

121. *Kamakura ibun*, vol. 16, doc. 12275, 3.30.1276 (Kenji 2) Higo Kubota *no shō* Sō Jōyū *chūshinjō*, 229. Translated by Thomas Conlan. See also Conlan, *In Little Need of Divine Intervention*, document 18, 216.
122. *Kamakura ibun*, vol. 16, doc. 12252, 3.5.1276 (Kenji 2) Ōtomo Yoriyasu *kakikudashi*, 220–21. Translated by Thomas Conlan. See also Conlan, *In Little Need of Divine Intervention*, document 16, 214–15.

—When crossing into foreign lands, record the names and ages of upper and lower [status] men, their arms, and their armor (*hyōgu*).

The preparations mentioned above should be completed prior to the twentieth day of this month and a report dispatched. You have the authority to severely punish those who flee. This is so conveyed.

The second year of Kenji [1276], fifth day, third month

The former Dewa *no kami* (monogram)

[To:] The Honorable Nokami Tarō

20. Petition for Reward (*gunchūjō*) by Shami Shukumyō Ōkami Korechika[123]

*Togō Korechika submitted the following petition to Kamakura in an attempt to receive rewards after the second Mongol invasions of 1281. His account describes the battle of Takashima and reveals that Korechika did not even know the first name of one of his witnesses, the novice (*nyūdō*) Kazusa Saburō.*

The Bungo *gokenin* Togō *Saemon* Gorō Ōkami Korechika *hōshi* (holy name Shukumyō) respectfully states:

I desire to receive immediately a [Kamakura] battle report (*onchūshin*) [that mentions my deeds], and to be singled out for rewards, as is customary [for service in] battles against the Mongols at Takashima, in Hizen Province, on the seventh day of the seventh intercalary month of the past year of 1281.

Concerning the above, when the Mongol rebels (*Mōko kyōto*) arrived on the shores of Takashima, in Hizen Province, Shukumyō galloped to Hoshika, of the same province, and on the seventh day, at the hour of the serpent [9–11 a.m.], crossed over to this island and performed battle service on its eastern beaches. Shukumyō's son, Shirō Koretō, managed to decapitate (*buntori*) the enemy. In addition, my retainer (*rōjū*) Saburōjirō Shigetō was wounded. The bannerman, one of the base (*genin*), Yaroku Suemori, was [also] wounded. These actions were witnessed by Shite Chikugo *no bō* Enhan, of the same province, and the novice (*nyūdō*) Kazusa

---

123. *Kamakura ibun*, vol. 21, doc. 15867, 3.1286 (Kōan 9) Shami Shukumyō Ōkami Korechika *gunchūjō*, 91–92. Translated by Thomas Conlan. See also Conlan, *In Little Need of Divine Intervention*, document 23, 220–21.

Saburō. Shukumyō desires to receive a [Kamakura] report [chronicling his deeds], and to be singled out for rewards with due haste. Respectfully stated thus.

The ninth year of Kōan [1286], third month

Shami Shukumyō (monogram)

21. Copy of a Letter by Shōni Kagesuke[124]

The following copy (utsushi) of a letter, dispatched by Shōni Kagesuke to Kamiyama Shirō, a witness for Kasai Norikage, shows that witnesses' statements had to be recorded under oath in order to be considered as "proof" of battle service. This document also reveals how battles were fought on the high seas before the typhoons slammed into the Mongol fleet.

The *jitō* Kasai Kotarō Norikage of Kigoya, Chikugo Province, states that on the fifth day of the seventh intercalary month of 1281, in the seas off the coast of Mizushizaki in Hizen Province, he managed to pursue a large vessel, one of three Mongol pirate vessels (*zokusen*), and do battle. [After] boarding [that] enemy ship, Norikage decapitated [the enemy], while his younger brother, Hironori, pursued the foreign pirates (*izoku*) into the sea. Some relatives and followers (*hikan*) were wounded, while [other] retainers (*rōjū*) were either killed, wounded, or managed to decapitate the enemy. Witnesses have stood [for Norikage] attesting that they saw [his actions]. Nevertheless, an oath should be written [by these witnesses] that verify the truth of Norikage's battle service. [Respectfully].

The seventh year of Kōan [1284], twelfth day, fourth month

Kagesuke ([ari]han)

[To:] The Honorable Kamiyama Shirō

---

124. *Kamakura ibun*, vol. 20, doc. 15150, 4.12.1284 (Kōan 7) Shōni Kagesuke *shojō utsushi*, 161. Translated by Thomas Conlan. See also Conlan, *In Little Need of Divine Intervention*, document 24, 221–22.

22. The New Laws (*Shin-shikimoku*) of Adachi Yasumori (1284–85)[125]

On 3.28.1284, the shogunal chief of staff (shikken) *Hōjō Tokimune suddenly died. His death was a surprise; he was signing documents not two days before. Tokimune's young son Sadatoki became the next Kamakura chief of staff* (shikken). *Nevertheless, Sadatoki's uncle, Adachi Yasumori, issued over ninety legal clauses from the fifth month of 1284 through the eleventh month of 1285. These laws, which have attracted considerable scholarly attention, represent an especially intense legislative period. As the subject is omitted from these clauses, it is most difficult to know if they were mostly designed for the* shōgun, *or Yasumori's nephew Hōjō Sadatoki.*

Yasumori's laws advocate the restoration of lands to shrines and temples because the transfer of land, through sale and inheritance, was thought to be a source of disorder. This well-intentioned edict served to undermine one of the bedrock clauses of the 1232 Kamakura law: that possession and use of lands for a period of twenty years established irrevocable ownership. Yasumori also advocated more frugality and better governance from the Hōjō. Ever suspicious, the Hōjō assassinated Yasumori.

The New Shikimoku (5.20.1284 [Kōan 7]). 38 clauses.[126]

Item (1) (491). The lands of temples and shrines shall be restored as of old; and their worship of the gods and Buddhas performed with the greatest attention. The construction of new temples and shrines shall cease, and old temples and shrines shall be restored.

Item (2) (492). For prayers, choose monks of ability, and reduce their number. Perform rituals in accordance with the law (*hō*) and do not be remiss regarding funds for them.

Item (3) (493). There should be tutoring (*gogakumon*).[127]

Item (4) (494). The martial way shall be promoted so as to ensure that it does not end.

---

125. Translated by Thomas Conlan with Horikawa Yasufumi.

126. The numbers appearing after "item" denote the numbering of these clauses in Satō Shin'ichi and Ikeuchi Yoshisuke, comp., *Chūsei hōsei shiryōshū*, vol. 1.

127. It is not clear if this refers to educating Hōjō Sadatoki, the young head of the Hōjō house, or Minamoto Koreyasu (age twenty-one) the *shōgun* and also an imperial prince or both. For one view, see Hosokawa Shigeo, *Kamakura Seiken tokusō senseiron*, 248–51.

Section IV • *The Age of Kamakura Ascendancy*

Item (5) (495). Three cases shall be discussed for each internal deliberation session (*naidan*).[128]

Item (6) (496). Intermediaries (*mōshitsugi banshū*) shall be appointed. When important people (*shikaru beki no hitobito*) call [Hōjō Sadatoki] they shall have a personal audience, while others will receive a response [from Hōjō Sadatoki] through other means.

Item (7) (497). The people staffing the [Hōjō] residence (*denchū*) should serve daily.

Item (8) (498). Women and monks should not intercede.

Item (9) (499). Frugality is encouraged in all things.[129]

Item (10) (500). Decorum and behavior (*reigi reihō*) at the [Hōjō] residence (*denchū*) shall be corrected.

Item (11) (501). Gifts from those who reside in the capital or dispatched as messengers throughout the land shall cease. Gifts from other people shall be prohibited if excessive.

Item (12) (502). Entertainment (*zasshō*) shall be prohibited.

Item (13) (503). Excessive, elaborate construction (*zōsa*) shall be prohibited.

Item (14) (504). Save for ceremonial visits for the New Year and directional taboos, [Hōjō Sadatoki] should not visit others lightly.[130]

Item (15) (505). People of the [Hōjō] residence (*denchū*) shall not dispatch messengers to the administrators (*bugyōnin*) regarding various affairs.

Item (16) (506). [Hōjō Sadatoki] should appoint and promote administrators who are straightforward (*renchoku*).

Item (17) (507). Provisional public levies should hereby cease.

Item (18) (508). Concerning levies of [Hōjō] territories. Every year accounts shall be sent and all the special taxes (*tokubun*) shall be paid.

---

128. *Naidan* were private consultations held by the Hōjō and their crucial administrators. According to the *Sata mirenshō*, "the important men of the *hyōjōshū* form the *yoriai* [Council]. They discuss policy in secret (*naidan*)" (*Hyōjōshū-chū ni mune no hitobito onyoriai ari, himitsu no on-naidan kore aru nari*). See Steenstrup, "Sata Mirensho," 416. Nevertheless, this could represent an attempt to restore shogunal authority, and because the subject is omitted, it is not necessarily clear whether these clauses apply to the *shōgun* or the Hōjō leader.

129. The likely subject here is Hōjō Sadatoki, the head of the Hōjō, and Adachi Yasumori's nephew.

130. The language here applies more to the *shōgun* rather than the Hōjō leader.

22. The New Laws (Shin-shikimoku) of Adachi Yasumori

Clauses concerning the Kubō (lord).[131]

Item (19) (509). Kyūshū Shrine lands shall not be purchased by the *hoi polloi* (*kō-otsunin*). As of old, they shall be administered by shrines.

Item (20) (510). From now on, the construction of new temples and shrines shall cease, and the provincial temples (Kokubunji) and the First Shrines (Ichinomiya) of each of the provinces shall be restored.

Item (21) (511). Frugality shall be practiced.

Item (22) (512). If landholdings are classified as being appropriable (*kessho*),[132] compensatory lands shall be granted;[133] rewards from the *shōgun* (*jun'on*) and benefices (*kyū'onrō*) shall be made in accordance with their previous service.

Item (23) (513). The administrators (*bugyōnin*) for appeals shall be decided.

Item (24) (514). "Lords of the land" (*myōshu*) of the nine provinces of the Chinzei (Kyushu) shall receive Kamakura edicts (*onkudashibumi*) [confirming their status].

Item (25) (515). Those that reside in the capital or who are dispatched as messengers throughout Japan shall be exempt from paddy taxes (*nengu*) levied on their holdings.

Item (26) (516). Yearly tax levies (*onnengu*) [of shogunal lands] shall be determined within a specific period of time. If this period is extended, then the land holdings [of the perpetrators] shall be confiscated.

Item (27) (517). *Gokenin* shall not be assessed with provisional public levies.

Item (28) (518). The great stable (*ōmaya*) shall be abolished.

Item (29) (519). Save for the provinces of Dewa and Mutsu, the eastern horse pastures (*maki*) shall be abolished.

Item (30) (520). Levies of roadside porters [from *gokenin*] shall cease.

---

131. The following clauses refer to the *shōgun*, who was after all an imperial prince. This language could have been added later, probably during the fourteenth century. Most likely, the name "The New Shikimoku" dates from this later time as well. Although the latter clauses mostly apply to the *Shōgun*, some of the earlier ones could apply to him as well.

132. This applied to lands confiscated from rebels, those who ran afoul of the law, or those whose properties were determined to actually be the legitimate possession of others.

133. *Shoryō no kae* or *kaechi* were cases in which lands granted were found to belong to others and were exchanged for other lands.

Item (31) (521). New Year Banquets (*ōban*) should be limited to three days; otherwise, they are prohibited.

Item (32) (522). Dress for the first ceremonial day of the Council (*gohyōjo*) on the fifth day [of the first month] shall consist of regular robes (*hitatare*) and a folded (*ori*) cap (*eboshi*).

Item (33) (523). Dress for the first archery practice of the year, on the seventh [of the first month] shall consist of regular robes (*hitatare*) and a standing cap.

Item (34) (524). Illustrations decorating screens (*byōbu*) and papered lattice windows (*shoji*) are prohibited.

Item (35) (525). Pictures on clothing shall be prohibited.

Item (36) (526). Ladies of the [shogunal] Palace (*gosho*) shall wear two layers of clothes while low-ranking women shall wear a thin robe.

Item (37) (527). Materials for side dishes (*okazu*) to be provided to the lord's pantry (*niedono*)[134] shall not be taken in the various places or harbors.

Item (38) (528). Those who chant the *nenbutsu* or who have taken religious vows (*tonseisha*) and the base (*bonge*) shall cease riding horses throughout Kamakura.

23. Excerpts from *The Confessions of Lady Nijō*[135]

The Confessions of Lady Nijō (Towazugatari) *survived as a single manuscript, discovered only during the mid-twentieth century in the imperial archives. Lady Nijō visited Kamakura in 1289, after she had taken Buddhist vows, and describes the city of Kamakura, as well as the moment when Kamakura's titular leader, Prince Koreyasu (1264–1326; shōgun 1266–89), the* Shōgun, *was deposed by his nominal chief of staff, the Hōjō. At this time, Kamakura's* Sei-i-tai shōgun *was an imperial prince, for scions of the Fujiwara Regent family, or imperial princes themselves, staffed this office after the death of Minamoto no Yoritomo's male descendants. The ever-suspicious Hōjō deposed these leaders at the first hint of their acting against Hōjō interests. Finally, Lady Nijō mentions seeing Ashikaga Sadauji (1273–1331) along with*

---

134. Here most likely refers to the pantry of the shogunal residence.
135. Tamai Kōsuke, ed., *Towazugatari*, 198–207. Translated by Thomas Conlan.

23. Excerpts from The Confessions of Lady Nijō

the Hōjō leader, which suggests that already the Ashikaga had a special social position in Kamakura not reflected by their receipt of any particularly notable offices within the Kamakura regime.

I set off for Kamakura at dawn. I first stopped by the temple called Gokurakuji (The Temple of Paradise). The monks acted no differently from those in Kyoto, and I watched them nostalgically. On crossing the mountain pass at Kewaizaka, I could look down over the city of Kamakura. It was so different from Higashiyama![136] Houses clung to the hills in rows and looked like stacks of parcels in little bags. It all seemed so wretched that it left me feeling uncomfortable. When I went to the beach, Yuigahama, I saw a large shrine gate (*torii*). It was the Wakamiya [Hachiman] Shrine. I reflected on the karmic bond that I had, for I was born into a lineage, the Minamoto, protected by this deity. . . .

On the morning of the fifteenth of that month, Lady Komachi told me, "Today is the day of the Liberation of Living Creatures Rites (*hōjōe*).[137] What do you remember of them?" I replied: "I have no use for them! The waters of the Iwashimizu Hachiman line no longer flow through me." She responded, "The gods show compassion on those who rely on them." Since Kamakura's Tsuraoka Hachiman had its own Hōjōe Festival, I was curious and decided to go there and take a look. Considering the place, the appearance of the *Shōgun* and his attendants was pretty impressive. The lords (*daimyō*) wore formal hunting robes (*kariginu*) while others wore regular robes (*hitatare*) with swords. It was all most remarkable. Nevertheless, at a place called Akahashi, the *Shōgun* alighted from his cart, and the appearance of the nobles and courtiers in attendance was shabby and pathetic. Taira Jirō *saemon*, heir to the Taira *saemon* novice (*nyūdō*), attended. He was head of the board of retainers for the *Shōgun*, but he looked as if he were an Imperial Regent (*kanpaku*).[138] He was most impressive. I was not interested in archery competitions (*yabusame*) or other festival events and returned home.

---

136. The eastern hills of Kyoto, which was (and still is) devoid of houses.
137. This is where animals, most generally fish, were released at Iwashimizu Hachiman Shrine.
138. Taira Yoritsuna, who was responsible for killing Adachi Yasumori in the eleventh month of 1285. A trusted heir to the Hōjō, he in turn, along with his son, was assassinated in 1293 for plotting to make one of his sons as *shōgun*. Yoritsuna's heir was Munetsuna, but the fact that the person here was named Jirō, or the second son, has caused some translators to assume that Lady Nijō was referring to another son named Sukemune. See Brazell, *The Confessions of Lady Nijō*, 189. Both Munetsuna and Sukemune were killed with Yoritsuna in 1293. For contemporaries voicing their fear of Yoritsuna, see *Sanemi kyōki*, 4.26.1293 (Shō-ō 6). The *Hōrakukanki* claims that Yoritsuna was killed for wanting to make his son Sukemune *shōgun*.

The Fall of the Shōgun Prince Koreyasu

Shortly after this, after not too many days had passed, we heard rumors of something that had happened in Kamakura. As we were wondering what it could possibly be, there were reports that the *Shōgun* would return to the capital immediately. I went to his palace and saw a strange and shabby simplified palanquin on the veranda. A lieutenant (*hangan*) named Tango Jirō was in charge until Taira *saemon* Jirō arrived.[139] Claiming that he was a representative of the Hōjō lord [Sadatoki], Jirō stated that there was precedent for the palanquin to be carried backward.[140] Even before the Prince left the palace, coarse servants walked into the mansion still wearing their straw sandals and started tearing down the bamboo blinds and other things. It was a terrible sight.

A while after the shogunal palanquin departed, groups of his ladies came out, but there were no palanquins waiting for them. They stood there with nothing to hide themselves from the gaze of others. Some sobbed, and others wondered where the *Shōgun* had been taken. Some lords (*daimyō*) felt sympathy with their plight and sent some young followers (*wakatō*) to escort them and see them off at dusk. The sight of them all going their separate ways was too sad for words. . . .

Although Koreyasu[141] was called the *Shōgun*, it is not as if he gained his power by quelling barbarians (*ebisu*) or anything like that. His father, Munetaka, was known as the second son of Emperor Go-Saga and was a few months or a year older than Go-Fukakusa.[142] Munetaka would have ascended the throne, but his mother was of insufficient status, so this did not happen.[143] Munetaka became *Shōgun*, and was no mere commoner, but was known as the Prince of the Central Affairs Ministry. His son Koreyasu was a worthy Prince as well, and rumors of his

---

139. A son of Taira Yoritsuna. Because Sukemune, another son, is referred to as Iinuma *Shinsaemon* in this text, this son of Yoritsuna named Jirō was in fact Taira Munetsuna.

140. Kamakura officials attempted to abide by precedent in their actions. Here, Koreyasu was treated in the same manner as his predecessor, Munetaka. Ranking officials accused of crimes were transported with the palanquin reversed like this.

141. Often people are referred to indirectly in the original, but they will be explicitly identified in this translation so as to avoid confusion.

142. Both Go-Saga and Go-Fukakusa reigned as emperors of Japan. Munetaka was the elder brother of Go-Fukakusa.

143. His mother had an honorary rank of *jugō*, but this implied that she was of non-imperial rank and thus relatively low status. The passage states that Koreyasu would have become "Lord of the Ten Good Acts," which was a euphemism for becoming emperor. It was assumed that one who ascended to the throne had to have been a Buddhist exemplar (who mastered the "ten good acts") in a past life.

23. Excerpts from The Confessions of Lady Nijō

illegitimacy were unfounded, as his mother was a daughter of the illustrious Fujiwara Regent family.[144] Tears came to my eyes when I thought of his magnificent lineage and his fall from grace. . . .

Soon word was out that Retired Emperor Go-Fukakusa's sixth son would come to Kamakura as the next *Shōgun*. . . . On the day of the new *Shōgun's* arrival, people lined Wakamiya Avenue. Many had gone to the toll barrier at the pass to welcome the new *Shōgun*, and the first of their party returned. Twenty or thirty horsemen, then forty or fifty, passed by in imposing procession, and next imperial attendants (*meshitsugi*) and servants (*kotoneri*), twenty in all, went by. Then came a procession of lords (*daimyō*), all crowded together and smartly dressed, which extended on and on, for seven hundred yards, and then there was a palanquin with its blinds rolled up. The *Shōgun* wore an embossed yellow robe (*ominaeshi oriamimono*). Later Iinuma *shinsaemon*,[145] wearing dark green hunting robes, accompanied the *Shōgun*. It was all most solemn. At the palace, the Provincial Governor (Hōjō Sadatoki),[146] and Ashikaga[147] and all the important people wore robes without crests. There was a splendid viewing of a parade of horses.[148] On the third day after his arrival, the *Shōgun* visited the Governor of Sagami's home, at a place called Yamanouchi.[149] He was entertained with a lavish banquet. I was moved, and remembered my earlier life at court.

---

144. Konoe Saishi, a daughter of Konoe Kanetsune. The rumors were understandable, for Saishi had an affair with her Protector Priest Ryōki, but this was after Koreyasu had been born. Ironically, when the *Shōgun* Munetaka discovered the affair, he wrote many missives to his father, Emperor Saga, but suspicious Kamakura officials thought he was plotting a rebellion and so divested him of the post and sent the hapless prince unceremoniously back to Kyoto. See Conlan, *From Sovereign to Symbol*, 25.

145. Taira Sukemune. Notably, he is referred to as *shinsaemon*, or the newly appointed *saemon*, and so a different person than the *Saemon* Jirō that she mentioned earlier.

146. The most important Hōjō leaders were invested with the office of governor of the provinces of Sagami, where Kamakura was located, and neighboring Musashi. Sadatoki was repeatedly invested as the governor of Sagami and is referred to by this office and not his name.

147. Ashikaga Sadauji, Takauji's father. That he would be mentioned by name shows that the Ashikaga were quite socially important, although they did not hold important offices within the Kamakura regime, even though Sadauji was the protector (*shugo*) of Kazusa Province late in life.

148. This sentence's translation is indebted to the approach offered by Karen Brazell, *The Confessions of Lady Nijō*, 195.

149. Hōjō Sadatoki sponsored a banquet at his home in honor of the new *Shōgun's* appointment.

Section IV • *The Age of Kamakura Ascendancy*

24. Excerpt from "The Light and Shadows of the Day," *The Clear Mirror* (*Masukagami*)[150]

In 1290, tensions generated by turmoil in the court and the rise of two competing imperial lineages culminated in a remarkable assassination attempt by a retired emperor against his reigning rival. A flamboyant warrior named Asahara Tameyori (?–1290) was ordered to carry out the assassination but proved spectacularly unsuited for such a delicate mission. Wearing brightly colored armor, he charged into the palace, whereupon the Emperor—the target of the assassination attempt—fled. Tameyori and his fellow marauders were killed (or forced to kill themselves).

This remarkable history, of unknown authorship, was written by a prominent courtier. Probable candidates include members of the Fujiwara Regent line, most likely a member of the Ichijō or Nijō families. This chronicle recounts the attempt of Retired Emperor Kameyama (1249–1305; r. 1260–74) to assassinate his rival, Emperor Fushimi (1265–1317; r. 1287–98). This account reveals that the warriors of thirteenth-century Japan did not rely on stealth when called on to assassinate someone. Rokuhara, the branch office of the Kamakura Shogunate, kept order in the capital and apprehended these would-be assassins, who certainly did not act like ninja! *This episode is significant because it reveals that courtiers and emperors, in their factional disputes, were willing to use violence to achieve their ends, and their actions would ultimately bring down the Kamakura Bakufu.*

At around the fourth or fifth day of the third month of Shō-ō 3 [1290], the statues of lions and guard dogs at the palace split down the middle. Surprised, the Emperor [Fushimi] consulted his diviners, who predicted that blood would flow. This caused great consternation. On the evening of the ninth, three or four ferocious mounted warriors (*bushi*) rode in from the western palace gate (*uemon no jin*) and entered the palace proper (*kokonoe no uchi*). One entered an outlying palace building. A handmaiden, standing nearby, heard someone say, "Hey!"; when she looked up, she saw a towering (*jō takaku*) formidable warrior wearing red-laced armor over red brocade, with the face of a red demon. "Where is the Emperor (*Mikado*)?" he asked. "In

---

150. Translated by Thomas Conlan. This translation is based on Wada Hidematsu's annotated transcription of the *Masukagami*; George Perkin's translation of this text was consulted as well. Wada Hidematsu, ed., *Shūtei Masukagami shōkai* (Meiji shoin, 1910), 437–69. In Perkins, *The Clear Mirror*, it appears in chapter 11, "Ornamental Combs," 141–42.

24. Excerpt from "The Light and Shadows of the Day," The Clear Mirror (Masukagami)

the bed chamber," she replied. Then he asked, "Where is that?" "At the northeast corner of the Main Palace."

While the warriors rode southward, the woman ran to alert the Provisional Grand Councilor's handmaiden and the new Mistress of Staff. The Emperor, who was with the Empress at the time, fled from one of the wings of the palace to the Kasuga Mansion; he was disguised most peculiarly as if he were a palace lady. The Dame of Staff took the sword and jewel, and a palace woman took the lutes Genjō and Suzuka; both women fled.[151] Lady Azechi, who attended the Empress, carried the Crown Prince to the Tokiwa Mansion. Words cannot describe how they all felt! Nearly everyone had fled by the time the red-faced, red-armored warrior—who was known as Asahara Whatever—reached the imperial bed chamber, hardly anyone remained. One of the empress's chief attendants, a man named Nagamasa, roared his own name in challenge, and fought well, but eventually he was wounded and withdrew.

After a while, the head of the Nijō Kyōgoku guard post galloped in, leading fifty odd horsemen and shouting battle cries. At first they were met with only a feeble response, and they were confident as they entered the palace grounds, violently smashing into buildings and destroying chairs in the palace. Hearing this, Asahara realized his situation was hopeless and killed himself in the imperial bed chambers. His son Tarō killed himself in the curtained dais. His younger brother Hachirō, just nineteen, crawled under a bench and slashed at the legs of his adversaries. But, knowing that he would be captured in the end, he eventually killed himself by pulling out his own entrails and holding them in his hands. All of the warriors' bodies were carted off to Rokuhara.

With the light of dawn, the Emperor and Crown Prince [Go-Fushimi (1288–1336, r. 1298–1301)] returned stealthily by cart to the palace. At noon, they then went to the Kasuga Mansion. Since the palace was defiled, a palanquin was brought to the Empress's sitting room, and the Emperor departed for the western palace gate. The Crown Prince traveled to the Tokiwa Mansion in a tasseled cart. The Empress also went to the Kasuga Mansion. Words cannot describe the chaos of the time.

As Rokuhara pursued their investigation of this incident, they arrested Sanjō Consultant Captain Sanemori. That was because "Catfish tail" (Namazu-o), an heirloom of the Sanjō house, which had been in Sanemori's possession, was used by this Asahara to kill himself. There were rumors to that the Retired Emperor Kameyama knew of these plans.[152] It all was most distressing.

---

151. These lutes were considered to be regalia of the emperor. See Conlan, *From Sovereign to Symbol*, 63, for more on their fate and ultimate loss in the fourteenth century.

152. Sanemori was a close confidant of the Retired Emperor Kameyama. He did not have the abilities to organize this assassination on his own but was, rather, perceived as acting on behest of his lord, Kameyama.

25. Kamakura's Response to the Asahara Assassination Attempt

In contrast to the vivid account of the Asahara assassination attempt, documents issued by Rokuhara are much more laconic. Rokuhara mobilized western warriors, including both gokenin *who came to the capital in haste, and* jitō *who resided farther afield and who arrived in the capital weeks later.*

Hiromine Chōyū's Report of Arrival (*chakutōjō*)[153]

The *gokenin* Hiromine Jibu Hōgan Chōyū of Harima Province has galloped here because of Asahara Hachirō. Let this be known without fail. Respectfully.

Tenth day of the fourth month of the third year of Shōō 3 [1290]. Hōgan Chōyū submitted

To: The magistrate's office

Received (monogram)

Shibuya Shigemura's Report of Arrival[154]

The *jitō* Shibuya Gorō Shirō Shigemura, of Kawakura district, Mimasaka Province, has arrived in the capital because of Asahara Hachirō. Let this be known without fail. Respectfully.

Twenty-first day of the fourth month

Taira Shigemura

To: The magistrate's office

Received (monogram)

---

153. *Kamakura ibun*, vol. 22, doc. 17311, 4.10.1290 (Shōō 3) Hiromine Chōyū *chakutōjō*, 381. Translated by Thomas Conlan.

154. *Kamakura ibun*, vol. 22, doc. 17321, 4.21.1290 (Shōō 3) Shibuya Shigemura *chakutōjō*, 384. Translated by Thomas Conlan.

26. Excerpts from *Mine'aiki*[155]

This account, a local history, was written in 1348 by an itinerant monk who visited Keisokuji, a temple near the mountain of Mine'ai, in Harima Province. There, he met an old monk, who told him the history of Harima. The passages here describe past events, and the old monk carefully distinguishes between what he read about in old histories, such as the Nihongi, *with things that he viewed "with his own eyes." Four passages are translated here. First, the history of a seventh-century Dog Temple at Awaga has been backed up by archaeological excavations, but the particulars of the narrative suggest a Kamakura era context. Although the story is purportedly of an earlier era, it does reveal the principle of warrior latitude in determining inheritance. The second passage reveals how ambitious warriors tried to profit from increasing trade by building harbors. The third selection, by far the most famous of this work, describes the rise of "evil bands," or akutō, and shows how these "bandits" went from being peripheral members of society to full-fledged warriors. The final passage, which by contrast is not widely known, describes rising animosity against Kamakura, a brief history of the age, and the events leading to the fall of Kamakura.*

Then there is the Dog Temple of Awaga.[156] The original lord of that area was a man known as Shūfu, a famous hunter. One of his followers violated Shūfu's wife, and on top of that he planned to kill Shūfu and marry her. Shūfu's wife and the follower had a secret pact. Out on their hunting ground in the mountains, the follower drew his bow against Shūfu and was about to loose an arrow. The moment had come. However, Shūfu had two faithful dogs, Big Black (Ōguro) and Little Black (Koguro). They launched themselves at the follower and seized both his arms in their jaws. Shūfu drew his dagger, rushed at the man, and demanded an explanation. The man confessed everything. Shūfu killed him, dismissed his wife, conceived aspiration to enlightenment, and renounced the world. At his death, since he had no children, he left his property to his two dogs. After the dogs died, the proprietor (*ryōke*) decided to build a temple (*in*) on his land, dedicated to the enlightenment of Shūfu and his dogs: halls, a pagoda, and monks' quarters. Buddhist practice flourished there. When the temple burned, the sacred statue of

---

155. *Hyōgo kenshi shiryōhen Chūsei* 4, 36-68. Translated by Royall Tyler with Thomas Conlan.
156. Recent excavations reveal that a seventh-century temple was founded there. See Kamikawa chō kyōiku iinkai, Kyōto furitsu daigaku bungakubu kokōgaku kenkyūshitsu comp. *Fukumoto Dōyashiki ni okeru hakkutsu chōsa no seika* (March 2017).

Section IV • The Age of Kamakura Ascendancy

Eleven-headed (Jūichimen) Kannon, together with those of Shūfu and his dogs, flew to the mountain to the north. They were worshipped there at a temple named Hōrakuji. A small hall was built on the site of the original temple.

The following passage reveals how warriors attempted to take advantage of increased trade by constructing harbors which, in this case, failed. Although the Mine'aki states that Andō Renshō completed this project, as early as 1293, the monk Gyō-en was soliciting contributions for the construction of this harbor of Fukutomari Island.[157] *Andō Renshō himself participated in the capture of* akutō *bandits.*

In Kangen 1 [1302], the novice (*nyūdō*) Andō Taira *uemon* Renshō (dubbed Tamenaga) constructed the Fukutomari harbor. He heaped up large rocks, spent several hundred *kan* of coin (*senzai*) and built a protected harbor of six acres (two *chō*) into the sea. It promised to be just as good as [the prosperous harbors of] Ura-tomari or Hyōgo Island. Wealthy merchants built many houses on it, and a great many ships, large and small, moored there. However, it was overwhelmed by silt from the mouth of the Kakogawa, which covered the interior of the island. Large ships no longer stopped there, and the island failed.[158]

The most famous passage of this account describes the rise of akutō, *or "evil bands." Some historians have seen this as a sign of an incipient class struggle, while others argue that it represents the rise of judicial violence among land managers.*

Question: Much the same things go on in all the provinces, but I gather that in this one [of Harima] *akutō* uprisings have been particularly prominent. When did they start being so severe?

Answer: Indeed, disputes over authority (*shomu sōron*) used to occur at Kamioka, Takaie, and elsewhere, but they were not that serious. After the eras of Shōan [1299–1302] and Kengen [1302–3] one saw or heard of little else. Violence everywhere, piracy up and down the coast, abductions, theft, banditry, and ruthless robbery occurred in varying forms and violated every norm of human behavior. In persimmon-dyed tunics and six-sided (*roppō*) hats,[159] or caps (*eboshi*) and trousers (*hakama*), they kept out of sight and snuck around with broken bamboo quivers on their backs, swords with battered hilts and sheaths at their waists,

---

157. *Kamakura ibun*, vol. 22, doc. 16682, Kurōdodokoro sahō tōro kugyōnin *kasanete* Tōdaiji imojira *kasanete mōshijō*, 78. The document, classified as dating from 1288 in this volume, more likely dates from 1293.

158. For an overview, see Wakita Haruko, "Ports, Markets and Medieval Urbanism in the Ōsaka Region," 31–32.

159. The color orange, or literally the color of persimmons, was a sign of the lowest status, while a six-sided hat was normally worn by women and obscured the face.

26. Excerpts from Mine'aiki

bamboo spears, and balance-pole staffs. Not one of them wore great armor (*ōyoroi*) or a corselet (*haramaki*).[160] Ten or twenty such men, banded together, would seek refuge in a stronghold,[161] then join the attackers, or else turn around and fight for their opponents' commander, in total disregard of any agreement reached with anyone. They enjoyed gambling and secretly engaged in petty thievery. Despite the efforts of military authorities, and despite the *shugo*'s orders to restrain them,[162] they increased in number daily. Under these circumstances, in the spring of Gen'ō 1 [1319], messengers were dispatched to twelve provinces in the San'yō and Nankai regions. In this province, *Hyōe-no-taifu* Tameyori, Shibuya Saburō *saemon-no-jō*, Kasuya Jirō *saemon-no-jō*, and the deputy *shugo* the Andō novice (*nyūdō*),[163] supported by oaths (*kishō*) from *jitō* and householders (*gokenin*), destroyed over twenty *akutō* bases and strongholds. Current criminals were executed. Fifty-one *akutō* were reported, and a *bakufu* directive (*mikyōjo*) was issued ordering the *jitō* and householders who had gone up to the capital from all over the province to pursue them relentlessly and arrest them. However, nothing came of it. In addition, two well-known men were appointed as envoys. A roster of *jitō* and housemen was drawn up, to assure turn-by-turn guards for Akashi and Nageishi. All was then calm for two or three years. However, after [Hōjō/Osaragi] Koresada[164] became the Mutsu Governor [and returned to Kamakura], the uprisings began again, increasing in frequency, until in Shōchū [1324–26] and Karyaku [1326–29] eras, to the astonishment of the entire realm, they surpassed anything seen in earlier years.

[These later *akutō*] rode good steeds in bands of fifty or a hundred, with spare mounts hauling chests[165] full of gear, bows and arrows, gold- and silver-inlaid weapons, great armor (*ōyoroi*), and corselets (*haramaki*) all glittering and gleaming. Claiming to represent the [rightful] proprietor, the *akutō* seized land the ownership of which had never been in dispute; formed leagues bound together by oaths; relied on groups of followers (*yoriki*) styled as their "guests," who built castles or captured

---

160. The most expensive style of armor, reserved for only the wealthiest of mounted warriors, was known as *ōyoroi* while *haramaki* represented a more simplified style, but still something that could only be worn by a warrior of means.

161. This shows that they were at times allied with powerful locals capable of building fortifications.

162. The *shugo* were "protectors" designed to provide order in their province.

163. The same Andō who built the harbor at Fukutomari.

164. Hōjō Koresada, also known as Osaragi Koresada, served as the "southern" Rokuhara *tandai* from 9.2.1315, until 8.17.1324, and as *rensho*, or cosigner, for the Kamakura regime from 4.24.1326, until 1327. The reference to hi as Mutsu, or the Governor of Mutsu, means that he became a cosigner for the Kamakura regime and returned there. Mutsu was a proprietary province of Kamakura.

165. Literally, *karabitsu*, or Chinese style chests.

them; built strongholds; constructed proper earthen walls; put up archery towers (*yagura*); set up an abatis (*hashiriki*); showered attackers with stones; erected watchtowers; employed shields in screen-like or box-like fashion; and covered them with leather hides or crushed bamboo. They readied themselves in various ways and contrived countless devices. Since most of the *akutō* came from Tajima, Tanba, Inaba, and Hōki Provinces [across the mountains from Harima to the north or northwest], they referred to their bribes as "fees for crossing the mountains" (*yama koshi*) and later they promised to ally with those who paid them.

The *akutō* showed no sign at all of wishing to go unnoticed or of feeling the least twinge of shame. Even warriors who were [willing to commit] *seppuku* (*seppuku ka tō*) when they felt shame praised them[166] as being "beyond the pale" (*sata no hoka*) in battle camp (*gunjin*) [and refused to attack].

For this reason, even *shugo* protectors stood in awe of their might, and warriors sent to suppress them turned back in apprehension. So it is that, in the end, hardly a single estate could escape the [depredations]—abductions, pursuit, riot, [illegal] harvesting of paddy and dry fields, break-ins, and robbery—of the bands. It seemed unlikely that any estate would be spared. It was as though [the *akutō*] walked with tigers and wolves and mingled with dragons and snakes. The authorities' judicial decisions (*jōsai*) were no doubt well-intentioned, but they seemed to lack either resources or courage. Failure to carry out orders from above resulted in no consequences; urgings from the *bakufu* mobilization directives (*mikyōjo saisoku*) just slipped through the cracks.[167] Since most people throughout the province, high or low, were in sympathy with [the *akutō*], honest and talented men, and those of good will, covered their ears and closed their eyes; so that the passage of time led in the end to the grave events of Genkō [1331–34]. However, such conduct constituted a lapse in warrior governance (*buke seidō*) [of Kamakura].

> *The closing passage of the* Mine'aiki, *which directly follows the passage on akutō, reveals historical attitudes about the Kamakura regime in the fourteenth century and how some in Harima perceived its later leaders to be arrogant. This province would be a hotbed of resistance to Kamakura during the Genkō era [1331–34]. This text ends with an account of the initiation of a rebellion against the Kamakura* Bakufu. *Other documents, which confirm the historical record, describe the crucial role of Harima Province warriors in the uprising.*

Question: Everyone knows how it went in Kyoto, Kamakura, and the provinces after Genkō [1331–34]. What happened in this province?

---

166. *Akutō.*
167. Literally, like a fish escaping from a net.

26. Excerpts from Mine'aiki

Answer: I need hardly remind you that the term *warrior house* (*buke*)[168] is a new one, but during Angen [1175–77] and Jishō [1177–81], the Taira Grand Minister (Taira *Shōkoku*) [Kiyomori] seized military power and ruled the realm as he pleased. He dismissed the Minamoto as chief of the Palace Guards (*buei*) and destroyed the Minamoto's entire house. Then the Genji seized power once more, and their head [Minamoto no Yoritomo] was appointed as the General of the Right (*utaishō*) and awarded the offices of Chief Envoy for pursuit and capture (*sōtsuibushi*) and over-*jitō* (*sōjitō*). They say that, as the protector (*kōken*) of the imperial house, he comported himself wisely in all circumstances and practiced virtuous government. However, after the child *Shōgun* [Fujiwara Yoritsuna] had gone down [to Kamakura], following the third *Shōgun*'s [Sanetomo's] death, the Hōjō family, as shogunal chief of staff (*shikken*),[169] seized control of the realm. The Imperial Way was lost, and government followed the will of the *buke*.[170]

This led to the extraordinary developments of Jōkyū.[171] Then there came the Sovereign's abdication, and conflict between the two imperial lineages. [Kamakura] appointed regents (*sesshō, kanpaku*), ministers, top court officials, empress, heirs apparent, and generals of the left and right. In addition, starting with Mt. Hiei and Nara, among other temples, and Ise and Iwashimizu among other shrines, the east[172] governed succession to the office of head priest, or temple chief (*zasu*) or intendants (*bettō*); appointed head shrine priests (*saishu*) [at Ise] and shrine administrators (*kannushi no shikken*); and controlled even the junior offices in the noble houses, as well as the ministers, provincial governors, and the Capital Police (*kebiishi*). All followed the will of the east. The entire realm submitted to the *buke*.[173] Therefore, the treasures of the imperial and the Retired Emperor's palaces, the valuables owned by the noble houses and the Princely Priests (*monzeki*), all went to support the *buke*, which became immensely wealthy—far more so than the richest houses—until gold, silver, pearls, and precious stones filled their storehouses. In the provinces, they generally monopolized the offices of *shugo* or of estate and local district headships, so that these houses prospered.

---

168. A synonym for the Kamakura *Bakufu*.
169. Technically, the head of the administrative office (*mandokoro*) of a shōgun; it is best translated as "chief of staff." Some scholars refer to the Hōjō as "regents" for Kamakura as a result of their ability to depose shoguns.
170. *Buke* refers to the Kamakura *Bakufu*, as well as the Hōjō.
171. The Jōkyū War of 1221, where the court forces of Go-Toba were soundly defeated by Kamakura.
172. A synonym for Kamakura.
173. Kamakura Shogunate.

The incumbents inhabited rows of mansions, markets grew up at their gates, their saddled mounts crowded the roads, and ancient houses of hereditary distinction insinuated themselves into their company. They held every worthy man—whether Confucian scholar or master in another line—to be beneath them, so that the etiquette of each encounter on the road, each judgment about a seating precedence, became even stricter than the proper comportment between lord and follower, to the point where even their household servants and retainers claimed exalted standing, and prided themselves on their influence. Everyone performed the seven rites of filial piety, the various houses fully acknowledged their service; therefore, acceptance or rejection of every opinion, judgment, or policy conformed to Kamakura's orders and followed their will. Each shogunal chief of staff (*shikken*) in succession acted with probity, gave first priority to loyal service, revered the Buddhas and Gods, and respected the nobility; wherefore the calm of the Four Seas obtained throughout the world, and the people took pride in orderly government (*kensei*). Plants and trees awaited no wind to yield but bent to authority; flying birds spread their wings in deference to wise counsel. In the same way, the current incumbent followed the example of earlier *shōgun*s and upheld their precedents. Or so they claimed.

However, such had been their excesses that they seemed to have forgotten the way of military strategy and abandoned the art of war. Their officials were still aware of established precedent, in outer and inner deportment, and their accoutrements surpassed those of any minister or great lord—indeed, they were hardly inferior to the palaces of the Empress or the Retired Emperor. However, in the present time of Genkō [1331–34] they have met their fate, and all five hundred and more of them have perished in an instant. In the historical records of the Other Realm, there appears the principle that the power of subject's lineage over the realm does not last more than three generations. However, the rewards of a succession of eight generations had proved great indeed. On the twenty-fifth day of the eighth month of last year, Genkō 1 [1331], half-way through the hour of the bird [5–7 p.m.], a messenger from the *shugo* raced here, opened a *bakufu* directive (*mikyōjo*), and read, "To the *jitō* and to the householders (*gokenin*): During the night of the twenty-third just past, the Emperor traveled elsewhere. You are to come up to the capital immediately." This was the start of disorder in the realm.

27. Excerpt from "The Dayflower," *The Clear Mirror* (*Masukagami*)[174]

This passage describes the uprising—led by Akamatsu Enshin (1277–1350), a disgruntled gokenin warrior, and carried out by the combined forces of the army of Ashikaga Takauji and the forces of Prince Itsuji Moriyoshi (a son of Emperor Kameyama)—that destroyed Kamakura's branch office in Rokuhara. By this time, the emperor Go-Daigo had already staged a revolt, been captured, and escaped from Oki Island. Resistance was also led by a son of Go-Daigo, also known as Prince Moriyoshi (1308–35).

Soon after the tenth day of the third month, the world became disordered. Akamatsu Enshin, so he was called, a novice (*nyūdō*) from Harima Province, decided to obey the previous emperor Go-Daigo's edict to attack the capital. The capital was plunged into confusion and, as was customary in such cases, Emperor Kōgon and both Retired Emperors fled from there to Rokuhara. Those of high and low status alike scrambled, horses and carts dashed in all different directions, and shouting warriors swarmed the streets. It was all most frightful!

Nevertheless, the Rokuhara forces were strong and the Akamatsu men retreated during that night. Though the fighting subsided, the situation remained chaotic and the emperors stayed in Rokuhara. On the twenty-sixth, the Crown Prince was sent to Rokuhara in order to be close to the Retired Emperors and Emperor. . . .

Imperial priests arrived in order to perform invocations.[175] There were reports of battles being fought here and there, and as the days passed, the Retired Emperors ordered even senior nobles and courtiers to muster warriors in a manner commensurate with their status. Accordingly, many warriors were mobilized, including even young *samurai* who could not easily wield a bow. It was now a world where one might deliberately break their elbow [to avoid military service]. So ended the rumor-filled third month.

On the tenth day of the fourth month, a great number of warriors arrived from the east. Many of them, including Ashikaga *jibu no taifu* Takauji, had attacked Kasagi two years before [during Go-Daigo's initial rebellion]. Retired Emperor Go-Fushimi was impressed with Takauji and dispatched an edict (*inzen*) ordering him to attack Go-Daigo.

When Takauji had departed from the east, he wrote an oath stating that he had undivided allegiance to Kamakura. But there were doubts about what he really

---

174. Wada Hidematsu, *Shūtei Masukagami shōkai*, 738–52. Translated by Thomas Conlan. For a variant translation, see Perkins, *The Clear Mirror*, chapter 17, "The Dayflower," 215–18.
175. Priests of the imperial family.

thought. This Takauji was a descendant of Yoriyoshi of old, and although he was a warrior of impeccable lineage, his Genji lineage had not been influential since the time of Jōkyū [1219–22].[176] Although [the Ashikaga were] obscure, a number of branch families had been established, and their influence extended far and wide. They gained the support of many in the provinces. Some people wondered if, during this time of crisis, Takauji would rise up in the world [through rebellion] and their suspicions proved to be correct.

Stating that he had been commanded to depart for the province of Hōki, Takauji stopped at Nishiyama Ōhara for a night, and then on the seventh day of the fifth month, just at the light of dawn, he broke through the barricades at Ōmiya Avenue. Dividing his forces into seven units, he then headed east on seven roads from Nijō, in the north, to Shichijō in the south. With their banners, he and his men, as thick as fog and clouds, headed toward Rokuhara. They encountered no opposition along the way. Having already received an edict from the previous emperor Go-Daigo, *Jibu no taiyū* Takauji had thus turned to conquer the capital.

Takauji and his men raised thunderous battle cries; the ground shook, and the Heavenly King Brahma (Bonten) must have been surprised in his palace. All who heard them were rattled by the clamor. It goes without saying that Emperor Kōgon, the Crown Prince, and the Retired Emperors Hanazono and Go-Fushimi were distraught. Accustomed more to beautiful melodies, they were shocked to hear such strange sounds.

Half of Rokuhara's warriors had been dispatched to Mt. Kongō; those who remained resolved to stay in the capital for as long as they lived. It was a ferocious battle, fought with reckless abandon. Many died in front of their comrades, brought down by arrows that fell like heavy rain. They fought day and night. Both Rokuhara leaders resisted until their forces were no more. But in the end their defenses collapsed, and the end appeared near.

The emperors, nobles, and courtiers could not have fled, even if they believed this day would be their last. Of course, none could have imagined the previous day's betrayal by Takauji, a man honored with a Retired Emperor's edict. All huddled together in fear.

Throughout the day, the sun was darkened by black smoke billowing from fires at Hachiman, Yamazaki, Takeda, Uji, Seta, Fukakusa, and Hosshōji. By nightfall, the sky was dark as ink. As the fires approached Rokuhara, and the situation became dire. Against the odds, the defenders somehow managed to break through the rear of Takauji's encampment, and their majesties escaped as if in a dream. Kōgon adopted the bizarre garb of a man too poor to afford decent clothes. Both Retired Emperors fled, hand in hand, with the help of others. Nobles and Grand Ministers fled in all directions, to the east and west of the river, and were too dazed to notice when they lost their caps.

---

176. At this time, Sanetomo, the last son of Minamoto no Yoritomo was assassinated and his line was eclipsed.

28. Kanesawa Sadamasa Letter (Fragment)

The two Rokuhara leaders, Nakatoki and Tokimasa, resolved to flee east, and the Emperor and Retired Emperors went with them. . . . When they were in Ōmi Province, at a place called Ibuki, there was some prince, who was a monk, with some skill in battle, who had allied with the former Emperor Go-Daigo. He ambushed them, shooting them with arrows. Hearing reports of a pursuing force from the capital, the northern Rokuhara leader Nakatoki took the Emperor [Kōgon], Crown Prince [Sukō], and both Retired Emperors [Go-Fushimi and Hanazono] into the hills at a place called Banba. A number of their warriors remained, but they could not attack; instead, they committed *seppuku* in these hills. The southern Rokuhara leader Tokimasa did not make it so far as Banba. Instead, we heard that he was lost in the vicinity of Moriyama. Words cannot express the wretchedness of it all. Of those who had accompanied the Emperor, only the Grand Councilor Toshizane, the Middle Councilors Tsuneaki and Yorisada, the Grand Councilor Sukena, the Consultant Sukeaki, and Takakage did not flee. Toshizane, Sukena, and Yorisada cut their hair [and took Buddhist vows]. Retired Emperor Go-Fushimi sent a letter to the Emperor suggesting that he, too, renounce the world, but Kōgon, who had never considered doing this, firmly refused.

28. Kanesawa Sadamasa Letter (Fragment)[177]

Kamakura easily quelled Go-Daigo's initial rebellion in 1331 and banished the emperor to Oki Island. Kanesawa Sadamasa (1302–33), son of powerful Kamakura official Kanesawa Sadaaki (1278–1333), penned the following letter in the tenth month of 1331. It was later recycled and survives in one of the few Kamakura temples not destroyed in 1333. The most notable general commanding this reinforcing army was Ashikaga Takauji, who was instrumental in bringing down the destruction of the Kamakura Bakufu.

Kusunoki Masashige has fortified a castle in Kawachi Province, the location of the previous Tendai chief of Nashimoto [Prince Moriyoshi].[178] I have learned that the

---

177. For a transcription of most of the document, see *Kamakura ibun*, vol. 40, doc. 31594, Kanesawa Sadamasa *shojō*, 307. For the discovery of a surviving separate fragment, Kanazawa kenritsu Kanazawa bunko, comp., *Kamakura Hōjōshi no kōbō* (Kanazawa, October 2007), 75. The rest of the letter has been lost, although the addressee was the head of Shōmyōji temple. Translated by Thomas Conlan.

178. This refers to Prince Moriyoshi, who renounced his vows and position as the head of the Tendai order. Nashimoto was a subtemple at Sanzenin, where Princely monks (*monzeki*) resided.

vast majority of Kamakura's military forces[179] departed on the past sixteenth day of the tenth month [of 1331]. From now, most assuredly we will be able to smite them. In addition, although my request is improper,[180] there is one type of tea.

29. Command (*ryōji*) of Prince Moriyoshi[181]

Several documents attest to the validity of the Clear Mirror *narrative (see "The Dayflower,"* The Clear Mirror, *p. 109). First, Prince Moriyoshi dispatched an edict to the monks of Taisanji, who fought under the command of Akamatsu Enshin.*

The eastern barbarian descendants of Hōjō Tokimasa, a former Governor of Tōtōmi province and a petty local official of Izu Province (*zaichō kanjin*), have since the time of Jōkyū (1221) controlled the four seas, and disdained the imperial house (*chōke*). Particularly in recent years Takatoki, the Sagami novice (*nyūdō*), and his family have not only relied on military force and stratagems but have also belittled imperial authority (*chō-i*) and degraded (*sasen tatematsuri*) the current Emperor by banishing him to Oki Province and bothering him greatly (*shinkin o nayamasu*). This disturbance in the country is the epitome of "the lower overcoming the higher" (*gekokujō*). This is all most strange (*kikai*); chastise them and return the Emperor. Mobilize forces in the western highways and fifteen provinces. This will allow for the return of imperial virtue for all. Assemble, gather, and lead your (*ichimon*) military forces, and immediately hasten to the battlefield. Hence, the edict of the Prince of the Second Rank of the Great Pagoda is thus.

Third year of Genkō 3 [1333], second month, twenty-first day

From: The Lieutenant of the Left Palace Guards (*sashōshō*) [Yoshida] Sadatsune

To: The Monks of Taisanji

---

179. They are actually referred to as the "Eastern Provinces" or the Kantō, a common name for the Kamakura Shogunate.
180. Literally, the left-handed path (*sadō*).
181. *Kamakura ibun*, vol. 41, doc. 31996, 2.21.1333 (Genkō 3) Ōtōnomiya Moriyoshi shinnō *ryōji* 192–93. Translated by Thomas Conlan. This language closely mirrors that of Go-Toba when he rebelled against Kamakura.

P.S.:[182] At the time (*itten*) of the hour of the tiger [4–6 a.m.] on the twenty-fifth day of this month, you led your forces and galloped to Akamatsu castle in this province [of Harima]. From that time, you have adorned yourself in high honor. You should state what you would like for rewards. It has been so commanded again.

30. Petition for Reward (*gunchūjō*) by the Monks of Taisanji, Harima Province[183]

After receiving the above document, the Taisanji monks went to war, committing acts of physical violence, wounding other monks, and performing Buddhist rituals. This record recounts their early campaigns. They started early in 1333 and had advanced as far as the capital by the third month of that year. Their petition for reward reveals that Akamatsu Enshin's forces were fighting in the capital during the same period as the events described in The Clear Mirror *(see "The Dayflower," p. 109).*

Witnessed [monogram][184]

Report:

At the will of the Prince of the Second Rank of the Great Pagoda,[185] the monks of Harima's Taisanji have performed battle service since the fifteenth day of the second intercalary month. Our prayers have also been outstanding.

The temple held unceasing Yakushiji *Nyorai* memorial rites.

We first fought in Settsu, Kohirano, and Hyōgo Island. It started on the fifteenth day of the second intercalary month. On the twenty-third day we fought in Amagasaki. The person named Tokinori *Taiyū* was wounded. On the twenty-fourth day we fought in Sakabe village, and *Gyōbu* Jirō, real name Yasushige, died. On the first day of the third month, we fought on Mount Maya, and *Hyōe* Saburō (real name Tomoshige) died. On the twelfth day of the same month, they fought

---

182. Unusually, this was written on an extra sheet of paper (*raishi* 礼紙), usually blank, that would be attached to such edicts.
183. *Kamakura ibun*, vol. 41, doc. 32148, 5.10.1333 (Genkō 3) Harima Taisanji shūto *gunchūjō*, 261. Translated by Joseph Henares and Thomas Conlan.
184. Akamatsu Enshin.
185. Prince Moriyoshi. See the above Command (*ryōji*) of Prince Moriyoshi of 2.21.1333 (Genkō 3).

in Kyoto, and *Taifubō Taishō* Genshin and Higo, whose real name is Yūkyō, died. On the same day, *Minbu*, whose real name is Chōshun; *Hyōbu*, whose real name is Ryōgen; *Shōyu*, whose real name is Enpan; and Tango, whose real name is Shinzen were wounded.

The castle on Mt. Maya is still being guarded.

The aforementioned occurred after we received the princely edict (*ryōji*) on the twenty-first day of the second month of this year. We fought first at Akamatsu castle, and then repeatedly at other places. This report is thus conveyed.

Genkō 3 [1333], fifth month, tenth day.

Presented to the magistrate's office.

31. Document of Praise (*kanjō*), Aso Harutoki[186]

The Clear Mirror (see "The Dayflower," p. 110) mentions that half of Kamakura's forces had been dispatched to Mt. Kongō. The following is a document of praise written by Aso Harutoki (1318–34), the general of these forces to a member of the Mikita family of Izumi Province. Harutoki's army survived the destruction of Kamakura and later surrendered to Go-Daigo. Harutoki is here using Shōkei, the era name of Emperor Kōgon (1313–64; r. 1331–33), instead of the era name of Genkō, which suggested allegiance to Go-Daigo after 1331 (Genkō 1).

In the mountains to the north of Chihaya Castle, you skirmished and took a head. This is most excellent. Therefore, [this report] shall be conveyed.

The second year of Shōkei [1333], fourth month, twenty-first day

Harutoki (Monogram)

To: The Honorable Mikita *Nakatsugi* [Sukehide]

---

186. Translated by Thomas Conlan and revised by the students of *Sources in Ancient and Medieval Japanese History*. For an image, transcription, and translation of the document, see https://komonjo.princeton.edu/migita-04/. Accessed August 26, 2021.

32. Document of Damages (*funshitsujō*) by the Nun Jikai (Excerpts)[187]

The following excerpt, drawn from a long list of damages (funshitsujō) *written by Jikai, a nun living in Kyoto, confirms the desperate nature of battles that were fought at Shichijō in Kyoto on the sixth and seventh days of the fifth month of 1333, when Ashikaga Takauji attacked Rokuhara. This document survived only as two separate pieces among the thousands of documents in the Tōji temple archives. In 2015, scholars determined that these two pieces were part of the same document, which dates from the eleventh month of 1333 (Genkō 3). As the list of damages is long, only the passage describing the battles is translated here.*

The aforementioned areas are the hereditarily transmitted property of Jikai. Nevertheless, on both the sixth and seventh days of the past fifth month, Rokuhara's powerful forces entered Jikai's residence to the south of the Seventh Avenue, and when they stole my valuables, my documents were lost.

33. Copy of Mino Washimi Tadayasu's Petition for Reward (*gunchūjō an*)[188]

The following document reveals how Kamakura's gokenin *relied upon imperial decrees to turn against the Rokuhara* tandai *forces and destroy them in the fifth month of 1333 (Genkō 3).*

The *gokenin* Washimi Tōsaburō Tadayasu, of Mino Province, Kujō district, received an imperial edict, and on the eighth day of the fifth month galloped forth to the mountain in front of Banba, in Ōmi, where we fought in battle. My retainer (*wakatō*)

---

187. Documents of loss (*funshitsujō*) from the nun Jikai, dating from the eleventh month of 1333 (Genkō 3) Ama Jikai *denchi monjo funshitsujō*, box E 92-8 and box Se 11-1, accessible online at http://hyakugo.kyoto.jp/contents/detail.php?id=15694 and http://hyakugo.kyoto.jp/contents/images/043_10706_0016.jpg. Accessed August 26, 2021. Translated by Thomas Conlan.

For the discovery and analysis of these documents, see the 2015 (Heisei 27) Tōji hyakugō monjoten kaisetsubun, http://hyakugo.pref.kyoto.lg.jp/wordpress_jp/wp-content/uploads/exhib_2015.pdf, accessed March 21, 2020. These records do not appear in the published *Kamaura ibun* series, although they can be searched on the Tokyo Historiographical Institute's *Kamakura ibun* database.

188. *Kamakura ibun*, vol. 41, doc. 32159, 5.12.1333 (Genkō 3) Mino Washimi Tadayasu *gunchūjō an*, 264. Translated by Thomas Conlan.

Mori Rokurō Tadashige was killed; and his brother Shichirō Shigenobu was wounded. Left knee shot. This was inspected and I received a monogram. I desire to let this be known for posterity. Let this be known without fail. Respectfully.

Twelfth day of the fifth month of Genkō 3 (1333)

Fujiwara Tadayasu submitted

To: Presented to the magistrate's office

Seen. Monogram copy

34. Command (*ryōji*) of the Fifth Prince (Moriyoshi)[189]

The author of The Clear Mirror (see *"The Dayflower," p. 111) correctly identifies Moriyoshi, the commander of the forces that annihilated Rokuhara. His name was a homonym of the eldest son of Go-Daigo, who initiated the uprisings of 1332–33, but he was in fact the fifth son of Emperor Kameyama. The Fifth Prince Moriyoshi is an obscure figure, but we know he commended lands to Taga Shrine shortly after Rokuhara's destruction. This is one of the few records of this victorious commander and indicates he saw his victory as being divinely preordained. Rokuhara's destruction has at times been inaccurately described as being caused by an* akutō *uprising, but this document reveals that Moriyoshi was ultimately responsible.*

Monogram

Commended: To Taga Shrine.

Total: Half of one place within the Taga Shrine estates[190]

Located in Ōmi province

I have heard that here, in an outer shrine, the grandson of the Sun Deity Amaterasu and his descendants reside in the Outer Shrine of Takamiya.[191] He is the ruling

---

189. This prince was the fifth son of Emperor Kameyama, not the eldest son of Go-Daigo, who shared a homonym name. *Kamakura ibun*, vol. 41, doc. 32160, 5.14.1333 (Genkō 3) Itsunomiya Moriyoshi shinnō *ryōji*, 264–65. Translated by Thomas Conlan.
190. This presumably constituted lands that previously had been divested.
191. Ninigi, the grandson of the Sun Goddess Amaterasu, descended from the Plains of the High Heavens, and was the first to rule the territories of Japan. Takamiya is located near Taga Shrine.

34. Command (ryōji) of the Fifth Prince (Moriyoshi)

god of the realm and this shrine is a place where the country is pacified and the people prosper. Here, on the days of shrine rites on the nineteenth day of the fourth month, I prayed for the chastisement of the enemies of the court (*chōteki*). I secretly (*hisoka ni*) worshipped at the shrine, day and night, and with my sincere belief, I saw remarkable mysterious signs (*reizui kechien*). My belief was unsurpassed and as a result, on this past ninth day, while the previous Emperor and both Retired Emperors were protected,[192] the eastern barbarians; the northern head of Rokuhara; Echigo *no kami* Nakatoki, the Eastern Messenger; the Ise novice (*nyūdō*) Gyō'i; and Sasaki Kiyotaka, the former governor of Oki—a force of several hundred horses in all—were annihilated here.[193] Now that the western capital is at peace, I pray to revitalize this shrine. Thus, I commend half of Taga Shrine's estate. From today onward, may this day of the ox be known. Hence, the Fifth Imperial Prince's edict (*ryōji*) and this commendation is thus.

The fourteenth day of the fifth month of Genkō 3 (1333)

From: The Lord Chamberlain (*jijū*) Noritada

---

192. Emperor Kōgon, who was "abolished" by Go-Daigo, as well as the Retired Emperors Hanazono and Go-Fushimi. The document states "within a castle" for protection, but no such structure existed.

193. In fact, 432 perished. Sasaki Kiyotaka was an important figure in the 1331 rebellion; the southern head of Rokuhara was killed before he could reach Banba.

SECTION V

The Rise of the Ashikaga and the Life of Ashikaga Takauji (1305–58)

This section focuses on Ashikaga Takauji's rebellion, which in 1333 brought down the Kamakura regime. Takauji perceived his victory and the triumph of his Minamoto lineage as both predetermined (as a result of his ancestors' prayers), and inevitable (because of a perceived Minamoto right to rule).

A series of records recounts Takauji's revolt and his prayers. One chronicle, Baishōron, written by a strong supporter from Munakata Shrine, describes an experience with Takauji during the tumultuous 1330s; the chronicle also describes how Takauji destroyed Kamakura and later rebelled against Go-Daigo, the triumphant emperor of 1333. This firsthand narrative varies from most fictional accounts in that it does not rely on extended dialogues and carefully distinguishes what the warrior himself would have seen on the battlefield.

1. Excerpt from Imagawa Ryōshun's *Nantaiheiki*[1]

Ideas of Minamoto warrior identity coalesced over the course of the thirteenth and fourteenth centuries. The wars of the Jishō (1177–81) and Jūei (1182–84) eras were originally conflicts against the center, with alliances not based upon family ties; the idea that the Minamoto were a cohesive identity became stronger, promoted by figures such as the Ashikaga, who used this myth as a justification to defeat their Hōjō (Taira) rivals. Retrospectively, the wars of the 1180s, between the Taira and the Minamoto, became known as the Genpei War even though they were not thought of in this way at the time. Ashikaga Takauji and Tadayoshi (1306–52) believed that their ancestors had written an oath to seize the realm in seven generations. Evidence for this comes from the retrospective account of Imagawa Ryōshun (1326–1420), who recounts a testament by Yoshiie stating he would accomplish this feat. Ashikaga Ietoki, Takauji's

---

1. Tyler, *Fourteenth-Century Voices II*, 236–38.

1. Excerpt from Imagawa Ryōshun's Nantaiheiki

The Descendants of Hachimantarō Yoshiie

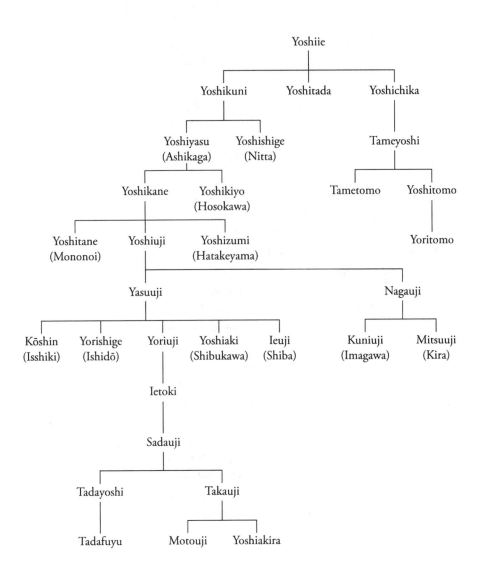

Section V • *The Rise of the Ashikaga and the Life of Ashikaga Takauji*

grandfather, who perished when Adachi Yasumori was killed in 1285, purportedly wrote a testament stating that his grandson Takauji would defeat the Hōjō and achieve a position of head of the warriors of Japan. Takauji and his brother Tadayoshi believed this to be true, as is revealed in a document from Tadayoshi (Ashikaga Tadayoshi Directive, p. 121) discussing Ietoki's testament—found in the Daigoji temple archives.

"Hachiman-dono" means Lord [Minamoto] Yoshiie, Governor of Mutsu and Chinjufu Shōgun. His son, Yoshikuni, was followed by Yoshiyasu, Yoshikane, Yoshiuji, Yasuuji, and so on. Yasuuji was known as Hiraishi-dono; his son, Yoriuji, as Jibu-no-Taifu-dono; and Yoriuji's son, Ietoki, as Iyo-no-kami. Ietoki's son, Sadauji, was referred to as Sanuki-no-nyūdō-dono. His sons were Takauji and Tadayoshi. Despite being Yasuuji's third son, Yoriuji followed his father as head of the house.[2] The men of Owari, the Shibukawa, and so on, his elder brothers, all became his juniors (*soshi*).[3] The Hosokawa and Hatakeyama lines seem to have parted after Yoshikane.

Yoshikane was over eight feet tall and supremely powerful. He was said really to be a son of Tametomo,[4] although Yoshiyasu had brought him up from infancy. Yoshikane kept this quiet, however, so that no one knew. He became particularly close to Yoritomo but feigned madness in order to avoid further attention, and he lived his life without incident. He is reported to have declared, "My spirit will possess my descendants for a time and madden them." For that matter, Yoshiie wrote in his testament (*okibumi*): "I shall be reborn seven generations hence and seize the realm." That generation was Ietoki's, who, no doubt realizing that the time was not yet ripe, prayed as follows to Hachiman: "Cut my life short, I beg, and have us seize the realm within three generations." He then slit his belly.[5] The testament written in his own hand gives further details. My late father and I read it in the presence of both Takauji and Tadayoshi. They said that they owed their conquest of the realm to this prayer. Ambition working over generations had made them masters of the world.

---

2. Ryōshun is suggesting that (as he states plainly below) his line is senior to the Ashikaga (Yoriuji's).
3. Yasuuji's first son, Ieuji, founded the Shiba line and Yoriaki, the Shibukawa. Both were elder brothers of Yoriuji.
4. Whose exploits are narrated in *Hōgen monogatari*.
5. This happened when Adachi Yasumori was killed in 1285.

2. Ashikaga Tadayoshi Directive (*mikyōjo*)[6]

Ashikaga Ietoki's testament is not extant. But the record of it below, created by Ashikaga Tadayoshi, predates 1350, and was written at a time when Tadayoshi wielded great power within the regime.

I viewed the document from the time of [Ashikaga] Ietoki's passing, which he gave to his retainer Kō no Morouji. Reading it brings tears to my eyes; I will not forget it. I am thus taking this document and will send you a copy. Thus

Fourth day, fifth month

Monogram (Tadayoshi)

To Kō Tosa *no kami* [Moroaki]

3. Ashikaga Takauji Prayer (*gammon*), Shinomura Shrine[7]

Though they were not trusted to hold major offices, the Ashikaga held an unusually high status within the Kamakura regime. Lady Nijō, for example, singles only them out among all the non-Hōjō in the record she kept of her 1289 visit to Kamakura (see The Confessions of Lady Nijō, *p. 99). The Ashikaga married into the Hōjō line; Takauji's wife was a member of their family. Nevertheless, as* The Clear Mirror *account (see "The Dayflower," p. 109) reveals, the Hōjō did not fully trust them, and forced Takauji to sign an oath of loyalty. He later ignored this oath, most likely because he was aware of the prophecy that he was destined to seize the realm. The best source for his perspective is a prayer written at Shinomura Shrine, to the northwest of Kyoto. An alternate version of this oath appears in* Taiheiki, *but it was derivative of an oath written by Minamoto Yoshinaka appearing in the* Tale of Heike *and so will not be translated here.*

Respectfully offered in prayer. The Hachiman Bodhisattva is the protector of the kingly realm [of Japan] and the ancestor of our [Minamoto] lineage. As Takauji is

---

6. *Dainihon komonjo iewake* 19 *Daigoji monjo*, vol. 1, doc. 160, 4.5 Ashikaga Tadayoshi *mikyōjo*, 117. Translated by Thomas Conlan.

7. *Kamakura ibun*, vol. 41, doc. 32120, 4.29.1333 (Genkō 3) Ashikaga Takauji *ganmon*, 245–46. Translated by Thomas Conlan.

the lingering trace of this God, and head of the lineage,[8] how can one be superior to him in the way of the bow and horse? Having destroyed, through the ages, enemies of the court, and having chastised rebels for generations, I now have received an imperial edict (*rinji*) from the enlightened lord of the current era (*genkō no meikun* [Go-Daigo]) who desires to revitalize the worship of the deities, to help the people of the realm prosper, and to save the world. Following this imperial command, I wish to raise a righteous army. While at the Shinomura station in Tanba province, I spied a white flag[9] at the base of a willow tree, and at the base of that tree there is a shrine altar (*shatan*). In response to our questions, the village residents explained this was a shrine for the Hachiman Bodhisattva. Our generals swiftly congregated at this holy spot, a sign of the future success of our righteous forces. Relying on faith in the Buddha to respond to our requests, and moved to tears, this prayer will meet with success, and the fortunes of our house will flourish again. Thus, we have respectfully commended paddy lands to this shrine altar. Our prayer is thus.

Reverently presented by the Former *Jibu no taifu* Minamoto *no ason* Takauji on the twenty-ninth day of the fourth month of the third year of Genkō (1333) (monogram on reverse)

4. Excerpts from *Baishōron*[10]

Among written accounts of medieval Japanese warfare, the Baishōron *remains relatively obscure.* Taiheiki, *the more popular chronicle of the age, overshadowed it for centuries. While* Taiheiki *recounts a generation of warfare in forty chapters (and over a thousand pages),* Baishōron, *just over a tenth as long, covers six years in detail.*

Baishōron's *survival is remarkable since the work was ideologically obsolescent when it was written. It recounts the glory of the Ashikaga brothers: Takauji, the first Ashikaga Sei-i-tai shōgun, and Tadayoshi. These two founded a warrior-based government and worked together until 1350, when they became embroiled in a mortal struggle known as the* Kannō no jōran *(the Kannō Anarchy, 1350–52). This conflict resulted in Tadayoshi's death and the near destruction of the Ashikaga regime. By presenting an early justification*

---

8. *Uji*, often translated as clan.
9. Sign of the Minamoto and completely unrelated to the modern symbol of surrender.
10. Uyenaka and Tyler, *Fourteenth-Century Voices II*, 47–52, 79–83, 85–90, 92–93, 97–98, 99–100, 102–5, 116–19.

4. Excerpts from Baishōron

of Ashikaga rule, Baishōron *is critical to understanding why Takauji and Tadayoshi were so successful from 1333 until 1350. The only comparable surviving monument of their authority consists of two remarkable portraits, one of Takauji and one Tadayoshi, likewise executed before 1350.*

Though the Baishōron *author has remained anonymous, analysis of the text provides ample clues to his identity. The text was completed between the eighth and tenth months of 1351.*[11] *Its author was a warrior from Kyushu who fought at the battles of Tatarahama and Minatogawa in 1336 and was somehow linked to Munakata Shrine. Unlike the formulaic description of battles in most literary accounts of warfare, the* Baishōron *author's accounts of these battles describe the coloring of armor or horses in a way consistent with how an actual observer would have noted them.*[12] *Details like the sunlight on the eve of battle, a sudden dust storm impacting the battle, or for that matter, the fact that the billowing cape* (horo) *of one warrior prevented his armor from being recognized suggests a careful narrator who recounted what he actually saw. This is a rare account of medieval Japanese warfare by a participant.*[13]

The next notable element of the text is its accuracy with respect to place and chronology. In comparison with Taiheiki, Baishōron *provides remarkably precise dates for major events, as well as a chronology consistent with actual geographical movement. For example,* Baishōron *correctly states that Takauji first rebelled on 4.27.1333 (Genkō 3) at Shinomura.*[14] Taiheiki, *by contrast, contains significant errors, most notably the notion that he switched sides on 5.7.1333.*[15] *Likewise, the* Baishōron *narrative lines up with that in other documents and is geographically and temporally possible. An example of this narrative accuracy is found in the* Baishōron's *account of Takauji's advance from Kamakura late in 1335. The chronology it provides for the battle of Minatogawa can also be verified.*[16] *Finally,* Baishōron *correctly states that the*

---

11. Koakimoto, *Taiheiki Baishōron no kenkyū*, Kyūko shoin, 2005, 352–61, 394–95. Koakimoto also showed that the work does not recognize Southern Court promotions and therefore betrays a Northern Court bias.
12. Fujimoto, *ibid.*, 181–83.
13. The only comparable work would be the Mongol Invasion Scrolls (*Mōko shūrai ekotoba*), which consists of Takezaki Suenaga's narrative of battle.
14. *Kamakura ibun*, vol. 41, docs. 32109–14, 4.27.1333 (Genkō 3) Ashikaga Takauji *gunzei saisokujō (an)*, 243–44.
15. Washio Junkei, ed. *Taiheiki (Seigen'in bon)* (Tōkō shoin, 1936), maki 9, "Gogatsu nanoka kassen no koto onajiku Rokuhara ochiru koto," particularly, 212–18. Similar variation appears in the *Kandabon* version. See *Taiheiki (Kandabon)*, maki 9, "Gogatsu nanoka miyako kassen no koto," 90–110.
16. Compare the narrative with Seno Seiichirō, comp., *Nanbokuchō ibun Kyushu hen*, vol. 1, doc. 616, 5.25.1336 (Kenmu 3) Ashikaga Takauji *kakikudashi an*, 193.

Section V • The Rise of the Ashikaga and the Life of Ashikaga Takauji

Protector Priest Kenshun brought an edict from the Jimyōin emperor (Kōgon) legitimating Takauji's rebellion midway through the second month of 1336. This is confirmed by a letter written by Takauji on 2.15.1336 and a mobilization order dating from two days later.[17] *Taiheiki* claims that this edict was not issued until nearly ten weeks later, on 5.1.1336.

Taiheiki exaggerates the size of armies and provides no consistency at all with respect to numbers.[18] Baishōron, *too, mentions impossibly large numbers, but these are invariably reported as hearsay, not as fact.*[19] *It describes actual encounters in far more limited, plausible fashion. For example,* Baishōron *mentions fifty troops dying in one encounter during the battle of Minatogawa, and it describes the destruction of the Kusunoki army as resulting in seven hundred deaths. Such numbers are consistent with the number of casualties in an overwhelming defeat.*[20]

Takauji Raises an Army

When Go-Daigo set off in the spring of the previous year, even those deeply indebted to the Bakufu grieved to see him leave on his long journey, and the most uncouth among peasant men and women joined those of more cultivated understanding in moistening the sleeves of their hempen garments with tears of sorrow. People everywhere prayed for the safety of the throne. It was therefore no mere coincidence that Akamatsu Nyūdō Enshin [Norimura][21] of Harima, and all the other forces in the Kinai and neighboring province had rallied to his support.

They awaited Go-Daigo's return, then on 3.12.1333 (Genkō 3) made a two-pronged attack on the capital from Toba and Takeda. Rokuhara forces quickly rode to meet them, fought them, and drove them back. A messenger rode from the capital to the Kantō with news of this attack. Ashikaga Takauji, now the *Shōgun*, therefore came up to the capital for the second time as one of the commanders of a punitive force. He entered the city late in the fourth month of the same year.

---

17. *Nanbokuchō ibun Kyushu hen* vol. 1, doc. 417, 2.15 Ashikaga Takauji *shojō an*, 144 and doc. 418, 2.17.1336 (Kenmu 2) Ashikaga Takauji *gunzei saisokujō*, 145.

18. See Conlan, *State of War*, p. 9 for one example of how *Taiheiki* exaggerates numbers.

19. The *Kandabon Taiheiki* states that 300 Ashikaga warriors fought 30,000 Kikuchi enemies. See maki 15, "Tatarahama kassen [no] koto," 221. The *Seigen'in* version has the same numbers. See maki 15, "Tatarahama kassen [no] koto," 424.

20. The battle, which resulted in the death of Kitabatake Akiie, resulted in seven hundred dead. See *Nanbokuchō ibun Kyushu hen*, vol. 1, docs. 1215–17, *urū* 7.6.1338 (Kenmu 5). Isshiki Dōyū *shigyōjō*, 367, and vol. 7, docs. 6995-8, *urū* 7.6.1338 Isshiki Dōyū *shigyōjō utsushi*, 15–16. [TDC]

21. The Akamatsu turned against Kamakura quite early in the conflict of 1331 and throughout the fourteenth century were staunch Ashikaga supporters.

4. Excerpts from Baishōron

Back in Genkō 1 [1331], too, he had been a commander of the force that attacked the stronghold on Mount Kasagi. This time, however, he received the order to go within a few days of his father's death.[22] He had not yet held the memorial service and was still overwhelmed with grief, but the lay priest [*zenmon*] Takatoki[23] nonetheless ordered him to start for the capital. He could only obey. No doubt his quality as a commander made him the Bakufu's best choice, but the order on this occasion was unreasonable, and Takauji apparently conceived a deep grudge. The other commander was Nagoe Takaie, the governor of Owari and a descendant of Tomotoki, of the Ministry of Ceremonial, who commanded the Hokurikudō force in the Jōkyū conflict. Both commanders reached the capital at the same time and also left at the same time, on the twenty-seventh of the fourth month. Takauji was to proceed to Hōki via the San'indō provinces of Tanba and Tango. Takaie moved to Hōki via the San'yōdō Harima and Bizen. Their goal was to attack Mount Funanoe, but in their first skirmish on the way there, at Koga Nawate,[24] Nagoe Takaie was killed. His men returned to the capital without fighting.

Takauji camped that same day at Shinomura, a holding of his in Tanba.[25]

His family had actually been harboring for generations the idea of destroying the Bakufu. Moreover, when he was at the Kagami post station in Ōmi, on his way to the capital, Hosokawa Kazuuji (Awa-no-kami) and Uesugi Shigeyoshi (Izu-no-kami) had conveyed to him the secret command that Go-Daigo had given them earlier. They had urged him repeatedly to take a stand for Go-Daigo, arguing that their receiving this command meant that the time had come to act.

Before the Hachiman Shrine in Shinomura, Takauji therefore flew his banner from the top of a huge willow. The spring sun rises in the east, and the willow is the tree of the east. By ruling the east the sun becomes the master of the realm. It is

---

22. According to *Sonpi Bunmyaku*, Takauji's father Sadauji (referred to in the original as Jōmyōji, his posthumous Buddhist name) died on 9.5.1331. This error appears also in the oldest (*Kanda-bon*) text of *Taiheiki* (Book 9, "Ashikaga dono jōraku no koto") but was corrected in the later *Jingū chōkokanbon*. See Hasegawa, *Taiheiki*, maki 9, "Ashikaga dono onjōraku no koto," 215–16. For analysis, see Koakimoto Dan, *Taiheiki Baishōron no kenkyū*, 397–99.
23. Hōjō Takatoki (1303–33), the fourteenth Kamakura *Bakufu* adjutant.
24. In present Fushimi-ku, Kyoto.
25. Takauji's mother, Uesugi Kiyoko, was born in the nearby Uesugi region and apparently gave birth to Takauji there as well, since much lore concerning Takauji's birth, as well as his grave and that of his wife and mother, can be found in nearby Ankokuji. In moments of crisis Takauji returned to Shinomura, and he made the shrine there an essential cultic site for the Ashikaga regime. Crucially, Takauji's earliest documents confirm that his rebellion dates from the twenty-seventh of the fourth month, showing that the *Baishōron* narrative is correct. The *Taiheiki* and other texts date his rebellion to approximately a week later. See *Kamakura ibun*, vol. 41, for Takauji's documents of 4.27 (1333).

also said that a great commander comes from the east, and that when spring turns to summer he will move west and destroy the enemies of the court. Accordingly, a great many of the troops that had crowded into the capital hastened to rally to Go-Daigo.

Takauji then moved his camp from Shinomura to Saga, and it was rumored that he would attack the capital in a few days. In the capital, the Bakufu forces, which had lost more than ten battles since the twelfth of the third month, fortified Rokuhara and established an imperial dwelling there.[26] Tens of thousands of men entrenched themselves inside.

Meanwhile the large Bakufu army that had surrounded Kusunoki Masashige's stronghold on Mount Kongō since the previous spring had not won a single encounter and had been losing ground. They were very frightened when they heard that Takauji, acting on Go-Daigo's orders, would soon invade the capital. Nonetheless, many residents of the city, as well as Shikoku and Kyushu warriors, continued to give the Bakufu impressive service.[27]

Takauji Attacks Rokuhara

On the seventh of the fifth month, at the hour of the hare [6 a.m.], Takauji's forces proceeded from Saga and occupied Uchino. The front ranks took up position in front of the Office of Shrines [*Jingikan*], facing east. The Rokuhara forces went up through Shirakawa and positioned themselves beyond the Nijō-Ōmiya crossing, facing west.

At the hour of the dragon [8 a.m.] the two sides advanced. The din of humming arrows resounded, war cries went up, and a battle to the death began. The thunder of hooves and the whistling of arrows filled the sky and shook the earth. The two sides charged again and again. The dead and wounded were beyond counting. Among them, on Takauji's side, was Shidara Gorō (*Saemon-no-jō*), whose loyal death in the vanguard of Takauji's forces was especially moving.

At the hour of the sheep [10 a.m.] the Rokuhara forces were defeated at Ōmiya and retreated. A loyalist force attacking from the south entered the capital via the Toba Road and Takeda, and occupied positions in several places around Kujō, while other forces attacking from various directions broke into the capital. The Rokuhara men therefore retreated into their fortress. Some braves among them,

---

26. See *Takemuki-ga-ki* 30, Kōgon, Go-Fushimi, and Hanazono moved to Rokuhara on 3.12.1333 (Genkō 3) (*Takemuki* has 3.16).

27. For example, the army of Aso Harutoki, who besieged Kusunoki Masashige in 1333. His army survived, long after other Kamakura institutions had been destroyed. For Harutoki's final document see "The Kamakura Age," doc. 31, Document of Praise (*kanjō*), Aso Harutoki. [TDC]

keen to win honor for their family and themselves, attempted sorties, and the battle continued for seven days.

Meanwhile, many on Go-Daigo's side favored using their great strength to surround the fortress immediately and kill all of the enemy. However, Hosokawa Kazuuji (Awa-*no-kami*) said, "If we do that, the enemy will fight desperately, and our casualties will be high. If instead we open one side of our siege and allow them to flee, they will be in retreat, and we will wipe them out easily." This suggestion was carried out.

Many in the fortress changed their minds and came over to Takauji. The two Rokuhara administrators (*tandai*), Hōjō Nakatoki (Echigo-*no-kami*) of the north Rokuhara compound and Hōjō Tokimasu of the south—discussed the situation and concluded: "If we are to die, we would prefer to fall in battle here in the capital, but this would give us only personal fulfillment. We have His Majesty with us, and it would not help him or the Retired Emperors[28] for us to die fighting or to kill ourselves. We must first escort them out of the capital and await reinforcements from the Kantō, or send word to the forces besieging Mount Kongō, and only then join battle. Then we can quickly re-enter the capital."

They reported their position to the Emperor, who replied that the warriors should do as they saw fit. Accordingly, they left Rokuhara at midnight on the seventh day, proceeded east along the Kuzume road, crossed the Seta bridge, and came to a path across a field. It was now light. As the attending courtiers made their way through the thick, dew-laden summer grass that lined this unfamiliar mountain path, their tears seemed to vie with the dew, for their sleeves were still wetter than the grass.

From roughly Moriyama on, skirmishers (*nobushi*) raced over hill and dale to attack the retreating force, of whom it is impossible to say how many were killed or wounded. That night the Emperor lodged at Kannonji in Ōmi.

The next day, the ninth of the fifth month [of Genkō 3, 1333], they were fleeing eastward when, at Banba in Ōmi, they were attacked by bandits [*akutō*] from Ōmi, Mino, Iga, and Ise. Claiming to be Go-Daigo partisans, the attackers raised their banner and blocked the road with their shields.[29]

Having fought in Kyoto on the seventh and survived the attacks of the roving warriors on the eighth, the previous day, the Rokuhara men and horses were too exhausted and could not go on. Nonetheless, some who valued their reputations

---

28. Emperors Go-Fushimi and Hanazono.
29. According to *Masukagami*, the fifth son of Emperor Kameyama, the Itsunomiya Prince Moriyoshi, led a "waiting imperial force." Documents issued by him, describing the destruction of Rokuhara, appear in *Kamakura ibun*, vol. 41, doc. 32160, 5.14.1333 (Genkō 3) Itsunomiiya *ryōji*. See Command of the Fifth Prince (p. 116). This Moriyoshi is not to be confused with another, the more famous son of Go-Daigo (e.g., Command of Prince Moriyoshi [p. 112]). [TDC]

fought all that day. However, there was no way out. The men agreed that they must perform the terrible act of killing the retired emperors, then all die in battle or by their own hand.

The commander, Nakatoki, said, "It would be disgraceful to survive and let His Majesty be captured, but what happens afterwards will not matter if we die first." At the hour of the bird [6 p.m.] he therefore killed himself, followed by several hundred fellow warriors. Tokimasu had been struck by a stray arrow on the night of the seventh at Shinomiya-gawara. After his death, one of his retainers took his head and brought it to Banba, where Nakatoki viewed it before he committed suicide. The names of those who slit their bellies on this occasion were recorded then in the temple at Banba and therefore are still known.[30]

After this battle was lost, Emperor Kōgon and the Retired Emperors learned that Former Emperor Go-Daigo had entered the capital. When the same news reached Mount Kongō, the great force attacking Masashige's fortress lifted their siege and withdrew to Nara. They did not know what to do next. However, once Takauji had destroyed Rokuhara and become *Shōgun* in the capital, on Go-Daigo's instructions he issued an order to all the warriors in the land to destroy the Bakufu, and the troops in Nara hastened to join him. Thereupon the commanders of the force attacking Masashige—Aso Tokiharu, Osaragi Takanao, and Nagasaki Shirōzaemon—surrendered in Nara and took holy orders in Nara. They were imprisoned nonetheless.[31]

The next passages of this account describe Takauji's flight to Kyushu after rebelling against Go-Daigo late in 1335. After briefly occupying the capital but then suffering defeat, Takauji fled to Kyushu, where he triumphed at the battle of Tatarahama and then returned to defeat Go-Daigo's forces at Minatogawa.

Akamatsu Advises Takauji to Withdraw to the Western Provinces and to Obtain a Decree from the Cloistered Emperor

Late that night, Akamatsu Enshin went in secret to see Takauji. He said, "Even if we were to defeat the enemy and invade the capital, we would be too tired to

---

30. This document, the *Ōmi Banba no shuku Rengeji kakochō*, survives (*Kamakura ibun*, vol., 41, pp. 252–58, doc. 32137) and shows that 430 perished. The days correspond to those in the narrative. Of this list, 189 have their names recorded. Almost all were close Kamakura confederates. Only one was an administrator (*bugyōnin*) of Rokuhara; another was a member of the Council. The rest, whose sympathies lay with the court, abandoned Kamakura with alacrity.

31. Documents from the Mikita collection reveal a document of praise written by Aso Harutoki (Doc. 31, Document of Praise [*kanjō*], Aso Harutoki). These men were killed by Go-Daigo in 1335, when Kamakura partisans launched a rebellion. [TDC]

4. Excerpts from Baishōron

accomplish anything worthwhile. Would it not be better to move your army to the western provinces for a while, let the troops recover their morale, rest the horses, and ready the weapons, and then only then proceed to the capital?

"In any battle," he continued, "the banners are fundamental. The Emperor's army follows the imperial banner. Our side has no comparable banner, and we therefore appear to be enemies of the throne. The Jimyōin Cloistered Emperor [Go-Fushimi] is, after all, of a legitimate imperial line (*shōtō*), and I doubt very much that the destruction of Hōjō Takatoki pleased him.[32] We should quickly obtain a retired emperor's decree (*inzen*) from him and fly the imperial banner before us.

"Our side was worsted in every battle last year," he went on, "because when we set out from the Kantō you were in the west, and we were therefore at a disadvantage. Nonetheless, you were fortunate enough after all to enter the capital. This time, when you attack from the western provinces the enemy in the capital will have to face you, you will accomplish your purpose.

"First, the Hosokawa should go to Shikoku. I myself will take control of Settsu and Harima. In Kyushu, the two sons of Myōe of Chikugo,[33] Saburō and Shōgen, will soon join you. Myōe recently received your summons, and they will certainly give you service.

"Ōtomo Sadanori was killed by Yūki Chikamitsu in Kyoto in the first month of this year, and his successor, Chiyomatsumaru, is still a child; but several hundred of his family's retainers are serving in your army. Can there be any doubt that you will return to the capital next month with forces from Chūgoku, Shikoku, and Kyushu? First, though, you should return to the foot of Mount Maya."

Akamatsu gave Takauji this advice repeatedly. Takauji therefore withdrew from his position at Segawa around midnight and entered Hyōgo on the twelfth day at the hour of the hare [6 a.m.].

Takauji's Army Moves from Hyōgo to Muro-no-tsu

When Tadayoshi returned to the foot of Mount Maya, he meant to go on to the capital without regard for his own life. Takauji therefore argued forcefully with him and persuaded him to return to Hyōgo. They boarded the ships at about the hour of

---

32. Kōgon had retreated with most of the Hōjō-related officials associated with the Rokuhara, although not their lower ranking administrators. In the end, over four hundred of these men were defeated and committed suicide. Although some courtiers were wounded, they did not die here like the Kamakura warriors. Some renounced the world but Go-Daigo refused to recognize this. Kōgon was then treated by Go-Daigo as if he had never reigned. This emphasis on Jimyōin legitimacy contrasts with the earlier narrative. As for the *inzen*, Go-Fushimi, the senior member of the Jimyōin line, fell ill at this time, so that the edict was ultimately issued by Kōgon, then styled Shin'in (Junior Retired Emperor).

33. Shōni Sadatsune, the deputy governor at Dazaifu in Kyushu.

the bird [6 p.m.] on the same day, without deciding who would board first, and the men's eagerness to do so showed how keen they were to get away.

Long ago, however, in Jishō [Jishō 4, 1180], when he first took up arms, Yoritomo was defeated in the battle of Ishibashi, and when he boarded a boat at Cape Manazuru there were only six men with him, including Doi Jirō Sanehira and Okazaki Shirō Yoshizane. Miura Kotarō Yoshimori joined him at sea, on the way to Awa or Kazusa. *Miura seemed truly loyal, and Yoritomo trusted him.*[34] The warriors of the eight eastern provinces joined him as soon as the boat reached Karishima, in Awa, and he accomplished his purpose. Also, when Yoriyoshi and Yoshiie went on a punitive expedition to the far north, their force was once reduced to only seven men. Therefore many said that with these initial reverses Takauji was following in his family's fine tradition.

Meanwhile, seven or eight[35] of those who had served Takauji with forces under their own command left for the capital. They were said to have surrendered. All had rendered Takauji distinguished service since the previous year, when they were fighting in the Kantō, but because of Takauji's defeats they quickly furled their banners, removed their helmets, and altered their crests.[36] It is sad to ponder their feelings. When those brave warriors who attached more importance to loyalty than to their own lives learned what they had done, they expressed their determination to render Takauji every possible service.

Takauji's ship set sail at about the hour of the dog [8 p.m.]. Suddenly, a wind blew up from the east: a following wind known as "the dragon."[37] The ship therefore reached Muro-no-tsu at about the hour of the tiger [4 a.m.]. Many who had been too late to board the ships the previous evening rode to Muro-no-tsu by land. Their service was admirable. Over three hundred ships accompanied Takauji's. The sea in the area where they made their passage is called Harimanada.[38] The passage is difficult and no one makes it without a favorable wind. Takauji's fortunes had depended on the wind. Tadayoshi attributed it entirely to divine protection. He dropped relics[39] and a sword into the sea during the passage as an offering to the Dragon God.

---

34. The Kyōdai, Kanshō, and other early copies of this text lack this sentence.
35. The oldest texts say eight or nine.
36. Warriors attached the family crest of the Ashikaga, printed on a piece of cloth, to their helmets or sleeves as an identifying badge (*kasajirushi*). Those who went over from Takauji to Yoshisada are said to have modified their Ashikaga crests to make them look like Nitta crests, since both families were of Minamoto descent and the crests were similar.
37. The dragon stands approximately southeast by east in the Chinese zodiac.
38. A *nada* is an area of ocean with strong winds and high waves.
39. *Shari*, in theory the bones of a Buddha or saint.

4. Excerpts from Baishōron

The Ashikaga Army Splits Up Among Several Provinces.
It Receives the Cloistered Emperor's Decree

The army stayed at Muro-no-tsu for a day or two, and a council of war was held there. Various opinions were expressed. One man said, "The imperial army will undoubtedly pursue us. Should we not station a commander in each province in order to protect Takauji's rear, until he reaches Shikoku and Kyushu?"

Takauji agreed. He immediately assigned these nine commanders to Shikoku: the three brothers Hosokawa Kazuuji, Yoriharu, and Morouji; and their cousins, the six brothers Hosokawa Akiuji, Jōzen, Kōkai, Tadatoshi, Masauji, and Shigeuji. He put Kazuuji and Akiuji in charge of rewarding warriors in Shikoku according to their services.

Akamatsu was assigned to Harima. Ishibashi Kazuyoshi of Owari was assigned to Bizen and stationed in Mitsuishi Castle, together with the Matsuda family. The Imagawa brothers Saburō and Shirō were assigned to Bingo, and took up positions at the ports of Tomo and Onomichi. Nunokawa Shosaku, of the Momonoi, and the Kobayakawa family were assigned to the province of Aki. Ōshima Yoshimasa of the Nitta was appointed commander and Ōuchi Nagahiro protector of Suō. Shiba Takatsune was appointed commander and Kotō Tarō Takezane protector of Nagato.

After making these assignments, Takauji proceeded to Tomo in Bingo, where Sanbōin Kenshun, acting as imperial messenger, presented him with Kōgon's decree.[40]

This was a cheering development. Takauji was no longer an enemy of the throne, and it was a joyful occasion when he sent instructions to his commanders in the provinces to raise the imperial banner.

The Ashikaga Army Sails the Inland Sea and Reaches Tsukushi (Kyushu)

Making a long, unforeseen journey was bad enough, but the sea route was unfamiliar to Takauji and many of his warriors. Afloat on the sea at high tide, the ships, numbering in the hundreds, seemed to be rising to the clouds and hanging in midair. Uncertainty filled the men, far from home and unsure of their destination. The clouds closed behind them. The noise of the wind forever blowing through the pine trees on the shore interrupted their sleep. Unable even to doze off, they could not stop thinking about their native lands. Words cannot express how discouraged they were in their desperate situation. Wretched and forlorn, they did not know whether

---

40. Kenshun was a crucial Ashikaga and Jimyōin supporter.

they would live to return. The weather was favorable, however, and Takauji's ship reached Akama-no-seki[41] in Nagato on Kenmu 3.2.20 [1336].

On the twenty-fifth of that month, Yorinao, the eldest son of Dazaifu Assistant (*Dazai no shōni*) Myōe, came to greet Takauji accompanied by over five hundred members of his family. He presented Takauji and Tadayoshi with brocade *hitatare*. The occasion seemed to foreshadow Takauji's future success.

On the twenty-ninth, Takauji and his army left Akama-no-seki by ship and after a day's journey on the Inland Sea reached the port of Ashiya in Chikuzen, in Kyushu.

Takauji's Army Leaves for Munakata and Yorinao Joins in a Council of War

The following day, the first of the third month, Yorinao was assigned to the advance guard. Takauji's army left the port of Ashiya and, at the hour of the bird [6 p.m.], reached the residence of Munakata Ujinori, the chief priest of the Munakata Shrine.[42] Ujinori presented Takauji and Tadayoshi with suits of armor and horses. Takauji learned there that Myōe had indeed committed suicide. He seemed to mourn him deeply.

Meanwhile, news came that the enemy had already taken up position at Hakata. That night Yorinao therefore did the same at Minoo Beach, some three miles ahead of Takauji's camp. He alone was summoned to Takauji's camp at Munakata, where they discussed the coming battle. Yorinao said, "My father was defeated in the recent fight at the Dazaifu Headquarters because I had taken my men to meet you and he therefore had too few. He knows that area well, however, and I am sure that he himself is safe. No doubt some of the local warriors will join you at tomorrow's battle. As for that Kikuchi Taketoshi, I will easily dispatch him with a single blow." He tossed off this speech casually, leaving the impression that one could fully rely on him.

One man said to Takauji: "The men who followed you from the Kantō are willing to die for you. However they are on foot, since they left their horses at Hyōgo, and it is uncertain whether they will arrive here tonight. I suggest that you stay here tomorrow, just one more day, and place them in the vanguard for the battle. It would be a pity to leave here without them."

---

41. The Shimonoseki strait that separates Honshu from Kyushu.
42. The Munakata, hereditary chief priests of the Munakata Shrine, were also administrators for Kamakura. Some lived in Kyoto, but many more fought for Takauji. They could well be the source of the *Baishōron* narrative.

4. Excerpts from Baishōron

There was no agreement, but about midnight there were reports from various quarters that Kikuchi had already left Dazaifu to attack Takauji. The question of the force left behind was therefore no longer relevant.

A Good Omen at the Kashii Shrine

At the hour of the dragon [8 a.m.] on 3.2.1336 (Kenmu 3), Takauji and his army left the camp at Munakata to meet the enemy. After some fifteen miles they passed at about the hour of the sheep [2 p.m.] before the Kashii Shrine, where priests brought Takauji cedar branches and said, "The enemy are all wearing as their emblem leaves of bamboo grass. Yours should be cedar." They attached cedar sprigs to the sleeves of Takauji, Tadayoshi, and the other warriors. This seemed truly auspicious. This shrine is named Kashii[43] because when Empress Jingū was here, at the time of her expedition against Silla, she touched a chestnut tree, and it gave off a sweet fragrance. The chestnut was therefore designated the shrine's sacred presence [*shintai*], while the cedar was made its particular treasure.

At any rate, an old man in white personally attached a cedar sprig to the sleeve of Takauji's armor. Takauji gave him a sword in a plain wooden scabbard. Later, when Takauji asked for the old man, the priests said that they had no idea who he was. Takauji took this as a sign of divine protection, the old man being a god in human form. He grew even more confident, and his army displayed heightened morale.

The Ashikaga Army Confronts the Kikuchi Army at Tatarahama

Takauji's army left Kashii and advanced to a place called Akasaka. Takauji sent out scouts. They discovered a dry beach known as Tatarahama, three and a half miles long and with a brook at its southern end. The Hakozaki Hachiman Shrine was there, surrounded by a hundred-acre pine wood. To the south was Hakata; there was a hill about a mile to the east; and to the west the sea stretched away to China. The place reminded one of the sad story of Lady Matsura, who pined away, waving her scarf.[44]

Between Akasaka, where Takauji took up position, and the pine wood, the sand sparkled like jewels. The enemy crossed the brook and drew up facing north, with the pine wood at their rear. They were reported to number over sixty thousand

---

43. Literally, "fragrant chestnut tree."
44. According to a legend recorded in the *Man'yōshū*, the *Hizen Fudoki*, and elsewhere, she climbed the hill mentioned and in vain waved her scarf to call back her departing lover, Ōtomo Sadehiko, who had been sent to lead an expedition to Mimana.

mounted men.⁴⁵ In the vanguard of Takauji's army were Kō no Moroyasu, as well as those who had followed Takauji from the capital: Ōtomo, Shimazu, Chiba, Utsunomiya, and over three hundred mounted warriors. These drew up facing the main enemy force. Takauji's advance guard to the east was Shōni Yorinao and his force of over five hundred mounted warriors; these dismounted and took up position. In all, Takauji's force numbered fewer than a thousand men.

Yorinao wore a yellow-braided breast protector and arm protectors bound at the edge with cord of the same color. This was the famous armor that his ancestor, Mutō Kojirō Sukeyori, had received from Yoritomo at the time of the Ōshū expedition in Bunji 5 [1189]⁴⁶ and that had been in his family for generations. Wearing this armor and his helmet, a drawn short halberd in hand, and riding a piebald horse, Yorinao went by himself to see Takauji and Tadayoshi. He said: "The enemy are many, but they may come over to your side. Kikuchi's own force cannot number over three hundred. If I sacrifice my life fighting at the forefront of your army, the enemy will be like dust before the wind. I suggest that we should advance under our banner." He seemed fully reliable. Naturally, everyone present agreed that Takauji and Tadayoshi should advance.

Takauji's Appearance, and His Orders

Takauji wore that day the red brocade *hitatare* that Myōe had presented to him through Yorinao; a suit of armor braided with Chinese twill; and two swords, one named Crunchbone,⁴⁷ which had been in his family for generations. He carried a rattan-wrapped bow and *kabura* arrows. His horse, a dark grey, was one that the chief priest of the Munakata Shrine had presented to him the previous day.

On that day Takauji had Atsutadaigūji Takanori⁴⁸ of Noda wear the suit of armor Kosode ("Short Sleeves"), which had been in the Ashikaga family for generations.⁴⁹ In general, that family has many secret traditions regarding battle dress. Long ago, when Minamoto Yoriyoshi went on his punitive expedition against Abe no Sadatō, he struggled hard for twelve years. Since they fought on dark nights and

---

45. Needless to say, a gross exaggeration.
46. Yoritomo's punitive expedition to Mutsu against the Fujiwara family in 1189.
47. Ōbami, according to *Genpei Jōsuiki* 16 the sword with which Minamoto no Yorimasa (1104–80) killed the *nue* (a monstrous creature with the head of a monkey, the body of a tiger, and the tail of a serpent) at the imperial palace. *Heike monogatari* 4 only mentions Yorimasa receiving a sword named Lion King (Shishi-ō) as a reward for his deed.
48. Originally Atsuta Daigūji ("chief priest of the Atsuta Shrine"). However, the title came to be used as the name of the Owari family, which held the office.
49. Perhaps Atsuta daigūji had been designated Takauji's double, a common practice.

in the snow, it was feared that in a melee Yoriyoshi might be mistaken for an enemy. Kiyohara Takenori got the idea of having him wear seven emblems, the so-called Seven Signs, all of them being items of military equipment, that would not allow the enemy easily to pick him out. It is said that Takauji gave some thought to his dress on this day, in accordance with this example, although he did not go as far as seven emblems.

Takauji said: "I never meant to come so far from the capital, but war involves both advance and retreat. If we meet this renowned enemy and for lack of a strategy lose our last battle, will our family not also lose its long-standing reputation for military skill, and will we not leave a bad name behind us? I have an excellent plan. If Tadayoshi and I were to advance together and find the going hard, who would be left to accomplish our purpose? If I stay in the rear, however, even by myself, the forces in the front will fight with some confidence. Even if the odds are against us, I would be able to take over with my guardsmen and defeat the enemy. Therefore Tadayoshi should advance first." Everyone praised this idea, saying that no one else could have thought of it. They also said that Takauji's tactics had won the battle at Ashigara the year before, after leaving Hakone, and they advanced under his banner.

Tadayoshi wore the red brocade *hitatare* given him by Myōe and armor braided with purple leather. His sword fittings were decorated with a bamboo grass leaf pattern, and he carried and a bow and arrows. He rode a chestnut horse that had been given him the day before by the chief priest of the Munakata Shrine.

The Battle Begins; Soga and Niki's Hard Fight

The warriors who had come with Takauji from the Kantō were all on foot, but all vied as they advanced to be first. Among them was Soga Morosuke, wearing a red-braided suit of armor, cut off below its cross-patterned borders, over a padded garment of shot silk. He carried two swords over four feet long; a large, unlacquered bow; and, on his back, a quiver with twenty or thirty arrows. With his helmet on, he cut a strange figure as he stood before Tadayoshi's mount.

Under the banner stood Niki Yoshinaga in a yellow-braided suit of armor. Tadayoshi had received this armor from the chief priest of the Munakata Shrine and then presented it to Niki, thus greatly honoring him.

When Niki rode his chestnut horse to the front, what seemed at least twenty or thirty thousand of the enemy charged out from the east wing, which faced the Shōni force, brandishing their swords and shouting battle cries. They were so powerful that it seemed not even demons could resist them.

However, Tadayoshi's force remained calm. First the foot soldiers shot arrows, and when the enemy hesitated for a moment, the mounted warriors seized the opportunity and charged. Just then, a north wind blew up clouds of sand, making things difficult for the enemy and causing them to falter. At the sight, Tadayoshi's center, too, fought fiercely.

Meanwhile, Soga Morosuke killed an enemy officer and cut off his head, and soon came before Tadayoshi riding on the officer's large red-tinged grey horse. When he showed Tadayoshi his prize, Tadayoshi was highly pleased. "Morosuke," he said, "you have gotten yourself a good horse. Now you can take on a thousand or even ten thousand of the enemy." Morosuke charged the enemy again, every inch a matchless warrior.

Niki Yoshinaga charged the enemy and fought without regard for his life, killing many, and rejoined the ranks with blood on his horse and armor.

Taking advantage of victory, Tadayoshi's force pursued the enemy past the Hakozaki pine wood and all the way to the Hakata beach.

Takauji's Offering at the Hakozaki Shrine

Tadayoshi quickly started with Yorinao in pursuit of the defeated enemy, even though it was the hour of the bird [6 p.m.]. They reached the Dazaifu that night at about the hour of the boar [10 p.m.]. Tadayoshi first inspected the remains of Myōe's residence, which had been reduced to ashes, and he seemed deeply grieved. The troops, however, had more confidence in Takauji than ever, for they believed that that his strategy had won the day.

Takauji camped at the Hakozaki temple.[50] The shrine priests welcomed him. He refrained from making a formal offering because he had been defiled by battle, but he bathed and saluted the Hachiman Shrine[51] from before the gallery. He then donated to the shrine a sword in a plain wooden scabbard, with a cord tied in a latticework pattern, given him by Kira Mitsuyoshi. Wishing also to donate land to the shrine, he asked to see the shrine documents in order to obtain a model for his letter of endowment. Among these he found a letter of endowment written long before by Chinzei Hachirō Tametomo.[52] Feeling truly grateful to his family's tutelary deity, he turned toward the shrine's main hall and pressed his palms together in veneration. His reverence seemed profound.

---

50. Presumably the temple (*jingūji*) associated with the shrine.
51. The Hakozaki Shrine proper.
52. Minamoto Tameyoshi's eighth son, who subdued most of Kyushu in the late Heian Period. *Heiji monogatari* tells his story.

4. Excerpts from Baishōron

Takauji and Tadayoshi Reunited

The next day, the third of the third month, Tadayoshi sent a messenger named Mutō Buzen Jirō, a Shōni kinsman, to Takauji to say, "Our victory in yesterday's battle was by no means due to our human prowess. I believe that we owe it to divine protection. Our triumph was auspicious. When we climbed the mountain near Dazaifu yesterday, at about the hour of the bird [6 p.m.], enemy warriors surrendered and joined us. Yorinao interceded with me on their behalf. We are expecting you here, but I am sending you this message in the meantime."

The distance from Hakozaki to Dazaifu is said to be about twelve miles. At the hour of the horse [11 a.m.] Takauji reached the monks' lodge on the mountain. While he and Tadayoshi met there, the warriors who had surrendered the previous day were assigned to guard the gate. This was a noble act indeed.

The victory had been due to Takauji's strategy, but it was said that the quick destruction of the enemy had been due to Shōni Yorinao's deeds.

Good Omens for the Ashikaga Army

Takauji reached Kojima in Bizen on the fifteenth of the fifth month. This area was held by the Sasaki family. Kaji Akinobu, therefore built him a temporary residence near the beach and prepared a bath and so on for him. Takauji rested there.

That night, two black lines of cloud were observed stretching for some time across the full moon. Takauji's troops joined their hands in worship. It was a very good omen.[53]

While Takauji was in Kyushu countless strange phenomena occurred at various shrines, and there were other good omens as well. A particularly auspicious one occurred while he was at Dazaifu in Kyushu. Speaking through a maidservant at the Sumiyoshi Shrine, the deity of the Kushida Shrine in Hakata said to Takauji, "I will be keeping watch over you and Tadayoshi all the way to the capital. You will arrive safely, but you will have to fight. Offer a white banner, a suit of armor, a sword, a bow, some arrows, and some humming arrows (*kabura*)." This oracle was so miraculous that Takauji had these things prepared. The woman who had received the oracle strung the bow and fitted a *kabura* to it in the presence of Takauji's messenger. She said: "Many doubt me, but here is the proof. If Takauji is to establish his rule over the realm, not one of these arrows will miss its mark." She then shot three arrows at a slender bead tree branch and never missed. No woman of humble birth could have done this.

---

53. The Ashikaga crest consisted of two dark horizontal bars in a circle.

Also, the spirit of Tenjin's messenger appeared, shining, in each battle, inspiring great confidence in Takauji's men.[54] Finally, Takauji had a sacred dream on his way down to Kyushu, as a result of which an old, pale grey horse was stationed to one side of his ship.[55]

Takauji Examines the Abandoned Enemy Banners

Meanwhile, the land force pitched camp at Kakogawa in Harima. The sea force reached the harbor of Muro in the same province. The next day, Akamatsu came to see Takauji at his ship and gave him a register of the warriors who had joined him in his castle, as well as over a hundred banners that the enemy had abandoned at their points of attack when they withdrew. Takauji examined each, and each family crest was identified. "Seeing these," he said, "I have nothing to say about those who were on the enemy side from the beginning. However, I also see here the banners of a few warriors who once rendered me distinguished service in war. It is sad to imagine the inmost thoughts of those who joined Yoshisada in order to avoid our temporary hardships. They will eventually rejoin us." Takauji looked very pleased, and people felt that his sentiment had been truly generous.

Takauji entrusted the banners to Akamatsu and told him to make a note of how many there were, saying that he would decide later what was to be done with them.

The Positioning of the Two Armies on Land and at Sea

At the hour of the hare [6 a.m.] on the twenty-fifth the Hosokawa commanders, whose more than five hundred ships from Shikoku made up the main naval force, spread their sails as on the previous day, since the following wind was still blowing, and sped along within sight, to port, of the Minato River, where the enemy had taken up position, and Hyōgo Island.[56] Their purpose was to block the enemy's line of retreat.

The imperial banner on Takauji's ship bore a gold sun disk and the names of the Sun Goddess and Hachiman in gold characters. It glittered in the sun. The banner was unfurled and fluttered in the breeze, and they beat the drum, as was the custom when Takauji's ship set sail. The thousands of ships spread their sails at the same

---

54. "Tenjin" is probably Tenman Tenjin, the deified Sugawara no Michizane enshrined at Dazaifu. Uesugi Kiyoko mentioned a comparable divine manifestation in the passage quoted as an epigraph to this volume.

55. The meaning of the original sentence is unclear.

56. Hyōgo-no-shima, a crucial port west of Sakai.

time, jostling one another so that even the three-mile-wide strait of Awaji seemed to be too narrow. As they rowed along in formation, one could not see the water.

The land forces likewise began to move. They seemed to fly through Ichinotani. Late in the hour of the dragon [9 a.m.] they came within sight of the island at Hyōgo. The enemy had taken up position from the mountains behind the Minato River down to the village, with their banners flying and their shields in lined. This was Kusunoki Masashige's force.

Also, a large force[57] proceeded to the Suma junction on the Harima Road and took up position there. At the beach front, an enemy force apparently over ten thousand strong stood with its back to a young pine grove on Wada Point, flying *nakaguro* banners.[58] Actually, it was divided into three.[59] The vanguard appeared to be about five hundred strong and the next force about two thousand. The third stood at the pine grove.

The Shōni Force Advances to the Van of the Ashikaga Army

Time passed. At the hour of the serpent [10 a.m.] Takauji's three forces—mountain, Suma junction, and beach—all began to advance at the same time. Perhaps because they were faster, Shōni's beach force of over two thousand mounted warriors took the lead under his banner.

Over five hundred of these warriors got some one hundred yards ahead of the rest, and over fifty of these were even further in front, when two of them raced about thirty yards ahead of all the others. One rode a black horse and wore a pink *horo*.[60] The color of his armor braiding was not clearly visible. The other rode a tan horse with a black mane and tail ("buckskin") and wore yellow-braided armor. Both were relatives of Shōni Yorinao.[61]

The one with the *horo* was Mutō Buzen Jirō, and the one with the yellow-braided armor was Mutō Tsushima Kojirō. Both were very young. The ships were only about a hundred yards from the shore, and those aboard could watch as though watching a performance from stands.

---

57. Tadayoshi's.

58. The Nitta family crest.

59. According to *Taiheiki*, these three were commanded by Nitta Yoshisada, his younger brother Wakiya Yoshisuke, and Ōdate Ujiaki.

60. A sort of cape that protected against enemy arrows. A crimson-dyed *horo* was thought to reflect a warrior's resolve to fight to the death in battle. A *horo* could also serve as a fallen warrior's funeral shroud.

61. Unusually, this passage does not describe a warrior's armor fully, but instead limits its description to what the narrator presumably observed.

Section V • *The Rise of the Ashikaga and the Life of Ashikaga Takauji*

Yoshisada's Defeat at the Battle of Hyōgo

When rapid drumbeats sounded from Takauji's ship, the men in the naval force raised their battle cry. The great land force responded three times, and the *kabura* arrows began to sound. The six earthquakes' roar could not have been louder.

Before this spectacle the enemy vanguard pulled back without shooting a single arrow. The two warriors in the lead changed direction and charged into the enemy's second rank.

Fearing that the two would be killed, the rest of the great force followed. As a result, the enemy was defeated. In this battle at Wada Point, while smoke rose from farmhouses at the edge of Hyōgo, the enemy force on the Harima road could not hold. The same was true for the mountain force.

Meanwhile, the Shikoku force was landing near at Ikuta Wood, to prevent the enemy at Hyōgo from retreating, when they encountered Yoshisada and some three thousand warriors, who were withdrawing in defeat from the battle at Hyōgo. The men on the ships hesitated to land, since the enemy being mounted. *However, the Hosokawa brothers and cousins advanced, each vying to be first.*[62] Among them were Jōzen, his younger brother Tatewaki Senjō, Furuyama Yūzō, Sugita, Usami, and Ōba. These disembarked their horses and mounted, and eight of them charged into the great force.

However, the enemy were too many. They were forced back into the water and returned to their ships. Then one Niinomi Kodayū, from Sanuki, declared that he would sacrifice his life for his commander. He dismounted and he remained alone on the shore to fight. At the sight, Jōzen and fifteen other mounted warriors rushed ashore again and fought. The rest of the force then disembarked and went up on the shore. As a result, Yoshisada was defeated and fled towards the capital.

Masashige's Death in the Battle at Minatogawa

Jōzen heard that Kusunoki Masashige was still at the Minato River and fighting fiercely against the center force. Ignoring Yoshisada, he rushed to join Tadayoshi in the fight. Late in the hour of the monkey [5 p.m.], Masashige, his younger brother Shichirō Masasue, and some fifty other warriors committed suicide together. Over three hundred others had died in action. It was said that, altogether, over seven hundred had died on the beach, at Hyōgo, and at the Minato River. In such a battle, there were naturally many killed and wounded on Takauji's side as well.

---

62. This sentence is missing from the Tenri text, one of the oldest variants.

4. Excerpts from Baishōron

The Most Reverend Musō's Praise of Takauji's Virtues

In the course of a sermon, the Most Reverend Musō[63] once praised Takauji's and Tadayoshi's virtues. Of Takauji he said, "A man born to become a king, a minister, or a leader of men is so destined by the power generated by his good deeds in previous lives; it is not a matter merely of what he does in this life. The *Shōgun*, especially, occupies a very important position, since it is his duty to assist the Emperor and suppress rebellion.

"I have heard only at second hand about affairs in China. In our own country, Sakanoue no Tamuramaro, Fujiwara no Toshihito, Minamoto no Yorimitsu, and Fujiwara no Yasumasa all suppressed rebels, but their authority did not extend over the whole country. From Jishō [1177–81] on, Yoritomo also held the office of *shōgun* and took affairs of state entirely into his own hands. He did not let his personal feelings affect his administration of justice, but the punishments he meted out were nonetheless too harsh, and he therefore appeared to lack humanity.

"Takauji, the present *Shōgun*, possesses not only benevolence, but also still greater virtues. First, he is courageous. Often, in his battles, his life seemed in danger, but he kept smiling and his face betrayed no fear. Second, he was born with charity and hates no one. He has forgiven many sworn enemies, treating each as if he were his only son. Third, he is generous; there is nothing stingy about him. To him gold and silver are like earth and stones, and when he gives weapons, horses, and so on away, he does not match the gift to the man but distributes them at random. I have heard that he has received gifts beyond counting on occasions like the first day of the eighth month, but that he has given them all away, so that by evening no one could remember what they had been. Truly, a *Shōgun* with these three virtues is rare in this latter age." Musō talked this way whenever he preached a sermon.

Takauji's and Tadayoshi's Deep Devotion to Buddhism

Prince Shōtoku built forty-nine temples and instructed the nation to observe the fast days. Emperor Shōmu built Tōdaiji and the Kokubunji, and Fujiwara no Fuhito built Kōfukuji. These things occurred in ancient times and were all a result of divine incarnation.

Likewise Takauji and Tadayoshi, in our own time, should not be regarded as ordinary men. They devote themselves to Buddhism above all, and they built Tenryūji, founded by Musō. Takauji offered a prayer in which he vowed to copy out

---

63. Musō Soseki, 1276–1351.

the Tripitaka,[64] and he personally painted a Buddhist image, wrote an inscription on it, and signed it. Even after a heavy bout of drinking he always holds a meditation session with everyone present.[65]

Takauji's and Tadayoshi's Good Government, and Their Respect for Musō

Tadayoshi built a temple named Ankokuji in each of the sixty-six provinces, and he similarly erected a stupa in each province. In this way he fulfilled his desire. His behavior shows him to be an upright, sincere man untainted by dishonesty. For this reason Takauji entrusted the government of the realm to him. Tadayoshi declined resolutely more than once, but he finally agreed after Takauji begged him to accept. Thereafter Takauji never interfered in government affairs, even in the most trivial matter.

Once, when they were together, Takauji said to Tadayoshi, "Since you rule the realm, please behave responsibly and never go sightseeing or waste your time. There is nothing wrong with viewing cherry blossoms or autumn leaves, but sightseeing and so on should be limited to special occasions. The reason I ask you to be prudent because I think that I myself will be mingling casually with retainers, eliciting their support, and guarding the imperial court." Tadayoshi appreciated this advice, which, he thought, an ordinary man would never have given him.

This is how Takauji and Tadayoshi came to accept Musō as their master. Before Genkō, when Hosokawa Akiuji was on his way through the northern provinces to Awa, to recruit troops for the imperial cause, he had an audience with Musō at Erinji Kai and received his teaching. Later, Musō gave spiritual guidance to Takauji and Tadayoshi. Thanks to the urging of the priest Musō and the layman Akiuji, Takauji and all those below achieved everlasting glory. This was wonderful and auspicious indeed.

Takauji's Magnanimous Rule and the People's Willing Submission

Takauji and Tadayoshi once came together, summoned Kō no Moronao and many members of the former Bakufu's Council of State, and enacted a number of government regulations. Takauji said, "According to what I have heard of ancient times, the Heike were wicked and tyrannical during the twenty years when Yoritomo suffered in exile in Izu and devised his farsighted plan of raising an army. In order to put an end to the inexpressible grief of the people, Yoritomo raised his army in

---

64. The *Gen'ishū* account of the battle of Tōji in 1355 describes Takauji's fulfillment of this vow.
65. The oldest Kyōdai text lacks these two paragraphs, although the 1466 (Kanshō 7) copy of the latter half of *Baishōron* contains them.

Jishō 4 [1180] and suppressed the rebels in Genryaku 1 [1184]. The war lasted for five years.

"What I have heard about his rule suggests that rewards and punishments were made clear, which is something that the ancient sages did well. However, there were still many harsh punishments and this gave rise to suspicion within the Minamoto family, and between it and others. As a result, many were executed for no particular misdeed. This was most unfortunate.

"The intention of this government is to rule without causing suffering. We should therefore placate even those who were our sworn enemies, assure continued tenure of their ancestral estates, and bestow especially generous rewards on those who perform military deeds. I trust that everyone will assist the government with this aim in mind."

Tadayoshi was particularly pleased. Moronao and all the members of the old Council of State appreciated Takauji's generous feelings. None among them did not wipe the tears from his eyes.

There is no need here to discuss Yao and Shun, since they lived in China. Here in Japan, however, those who were born under such a *Shōgun* as Takauji, even in this Latter Age, have had the good fortune to enjoy prosperous and peaceful lives.

5. Copy of a Letter (*shojō an*) by Ashikaga Takauji[66]

The following document was sent by Takauji after he first received legitimation from Kōgon—the Emperor who fled to Banba with Rokuhara in 1333—and was then abolished before being recognized by Takauji again.

By the pleasure of the New Retired Emperor (Kōgon), I am departing for *Chinzei* [Kyushu]. For your military service (*chūsetsu*) to be undivided, older and younger brothers should act as if they are adopted father and son. Respectfully.

Second month, fifteenth day of the third year of Kenmu (1336) Takauji (copy of seal)

[To]: The Honorable Ōtomo Chiyomatsu

---

66. Seno Seiichirō, comp., *Nanbokuchō ibun Kyushu hen*, vol. 1, doc. 417, 2.15 Ashikaga Takauji *shojō an*, 144. Translated by Thomas Conlan.

6. Mobilization Order (*gunzei saisokujō*), Ashikaga Takauji[67]

Takauji, having received an edict from the Retired Emperor Kōgon, used it to attract support from warriors to attack Go-Daigo's general Nitta Yoshisada. He deferred to Go-Daigo and did not openly call for his removal.

I have received a Retired Emperor's edict (*inzen*) ordering me to immediately chastise Nitta Yoshisada and his supporters. Quickly, lead your family and ride for Akamaseki. As for rewards: if you perform military service, we will personally distribute them.

The seventeenth day of the second month of the third year of Kenmu (1336)

To: The Honorable Aki *Daiku no suke*

7. Ashikaga Takauji Prayer (*ganmon*)[68]

Ashikaga Takauji issued the following prayer at Kiyomizu temple on 8.17.1336. He had just installed Kōmyō, Kōgon's son, as Emperor two days before and was well on his way to establishing the Muromachi shogunate. This document gives no sense of the fact that he had attained victory. Ironically, although Takauji would delegate authority to his brother Tadayoshi, the two brothers would, in the end, wage war against each other, resulting in Tadayoshi's death in 1352.

This world is nothing but a dream. I, Takauji, feel compelled to enter religious orders. Please let my later incarnations achieve enlightenment. Now, as I wish to take the tonsure, please let me have the peace of mind (*dōshin*) to do so. As for the karma of this world, please transfer it to later incarnations. As for the karma of my life, please transfer it to [my brother] Tadayoshi. Protect him in all ways.

---

67. *Nanbokuchō ibun Kyushu hen*, vol. 1, doc. 418, 2.17.1336 (Kenmu 3) Ashikaga Takauji *gunzei saisokujō*, 145. Translated by Thomas Conlan.

68. *Dainihon shiryō* series 6, vol. 3 (1903), *hoi*, 3. 8.17.1336 (Kenmu 3) Ashikaga Takauji *ganmon*. Translated by Thomas Conlan.

8. Document (*kakikudashi*) by Ashikaga Tadayoshi[69]

In fact, Takauji did not enter religious orders. He tended to entrust most affairs to his brother Tadayoshi. The rift that developed between the two brothers resulted in the splitting of the Ashikaga regime. Here Tadayoshi issues an edict to attack the Kō brothers Moronao, Takauji's trusted chief of staff, and Moronao's brother Moroyasu in 1350.

Chastise Moronao and Moroyasu.
You shall quickly perform military service.
Thus.

Eleventh month, twenty-first day of the first year of Kannō (1350) (monogram)[70]
To: The Honorable Tannowa Hikotarō

9. Reminiscences by Aiba Ujinao[71]

Takauji later dreamed his brother tried to kill him. Tadayoshi's supporters killed Kō Moronao and Moroyasu, and in the ensuing conflict Takauji attacked and defeated Tadayoshi, resulting in Tadayoshi's ultimate death. Here, thirty-three years after Takauji's death his confidant Aiba Ujinao explained why Takauji often drew images of Jizō *(Sanskrit* Kṣitigarbha*), revealing that Takauji was as devout as* Baishōron *suggests, and that he perceived himself as directly communicating to bodhisattvas through dreams.*

Takauji had a dream in which he was pressed by enemy forces. He fled to the mountains. At the peak, the road came to an end and he was in danger of falling. He looked back and was grabbed by Tadayoshi, who exerted all his strength in trying to throw Takauji into the abyss. Then, suddenly, Takauji saw a single priest (*bikuni sō*) in the form of *Jizō* bodhisattva who took him by the hand and led him

---

69. 11.21.1350 (Kannō 1) Ashikaga Tadayoshi *kakikudashi*. https://komonjo.princeton.edu/tannowa/view.html?t=2-1. Accessed August 27, 2021. Translated by the students of *Sources in Ancient and Medieval Japanese History* with Thomas Conlan.

70. Ashikaga Tadayoshi.

71. Gidō Shūshin, *Kūge nichiyō kufū ryakushū* (10.1.1382 (Eitoku 2), 175–76. Translated by Thomas Conlan.

to the safety of the plains where the Kō brothers and an army of thousands greeted him. Later, when reaching Kyushu, he encamped at just such a plain, proof of his dream. Thereupon, Takauji drew a picture of the *Jizō* in which he celebrated his ability to sense [*Jizō*] through his dreams.

10. Letter (*shojō*) by the Protector Priest (*gojisō*) Kenshun[72]

Early in 1351, when the defeat of his patron seemed inescapable, Sanbō'in Kenshun (1299–1357), a Protector Priest (gojisō) for the Northern Court Emperors and Ashikaga Takauji, wrote the following remarkable letter to his nephew and disciple Kōzei (1326–79). The letter shows that gojisō *like Kenshun were Takauji's most trusted and most loyal supporters—even more loyal and trusted than his own warriors. Although Takauji was defeated and the Kō brothers killed, Tadayoshi's young son died at the moment of Takauji's surrender. This death allowed Takauji to reward his followers and undermine his brother. Some allies of the Kō brothers eventually poisoned Tadayoshi. Kenshun, who was a Protector Priest devoted to Takauji, died in 1357, but not before offering to exchange his life so as to extend Takauji's (see Prayer by the Protector Priest Kenshun, p. 147). Takauji himself died in 1358.*

Last winter, at the time when I thought about how best to convey my ritual knowledge (*hōryū*), I transmitted to you our sect's (*shū*) most important practices. Nevertheless, you have again offered to help at this difficult time. I have spoken to the monk (*hōin*) Jōchō. Last year when we worshipped at the shrine (*jingū*), I spoke with him, and you should be assured. You should question him most closely. I have written out a testament concerning the transmission of the *monzeki* and other rights.[73] There should be no disturbances. Everyone should follow this document and there should be no disturbances.

As my future is intertwined with his life, I am now traveling on the same path as the *Shōgun* [Takauji]. To follow the *Shōgun* into battle goes against the way of the Buddha (*shakamon*) and is a source of shame for my lineage (*ichiryū*) and a deep cause for concern in both this world and the unseen world known only to the gods and Buddhas (*myōken*). Nevertheless, please understand that I have no other choice.

---

72. *Dainihon komonjo iewake* 19 *Daigoji monjo* vol. 6, doc. 1258, 1.14 [(1351/Kannō 2)], *Zen daisōjō* Kenshun *shojō*, 253–54. Translated by Thomas Conlan.
73. Buddhist priests of an aristocratic or imperial lineage and their offices.

11. Prayer (ganmon) *by the Protector Priest* (gojisō) *Kenshun*

If I perish in the course of my travels, wait until peace returns and then restore these teachings. During the time of the 1333 disturbance, I received the transmissions of my master [Kenjo], and during later difficult moments, I briefly lost honor (*menboku*). But, after the realm returned to peace, my earlier decision was ultimately one of wisdom and not shame and all was restored. As a sign of otherworldly help (*myōjo*), I have come to exceed all others. Pray fervently so as to receive the support of the otherworld. Respectfully.

The fourteenth day of the first month [of 1351]

Kenshun

[To:] Hōchi-in *hōin gobō* [Kōzei]

11. Prayer (*ganmon*) by the Protector Priest (*gojisō*) Kenshun[74]

Kenshun was Takauji's most trusted Protector Priest and adviser. Knowing the general was ill, Kenshun prayed to the gods that he might die first so as to trade his life for Takauji's. No warriors were willing to die for Takauji but not so Kenshun! Kenshun's prayer inspired his later successor, the powerful Protector Priest Manzei (1378–1435). Such devotion to lords would later become expected of higher-ranked warriors in later centuries.

Respectfully Submitted Before the Treasure Hall of the Iwashimizu Hachiman Shrine, a Prayer:

This prayer is as follows: The Minamoto Grand Minister (*Ashō*) Lord Takauji is in a dangerous year [of his life]. The general is grateful to the gods and Buddhas; may his years in the world be extended. The general and I, Kenshun, disciple of the Buddha,[75] have for many years been blessed with a bond (*hōkei*) that is deep, and for the last few years, our obligation has become even deeper. His kindness is manifest; and in order to pay back his benefice (*on mukuimugatame*), I pray that I can substitute my life for the *Shōgun* (*daiju*). May the majesty of the gods descend, and may my prayer not be in vain; so to the three gods of Hachiman (Ōjin, Jingū, and Himegami), and the Wakamiya and Takeuchi Shrines and [all of the shrines]

---

74. *Dainihon shiryō* series 6, vol. 21 (1924), 206–7. Manzei was a powerful monk who mastered Kenshun's ritual knowledge. Translated by Thomas Conlan.

75. A Shingon monk.

affiliated with this mountain [complex] (*manzan*) receive the protection of the Buddhist law, and through the expedient means of great compassion, may the power of the Buddhas and the power of the Buddhist law be added. Thus, my request is such. Respectfully.

Second month, tenth day of the second year of Enbun (1357)

The *Kongō busshi* Kenshun, respectfully,

(copy of monogram)

A copy of this prayer was written by my grandfather, master Kenshun, in his own hand. The original is to be found at the treasure hall of the Treasure Hall. His request was fulfilled because of his fervent prayer. I am incredibly moved. So that others know this, I have recorded this year.

Manzei (Monogram)

12. Sutra Colophon Written by Ashikaga Takauji[76]

Ashikaga Takauji copied out the Perfection of Wisdom Sutra (Japanese Rishukyō Sanskrit Prajñāpāramitā-naya-śatapañcaśatikā), a foundational Buddhist sutra, for Kenshun's Shingon sect. In his copy he praised Kenshun's sacrifice of his life in order to give more years to Takauji. Kenshun died on the sixteenth day of the seventh intercalary month of 1357 (Enbun 2). On the forty-ninth day after Kenshun's death, Takauji wrote the following postscript. Takauji himself would die during the fourth month of 1358 (Enbun 3).

On the day that corresponds to the Buddhist services held on the forty-ninth day (after the death of) Sanbō'in Primary Prelate (*daisōjō*), I have copied one volume of the *Hannya Rishukyō*.

Twenty-eighth day of the eighth month of Enbun 2 (1357)

The Minamoto *ason* of the Second Rank Takauji (monogram)

---

76. For a good illustration of this sutra, see *Ashikaga Takauji: Sono shōgai to yukari no meihō*, 48. Translated by Thomas Conlan.

SECTION VI
Warfare in the Fourteenth Century: Warrior Experiences (1331–92)

The documents of the fourteenth century are unusually rich, as they provide a detailed record of warriors' actions and tribulations. Many families relied on oaths to shore up their internal support; others complained about insufficient rewards or compensation. The burdens of waging war are most evident in a series of letters written by a warrior, Yamanouchi Tsuneyuki, who perished in 1340. Ultimately, after 1350, the Ashikaga would allow *shugo* to use half of a province's revenue for military provisions: this allowed them to better supply warriors, establish standing armies over time, and become incipient provincial magnates.

The letters written by Yamanouchi Tsuneyuki to his family tell of the great burdens imposed upon Japan's warriors by the civil war. These records, which were only discovered in the 1990s, make clear the precarious position of these warriors, many of whom did not survive the conflict. These sources show that both warriors and commoners (*hyakushō*) could ride horses and fight in battle. They also illustrate warriors' efforts to equip their families and followers for campaigns—a crushing financial burden.

Most translations have focused on the drama of the earlier years of the conflict, but an entertaining passage from the latter half of *Taiheiki*, a lengthy and famous text that serves as one of the most influential tales of the age, recounts the tedium of besieging castles, warrior knowledge of Chinese military manuals, and the enduring competition by warriors for recognition. This section ends with a passage from *The Chronicle of Meitoku*.

Section VI • *Warfare in the Fourteenth Century: Warrior Experiences*

1. An Oath by Members of the Nejime Family[1]

When confronted with the renewed outbreak of warfare late in 1335, some families took steps to shore up their bonds and refrain from discord. When they heard of Takauji's rebellion against Go-Daigo early in 1336, warriors in southern Kyushu relied on oaths to bolster their familial ties in an attempt to ensure their survival during the civil war.

As the world is in turmoil, this clan (*ichimon*) agrees to be unified, [as if of] one body and one mind (*ichimi dōshin*).

Concerning the above, we shall act of one mind in thought in action (*ichimi dōshin*) concerning various things. There should not be the least difference of opinion (*igi*). Everything shall be discussed in council (*shūgi*). Those who disobey this oath shall suffer the otherworldly (*myōdō*) punishment of all of the small, middling, and great gods of the country of Japan. This document is stated thus.

The eleventh day of the first month of the third year of Kemmu (1336)

Kiyoyoshi	(Copy of Monogram)
Kiyotane	(Copy of Monogram)
Kiyotake	
Yorisumi	(Copy of Monogram)
Dō'e	
Kiyonari	(Copy of Monogram)

2. A Petition for Reward (*gunchūjō*) by Hatano Kageuji[2]

In a petition, Hatano Kageuji recounted his remarkable experiences. He joined Takauji shortly after his rebellion. But when Takauji was defeated and fled to the west early in 1336, Kageuji was trapped and left behind. He somehow

---

1. Seno Seiichirō, *Nanbokuchō ibun Kyushu hen*, vol. 1, doc. 383, 1.11.1336 (Kenmu 3) Torihama Kiyoyoshi *rensho keijō utsushi*, 132. Translated by Thomas Conlan.

2. Matsuoka Hisato, comp., *Nanbokuchō ibun Chūgoku shikoku hen*, vol. 1, doc. 259, 2.25.1336 (Kenmu 3) Hatano Kageuji *gunchūjō utsushi*, 125. Translated by Thomas Conlan.

The Nejime Clan (*Ichimon*)

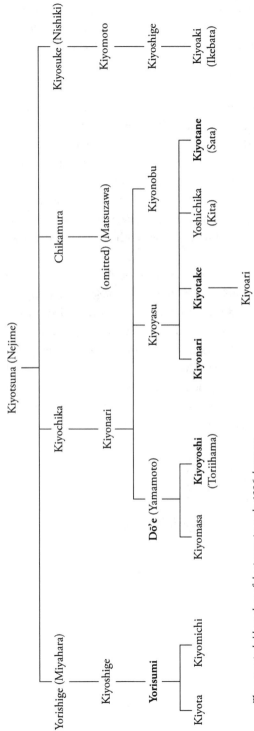

The names in bold are those of the signatories to the 1336 document.

managed to escape. In the following excerpt from his petition, he argues that because he thought about dying in battle—which, to him, is the same as actually dying in battle—he made the ultimate sacrifice, which was, among these autonomous warriors, rather rare.

Hatano Hikohachirō Kageuji states: On the past twelfth day of the first month, I joined the forces that entered the capital and, on the thirteenth, followed them as they forded the river. On the sixteenth, the mountain monks [of Mt. Hiei] and other rebels descended to the lower wards of the capital and tried to encircle our encampment. I traveled to Hosshōji where I performed great service before the temple, pursuing defeated enemy forces up the mountain [Mt. Hiei]. On both days of the seventeenth and the eighteenth, we went to Nishi Sakamoto [to the east of Mt. Hiei] and on the nineteenth we defended Yawata castle [to the south of Kyoto].

My military service continued through the seventh day of the second month. While we were fighting in battle, the *Shōgun* [Ashikaga Takauji] departed for Hyōgo Island, and the victorious enemy surrounded my castle. I wanted to join the *Shōgun*'s forces but could not. I thought I would die where I stood. I had all but resolved to kill myself in the garden any number of times, but, somehow, I managed to preserve my unworthy life. If one were to carefully consider the extent of my service (*chūkin*), then it would be the equivalent of dying in battle. Regardless, many have abandoned the general, and most of our army has fled. In order to prove the veracity of my claim, I desire to receive a commander's monogram. Respectfully.

Second month, twenty-fifth day of the third year of Kenmu (1336)

To: The administrators

Received (monogram) [Takeda Nobutaka]

3. Takeda Nobutaka Document of Praise (*kanjō*)[3]

In the following extant copy (utsushi) of a document, Takeda Nobutaka recognizes the service, and praises the accomplishments of Hatano Kageuji.

A document viewed by the Honorable Takeda *Hyōgo no suke*

During the battle for Yawata, several thousand horsemen of our army—the vast majority—fled. Those who remained performed splendid battle service. As for rewards, let [your] receipt [of them] not be a matter of dispute. This report (*chūshin*) is thus.

The second month, twenty-fifth day of the third year of Kenmu (1336)

Hyōgo no suke (copy of monogram)

To: The Honorable Hatano Hikohachirō

4. A Cosigned Document (*rensho shojō*)[4]

In the following document, warriors from the Gotō islands of northern Kyushu complain about the lack of compensation for their military service and emphasize their unified resolve in pressing their claims. Such complaints were not invariably successful, but they reveal that no notion of loyal obligation existed. To the contrary, military service required compensation.

Our rewards are insufficient, and we were told to speak of this publicly (*oyake*). This family (*ichizoku*) is in agreement (*ikki tokoro sōrō nari*) that there should not be any problems [with our claims]. Respectfully.

The fifth day of the eleventh month of the second year of Ryakuō (1339)

Tomo (Monogram)

Tsumu (Monogram)

[To:] The Honorable Madarajima Genji

---

3. Matsuoka Hisato, comp., *Nanbokuchō ibun Chūgoku shikoku hen*, vol. 1, doc. 260, Takeda Nobutake *ikenjō utsushi*, 125. The copyist mistakenly copied the character for year as the number three. Translated by Thomas Conlan.

4. Seno Seiichirō, *Nanbokuchō ibun Kyushu hen*, vol. 2, doc. 1418, 11.5 Terada Tomo Tsumo *rensho shojō*, 36. Translated by Thomas Conlan.

Section VI • *Warfare in the Fourteenth Century: Warrior Experiences*

5. The Letters of the Yamanouchi[5]

One of the most remarkable sources for the study of the wars of the fourteenth century is a cache of letters later discovered inside a Buddhist statue (Takahata Fudō). Cut into small pieces and stamped with images, it is possible these letters were considered magical talismans, and that they were given to the temple by Tsuneyuki's surviving wife and son in his memory and to aid his salvation. Piecing the letters back together proved to be painstaking work. These letters recount the actions of one warrior, Yamanouchi Tsuneyuki, who participated in the early battles fought in Hitachi Province. Tsuneyuki's letters reveal the great costs of the war in Hitachi, which lasted from 1339 through 1344, as well as the intensity of the battles. Yamanouchi Tsuneyuki fought under the command of Kō no Morofuyu (?–1351) and traveled to Kamakura during the eighth month of 1339. In the early years of the war, Morofuyu's forces were at a disadvantage as he tried to conquer the Southern Court strongholds of Seki and Taihō castles, located in Hitachi Province.

Kitabatake Chikafusa (1293–1354), whose son Akiie (1318–38) died in battles in 1338, was the able opposing commander. He described Morofuyu's forces as being "unusually weak" early in 1340.[6] It was probably around this time that Tsuneyuki died. Other Yamanouchi would survive this conflict and prosper, but nothing more is known of Tsuneyuki, his wife, or his son.

Tsuneyuki's records show the great burden placed on families by the waging of warfare. Notable, too, is that hyakushō—*a term commonly translated as "peasants"—had horses and weapons. The term is translated here as "commoners" to reveal their relatively elite status in provincial society. Tsuneyuki also relied on several figures, such as the Arai and Takahata, for support, but of them, little is known.*

Though the Kō were valued followers of the Ashikaga, and though Morofuyu ultimately triumphed, they would be almost completely annihilated in the political disturbances of Kannō. Two of Morofuyu's documents, which were preserved by some of Tsuneyuki's surviving relatives, are reproduced here as well.

---

5. Documents drawn from *Hino shi shi shiryōshū Takahata Fudō tainai monjo hen*. All were translated by Thomas Conlan.

6. *Sekijō chōshi, shiryōhen III, chūsei kankei shiryō*, 1.22 Shirakawa Yūki Chikatomo *ate* Kitabatake Chikafusa *mikyōjo utsushi*, 346–47. This weakness continued, according to Chikafusa, through 4.3.1340, with no signs of enemy reinforcement arriving. See Ibid., 4.3 Shirakawa Yūki Chikatomo *ate* Kitabatake Chikafusa *mikyōjo utsushi*, 348–49.

5. *The Letters of the Yamanouchi*

Part One: Preparations for War

Organizing and dispatching an army required months of efforts. The following letters reveal the length of time required before an army embarked on an offensive.

YAMANOUCHI TSUNEYUKI LETTER, UNKNOWN DATE, TO MATAKESA (1)[7]

This letter confirms that Tsuneyuki was in Kamakura and involved in some unspecified court case in 1339. Officials required that Tsuneyuki buy them sake *before they would hear his case. In later letters, he mentions (28) how he received a dwelling, which suggests he was successful in this case.*

[Beginning of letter missing/fragmentary]. As for my judicial dispute, after the initial court (*honbugyō*) [proceedings] I dispatched a messenger. I was well-known there [in Kamakura] and, when my case was transferred to another court,[8] they decided to hear my case. Unfortunately, right now, I don't have any *sake* [for the administrators] but need to buy five gallons (one *to*)[9] before I can do anything in the matter. At this stage, there are many people [waiting for their day in court] and so I want to be able, somehow, to buy *sake*. . . .

YAMANOUCHI TSUNEYUKI LETTER, UNKNOWN DATE, TO MATAKESA (4)[10]

Here Tsuneyuki discusses the need to get funds from the commoners of his estate. The provisional levies are undoubtedly to be used to pay for his provisions. He relied upon someone named Hachirōshirō to help his son collect these funds.

Even though we levied a provisional tax (*tenyaku*) on the commoners (*hyakushō*), I have heard they [these funds] have not been distributed. Speak to Hachirōshirō

---

7. *Hino shi shi shiryōshū Takahata Fudō tainai monjo hen* (Hino, 1993), doc. 1, Yamanouchi Tsuneyuki *shojō*, 14–15.

8. In Muromachi court cases, the *honbugyō* was responsible for the initial hearing of the case, while another court, the *ai-bugyō*, was responsible for the supplementary function of interrogating the plaintiff. Tsuneyuki, in referring to the change in court, is referring to the *ai-bugyō*.

9. One *to* equals just under 5 gallons (1.05 *to* constitute 5 gallons, or 18 liters).

10. *Hino shi shi shiryōshū Takahata Fudō tainai monjo hen*, doc. 4, Yamanouchi Tsuneyuki *shojō*, 20–21.

and the Tarōjirō novice (*nyūdō*) and have them attach a notice (*fuda*) on the agricultural produce [designating it for these taxes]. If anyone has a problem with this (*igi*), please inform me.... Show them a document explaining why this is the case. If you do not do this, they will not be at ease (*ando dekinai*).

Yamanouchi Tsuneyuki Letter, Unknown Date, to his Son Matakesa (5)[11]

This letter indicates that while Tsuneyuki was away, he had continuing problems collecting taxes and dispatched either Hikosaburō or Kosaburō to help Matakesa, his young son, govern these lands.

The commoners (*hyakushō*) are not paying their taxes (*tokubun*) at all, but there is nothing that I can do about it. They will not listen to me. I find this most surprising (*kokoro yori hoka ni zonji sōrō*). As [most of my followers] are away, I will dispatch [name missing] Saburō there....

Letter, of Unknown Date, from Yamanouchi Tsuneyuki to Shōshin, a Monk at Takahata Fudō (22)[12]

Tsuneyuki expresses his regrets for not being able to return but asks that the Arai help his family secure revenue from the commoners of his lands.

I am delighted to have the chance to speak with you. At this time, I would once again like to worship at your temple, but because of preparations, I am acting most improperly,[13] and contrary to my wishes, there is no way that I can return.... In all affairs.... The Honorable Arai has requested that Tōken, a servant of the monastery, should visit and speak with him. As for the commoners (*hyakushō*) and their affairs, speak to the Honorable Arai and gain a real understanding of the true situation at the temple so that we can prepare. Explain this to the people there in detail and report this directly to the Honorable Arai, regarding all things....

---

11. *Hino shi shi shiryōshū Takahata Fudō tainai monjo hen*, doc. 5, Yamanouchi Tsuneyuki *shojō*, 22–23.
12. *Hino shi shi shiryōshū Takahata Fudō tainai monjo hen*, doc. 22, Yamanouchi Tsuneyuki *shojō*, 60–61.
13. Literally, the way of the left hand (*sadō*).

5. *The Letters of the Yamanouchi*

Yamanouchi Tsuneyuki Letter, Eighth Month (23)[14]

The following letters recount delays in Morofuyu's force departing for Hitachi.

Because I can easily dispatch [something to you], I am writing this letter. Our departure to Hitachi is delayed again for who knows how long. Everyone is lamenting how long they must stay here. I thought that we would leave on the thirteenth, but that has not happened. . . .

Yamanouchi Tsuneyuki Letter Fragment to a Monk from Sekidō Kannon (24)[15]

I would like one or two *da* of commissariat rice.[16] I entrust everything to you.

Yamanouchi Tsuneyuki Letter to a Monk from Sekidō Kannon (25)[17]

I read your letter carefully. They say that we will set off for Hitachi either today or tomorrow, but I am not sure exactly when this will be. I feel bad about this, but can you borrow money from the Honorable Arai, and please send it me? There are reports that we will depart on the sixteenth . . . .

Yamanouchi Tsuneyuki Letter to Matakesa, Eighth Month 1339 (26)[18]

Here Tsuneyuki continues to wait for the army to depart. He requests more funds for provisions.

[First part of letter missing] . . . In addition, today. . . Shichirōjirō [text missing]. I really want to hear all about this. As for your letter, I have been told it will arrive

---

14. *Hino shi shi shiryōshū Takahata Fudō tainai monjo hen*, doc. 23, Yamanouchi Tsuneyuki *shojō*, 62–63.
15. *Hino shi shi shiryōshū Takahata Fudō tainai monjo hen*, doc. 24, Yamanouchi Tsuneyuki *shojō*, 64–65.
16. One *da* weighs approximately 240 lbs. (110 kg).
17. *Hino shi shi shiryōshū Takahata Fudō tainai monjo hen*, doc. 25, Yamanouchi Tsuneyuki *shojō*, 66–67.
18. *Hino shi shi shiryōshū Takahata Fudō tainai monjo hen*, doc. 26, Yamanouchi Tsuneyuki *shojō*, 68–69.

soon. Even if it does not make it on the seventh or eighth, it will arrive eventually. The Honorable Mikawa [governor Morofuyu] will depart around the twentieth. I hope your letter arrives before then. I will need two *kanmon* in expenses before I depart.[19] You must get these funds somehow, even if you have to sell a house (*zaike*)... [text missing] ... Shirōjirō ...

YAMANOUCHI TSUNEYUKI LETTER TO WIFE, EIGHTH MONTH (27)[20]

... The Mikawa Governor (Kō no Morofuyu) has decided the army will set off on the twentieth. I will be with those forces through their arrival at the Musashi Provincial Headquarters.... I will have to sell one house (*zaike ikken*). I would some tea, and also two or three dyed robes. It finally looks like we will be setting off soon. Every day, [regardless of] whatever happens, I will write.[21]

YAMANOUCHI TSUNEYUKI LETTER TO HIS SON MATAKESA (28)[22]

Thank you for sending a messenger with a letter. The Mikawa [Governor Morofuyu] will soon be departing and I will go with him to Musashi Province. I hoped that you would come to Kamakura, but you said that you are from the countryside, you would not look good there, so it is best that you remain, although I worry as it is difficult to remain there. Gorō is also exhausted... I was given a dwelling (*zaike*) as a result of a successful court case, and some cash remains. Please take it and buy a bow and send it my way. I am sending them to you. Give your mother my very best regards....

Eighth month, sixteenth day ...

---

19. This is roughly the equivalent of two thousand dollars.
20. *Hino shi shi shiryōshū Takahata Fudō tainai monjo hen*, doc. 27, Yamanouchi Tsuneyuki *shojō*, 70–71.
21. He states, literally, I will speak to you.
22. *Hino shi shi shiryōshū Takahata Fudō tainai monjo hen*, doc. 28, Yamanouchi Tsuneyuki *shojō*, 72–73.

Part Two: The Campaign Commences

The following letters reveal the frantic activity and stress of Tsuneyuki as Morofuyu's armies prepared to besiege the enemy castles in Hitachi, located near Shimokōbe estate.

YAMANOUCHI TSUNEYUKI LETTER, EARLY NINTH MONTH (31)[23]

From various messengers on fast horses, I know that we are now going to Shimokōbe estate, where eventually a battle will most likely be waged, although I cannot confirm this. We will reach Shimokōbe estate on the fourteenth or fifteenth, or perhaps later, on the sixteenth or seventeenth. . . .

YAMANOUCHI TSUNEYUKI LETTER TO YAMANOUCHI ROKURŌ, A RETAINER (34)[24]

I am happy to receive your letter. You have sent many, even before waiting for my replies. We are setting off for Shimokōbe estate. According to rumors, it has been ordered that all who remain behind will have [some of] their holdings confiscated. In addition, anyone who mentions this [policy] in a petition[25] will lose [all] their homelands (*honryō*). . . . By all means [secure] two to three *kan* [of cash], which I really need. Speak to Daishinbō[26] and borrow five *kanmon*. . . .

YAMANOUCHI TSUNEYUKI LETTER TO MATAKESA (35)[27]

This fragmentary letter reveals Tsuneyuki's impatience to receive military accoutrements before battles commenced.

[First part missing] . . . borrow. . . messenger. I need to receive this most quickly, for on the ninth day of this month, I am convinced that battles will begin. [text missing] day would be most welcome, as forces are approaching the castle [at Koma]. . . speak to the military council. . .

Tenth month

---

23. *Hino shi shi shiryōshū Takahata Fudō tainai monjo hen*, doc. 31, Yamanouchi Tsuneyuki *shojō*, 80–81.
24. *Hino shi shi shiryōshū Takahata Fudō tainai monjo hen*, doc. 34, Yamanouchi Tsuneyuki *shojō*, 86–87.
25. In other words, those who complain about this policy.
26. Unknown, but most likely some sort of money lender affiliated with a monastary.
27. *Hino shi shi shiryōshū Takahata Fudō tainai monjo hen*, doc. 35, Yamanouchi Tsuneyuki *shojō*, 88–89.

Yamanouchi Tsuneyuki Letter to His Wife (36)[28]

I am delighted to receive your letter. . . . We expect to arrive at Shimokōbe estate on the twelfth. Tomorrow they will decide exactly when we will arrive. Don't worry about the battle. As a number of people have gathered, we may leave by noon today. If not—even if we are delayed—we will definitely leave tomorrow. I am waiting for our departure. I miss you so much already!

Yamanouchi Tsuneyuki Letter to His Son Matakesa (37)[29]

[First part missing]. Bring two [containers]. If it is not too difficult to do so, speak with the temple, and get old [powdered?] tea for the first. In the other, buy some tea. In addition, get dried persimmons and dried peeled "victory" chestnuts (*kachikuri*).[30] Buy them and bring them to me. Respectfully,

Thirteenth day of the tenth month.

[Yamanouchi] Tsune[yuki]

Ink mark of a cut seal[31]

Letter, Sent by Yamanouchi Tsuneyuki in the Yamakawa Region, to His Son Matakesa (38)[32]

This would have been written while Tsuneyuki was part of Morofuyu's army. His request to borrow horses and armaments from the commoners (hyakushō) *of his lands indicates he suffered from a lack of adequate supplies.*

[First part missing] borrow horse . . . notify the commoners (*hyakushō*) and make this happen. Borrow a saddle and accoutrements (*gusoku*) and put them on the

---

28. *Hino shi shi shiryōshū Takahata Fudō tainai monjo hen*, doc. 36, Yamanouchi Tsuneyuki *shojō*, 90–91.

29. *Hino shi shi shiryōshū Takahata Fudō tainai monjo hen*, doc. 37, Yamanouchi Tsuneyuki *shojō*, 92–93.

30. These chestnuts had been dried and shelled. Their name represented a homonym for victory (*kachi*); hence, they were favored in battle. See *Hino shi shi shiryōshū Takahata Fudō tainai monjo hen*, doc. 37, Yamanouchi Tsuneyuki *shojō*, 92–93.

31. A "cut seal" (*kirifu*) was where the end of the document was cut vertically and used to wrap the document and seal it with an ink marking, which is evident here. For more on *kirifu*, see https://komonjo.princeton.edu/uesugi-01/. Accessed August 29, 2021.

32. *Hino shi shi shiryōshū Takahata Fudō tainai monjo hen*, doc. 38, Yamanouchi Tsuneyuki *shojō*, 94–95.

horses. If they do not have saddles or accoutrements, please have them lead a horse on foot. In everything, consult with your mother. As you are not so young, please plan this all out. Respectfully.

Sixteenth day of the tenth month. Tsuneyuki (monogram)

Ink mark of a cut seal

From Yamakawa. To Matakesa. A response from Tsuneyuki

Letter, Dated 10.28, from Yamanouchi Tsuneyuki to His Son Matakesa Regarding the Desertion of Many of His Followers after Their First Battle (39)[33]

Whether you call it a battle, or guard duty, one should not be discouraged. I will write down the number [and names] of our retainers (*matadomo*) who fled.[34] You should make sure that every single one of them is returned without fail. If you do not do this, I will no longer consider you to be my son. Etchū Hachirō, Yatsu, Kiheiji. . . if those people do not come, then send their parents here. Tell Okubō's Yasaburō that he should have those who have not yet arrived bring up the rear.

Twenty-eighth day of the tenth month

Take this and speak [of its contents] Ink remains of cut seal

To: The Honorable Matakesa   From: Yamakawa   Tsuneyuki (monogram)

Reply from Shikime . . . no Hi[ko]saburō

Letter from Hikoshirō to Aoyanagi Saburō (53)[35]

Hikoshirō commiserates with Aoyanagi Saburō on the death of the "wet nurse mother" who raised Saburō. Hikoshirō also comments on comrades performing guard duty.

Now it is the eleventh month . . . final turn of guard duty. People from Chisagata district [of Shinano Province] are performing [this guard service]. They are doing

---

33. *Hino shi shi shiryōshū Takahata Fudō tainai monjo hen*, doc. 39, Yamanouchi Tsuneyuki *shojō*, 96–97.

34. The meaning of the term *matadomo* is unclear. It seems to be a colloquial term for Tsuneyuki's core retainers.

35. *Hino shi shi shiryōshū Takahata Fudō tainai monjo hen*, doc. 53, Aoyanagi Saburō *shojō*, 124–25.

this adequately, as one would expect. Consult with the Honorable Nyū about everything. The current world is one where everything is unsettled. I am happy to hear that you are passing the time without having to collect anything [e.g., taxes, revenue, supplies of people]. I am really sorry to hear about your wet nurse mother (*menoto*) and am thinking of how deep your laments must be. I will discuss all things and convey them to [my retainer] Aoyanagi.

Eighth day of the eleventh month

Hikoshirō (monogram)

To: The Honorable Aoyanagi Saburō

Letter from Yamanouchi Tsuneyuki to His Son Matakesa (40)[36]

We are having Satō Saburō's son sent here. Make sure he is prepared and have him gallop here. Please inform Oku (the Governor of Michinoku?). As I previously requested, Matamera, who has already fled and returned, should be arrested without fail, [along with his people]. As you are taking care of affairs at home, you must have much to worry about. I will write further regarding everything.

Second day of the eleventh month   Tsuneyuki (Monogram)

Reply to The Honorable Yamanouchi Matakesa

[P.S.] I did not mention it in my letter to your mother, but people should continue to live at the temple houses (*zaike*). In addition Yatsu . . . respond to . . . *emon* Tarō Hachirō

Ink mark of cut seal

To: The Honorable Yamanouchi Matakesa

---

36. *Hino shi shi shiryōshū Takahata Fudō tainai monjo hen*, doc. 40, Yamanouchi Tsuneyuki *shojō*, 98–99.

5. The Letters of the Yamanouchi

Part 3: The Tribulations of Battle and Death

The following, final letters of Tsuneyuki, reveal the intensity of battle, and in the end, the hopelessness of Tsuneyuki, who did not expect to return from the campaign alive.

Letter from Yamanouchi Tsuneyuki to His Son Matakesa (42)[37]

I need a horse. As some of our reinforcements have brought horses, I asked for and received one from Lord Ebina's herd. I was also able to borrow a helmet from someone. War has arrived here [at Koma castle]. I have not yet been injured, but many have been killed or wounded. You must wonder what battle is like. Don't think that it is no big deal. As for this battle, a variety of important people have been wounded . . . or dead. . . will speak with . . .

Eleventh month

Letter from Yamanouchi Tsuneyuki to His Son Matakesa (43)[38]

Tsuneyuki wrote to his son during the twelfth month of 1339, at the start of the battle for Koma castle. Since the castle was not likely to be conquered, Tsuneyuki wanted to return home.

I read with care the letter from Kosaburō. I have no particular response regarding what he said. This castle will not fall within the year. I am thinking that I might take my leave and return. From now it will just be getting colder. . . . I am worried about [your finances for] at the end of the year, . . . if not there, Okubō's Ya[saburō]

Ink mark of cut seal

Reply to the Honorable Matakesa   Tsuneyuki (monogram)

---

37. *Hino shi shi shiryōshū Takahata Fudō tainai monjo hen*, doc. 42, Yamanouchi Tsuneyuki *shojō*, 102–3.

38. *Hino shi shi shiryōshū Takahata Fudō tainai monjo hen*, see doc. 43, Yamanouchi Tsuneyuki *shojō*, 104–5, for people leaving his forces, presumably during the twelfth month of 1339.

Letter from Yamanuchi Tsuneyuki to a Monk (44)[39]

This letter reveals the difficulties caused by the military campaign—such as the fact he was running low on provisions and his need to borrow money from Daishinbō again.

Thank you for your letter. When the retainer (*wakatō*) of the Honorable Takeda came here, I said that I would like to receive a letter at Kawamata.[40] I hope to hear about the Kiheiji affair. My military provisions (*hyōrōmai*) are exhausted. . . . From Nuta, send a messenger to Daishinbō and say . . . [text missing]

Letter from Yamanuchi Tsuneyuki to His Son Matakesa (45)[41]

I carefully read your last letter. As you said in your letter, things [back home] are difficult as no one is there to help you. I have, however, explained everything, and as recently you seem to be in good spirits, there is nothing more for me to say. By the way, the Governor of Mikawa (Kō no Morofuyu) is quite pleased about my actions in this battle. . . . Even if I end up dying, as long as the general or members of this unit (*ikki*) survive I am at ease [as they will help to take care of you].

Letter from Matakesa to the Honorable Arai, or a Takahata Monk (58)[42]

My father fought in many battles but has not been killed; it gives me great joy. We received a document . . . [of praise] that had been sent by the General (*taishō*) [Morofuyu].

---

39. *Hino shi shi shiryōshū Takahata Fudō tainai monjo hen*, doc. 44, Yamanouchi Tsuneyuki *shojō*, 106–7.
40. Located in Saitama district of Musashi Province. It is not clear whose opinion he wanted regarding Kiheiji, but the language suggests a social superior.
41. *Hino shi shi shiryōshū Takahata Fudō tainai monjo hen*, doc. 45, Yamanouchi Tsuneyuki *shojō*, 108–9.
42. *Hino shi shi shiryōshū Takahata Fudō tainai monjo hen*, doc. 58, Bō *shojō*, 134–35.

5. *The Letters of the Yamanouchi*

Letter by Yamanouchi Tsuneyuki (46)[43]

In his letters, Tsuneyuki would often complain of the difficulties of guard duty and the counterattacks being launched by the enemy.

[First half missing.] This leaves me ill at ease (*kokoromoto naku*). Regarding guard duty (*tono-i*),[44] you should have the commoners (*hyakushō*) do it. Keep them appeased until I return, but please ensure that they perform guard duty. . . . I received a letter. I want to reply to it, but we are fighting battles every day . . . attack . . . [text missing or fragmentary]

Ink mark of cut seal

[To: The Honorable Mata] ke[sa]

Letter from Yamanuchi Tsuneyuki to His Son Matakesa (47)[45]

Tsuneyuki complained to his son about the lack of reliable followers at home and the difficulty of extracting revenue from commoners. Tsuneyuki's letter to his wife is most likely his last letter. He apparently died in this campaign shortly after it was written.

I saw the letter from Yasunobu. As he says, no words can describe the hardships here. Nevertheless, I am reconciled with things. To the contrary, I am most worried that there is no one to help protect you as you remain behind. You, as a responsible adult (*ichinin mae no hito to shite*) are to consult with your mother in all matters. Ensure that the commoners (*hyakushō*) pay their taxes and are not remiss. . . . [latter half missing]

---

43. *Hino shi shi shiryōshū Takahata Fudō tainai monjo hen*, doc. 46, Yamanouchi Tsuneyuki *shojō*, 110–11.
44. In this case at Yamanouchi Tsuneyuki's home or temple.
45. *Hino shi shi shiryōshū Takahata Fudō tainai monjo hen*, doc. 47, Yamanouchi Tsuneyuki *shojō*, 112–13.

Section VI • *Warfare in the Fourteenth Century: Warrior Experiences*

Letter from Yamanouchi Tsuneyuki (48)[46]

I am delighted with your letter. . . . In addition, Shiomoto is setting off, and although it will be to the same battle[field], it will be most difficult [for him] as he [commands] only limited forces. . . . Regarding what has happened until now, I wanted to send a letter to the Honorable Arai, but there was nothing in particular to report. In addition, last night we had reports that enemy forces would attack our castle. I decided to be careful [and not write a letter]. . . . Please do not worry regarding anything, as I have now sent a messenger with a letter to the Honorable Arai.

Letter from Yamanouchi Tsuneyuki to Matakesa (50)[47]

Everything is so confused here—I think that I cannot send you even a trifle. Nevertheless, the battles continue, and I think that I cannot get the time to return. The enemy castle is located nearby so taking leave is impossible. I don't think I will be able to survive this battle and I am most worried that there is no one there to take good care of you. . . . Talk to Hachiroshirō about guard duty [of our house and temple]

[Latter half of letter missing]

Letter from Yamanouchi Tsuneyuki to His Wife (21)[48]

. . . As for everything, I will entrust affairs to the Honorable Arai. You should speak to him regarding all things; he will listen to you regarding anything. I know my abilities (*mi no hodo*). I thought that I would have Hikosaburō remain in Hitachi before returning, but Gorō states that he really wants to come back. . . so he will bring this. I am repeating myself, but as for our holdings (*shitaji*),[49] you should rely on the Honorable Arai for everything. Do not unburden yourself with others. In

---

46. *Hino shi shi shiryōshū Takahata Fudō tainai monjo hen*, doc. 48, Yamanouchi Tsuneyuki *shōjō*, 114–15.

47. *Hino shi shi shiryōshū Takahata Fudō tainai monjo hen*, doc. 50, Yamanouchi Tsuneyuki *shōjō*, 118–19.

48. *Hino shi shi shiryōshū Takahata Fudō tainai monjo hen*, doc. 21, Yamanouchi Tsuneyuki *shōjō* A B, 56–59.

49. This refers to a lord's paddies, forested lands, tax revenues, and public duties.

everything, the Honorable Arai . . . [text missing] and even regarding yourself all is the same. It is no big deal regarding me. People come into the world and leave it. . . .

6. A Document by Kō no Morofuyu (*hōsho*)[50]

This document, written by the general Kō no Morofuyu, recounts the battles for Koma castle and suggests the difficulty his army had during the campaign. Tsuneyuki's letters ceased around this time.[51] It survives in a documentary collection of the Yamanouchi Sudō house. They were relatives of Tsuneyuki who survived the campaign.

Concerning our attack on the rebels of Hitachi and Shimōsa provinces. We are in the midst of battles at the Castle of Koma Mansion. Most of our military forces have returned to their provinces. Your current service (*chūsetsu*) is outstanding. Henceforth, you should exhibit outstanding military service (*gunchū*). This order is thus conveyed.

Thirteenth day of the twelfth month of Ryakuō 2 [1339]

Mikawa *no kami* (monogram Kō no Morofuyu)

To: The Honorable Yamanouchi Sudō Saburō

---

50. *Dainihon komonjo iewake* 15 *Yamanouchi Sudō ke monjo* (Tokyo teikoku daigaku, 1940), 12.13.1339 (Ryakuō 2), Kō no Morofuyu *hōsho*, 46–47. Translated by Thomas Conlan.
51. *Hino shi shi shiryōshū Takahata Fudō tainai monjo hen*, 195, 197–205, particularly 205.

Section VI • *Warfare in the Fourteenth Century: Warrior Experiences*

7. Yamanouchi Tokimichi Report of Arrival (*chakutōjō*)⁵²

The following report of arrival, monogrammed by Kō no Morofuyu, marks the end of the campaign against the forces of Kitabatake Chikafusa, and the fall of his castles. Tsuneyuki did not survive the campaign, but Yamanouchi Tokimichi, one of his relatives, did.

11.13.1343 (Kōei 2) Yamanouchi Tokimichi report of arrival (*chakutōjō*)

Arrived: Yamanouchi Sudō Saburō Tokimichi

The aforementioned Tokimichi performed military service from the beginning at Shidariyanagi until the fall of the Seki and Taihō castles.⁵³ His arrival is thus.

The thirteenth day of the eleventh month of the second year of Kōei (1343)
(Monogram)⁵⁴

8. Oaths and the Kannō Disturbance⁵⁵

The Kannō Disturbance of 1350 pitted Ashikaga Takauji against his brother Ashikaga Tadayoshi. Warriors of the provinces (kokujin) had to decide whether to ally with one of the Ashikaga brothers or with the forces of the Southern Court. This period marks the ultimate division of higher authority during the fourteenth century. In this case, numerous members of the Yamanouchi decided to side with Ashikaga Tadayoshi. Many Yamanouchi did not agree, preferring instead to fight for Ashikaga Takauji.

Agreed (*keiyaku su*): The particulars of this family in accord (*ichizoku ikki*)

Concerning the above: since the Genkō era [1331–34], this family has been of one mind (*dōshin*) and has received rewards from the *Shōgun*'s house. There have been no disturbances regarding our possessions (*chigyō*). Nevertheless, since

---

52. *Dainihon komonjo iewake* 15 *Yamanouchi Sudō ke monjo*, doc. 46, 11.13.1342 (Kōei 2) Yamanouchi Tokimichi *chakutōjō*, 48–49. Translated by Thomas Conlan.

53. These castles were the headquarters of Kitabatake Chikafusa. Their fall marked the end of Southern Court resistance in Hitachi and the ultimate triumph of Kō no Morofuyu's campaign.

54. Kō no Morofuyu.

55. *Yamanouchi Sudō ke monjo*, doc. 25, 10.2.1351 (Jōwa 7) Yamanouchi *ichizoku ikki keiyaku rensho kishōmon*, 30–31. Translated by Thomas Conlan.

8. Oaths and the Kannō Disturbance

autumn of the last year, due to the conflict between both [Ashikaga] lords, peace and stability have not returned. Claiming to support the [Southern] Court side, or the *Shōgun*'s house, or the Nishiki-kōji Lord [Tadayoshi],[56] the opinions of the people of the province (*kokujin*) are divided, and yet this family (*ichizoku*), basks in the rewards (*go-on*) of military houses (*buke onshō*).[57] How can we forget such rewards? Thus, we shall fight for our allies[58] and hope to display our prowess and honor in war through our final generations. Of the above, there must be no duplicity. In the future, if someone violates these provisions, it shall be discussed within the council (*shūchū*) and opinions should be unanimous. If anyone utters even the slightest lie, may they endure, first, the punishments of Bonten, Taishaku, the four Heavenly Kings, and the otherworldly (*myōdō*) punishment of the small, middling, and great gods of the nation of Japan, and in particular Suwa, Hachiman *Daibosatsu*, and the Kibi-tsu *Daimyōin* of this province shall be inflicted upon each. Thus, this vow (*ichimi keiyaku kishōmon*) is stated as such.

The second day of the tenth month of the seventh year of Jōwa (1351)

Fujiwara Toshikiyo		Monogram
" "	Morimichi	Monogram
" "	Sanetsuna	Monogram
" "	Michihiro	Monogram
" "	Michitoshi	Monogram
" "	Sukesada	Monogram
" "	Michiaki	Monogram
" "	Suketsuna	Monogram
" "	Michiyuki	Monogram

Shami Jōkaku   Monogram

Kumajūmaru [Michitsugu] representative (*dai*) Dōen   Monogram

---

56. The three references are to the Southern Court forces, and those of Ashikaga Takauji and his younger brother Tadayoshi, respectively. This period marks the ultimate division of higher authority during the *Nanbokuchō* period.

57. The Ashikaga.

58. This evidently refers to Ashikaga Tadayoshi's forces. See Satō Shin'ichi, *Nanbokuchō no dōran*, 358.

Section VI • Warfare in the Fourteenth Century: Warrior Experiences

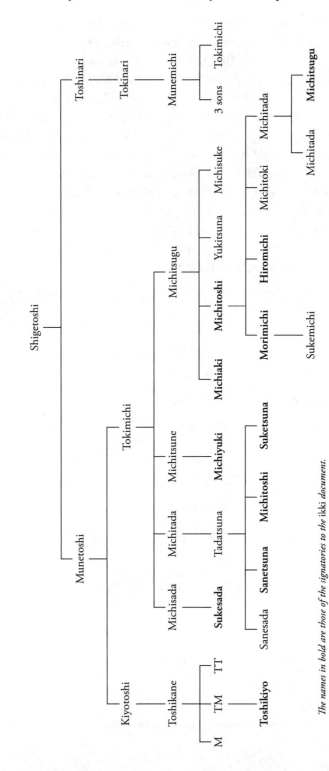

The Yamanouchi Clan (*Ichimon*)

The names in bold are those of the signatories to the ikki document.

9. Petition for Reward (*gunchūjō*) by Aso Koresumi[59]

Aso Koresumi fought for the Southern Court. He experienced difficulties similar to those encountered by Yamanouchi Tsuneyuki. Though this document is not dated, it most likely dates from late 1350. Although written from the perspective of Koresumi, he refers to himself in third person and this document is translated accordingly.

Aso Chikugo *no kami* Koresumi, of Higo Province, respectfully states:

Having accrued merit in more than a hundred battles since the Genkō era [1331–34]—and in order to continue to excel in my service—I wish to be granted land holdings (*ryōsho*).

Since the Genkō era, Koresumi, of no great renown, has fought several hundred battles and submitted battle reports (*chūshin*); he has even received imperial edicts. Since the beginning of this conflict, Koresumi has performed military service, unceasingly aiding members of both his and other lineages. Other men—even those who have surrendered or are simply members of families that have performed military service for our forces—have all received land holdings (*ryōsho*). It's easy to [speak of] honor, but Koresumi has not received a single land holding even though he is exhausted and struggles to perform unceasing service. [Koresumi's inability to continue serving] would render worthless his previous efforts. In addition, Koresumi's homelands and new rewards (*honryō shin'on*) were not confirmed when [his rival Aso] Koretoki allied [with the Southern Court].[60] Furthermore, tax-exempt paddies within these holdings were taken from us and restored to the Aso Shrine this past autumn. Our exhaustion increases. We wish to be granted to land (*ryōsho*) in this or some other province. Such a grant would support our military forces, depleted after many years, and allow us to perform increasingly noteworthy military service (*chūkin*) from now on.

Item: Concerning Moritomi estate. Koresumi, allied [with Southern Court forces] and in accord with the Council, has received imperial edicts [from Emperor Go-Murakami] and princely edicts [from Prince Kaneyoshi]. Nevertheless, because Kawajiri Shichirō surrendered, these lands have yet to be confirmed. The holdings

---

59. Seno Seiichirō, *Nanbokuchō ibun Kyushu hen*, vol. 3, doc. 2835, Era Koresumi *mōshijō an*, 125–26. Translated by Thomas Conlan.

60. Warriors' core lands were known as "original holdings," and they, as well as more recent land grants, were typically confirmed when warriors fought. In this case, Koresumi lost his lands when a rival relative joined his army. Presumably the more powerful Koretoki received Koresumi's holdings.

of Kawajiri Shichirō were actually grants from Takauji, the enemy of the court (*chōteki*). Koresumi has fought according to the wishes of his commanders and received [praise] from emperors and princes. Koresumi wishes . . . [text missing] to receive a just settlement so as to perform noteworthy military service. Spoken roughly, thus. . . [rest of document missing].

10. A Document of Loss (*funshitsujō*) by Tannowa Nagashige[61]

*A statement from Tannowa Nagashige, penned in the third year of the Ōei era (1396), regarding the loss of documents concerning managerial (*gesu*) rights. That Nagashige's compatriots signed this document suggests they supported the veracity of his claims. But the fact they felt they had to sign indicates that the protector (*shugo*) of the province did not support Nagashige.*

Concerning the loss of documents pertaining to the managerial (*gesu*) rights in and to the homelands of Tannowa Inaba *no kami* Nagashige of Izumi Province.

As for the aforementioned, two Rokuhara orders (*gechijō*),[62] one letter of appointment from the proprietor (*ryōke*), and a house genealogy were entrusted to Nagao Munehide of Kii Province. During the disturbance (*sekiran*) of the Ōan era (1368–75) these documents were burned and lost. The *jitō* and *gokenin* of this province collectively sign this document of loss. Thus.

Twenty-second day of the eighth month of the third year of Ōei (1396)

Tottori

Kadeno *saemon no jō* Masakatsu (monogram)

Imai

Saburō *saemon no jō* Munesada (monogram)

Sakō

---

61. https://komonjo.princeton.edu/tannowa/view.html?t=4-0. 8.22.1396 (Ōei 3) Tannowa Nagashige *funshitsujō*. Accessed August 26, 2021. Translated by the students of *Sources in Ancient and Medieval Japanese History* with Thomas Conlan.

62. Documents issued by the Rokuhara *tandai*, which was destroyed in 1333.

11. Excerpts from "The Battle of Ryūsenji," Taiheiki

Shirō *saemon no jō* Yoritada (monogram)

Tottori

Tōtōmi *no kami* Tadatsugu (monogram)

Tadokoro

Shūri no suke Motoie (monogram)

Sōkan

Shirō *saemon no jō* Kagetoshi (monogram)

Kashii

Iwami *no kami* Sadaaki (monogram)

Sano

Hayato *no suke* Tomokage (monogram)

Sukematsu

Saburō *saemon no jō* Masakatsu (monogram)

Sueki

Mimasaka *no kami* Masatomo (monogram)

Tashiro

Buzen *no kami* Suetsuna (monogram)

11. Excerpts from "The Battle of Ryūsenji," *Taiheiki* [63]

The Taiheiki, *an epic tale of the fourteenth century, comprising over forty volumes, contains in its final third detailed accounts of battles which are, at times, humorous. The following passage recounts the valor of Hosokawa Kiyouji (?–1362), a prominent supporter of the Ashikaga shogunate. This section recounts events which occurred in 1359–60, shortly after the death of Ashikaga Takauji, against the Southern Court forces in their central Japan*

---

63. This version was drawn from Hyōdo Hiromi, *Taiheiki*, vol. 5 (Iwanami shoten, 2016), maki 34, 319–23. Translated by Thomas Conlan.

Section VI • Warfare in the Fourteenth Century: Warrior Experiences

heartlands. This account also shows that some Chinese military manuals (but not the famous Sunzi Art of War) were known to Japanese warriors and writers.

The Kusunoki and Mikita generals stationed a thousand warriors from nearby Yamato and Kawachi Provinces at Ryūsenji castle.[64] The enemy would not attack them, and the soldiers complained. "Why in the world are we here? Let us attack the plains and scatter our enemies!" They left one hundred skirmishers (*nobushi*) of no great skill behind as decoys, disguised treetops as archers' blinds and attached banners, making it look as if a great army remained.

The besieging forces of Tsuzuyama looked at the castle and exclaimed in fear: "How terrible! A mighty enemy army occupies this looming castle, perched high on a mountain. There is no way we can take it." Not a single warrior dared to attack. Pointlessly, 150-odd days passed with the men merely looking up at the enemy's banners.

At a certain time, a resourceful old warrior who belonged to the Toki family's Bellflower unit (Kikiyo *ikki*) intently observed the Ryūsen castle. Speaking to his comrades, he said: "Taigong (Jiang Ziya) wrote in the 'empty fortifications' volume of his military manual that 'When looking above enemy castles, if you do not see flying birds startle then certainly you shall know your enemies have created false figures of deception.'[65] I have been closely observing the Ryūsen castle for the last three or four days: the kites flying in the sky and the crows returning to forest have not been disturbed. Our enemy must have made it look as if a large force was holed-up by planting some banners over there. Without mingling with other troops this *ikki* alone should advance and take Ryūsen—it will make us famous throughout the realm."

Upon saying this, the five hundred-odd horsemen of the Toki Bellflower *ikki*, realizing that the old man's advice was excellent, agreed and decided to attack immediately. At the break of dawn on the twenty-ninth of the fourth intercalary month, the five hundred-odd horsemen of the Bellflower unit crept away from Tsuzuyama. Then, under the cover of the morning fog, before the eastern sky began

---

64. Kusunoki Masanori and Mikita Masatake were two prominent Southern Court generals. Yamato and Kawachi Provinces now constitute modern Nara and Ōsaka, respectively. The castle was located in Izumi Province, which is now part of Ōsaka as well.

65. Taigong (T'ai Kung)'s *Six Secret Teachings* (*Liù Tāo*) has been translated by Ralph Sawyer, *The Seven Military Classics of Ancient China*, 40–106. For the relevant passage about empty fortifications, see p. 88, which states: "The T'ai Kung said: 'Listen to see if his drums are silent, if his bells make no sound. Look to see whether there are many birds flying above the fortifications, if they were not startled [into flight]. If there are no vapors overhead, you will certainly know the enemy has tricked you with dummies.'"

11. Excerpts from "The Battle of Ryūsenji," Taiheiki

to brighten, they swept toward one gate of the Ryūsen and in unison screamed their battle cries.

Hosokawa Sagami *no kami* Kiyouji and Akamatsu Hikogorō Norizane both were in the headquarters at Tsuzuyama, but when they heard the war cries from Ryūsen, Kiyouji cried out: "Already others are charging ahead of us! We must cut our way into the fort first. *That* is what is known as the real vanguard! Saddle the horses! Bannermen, come quick!" Just as he said this Kiyouji and Hikogorō grabbed their armor and threw it on their shoulders, tightened their shoulder straps,[66] and galloped toward Ryūsen's western gate, located under a tall wooden turret. There they jumped off their horses. Glancing behind, they saw three horsemen—Tamiya *danjō no chū*, Kidokoro no Hikogorō, and Takami Hikoshirō, all Akamatsu men—following. Behind them, Kiyouji's retainers (*rōjū*) were coming, strung along in no particular formation, each vying to be first.

Hosokawa Kiyouji's bannerman crashed his horse headfirst into a steep embankment. Seeing that he could not easily rise, Kiyouji himself ran over and snatched the flag. Plunging it into the front of the embankment, he cried out in a thunderous voice: "Kiyouji is first in the van!" Then Akamatsu Hikogorō entered the fort and yelled repeatedly: "The first one in the van is Norizane. Those who saw me, come forth as witnesses!" He then clambered over the castle walls.

Seeing this, Hiyoshi *shuri no suke*, Fujita Hyōgo *no suke* and Utsumi *shuri no suke* Mitsunori of the Toki Bellflower *ikki* wrenched open the gate and plunged inside. The soldiers inside the castle continued fighting for a while but, aware of their enemy's great strength and their own utter weakness, must have felt that there was nothing that they could have done and retreated toward Akasaka under a calm and deliberate cover fire of arrows.[67]

After a while, the great multitude of besieging warriors, huddled together in many encampments, realized that the Toki Bellflower *ikki* had advanced and attacked Ryūsen. Surely, they thought, the *ikki* could not take that fort easily. "Put up the shields! Archers to the fore!" Calmly they mobilized for battle, their army consisting of over a hundred thousand horsemen, and set off for the base of Ryūsen mountain. By that time, the castle had already been taken and its turrets and wooden palisades were torched. The advancing force's tens of thousands scratched their heads and lamented their misfortune. Without knowing how puny enemy forces were—and to their everlasting regret—they did nothing while Toki and Hosokawa achieved great names for valor. They all gritted their teeth in disappointment.

---

66. *Takahimo*, the straps which helped attach armor to a warrior's torso.
67. Akasaka Castle was a Southern Court stronghold held by Kusunoki Masanori.

12. Excerpts from *The Chronicle of Meitoku*[68]

The following excerpt recounts one of the last major uprisings of the fourteenth century, when members of the Yamana rose against the forces of Ashikaga Yoshimitsu, who appears in the narrative as "the Shōgun." Note the long swords favored at this time, and how adequate preparation for death, and prayer to Amida Buddha for rebirth, elicit great praise by the chroniclers of this tale.

The deaths of Kakiya and Namera

The two charged into the thick of the mass. Kakiya with his five-foot, three-inch long sword[69] and Namera with his five-foot, two-inch glaive slew six. "Look!" Ujikiyo cried when he saw them. "A mere two of the enemy have killed many of our men. You should be ashamed of yourselves! Level your blades, charge them, engage with them, kill them!" Yamaguchi Danjō, Fukutomi Bitchū and other mighty warriors, fourteen or fifteen of them, promptly dismounted, ranged their spear and glaive points in a serried row, and attacked.

"There's no escape, Namera." Kakiya said. "Dismount! We're going to die." Armed as he was with a long sword, Kakiya moved to slash vertically at men and horses, meanwhile avoiding the foe's daggers; but his blade, entangled in cut strips of armor sleeves, stabbed deep into the soil. He was striving to extract it when, in the struggle, a lance and a glaive penetrated his armor. He certainly knew he was finished. "You there, Namera?" he shouted. "I'll go on ahead!" He called the Amida's Name four or five times, and a blade thrust killed him.

Namera heard him. "Right!" he replied. In battle frenzy he charged into the enemy and fought to the death. "That must be Namera Hyōgo," Ujikiyo said to himself, "famed throughout the nine provinces of Tsukushi. And he continued aloud, "Get him, men! Use your long weapons [*nagagusoku*]! Move your sword-bearer around behind him and cut his armor skirts!"

Five men, already in place with thrusting spears and glaives, sent their sword-bearers dashing around behind Namera. These cut the back plate [*okubyō-gane*] of the shin guard on each leg. Badly wounded, Namera collapsed to a sitting position, braced upright by his arms. When a new thrust slipped past his skirts, he dropped his glaive, drew a three-foot sword, and with it kept the attackers at bay.

He then looked up at them. "I am exhausted," he said. "Please just let me lie down. Gentlemen, see me welcomed by Amida and go to rebirth in his Pure Land."

---

68. Tyler, *Iwashimizu Hachiman in War and Cult*, 55–56.
69. *Ōdachi*, a weapon carried across the back or over the shoulder.

12. Excerpts from The Chronicle of Meitoku

He faced west and died seated, braced by his arms. Every witness, friend or foe, was deeply moved.

At that very moment Tokihiro raced to join the Ōuchi force stationed by the Jingikan. He had barely escaped death. Once the fight was over he rushed to the *Shōgun*, reported briefly on the battle, and described the deportment of friend and foe.

The *Shōgun* looked pleased. "Is Kakiya really dead?" he asked.

"Yes, my lord, he is. With fourteen or fifteen enemy warriors around me I thought I was finished, but then Kakiya and Namera rushed to me." He wept until he could no longer speak, and his tears moistened his armor sleeves.

"I understand how you feel," the *Shōgun* said with emotion. "Those two will stand as models for every man of bow and arrow. They are a great loss."

Every witness envied Tokihiro. "Not only did he stay alive thanks to Kakiya and Namera," they said to themselves, "but now the *Shōgun* also heaps praise on him!"

SECTION VII

The Ashikaga Decline and the Ōnin War (1441–77)

The period of Ashikaga dominance lasted from the time of Yoshimitsu (1358–1408) through the 1441 assassination of the sixth shōgun Ashikaga Yoshinori (1394–1441). The accession of the incompetent eighth *shōgun* Ashikaga Yoshimasa (1436–1490) led to the civil war most commonly known as the *Conflict of Ōnin* (1467–77). Surviving documents also explain how the Ōnin conflict led to warriors entrenching and building mighty watchtowers, as the battles of this war were fought mostly by foot soldiers in a manner not too dissimilar from the defensive tactics, and entrenched armies, of the Western Front in World War I.

1. Prince Sadafusa's Account of the Assassination of Ashikaga Yoshinori (1441)[1]

Beginning in 1350, extensive rites were delegated to shugo, *as was the* hanzei—*the collection of up to half of a province's revenue for military provisions. Yet, despite this allocation of power to the* shugo, *the Ashikaga shōguns managed to establish themselves as the dominant warlords of Japan. Some of the shōguns, such as Yoshimitsu, simply overpowered the* shugo, *while others, like Yoshimochi, adopted a more conciliatory approach. A powerful ruler, Yoshinori's capriciousness—and his tendency to attack* shugo—*eventually led to turmoil. Akamatsu Mitsusuke, one of the most trusted* shugo, *boldly assassinated Ashikaga Yoshinori on 6.24.1441 (Kakitsu 1), at a performance of the Noh* (sarugaku) *play* Unoha *(Cormorant Feathers), staged in the Akamatsu mansion.*[2]

---

1. *Kanmon gyoki*, in *Zoku gunsho ruijū hoi* 2, 6.24–25.1441 (Kakitsu 1), 630–31. Translated by Thomas Conlan with Mai Yamaguchi and Skyler Negrete.
2. This reference to the Noh play comes from the chronicle *Kakitsuki*.

1. Prince Sadafusa's Account of the Assassination of Ashikaga Yoshinori

The following account, excerpted from the diary of the Imperial Prince Sadafusa (1372–1456), vividly recounts the tumult of this time. Legend has it that the assassination occurred at the climactic moment of the play, just as a fisherwoman appeared onstage as the sea goddess Toyotahime. But according to Sadafusa's account, the plot seems to have been set in motion at the beginning of the play. Ashikaga prestige never fully recovered after Yoshinori's "dog's death."

Twenty-fourth day. Rain. They said that the Akamatsu invited Lord Yoshinori for a *sarugaku* performance. That evening, in their mansion, a fight broke out. Sanjō returned, wounded, before I'd heard the details of this disturbance.[3] We do not know what precisely happened to the Lord. Fires raged at the Akamatsu mansion. Warriors galloped east and west. I will not recklessly repeat slander. Later that evening, the mansion of Akamatsu Yoshimasa, the Iyo Governor, went up in flames. Akamatsu retainers also set fire to their houses. They killed the Lord, took his head, and fled. I am utterly astonished and concerned.

Twenty-fifth day. Clear. I heard roughly what happened yesterday. There was a banquet, first with three cups of *sake* imbibed (*ikon*), then nine (*sankon*). Then, as a *sarugaku* performance began, there was a rumbling sound. "What was that noise?" Yoshinori asked, and Sanjō replied, "It sounds like thunder." At that moment, the *shoji* screen behind him opened, a great number of warriors appeared, and they attacked and killed Yoshinori. Sanjō picked up a sword (*tachi*) that had been given to Yoshinori as a gift (*onhikidemono*) and slashed away. But he fell and was cut down and injured. Yamana *taifu* [Hirotaka], the Kyōgoku Kaga novice (*nyūdō*) [Takakazu], and Toki Tōyama, a guard,[4] were cut down and killed. Although the Governor of Shimotsuke Hosokawa [Mochiharu] and Ōuchi [Mochiyo] fought with short swords, they could not take an enemy. They were injured and retreated. The Shogunal Chancellor (*kanrei*) Hosokawa [Mochiyuki], the Hosokawa Governor of Sanuki Province [Mochitsune], Isshiki Gorō [Norichika], and the Akamatsu Izu Governor [Sadamura] ran away.[5] In addition to them, everyone else scattered away in all directions. Nobody committed *seppuku* in front of our Lord. The Akamatsu fled, but nobody pursued them.

This was not just due to unpreparedness. Perhaps various *daimyō* were complicit. I don't know. Anyway, it was well known that Yoshinori was planning to kill the Akamatsu, but they put an end to that by killing him. This serves him

---

3. Sanjō Sanemasa. The older brother of Yoshinori's official wife and a confidant of Yoshinori.
4. The Tōyama were an offshoot of the Toki family, serving as Yoshinori's personal guard.
5. These four were singled out because Sadamura and Norichika were close confidants of Yoshinori, while the Hosokawa had the most important offices within the regime after that of *shōgun*.

right. Nothing can be done. This *Shōgun* died like a dog, and I have never heard of a case like that ever happening before. The head of the Zuisō subtemple[6] searched for the corpse in the burned-out ruins and sent it to Tōji-in.[7] A messenger from the Akamatsu reported that Yoshinori's head is now at Nakajima in Settsu Province. The Shogunal Chancellor (*kanrei*) beheaded this messenger. Numerous unfounded rumors abound.

My wife[8] went to the Muromachi mansion to visit the *Shōgun*'s wife (*uesama*).[9] Then, last night, she started wearing [a nun's] black robes.[10] The head of Rokuonin administered her vows. The Lady in Waiting (*jōrō*)[11] also became a nun. Since she is pregnant, the one who faces the north[12] did not take vows. All of Yoshinori's prostitutes—and all of his maids of suitable status who bore his children—also became nuns. His wife (*uesama* [Sanjō Tadako]) was about to leave, but the Shogunal Chancellor (*kanrei*) strictly prohibited her from doing so. The principle that the proud and mighty invariably fall (*jōja hissui no kotowari*)[13] became clear before my eyes. Save for tears of sorrow, nothing else remains.

2. The Poems of *Ikkyū* (1394–1481)[14]

The Zen monk Ikkyū wrote a variety of sardonic poems. One, "Acts of Grace," refers to the tokusei *edicts of the Ashikaga. Originally,* tokusei, *or Virtuous Government Edicts, served as debt relief. They were first promulgated by the court in 1242. Kamakura issued one such edict to its warriors in 1297 as well. The Ashikaga issued similar edicts, but they allowed either the debtor or the creditor to pay 10 percent. If the former did so, the debts were forgiven, but if the latter did, the debts would remain. As creditors had more money, they could*

---

6. A subtemple of Chionji, a Pure Land temple. This person was well known to Sadafusa but is not named.
7. The Ashikaga mortuary temple. Statues of most of the Ashikaga shoguns exist there to this day.
8. Niwata Yukiko. She is referred to here as the "Southern person" (*minami no onkata*).
9. Yoshinori's wife Sanjō Tadako.
10. She had renounced the world and became a Buddhist nun.
11. A younger sister of Sanjō Tadako.
12. Yoshinori's concubine, Hino Shigeko, the mother of the shoguns Ashikaga Yoshikatsu and Yoshimasa. Shigeko was the younger sister of Yoshinori's first primary wife, Hino Muneko.
13. This phrase appears at the beginning of *The Tale of Heike*.
14. Arntzen, *Ikkyū and the Crazy Cloud Anthology*, 139–40.

almost invariably pay what amounted to a 10 percent tax on debt. Ikkyū's second poem discusses how the common sense of earlier ages was stupidity in the present.

Acts of Grace[15]　　　　　　　　　　　　　　　　　徳政

Robbers never strike poor houses.　　　　　　　　　賊元来不打家貧
One man's wealth is not wealth for the whole country.　孤独財非万国珎
I believe that calamity has its origin in good fortune.　信道禍元福所復
You lose your soul over 100,000 pieces of copper.　　青銅十万失霊神

The Correct Skill for Great Peace　　　　　　　　太平正工夫

Natural, reckless, correct skill;　　　　　　　　　　天然胡乱正工夫
Yesterday's clarity is today's stupidity.　　　　　　昨日聡明今日愚
The universe has dark and light, entrust oneself to change.　宇宙陰晴任変化
One time, shade the eyes and gaze afar at the road of Heaven.　一回斫額望天衢

The Correct Skill for a Disorderly Age　　　　　　乱世正工夫

The strong one must equip himself with the right view;　丈夫須具正見
Deluded notions in keeping with the object manifest themselves.　諸妄想随境現
About a horse, one asks, "Do you have a good one or not?"　馬問良馬麼無
They reply, "This sword is sharp."　　　　　　　　　人答此刀利剣

3. The Ōnin War (1467–77)

The Ōnin War (circa 1467–77) pitted the forces of the western lord Ōuchi Masahiro and his ally, Yamana Sōzen, against those of Ashikaga Yoshimasa, Yoshimasa's Shogunal Chancellor (kanrei) Hosokawa Katsumoto, and other lords throughout the realm. An increased use of defensive tactics quickly brought the war to a tactical stalemate.

---

15. Acts of Grace: Term for the Muromachi shogunate's proclamations of moratorium for debts. Throughout the period, when particularly hard-pressed groups of farmers and sometimes townfolk would rise in revolt to demand cancellation of debts.

The superior logistical powers of the shugo, which expanded over the course of the late fourteenth and early fifteenth centuries, allowed them to maintain standing armies. These standing armies could be trained to fight using pikes and other weapons in massed formations like the phalanx. This change in training methods seems to have occurred before the outset of the war, as documents describing the early conflict—some of which are translated below—describe extensive pike wounds. With this change in strategy came a change in the way battles were recorded: instead of recording their movements as they did in the earlier petitions, warriors instead began to merely record lists of the wounded. These rosters rarely survive (although many documents of praise received from commanders are extant). The lack of more descriptive records makes it harder for historians to study and understand the wars of the fifteenth century and later.

In addition to the use of new tactics, new weapons—including early guns and catapults (see the Inryōken Nichiroku *Concerning Guns*, p. 186; and Hekizan Nichiroku, p. 188)—were also used for the first time in this conflict. Parts of the capital of Kyoto came to resemble the Western Front of World War I as armies dug trenches, built watchtowers, and generally fought differently from before. Ōnin was long remembered as an epochal conflict. Records from a court family show that they, too, fought in the war and describe how their deeds during the "Great Conflict" of Ōnin were recognized and remembered as late as 1546 (see *Remembering the Ōnin War*, p. 190).

A Document of Praise (*kanjō*), Issued by Hosokawa Tsuneari[16]

Tsuneari, a commander of the Eastern Army, issued this document on the twenty-seventh day of the fifth month of the first year of Ōnin (1467), to the Tannowa. Warriors such as the Tannowa now fought solely for their shugo and exhibited no autonomy as was typical before.

On this past twenty-sixth day, you fought well in the battle at the crossroads of Ichijō and Ōmiya. You and your retainers and low-ranking followers were all injured. This is very impressive.

Respectfully,

On the twenty-seventh day of the fifth month. Tsuneari (monogram)

To: The Honorable Tannowa Jirō *saemon no jō*

---

16. http://komonjo.princeton.edu/tannowa/view.html?t=2-16. Translated by the students of *Sources in Ancient and Medieval Japanese History* with Thomas Conlan. Accessed August 27, 2021.

3. The Ōnin War

Yamana Sōzen Document of Praise[17]

Here Yamana Sōzen, commander of the opposing Western Army, issues a document of praise, revealing that no one—not even ladies of the court—was safe from the internecine war.

On the seventeenth, during the battle of Funabashi, you beheaded the Naitō Palace Maid (*uneme*).[18] This is most splendid. This document is thus.

The twentieth day of the seventh month [Ōnin 1/1467][19]

[Yamana] Sōzen (monogram)

To: The Honorable Kakiya Suruga *no kami*

Order concerning provisions (1467)[20]

This order, issued by Ashikaga officials to Yamana Sōzen, reveals how commanders struggled to secure adequate provisions for their armies, with ultimately half the revenue and produce from lands near the capital (with a few exceptions) being confiscated for military provisions.

Concerning the various temple and shrine homelands of Yamashiro province's Nishioka and Nakasuji: excluding the lands of Kamo, Hachiman, Kasuga, and Kitano, half [shall be confiscated for military provisions]. This document was generated in response to Hosokawa *sakyō no taifu* Katsumoto's order. Quickly dispatch a representative and take control of these lands. If by chance anyone should dispute this, record their names and their lands. Those so recorded shall be punished. It has been ordered. Thus, this is conveyed as follows.

Twenty-seventh day of the eighth month of the first year of Ōnin (1467)

[Saitō] Chikamoto

[Fuse] Sadamoto

The Honorable Censor (*Danjō no chū*) Yamana

---

17. Kakiya monjo, doc. 1, 7.20 Yamana Mochitoyo *kanjō*, *Hyōgo kenshi shiryōhen Chūsei* 9, 631. Translated by Thomas Conlan.
18. *Uneme* were low-ranking women who served food to the emperor.
19. This year was written later on the document.
20. *Dainihon shiryō* series 8 vol. 1, 379. Translated by Thomas Conlan.

4. The Process of Praise and Rewards: A Case Study

Few complete sets of documents recounting the Ōnin War remain, but the Kikkawa family—who were allied with the Eastern Army even though they hailed from western Japan—preserved all of their paperwork. The following Kikkawa documents contain rosters of the wounded, which rarely survive, as well as documents of praise issued by the kanrei Hosokawa Katsumoto and the shōgun Ashikaga Yoshimasa.

Kikkawa Mototsune Roster of Wounds (*teoi chūmon*)[21]

Listed here are those who were wounded during the battle at the crossroads of Ichijō and Takakura on the thirteenth day of the ninth month of the first year of Ōnin (1467):
 [same name] Asaeda Kōzuke *no suke* two arrow wounds
 [same name] Asaeda Shingorō one arrow wound
 One follower (*chūgen*) one arrow wound

Kikkawa Jirōsaburō Mototsune (monogram)

Received.[22]

Kikkawa Mototsune Roster of Wounds (*teoi chūmon*)[23]

This second document was issued on the same day as the previous. Note the high number of pike wounds. Pikes became a dominant shock weapon sometime between the end of the wars of the fourteenth century and the onset of the Ōnin War.

Here is a list of my men killed and wounded during the battle at the crossroads of Ichijō and Takakura on the thirteenth day of the ninth month of the first year of Ōnin (1467):
 Yuasa Yajirō killed
 same name Asaeda Magotarō

---

21. *Kikkawa ke monjo*, vol. 1 (Reprint ed., 1970), doc. 320, 9.13.1467 (Ōnin 1) Kikkawa Mototsune *jihitsu kassen teoi chūmon*, 272–73. Translated by Thomas Conlan.
22. Hosokawa Katsumoto.
23. *Kikkawa ke monjo*, vol. 1, doc. 321, 9.13.1467 (Ōnin 1), Kikkawa Mototsune *jihitsu kassen tachiuchi chūmon*, 273–74. Translated by Thomas Conlan.

same name Asaeda Matajirō

same name Asaeda Magogorō

Yamagata Mago *saemon no jō* pike (*yari*) wound in one place

Wada Saburō *saemon no jō* pike wound in one place. Arrow wound

Ono Yaroku same as above

Miyoshi *saemon* Tarō

Saeki Shoroku pike wound

Tahara *Toshō no suke* pike wound

Hiyoshi Shin *saemon no jō* same as above

Kikkawa Jirōsaburō Mototsune (monogram)

Received (monogram)[24]

Hosokawa Katsumoto Document of Praise (*KANJŌ*)[25]

Upon receiving the Kikkawa document translated above, Hosokawa Katsumoto wrote the following document of praise. It was on a kirigami, *or small sheet of paper. Though such documents of praise have often survived, the rosters of wounds translated above usually do not. Here, only the battle death of Yuasa Yajirō merits specific mention.*

During the battle of the past thirteenth, you exchanged blows with your sword. I received a report that your retainer (*hikan*) Yuasa Yajirō was killed, and, in addition, many others were wounded. I am extremely pleased and moved. It is my sincerest desire that you shall continue your military service. Respectfully.

Twenty-third day of the ninth month of the first year of Ōnin (1467)

To: The Honorable Kikkawa Jirōsaburō

Katsumoto (monogram)

The Honorable Kikkawa Jirōsaburō

---

24. Hosokawa Katsumoto

25. *Kikkawa ke monjo*, vol. 1, doc. 327, 9.23 [1467 (Ōnin 1)], Hosokawa Katsumoto *kanjō* (*kirigami*), 279. Translated by Thomas Conlan.

Section VII • *The Ashikaga Decline and the Ōnin War*

Ashikaga Yoshimasa Document of Praise (*kanjō*)[26]

The Kikkawa were so worthy of merit that they received this second document of praise from Ashikaga Yoshimasa for the same battle. This document was issued weeks after Hosokawa Katsumoto's document of praise.

Since this past first year of the Ōnin era [1467], I have heard that your relatives and retainers have fought strenuously many times, with [some being] injured or killed. In particular, in the battle fought during the waning days of the eighth month of the second year of Ōnin [1468], at the burned-out remains of Shōkokuji, you yourself were wounded in battle. Your repeated service (*chūsetsu*) is without compare. I am particularly moved by your accomplishments. If you continue your military service, you shall be rewarded.

The third day of the ninth month [Ōnin 2/1468] [*gohan*][27]

To: The Honorable Kikkawa Jirōsaburō

5. Selection from the *Inryōken Nichiroku* Concerning Guns[28]

A fifteenth-century diary records how an official from the Ryūkyū Kingdom surprised many bystanders in Kyoto by firing a gun (teppō) *on 7.28.1466 (Bunshō 1). Such firearms were primitive three-barreled affairs that did not, however, significantly impact the waging of war. This diary entry was written by Kikei Shinzui, a monk at the sub-temple Inryōken, part of Rokuōnin, which was a temple in the Shōkokuji Zen monastic complex. Kikei was a close adviser to, and representative of, the Shōgun Ashikaga Yoshimasa.*

Twenty eighth day... Ryūkyū officials arrived. After bowing three times, they left. Suddenly they provided us with souvenirs.[29] In an area outside of our main gate

---

26. *Kikkawa ke monjo*, vol. 1, doc. 50, 9.3 [1468 (Ōnin 2)], Ashikaga Yoshimasa *gonaisho an*, 30. Translated by Thomas Conlan.
27. This document survives as a copy and so Yoshimasa's signature is represented by the honorific term for "monogram."
28. *Inryōken Nichiroku* (Kikkei Shinzui). (5 Vols. *Dainihon bukkyō zensho*, no. 133–373), vol. 2 (134), 7.28.1466 (Bunshō 1), 670. Translated by Thomas Conlan.
29. Literally, *hōbutsu*, or objects from their locality.

(*sōmon*) they fired a gun (*teppō ichiryō hanasu*). All the people who heard the sound were astonished. The king of their land is an old man,[30] but he sends many gifts and letters. We, too, send letters and are on good terms. The king is most thoughtful (*ninjō no tsune*). Someone with such fidelity is rare [nearby] but even rarer is someone like this, who comes from a distant land, thousands or tens of thousands of leagues (*li*) away.

6. The *Chronicle of Ōnin* (Excerpt)[31]

The Chronicle of Ōnin, *the main source for our understanding of the conflict, was originally thought to have been an eyewitness account but more recent research reveals that it was written a generation after the conflict. In the oldest version of this text, the war starts with a prophecy, the* Yamataishi, *which emphasized the "lower overthrowing the upper"* (gekokujō) *and also predicted that a monkey and dog would compete for hegemony. This was thought to represent Yamana Sōzen and Hosokawa Katsumoto.*

The following passage describes the powerful forces of Ōuchi Masahiro, who attempted to cut off the Hosokawa forces at Nanzenji but were thwarted by adversaries.

First the Ōuchi attacked from Nanzenji. Enemy forces were of great number, and already the Fujiwara of Owari[32] tried to advance from Miidera, but the mountains were steep, and there was only one path to advance. "Destroy them with rocks," the enemies said and threw mighty boulders, so even the strong Ōuchi forces, which somehow should have stopped here, instead collapsed deep in the valleys.

---

30. This statement is curious, as the commonly accepted King of the Ryukyu kingdom in 1466 was Shō Toku (1441–69), the last of the first Shō Dynasty, who was born in 1441. Most likely he is confused with his father, Shō Taikyū (1415–60), although the emissary could also be another Okinawan lord. Shō Toku led a campaign against Kikai Island in 1466 and was posthumously remembered, being the last of his line, as being cruel.

31. Wada Hidemichi, ed., *Ōninki*, "Higashiyama Iwakura kassen narabi ni Nanzenji enjō no koto," 91–92. Translated by Thomas Conlan.

32. A reference to the deputy of Owari Province, with the Fujiwara surname—the Oda.

Section VII • *The Ashikaga Decline and the Ōnin War*

7. Observations from *Hekizan Nichiroku*[33]

In the following passages, drawn from his diary for the year 1468 (Ōnin 2), the Zen monk Unsen Taikyoku describes the importance of defensive tactics in the aftermath of the stalemate at Hosshōji. Taikyoku describes fortifications, watchtowers, catapults, and guns. He also shows off his erudition in making references to catapults in history and goes to great lengths to claim that they were not new weapons—even though they, as well as the extensive fortifications in the capital, had not been seen in Japan for centuries.

Twenty-ninth day of the first month
    Eastern Army . . . trenches are deep and their earthworks imposing; such strong defenses have never been seen, nor imagined before.
    A craftsman from Izumi Province came to their encampment and built a contraption (*hasseki boku*), which tosses stones and unleashes limitless destruction where it hits. It is called a *hō*. It is said that Li Mi (722–89) of the Tang used such a such a contraption (*kihasseki*) to attack enemy castles . . . Tsao Tsao (220–66) of the Wei fired such stones to destroy chariots. . . and in the military manual of Fan Li of Yue, rocks weighing 16 pounds (12 *kin*) were shot 250 yards (300 *ho*). The Izumi Province craftsman knows weapons (*heiki*) very well, but this is not new.[34]
    Fourteenth day of the fourth month. Sōzen of the Western Army built a watchtower, called Seirō, in front of his fortifications. They say that it was 77 feet (7 *jō*) tall.[35]
    Twenty-fifth day of the fourth month. Ōuchi Masahiro of the Western Army built a tower to the southwest of Rokuonin,[36] called the Great Seirō (Daiseirō).[37]
    Twenty-first day of the sixth month. The Western Army dispatched a large force to attack the Eastern Army's fortifications. They unleashed two thousand fire arrows (*hiya*) but did not burn the castle. The defenders within the castle were good shots, and several hundred of the attackers were wounded.[38]
    Sixth day eleventh month. . .

---

33. *Dainihon kokiroku Hekizan nichiroku*, vol. 2. Translated by Thomas Conlan.
34. *Hekizan nichiroku*, 1.29.1468 (Ōnin 2), 35–36.
35. *Hekizan nichiroku*, 4.14.1468 (Ōnin 2), 60.
36. Shōkokuji.
37. *Hekizan nichiroku*, 4.25.1468 (Ōnin 2), 62. This tower is later described as being nearly 110 feet (10 *jō*) tall. One *jō* is 3.3 meters so this would be 109 feet. See Ibid., 11.6.1468 (Ōnin 2), 113–14 (translated below). For how they allowed warriors to look down on opposing armies, see *Hekizan nichiroku*, 5.27.1468 (Ōnin 2), 70.
38. *Hekizan nichiroku*, 6.21.1468 (Ōnin 2), 76.

To the southeast of Rokuonin there is a military tower. It is 109 feet (10 *jō*) tall, they say. It is just about as tall as the Shōkokuji pagoda. A myriad of small watch towers, high earthworks, and deep moats fully covered (*shūsō jūjū*) the region; the same holds true for enemy camps. Millions (*okuman*) of soldiers traversed this area. The encampments of Hosokawa Katsumoto, Hatakeyama Masanaga, Yamana Koretoyo, Akamatsu Masanori, and Takeda Kenshin were lined up and acting as support. Hosokawa Sanuki *no kami* Shigeyuki's encampment was a linchpin of the defenses, and here at the Kushirōsō tower, it was well stocked with offensive weapons, including flying projectile fire spears (*hihō hisō*),[39] which were also reportedly discharged from a besieged tower.[40] The open area in front of the fortifications consists of some ten acres.[41] In addition, the facing enemy camps of Yamana Sōzen, Hatakeyama Yoshihiro,[42] Tamado[43] Yoshikado, Isshiki Yoshinao, Toki Shigeyori, and Tatara[44] Masahiro are set up the same.

8. Kikkawa Mototsune Roster of Wounds[45]

This, another Kikkawa document, describes fighting occurring in the vicinity of towers at Rokuonin, where Ōuchi Masahiro was later described by Unsen Taikyoku as building a tall tower. The injuries, said to have been caused by rocks, may have been caused by the early guns, which used rocks for bullets.

Here is a roster of those killed and wounded when coming to blows (*tachi uchi*) on the third day of the tenth month of Ōnin 1 (1467), during the battle of the crossroads of Kitaōji and Takakura:
same name Asaeda Magotarō   one pike wound
same name Asaeda Matajirō   same as above

---

39. The meaning of this phrase is opaque. It could refer to a single weapon, or, perhaps, two; *hihō* could refer to stone catapults and to *hisō*, fire spears, which may be a reference to the early Okinawan guns mentioned in the *Inryōken Nichiroku* in 1466. Or this phrase may express a single weapon.
40. *Hekizan nichiroku*, 11.6.1468 (Ōnin 2), 113–14.
41. Literally 80 *li* (里) with each *li* equaling approximately 500 square meters.
42. Otherwise known as Hatakeyama Yoshinari.
43. Shiba.
44. Ōuchi.
45. *Kikkawa ke monjo*, vol. 1, doc. 324, 10.3–4 1467 (Ōnin 1), Kikkawa Mototsune *jihitsu kassen tachi-uchi chūmon*, 276–77. Translated by Thomas Conlan.

One follower (*chūgen*) Yo-ichi *saemon* killed
Those wounded one the same day at the tower by the entrance to Rokuonin
Same name Asaeda Kōzuke *no suke* rock wound (*tsubute*)
Same name Asaeda Magogorō same

Kikkawa Jirōsaburō Mototsune (monogram)

Received.[46]

9. Remembering the Ōnin War

The three documents offered here are related to the Awazu, a family of courtiers who rescued the imperial wardrobe from battles fought in Yamashina in 1471. The first document is the official recognition of the family's actions, sent by a court lady writing on behalf of Emperor Go-Hanazono (1419–71; r. 1428–64). The second document is the original imperial document of praise, sent by Awazu Kiyonori's lord Hirohashi Morimitsu. The final document here, dated 1546, shows that the Awazu continued to be rewarded for this action four generations after the events of 1471.

A Court Lady's Communiqué[47]

This Communiqué was sent to the Retired Emperor Go-Hanazono (jōkō nyōbō hōsho)

(Label on the back of document)

[The second year of Bunmei (1471)]

[The Command of the Retired Emperor. Seventh month, twenty-second day]

[Go-Hanazono-in]

We have heard that your retainer went to Yamashina and rescued the storage chest (*karabitsu*) with the ceremonial robes. It would be most excellent if you would have him bring them to the palace. Speak of this to your retainer.

---

46. Hosokawa Katsumoto.

47. http://komonjo.princeton.edu/awazu-01/. 7.22.1471 (Bunmei 2) Go-Hananzono *jōkō nyōbō hōsho*. Translated by the students of *Sources in Ancient and Medieval Japanese History* with Thomas Conlan. Accessed August 27, 2021.

9. Remembering the Ōnin War

Sincerely yours,

Kirifu (piece cut from the document), *sumibiki* (ink mark)

[Takakura Nagatsugu, Acting Middle Councilor]

To: The Honorable Tō *no saishō*

LETTER OF HIROHASHI MORIMITSU[48]

Although Awazu Kiyonori was a courtier, his naming style and behavior shows that he fought in Yamashina to secure the clothes from the Western Army forces. He is referred to with a martial office and by his Taira lineage name. These naming practices make him indistinguishable from a warrior.

Recently, the imperial ceremonial robes were retrieved in the face of the enemy depredations in Yamashina district. *Saemon no jō* Taira Kiyonori's guarding and presenting them to us is most wonderful. As a reward for his service, he is to take up the post of Governor of Chikuzen. The letter that shall make this known is thus.

[Transmitter: The Honorable Grand Minister Hirohashi Tsunemitsu]

Twenty-fifth day, seventh month [1471 (Bunmei 2)]   (Monogram)

LETTER OF HIROHASHI KANEHIDE[49]

Hirohashi Kanehide, Kiyonori's great grandson, received court rank for his ancestor's exploits.

The Emperor viewed a court lady's communiqué praising the outstanding service of Awazu *shuri no suke* Michikiyo's grandfather [*sic*] Kiyonori who rescued garments and ceremonial robes during the "great conflict" (*gekiran*) of Ōnin. The Emperor, moved beyond measure, issued an edict promoting Michikiyo to the ranks of the nobility. "It is a great honor, and most rare, for rewards to accrue to one's

---

48. http://komonjo.princeton.edu/awazu-04/. 7.25.1471 (Bunmei 2) Hirohashi Tsunemitsu *shojō*. Translated by the students of *Sources in Ancient and Medieval Japanese History* with Thomas Conlan. Accessed August 27, 2021.

49. http://komonjo.princeton.edu/awazu-14/. 9.3 Hirohashi Kanehide *shojō*. Translated by the students of *Sources in Ancient and Medieval Japanese History* with Thomas Conlan. Accessed August 27, 2021.

descendants like this. Devote yourself to further service. So this shall be heard." Respectfully.

[Hirohashi Kanehide: The Palace Grand Minister. At the time, Transmitter of Messages for the Ashikaga (*Buke tensō*) and Former Grand Councilor]

Kanehide

Third day, ninth month

Ink mark of a cut seal (*Kirifu sumibiki*)

To: The Honorable Takakaura

SECTION VIII

The Rise of Regional Hegemons (Daimyō) (1450–1557)

In the fifteenth and sixteenth centuries, some regional hegemons, or *daimyō*, attempted to restore order in their domains. The Ōuchi wall codes depict a stable and ordered society; one of the prohibitions mentions that uninvited guests would sometimes wander into the lord's garden and peek into his house. By contrast, the Date family codes show that northern Japan was a much poorer and more chaotic place. A series of Mōri family oaths demonstrates how Japan's warriors tried to create durable organizations without instituting a law code.

1. Ōuchi Laws Regarding Violence[1]

The Ōuchi were among the most powerful warlords of western Japan. The Ōuchi law codes, of greater antiquity than most daimyō *laws, reveal much about warrior life in the fifteenth and early sixteenth centuries. The earliest of these laws were designed to establish order in the newly founded town of Yamaguchi. Since they were apparently written on the walls surrounding the mansion of the Ōuchi lord—where they could be seen and known by all—the laws became known as* sekisho, *or "wall writings." It seems likely, however, judging from their length, that only the newest regulations would appear on the walls, with administrators keeping track of the previous regulations. These wall writings also reveal how the town of Yamaguchi was ordered and purified. Finally, regulations concerning adultery and violence reveal that the Ōuchi relied on some elements of Kamakura law, which by this time had become customary practice.*

Ōuchi regulations for Yamaguchi. 5.22.1459 (Chōroku 3).

Monogram[2]

---

1. *Chūsei hōsei shiryōshū* vol. 3, *Bukehō* 1, 5.22.1459 (Chōroku 3) Ōuchi shi *sekisho*, clauses 2–8, 36. Translated by Thomas Conlan with Horikawa Yasufumi.
2. The Tsukiyama lord, Ōuchi Norihiro.

Section VIII • The Rise of Regional Hegemons (Daimyō)

Prohibited:

Item (2). Wandering along major roads at night.

Item (3). Sumō wresting at the crossroads.

Item (4). Taking women on the roadside (*rotō*).[3]

Item (5). Entering the Yuta hot springs at night. However, this does not apply for visitors to Yuta,[4] women, and cultivators (*nōnin*).

Item (6). People fleeing from other provinces, and those whose reason for coming here is not known. They should not be taken into service.

Item (7). Wearing strange clothes, claiming that it is the style of the capital.

Item (8). Use care in taking people from different provinces into your service.

The aforementioned seven clauses were decided on this past twentieth day in Council meeting. The high, middle, and low people of our lands should abide by these clauses. This Wall Writing (*hekisho*) is thus.

Twenty-second day of the fifth month of the third year of Chōroku (1459).

[Sugi] *Saemon no jō* Hideaki   Received.

[Sugi] *Saemon no taifu* Masayasu   Received.

2. Ōuchi Regulations for Yamaguchi, 4.29.1486[5]

The 1459 regulations, some of which had become widely accepted, were revised.

Item (89). Walking along major roads at night. This prohibition became well known during the previous rule [of Ōuchi Norihiro]. Different, suspicious people should be banned. Nevertheless, travelers should be exempted (from this prohibition) after their lodgings have been investigated.

---

3. Although the laws only refer to "taking" women, the context suggests prostitution rather than abducting women.

4. The Yuta springs were thought to have medicinal value.

5. *Chūsei hōsei shiryōshū*, vol. 3, *Bukehō* 1, 4.29.1486 (Bunmei 18), Ōuchi shi *sekisho*, clauses 89–93, 69–70. Translated by Thomas Conlan with Horikawa Yasufumi.

Item (90). Wandering monks, itinerant musicians, and monkey trainers should be expelled from here and nearby villages.

Item (91). People from other provinces who are not craftsmen (*shokunin*) or retainers (*hikan*) of various people (*shonin*) should not lodge here.

Item (92). Evening chanting of the *nenbutsu* at the roadside (*rotō*) is prohibited.

Item (93). Pilgrims (*junreisha*) can stay here for five days. Stays lasting more than five days will not be permitted.

The aforementioned five clauses were decided on this past nineteenth day in Council meeting. The lord has thus ordered that these clauses should be strictly followed. This judgment is thus.

The ninth day of the fourth month of the eighteenth year of Bunmei (1486)

Handa *Ōi no suke* (Hiro-oki)

Toida *Kamon no kami* (Hirotsuna)

3. Ōuchi Regulations for Yamaguchi, 4.20.1487[6]

Further revisions of the previous year's clauses.

Prohibitions Regarding walking along major roads at night.

Item (117). Long weapons,[7] bows, and quivers. However, travelers and those greeting or seeing off travelers are exempt. All others will be rigorously inspected.

Item (118). Those with hats (*kasa*), *haori*,[8] or *jutoku* or other strange clothes. Even if they are seen during the day, such people will be punished (*seibai seraru beki nari*).

Item (119). People who claim to be worshipping [at shrines and temples].

Item (120). People who cover their faces (*hōkaburi*) or show their underclothes [without wearing jackets (*jutoku*)].

---

6. *Chūsei hōsei shiryōshū* vol. 3, *Bukehō* 1, 4.20.1487 (Bunmei 19) Ōuchi shi *sekisho*, clauses, clauses 117–21, 77–80. Translated by Thomas Conlan with Horikawa Yasufumi.

7. *Nagagusoku*. Refers to glaives (*naginata*), long swords (*ōdachi*), or pikes (*yari*).

8. This presumably refers to a formal jacket, but why it would be prohibited is not clear. The term clothing is referred to as a *hōri*.

Section VIII • *The Rise of Regional Hegemons* (Daimyō)

Item (121). Those with flutes, *shakuhachi*, or other instruments. However, they are exempt within 100 to 200 yards of their lodgings.

The aforementioned people are strictly prohibited. If someone disobeys these orders, or if they are a suspicious person wearing strange clothes, they should be held in their lodgings and investigated. If their [identity] is not clear, then in pursuance to the law, the lord will be notified and the person will be punished. Arsonists, rock throwers, and thieves shall be bound and reported without notifying the lord. Next, as for householders (*gokenin*) and retainers (*hikan*) of various people: their work is never done, so such people, whether male or female, may go back and forth even in the depths of the night. These people should not be investigated. These clauses should be known to night watchmen, who should be prepared to enforce them. The lord has ordered thus. This Wall Writing (*sekisho*) is thus.

The twentieth day of the fourth month of the nineteenth year of Bunmei (1487)

4. Further Prohibitions Regarding Killing[9]

Having established regulations concerning the control of people, Ōuchi Masahiro then issued prohibitions regarding the killing of animals and tried to make Yamaguchi a purified area.

Item (106). Concerning the cleaning of Tsukiyama.[10]

Cleaning, from the Tsukiyama Shrine to the small gate of Matsubara, shall take place on the last day of every month. The cleaning and construction crew (*fushinshū*) shall be conscripted [from a pool of retainers] at a ratio of one person per one hundred *koku* of revenue. The administrators in charge, and the allocation of the number of the crew, shall be determined beforehand [by the Ōuchi lord]. If, however, there is inclement weather, [the crew] shall wait for the weather to clear. The lord has thus ordered this process. This Wall Writing is thus.

The last day (*misoka*) of the third month of the nineteenth year of Bunmei (1487).

---

9. *Chūsei hōsei shiryōshū* vol. 3, *Bukehō* 1, 3.30.1487 (Bunmei 19), Ōuchi shi *sekisho*, clause 106, 76, and ninth month 1487 (Chōkyō 1), Ōuchi shi *sekisho*, clause 124, 82. Translated by Thomas Conlan with Horikawa Yasufumi.

10. This, the former dwelling of Ōuchi Norihiro, is the area where he was enshrined as a deity.

Item (124). The killing of soft-shelled turtles (*tochigame*) for use as hawk bait is prohibited.

Soft-shelled turtles and snakes shall not be used as hawk bait. That is because they are the manifest messengers of the [North Star God] Hikamisan. Those who do not fear the God, and kill turtles and snakes, shall not escape divine punishment. Henceforth, that practice shall be strictly prohibited. Falconers should only use wild animals as bait. Anyone who cannot secure adequate bait should not possess falcons. If any *samurai* disobey this prohibition and seek soft-shelled turtles, they shall have their benefice lands confiscated. Violators who don't own land shall be banished. As for the common rabble (*bonge no tomogara*): if they are seen, or rumored to be, killing turtles, they shall be arrested or cut down at the place where it happened, according to the situation. The lord has ordered thus. This Wall Writing is thus.

The fourth day of the ninth month of the first year of Chōkyō (1487)

5. Prohibitions of Loitering[11]

Even during the "Warring States" era, the Ōuchi experienced problems with people leering into their mansions. They never did fortify their dwelling.

Item (138). People shall not sightsee at the lord's mansion

Gawking at the lord's mansion is strictly prohibited. Some people get their friends to sneak them into [the lord]'s living quarters; this is most surprising. Henceforth, sightseers shall not be allowed to enter the mansion, even to see the gardens. Autonomous warriors (*tozamashū*)[12]—even those who serve at the mansion—shall not be allowed into the inner chambers. The lord has ordered that anyone disobeying these orders should be punished. This Wall Writing is thus.

The nineteenth day of the twelfth month of the first year of Entoku (1489)

---

11. *Chūsei hōsei shiryōshū* vol. 3, *Bukehō* 1, 12.19.1489 (Entoku 1), Ōuchi shi *sekisho*, clause 138, 89–90, and 6.1492 (Entoku 4) Ōuchi shi *sekisho*, clause 146, 96. Translated by Thomas Conlan with Horikawa Yasufumi.

12. Not direct retainers of the lord but still, in this case, having some ties and obligations to the Ōuchi with at the same time maintaining a modicum of independence. For more on the distinction of *tozama* and *miuchi*, see Conlan, "Largesse and the Limits of Loyalty in the Fourteenth Century," 39-64. By contrast, followers with greater obligation, known in earlier times as *miuchi*, would be described by terms such as *nainai*, or "interior" followers.

Item (146). The prohibition of people sightseeing from atop the earthen walls of Tsukiyama

People spontaneously (*shizen*) climb atop the earthen walls of Tsukiyama to view the Gion Festival or to see other various things—this is strictly prohibited. In particular, people tend to congregate near the main hall (*gohōden*) or other shrines (*chinju*). Some climb the stone walls and set up seats to view events (*saijiki*). This is strictly prohibited. From now on, when [the Lord Masahiro's sister, and head of the subtemple] Shinhō-in[13] wants to sightsee from the walls, she must first make a request, through the temple administrators, to the person in charge of temple affairs. The lord has ordered that anyone disobeying these orders should be punished. This Wall Writing is thus.

The sixth month of the fourth year of Entoku (1492)

6. Ōuchi Reverence for Kamakura Law[14]

Ōuchi Norihiro upheld the legal tradition of the Kamakura Bakufu (1185–1333) and used principles espoused in its laws as the basis for common law in his domains. In 1462, Ishikawa Sukegorō was killed by a commoner (heimin) *named Saburō, who had discovered his wife and Sukegorō in flagrante delicto; Saburō killed Sukegorō but not his wife. Norihiro adjudicated the case, banishing Saburō, his wife, and their child to Mishima Island. He justified this decision through an appeal to the principles of the 1232* Goseibai shikimoku (The Jōei Code) (*see* The Formulary of Adjudication, *p. 42*). *Norihiro issued the law to the deputy shugo of Nagato Province, who was entrusted with enforcing the decision.*

Concerning the Crime of Killing People in Revenge.[15] The last day of the eighth month of the third year of Kanshō (1462).

---

13. This identity of Masahiro's sister is known from the sixteenth-century account known as *Towazu monogatari*. See Hagihara Daisuke, "Ashikaga Yoshitada seiken kō," 90.

14. *Chūsei hōsei shiryōshū* vol. 3, *Bukehō* 1, 8.30.1462 (Kanshō 3), Ōuchi shi *sekisho*, clause 14, 43. Translated by Thomas Conlan with Horikawa Yasufumi. This proved to be a much stronger authority over house law than evidence in other regions, such as by the *Jinkaishū*, which dates from the sixteenth century and is translated below.

15. Violence for self-redress of wrongs.

6. Ōuchi Reverence for Kamakura Law

Item (14). Laws concerning those who rely on some pretext to kill people for revenge.

On the night of the past seventeenth day [of August], Ishikawa Sukegorō, a retainer (*rōjū*) of Iida Ōinosuke Sadaie, was killed by the commoner (*heimin*) Saemon Saburō of Misumi estate, in Nagato Province.

Concerning the aforementioned, Sukegorō had an affair with the wife of *Saemon* Saburō. She is known as the mother of [the child] Saimatsu. *Saemon* Saburō cannot avoid punishment for his crime of killing Sukegorō for revenge. In the domains governed by this house, the commoners (*domin*) should either notify their lords or state the particulars of a dispute in our courts and receive a judgment. The Ōuchi will judge cases concerning matters of our domain, based on the right or wrong of the matter. Anyone who seeks vengeance for a grudge are liable to lose their judgment. Their actions are disloyal and unfilial, and similar to those who come to ruin over prostitutes (*keisei*).[16] What indiscreet people they are! It follows that henceforth we shall uphold this judgment and establish a law that should not be violated. If anyone happens to disobey this law—even if they are completely different types of people (*iruishin*), or devoted retainers who have served a house for generations—they, their children, and their grandchildren shall all be punished.

In order for this regulation to be widely known, it has been decided that, in accordance with the laws of the Jōei Code, *Saemon* Saburō and [his wife] the mother of Saimatsu, shall be banished. Quickly dispatch both of these people to Mishima Island, Nagato Province.[17] Thus.

The last day of the eighth month of the third year of Kanshō (1462)

The Tsukiyama Lord [copy of monogram]

To: The Honorable Naitō Shimotsuke *no kami* [This is Moriyo].

---

16. This phrase literally means "became prostitutes and came to their ruin." Originally the text must have said "for the sake of prostitutes" (*keisei no tame ni*), but at some point this code was misread or miscopied as *keisei to shite*, or "as prostitutes," which makes less sense here.

17. This island is located approximately an hour north of Hagi by boat.

7. More Laws Concerning Violence[18]

The following law was written shortly before Ōuchi Masahiro's death, and shows that his son decided to adopt a more hands-on approach in dealing with quarrels, which were given great latitude during the turmoil of the Ōnin War and its aftermath.

Item (155). Laws concerning quarrels.

Quarrels should be decided by the participants. They should not become a source of public or private concern. It is Lord Ōuchi Masahiro's belief, held since the time of the Bunmei era [1469–77], when he resided in the capital,[19] that he would not intervene in such disputes and this has become established law. Later, he naturally heard examples of quarrels breaking out, but they were not adjudicated. From now on, quarrels should be settled by participants themselves. Yet it is rumored that other people are getting involved, providing military aid to one or another of the sides in a quarrel, or otherwise acting selfishly and loudly, and causing disturbances. Such behavior will cause problems for many and lead to a disregard for [our] laws. Thus we are now changing the recent law: from now on, if the lord hears of such quarrels, he will adjudicate them. He and he alone will determine the rightness or wrongness of a given case and in all matters. Should someone violate this law, they should be prepared for their own destruction. From now on, no one will give any help to either side in a quarrel, regardless of whether the quarrel involves parents and children, older and younger brothers, retainers within a house, or people with some other bond; instead, the will of the lord must be followed. This law is established, once again, thus. Let the people know this. This Wall Writing is thus.

[Sagara] *Shami* Masatō received

[Sugi] *Saemon no jō* Takeaki received

The eighth month of the fourth year of Meiō (1495)

Item (173). Regulations concerning quarrels in military encampments.

Quarrels arising within military encampments should be settled in a peaceful manner, regardless of the rights or wrongs of the matter. If one of the aggrieved parties has something to say, they should say it to the lord after the campaign has

---

18. *Chūsei hōsei shiryōshū* vol. 3, *Bukehō* 1, 8.1495 (Meiō 4), Ōuchi shi *sekisho*, clause 155, 99, and 1.13.1521 (Dai'ei 2), Ōuchi shi *sekisho*, clause 173, 110. Translated by Thomas Conlan with Horikawa Yasufumi.

19. This passage refers to the latter states of the Ōnin War. Masahiro was in fact in the capital from 1467 through 1477.

ended. Conversely, anyone who acts selfishly and violates this law shall be punished, even if they are in the right.[20]

The thirteenth day of the first month of the second year of Dai'ei (1521)

8. Regulations Concerning Shipping[21]

The Ōuchi were a major maritime power, and they twice led armadas to the capital. The first such voyage, undertaken by Ōuchi Masahiro in 1467, allowed him to maintain a presence there until 1477. Masahiro's son Yoshioki also led an army to Kyoto in 1508, which he occupied until 1518. The first regulation below concerns the crossing of the Straits of Shimonoseki in order to quell a rival of the Ōuchi, the Shōni.

Item (58). Regulations concerning levies of war boats crossing the Straits of Shimonoseki

When the [Ōuchi] lord was at Akamagaseki in order to conquer Kyushu, it was decided at the Council that the residents of Akamagaseki should, as their military duty, outfit war boats to cross the Straits of Shimonoseki. This law has been established in accordance with precedent. [Today] it has been decided at the Council that this law shall continue to be followed.[22] This [was added] to the daily record for the Council. This Wall Writing is thus.

The first day of the eighth month of the fifteenth year of Bunmei (1483)

Item (105). Concerning waivers of tax levies for various merchant ships: although some want these taxes waived, henceforth [retainers] shall not entertain requests [as intermediaries from others to the lord]. Such exemptions are granted solely at the lord's discretion. This Wall Writing is thus.

The twenty-ninth day of the third month of the nineteenth year of Bunmei (1487)

Saemon no jō Takeaki

---

20. The term *seibai* here refers to punishment.
21. *Chūsei hōsei shiryōshū* vol. 3, *Bukehō* 1, 8.1.1483 (Bunmei 15), Ōuchi shi *sekisho*, clause 58, 56, 3.29.1487 (Bunmei 19), Ōuchi shi *sekisho*, clause 105, 75, and 4.20.1487 (Bunmei 19), Ōuchi shi *sekisho*, clauses 108–16, 77–79, and 1.20.1488 (Chōkyō 2), Ōuchi shi *sekisho*, clause 128, 84–85. Translated by Thomas Conlan with Horikawa Yasufumi.
22. Here, the term *denchū* refers to the place where the Council was held.

Section VIII • The Rise of Regional Hegemons (Daimyō)

Ōi no suke Hiro [missing]

Tolls for Akamagaseki

Stipulated Articles

For the crossing between Akamagaseki, Kokura, Moji, and Akasaka.[23]

Item (108). Akamagaseki to Kokura: three *mon*.[24]

Item (109). Akamagaseki to Moji: one *mon*.

Item (110). Akamagaseki to Akasaka: two *mon*.

Item (111). Chests for armor:[25] fifteen *mon*.

Item (112). Long chests (*karabitsu*): same as above.

Item (113). One horse: same as above.

Item (114). One palanquin: same as above.

Item (115). One dog: ten *mon*.

Regarding those eight clauses about tolls: though these laws were established previously, it has been reported that ferrymen (*funagata*) are not honest in their pricing, and that this has become a nuisance for people traveling back and forth. Starting now, ships from Akamagaseki to Kokura shall not charge an additional two *mon* per person; neither shall ships returning from Kokura to Akamagaseki charge an additional *mon* per person. When [the Ōuchi] discussed tolls [with the ferrymen] last year, they never mentioned these additional tolls (*agesen*). Tarō *saemon*, Jirōsaburō, and Jirō *uemon* of the Amidaji lands (*ryō*), both from Akamagaseki, requested this ruling for the first time this year. Laws regulating the tolls have been firmly established. Yet when the wind and waves are strong, the ferrymen have been taking [extra] tolls as they wish and thus disobeying the laws.

These regulations should be followed even when the wind and waves are strong. Whoever disobeys these laws, and harasses the people crossing back and forth, will be imprisoned by the representatives (*daikan*) of Akamagaseki or Kokura. From there [the situation] will be reported to officials in Yamaguchi, where the matter will be investigated carefully, and the criminals executed. Hence, this order is thus.

---

23. All separate ports on the straits of Shimonoseki, with Moji, Kokura, and Akasaka all being harbors in Kyushu, and Akamagaseki the only port involved at the tip of western Honshu.

24. A copper coin, a small unit of currency. In current purchasing power, equivalent to one dollar. Akamagaseki is referred to in these classes in an abbreviated fashion as "Seki," but to avoid confusion it will be referred to as Akamagaseki.

25. *Karabitsu*, or literally "Chinese chests."

8. Regulations Concerning Shipping

The twentieth day of the fourth month of the nineteenth year of Bunmei (1487)

From the administrators at that time

[Handa] *Ōi no suke* Hiro[oki]

[Yasutomi] *Ōmi no kami* Fusayuki

[Sugi] *shami* [Shūsai]

[Naitō] *Danjō no chū* Hironori

[Toida] *Ōkura no shōyū* Hirotane

Item (116). Contracts (*ōsho*) with Locals Concerning the Established Law about the Ferries at Akamagaseki

Concerning the ferries at Akamagaseki: if we hear about someone failing to obey the posted prohibitions, we will investigate them and report back to you. Should we fail to keep you informed, we should be immediately punished. Respectfully.

The twentieth day of the fourth month of the nineteenth year of Bunmei (1487)

Tarō *saemon* (*han*)[26]

Jirōsaburō (*han*)

Jirō *uemon* (*han*)

Item (128). Concerning the Boats Commandeered for War

When we provide our retainers with commandeered boats for the advance to the capital (and a variety of other purposes), we also supply a daily ration of rice. Because we pay for these provisions, we do not pay retainers for boat fees or wages for sailors. This has long been the arrangement. Nevertheless, last year, when war boats were allotted to retainers,[27] some of them improperly requested boat fees. Acting as if they were merchant ships or ferries (*kaisen*), our retainers willfully requested rice as well as boat fees and wages for sailors. When the forces advancing to the capital boarded the boats, they insisted on making this selfish request (*watakushi no kojitsu*), which is most surprising. In the end, if this law is disobeyed, or if someone disputes this or hides boat gear, that boat shall be confiscated from those who were allotted the said boat [such as the Ōuchi, or the Sue][28] and will be

---

26. Copy of monogram. This oath was copied, dispatched to the representatives at Akamagaseki, and then transmitted to Yamaguchi.

27. This was during the twelfth month of 1487, when Toida Hirotane led an expeditionary force to aid Ashikaga Yoshitane.

28. That is because the Sue received this law and were presumably responsible for this allotment to retainers.

used however the leader of the campaign pleases. The Council is in accord. This order shall be made known. The order is thus. This is so conveyed.

Twentieth day of the first month of the second year of Chōkyō (1488)

Handa *Ōi no suke* Hiro[oki]

Sugi *Saemon no jō* Takeaki

Sugi *Saemon no jō* Takemichi

Yasutomi Ōmi *no kami* Fusayuki

Naitō Higo *no kami* Hironori

To: The Honorable Sue *Nakanotsukasa no shōyū*

9. Portrait of Hosokawa Sumimoto

The following portrait of Hosokawa Sumimoto (1489–1520) was completed sometime before 1518, as the monk Keijo Shūrin commented that Sumimoto had this portrait commissioned as a sign of his victory in a familial dispute. He did so after seeing a portrait of Ashikaga Takauji in armor, showing the enduring influence of the Ashikaga leader.[29] Sumimoto is wearing a style of simplified armor, known as haramaki, *which was tied under his right shoulder. The shoulder boards* (sode) *are flexible and are more for decoration than the inflexible* sode *of earlier times. The helmet is of a style favored in his time, known as* akoda-bachi, *and it is decorated with horns, called* maidate, *attached at the front. Sumimoto holds a long sword with a wrapped handle that covered three feet of the blade. This style of sword, known as* nagamaki, *was popular in his day, but later fell from favor. Equally notable, inserted in his belt one can see a short sword with* katana-style fittings. *This portrait is one of the oldest showing swords with these fittings. Finally, partially visible on his left is a sword hanging from his belt in the earlier tachi style. The leg armor is also notable, as it completely covers the lower leg, including the knee, and the rear of the leg. Finally, the haunch of his horse is branded with a three diamond* (mitsumeiyui) *crest.*

---

29. For this explanation, see http://www.eiseibunko.com/collection/hosokawa1.html. Accessed August 27, 2021.

9. Portrait of Hosokawa Sumimoto

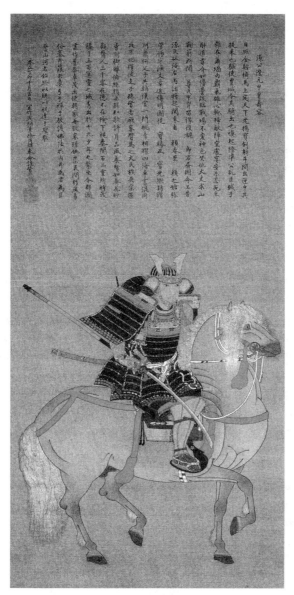

A portrait of Hosokawa Sumimoto. This painting accurately depicts sixteenth-century Japanese armor and is unusual in offering one of the earliest-known images of a sword (tucked in Sumimoto's belt) with katana-*style fittings.*

Section VIII • *The Rise of Regional Hegemons* (Daimyō)

10. The *Jinkaishū*, Laws of the Date[30]

In 1536 (Tenbun 5), Date Tanemune (1488–1565), a lord of Mutsu, in northern Japan, wrote a set of laws that he called the Jinkaishū. *The phrase means "dust and dirt," and was used to describe worldly (as opposed to Buddhist) affairs. Unlike the Ōuchi laws, Tanemune's regulations were not apparently publicly displayed as "wall writings."*

Tanemune felt the need to codify local practice by writing laws but struggled greatly in crafting them. Tanemune was a very poor writer. He wrote the codes in the local dialect. Although people in his domains most likely understood the laws, later scholars struggle to decipher them. Tanemune ended his new code with the 1232 Jōei Formulary's final oath (see The Formulary of Adjudication, *p. 42), thereby revealing the esteem with which he held the earlier laws. Passages lifted directly from that code are reproduced here in bold type.*

Tanemune's world was one where local warrior authority remained strong. Warriors were still referred to with the title of jitō, *a holdover from Kamakura times. Their houses were autonomous legal spheres, and Tanemune freely admitted that his writ did not apply there. Here, he exercised far less authority than the Ōuchi, who could interfere in house affairs. He also recognized their right to feud with other houses. These local warriors (jitō) also began to assert greater authority over the region's commoners. Indeed, the old term for commoners,* hyakushō, *was increasingly used to refer to peasants instead of people who could serve as military retainers.*

Though evidence was still required in the processing of legal matters, the use of torture to generate confessions was becoming ever more common in judicial affairs. Still, older practices, such as allowing women to inherit lands, remained.

Tanemune's code contains 171 clauses; 52 of them are translated here. The clauses reproduced below mostly refer to criminal cases, which illuminate the lives and judicial ideals and practices of warriors and their followers in the north. Laws that refer to financial matters, loans, or religious institutions are omitted.

Item (13). People who have renounced the world should not carry (*sasu*) swords.

Item (16). The punishment of murder.

For those who aid murderers: if they have unsheathed their swords, they shall be punished for the same crime as the murderer. But accessories to murder who want

---

30. Ishii Susumu, et al., eds., *Chūsei seiji shakai shisō*, vol. 1, 210–43. Translated by Thomas Conlan with Horikawa Yasufumi.

10. The Jinkaishū, Laws of the Date

to avoid this punishment will be pardoned if they kill the perpetrator before turning themselves in. Any abettors (*toritabane*) who have not used their own swords but have been involved with the perpetrator are to be convicted of the same crime and punished in the same way.[31]

Item (17). In violent contest (*kakemukai*), there are cases where one party claims that they were ambushed and suffered fatalities but in fact they were the ambusher; or in other cases they claimed that through skill they killed ambushers when in fact they ambushed their rival in a surprise attack. In such cases, officials should search for proof. If there is no proof, it shall be judged that the killed party was in the right.

Item (18). If a retainer or a low-ranked person kills someone and then flees, their lord should not be punished. But if the lord harbors a known killer, that lord should receive the same punishment as the murderer. Furthermore, in such cases, if someone associated with the victim claims that a lord aided or protected the killer during the murder, then the lord's residence (*zaisho*) should be searched.[32] If the aggrieved party claims that the lord aided and abetted the killer after the murder took place—and if these claims are proven to be true—then the lord shall be punished in the same way as mentioned above. If no clear proof is produced to support these claims, then the lord shall not be blamed. If a retainer, in an attempt to placate a lord's anger, killed someone without the lord's knowledge and then fled, it will be difficult for the lord to escape punishment. In such cases the lord shall be pardoned if he kills the murdering retainer and then turns himself in.

Item (19). If a criminal attempts to escape execution by seeking sanctuary in another lord's lands, the lord of those lands should quickly expel the criminal. If the lord does not expel the criminal, his holdings should be searched. The same holds for criminals seeking sanctuary on temple lands; these temples shall not protect them.

Item (20). If a quarrelsome and combative person willfully (*watakushi ni*) attacks another's place without first asking the Date to rule on the right and wrong of the matter, then that person shall be found guilty even if he is completely in the right in terms of the legal case.

Item (21). When crazed drunkards kill people, they often use their inebriation as an excuse, but they should be punished. Drunks who slash or beat people should suffer the same punishment they would receive if they were sober.

---

31. The word used to describe abettors is *toritabane*. It refers not to plotters but to people who captured or held down the victim so that he or she could be killed.

32. With the assumption that the lord was harboring the criminal. If the criminal was discovered in such cases, he would be apprehended.

Section VIII • The Rise of Regional Hegemons (Daimyō)

Item (22). The slander of drunkards shall be evaluated on a case-by-case basis, even if the drunks are women or those who have renounced the world.

Item (23). When criminals are killed, they are still at fault regardless of how many of their confederates were killed in the process of their capture.[33] But if the criminals' confederates are men of worth, you should let them escape, notify the Date, and wait for the Date's judgment.

Item (24). Enemies of one's family should not be killed impulsively.[34] Nevertheless, if such an enemy, after his punishment has ended, is loitering in rival lands and runs into someone who then proclaims that they are an enemy of their parent or child and kills them, the avengers are not at fault.[35]

Item (25). Punishments of parents and children in affairs that may or may not bind them.

Concerning the aforementioned: in cases where people impulsively quarreled, or were crazed at a banquet, and unpremeditatedly killed someone, they shall be punished, and their lands confiscated. However, if their father or son was not involved, they should not be punished. The same is true in the case of crimes where someone cuts down another person. Next, when sons or grandsons are convicted of having killed their parents' or grandparents' enemies (*ada*), the parents or grandparents shall suffer the same punishment even if they were unaware of their sons' or grandsons' plans. This is because such murders are plotted and carried out in order to seek revenge on a parent's or grandparent's behalf. If, in the course of committing a crime, a son kills the person from whom he is stealing land or possessions, his father shall not be punished so long as his ignorance of his son's plans can be proven beyond a doubt. The same principle shall apply in cases involving crimes committed by brothers.

Item (26). When criminals from different domains are killed, people from those domains should not interfere.

Item (27). In cases where a retainer abandons his original lord and takes a new lord, the original lord should inform the new lord of these existing bonds of lordship. If the new lord keeps the retainer and does not return him to the original lord, the original lord should inform the new lord that he will kill the retainer. The original

---

33. This means that the people who killed the criminal should not be responsible for any collateral deaths.
34. This clause states literally "enemies of parents, children, or siblings." In other words, enemies of a family could be killed after they were first punished by the Date and then were proclaimed as being enemies by their rivals.
35. This is tacit recognition of feuding, in that a warrior could kill an enemy of any of their close relatives even if they did not have a personal grudge or conflict with them. Date Tanemune only prohibits hasty attacks, but he otherwise permits these feuds to take place in due course.

lord can kill the retainer wherever he finds him. Furthermore, if the new lord does not respond to the original lord's letter, the details of the case shall be made known to the Date. Depending on the facts, the aforementioned retainer, or those who permitted him to switch lords, shall be punished.

Item (28). When a guest is killed, the master of the house shall be punished. In cases where the perpetrator can be clearly identified beyond any doubt, the master shall not be punished, depending on the circumstances.

Item (29). In cases where two guests get in a fight, and one is killed by the other, the master of the house should apprehend the murderer and notify the authorities. In cases where the murderer is not apprehended, the master of the house should consider the circumstances and explain[36] the particulars.

Item (30). In cases where people are called out from their residence (*zaisho*) only to go missing and then be found assassinated (*yamiuchi*): in such cases, the person who called out the victim shall be punished. But he shall not be punished if there is unmistakable proof of his innocence.

Item (31). In cases where someone is called out, then assassinated (*yamiuchi*) on their way home, the person who called out the victim shall be responsible to investigate this murder.[37]

Item (37). It is prohibited to kill a criminal without first notifying the lord of the residence (*zaisho*) where the criminal is being harbored. If the lord is notified but ignores this notification and continues to protect the criminal, then this case will be made known to the Date and that lord's residence will be searched.

Item (38). In quarrels or disputes where people have been cut down on both sides, the judgment will be made in favor of the party that suffered the greatest number of casualties. But if they attacked first (*kakarite*), they will be at fault and will be punished even if they suffered the greater number of dead and wounded.

Item (39). When people are apprehended for the crime of cutting down others, report the case to the Date and wait for their ruling. No one should willfully (*watakushi ni*) strike back without waiting for the Date's judgment. Those that do, even if they have ample right on their side, are disobeying the law and will be punished.

Item (40). As for those who assault others: if *samurai*, they shall have their lands confiscated. Those with no lands will be banished to other provinces. Victims who seek

---

36. *Mōshiwaku*, to explain or make an excuse.
37. The implication is that if the person who called someone out does not find proof that another murdered the victim, then he would be punished as an accessory to murder as outlined in Item 30.

revenge without waiting for our judgment will lose their land holdings. Any landless victims found guilty of seeking revenge will be banished to another province.

Item (41). Stealing, banditry, robbery, and piracy.[38] If evidence is lacking in the case of the aforementioned crimes, suspects shall be apprehended and questioned (*ikeguchi*). Accomplices named in a suspect's confession shall also be apprehended. If such named accomplices claim innocence of the crime, they can name their own suspects, and both groups will be taken to the court (*satasho*) where they will be questioned for fifty days. The guilty party will be punished.

Item (47). If someone discovers people who ran away from their master, he should return the fugitives to the original master. If, after the fugitives have been captured and the master notified, the lowly people (*genin*) flee again, then the person who found, then lost, them is liable. In such cases, the discoverer will have to pay three hundred *hiki* in compensation for the loss of male fugitives and five hundred *hiki* in compensation for the loss of females.

Item (48). If someone discovers people who ran away from their master and notifies the master, he should receive, as a show of gratitude, thirty *hiki* for each person he returns. But if the capturer has to return the escapees from far away, miscellaneous expenses and tolls should be paid by the original master. All items used by the escapee should be returned.[39] If the discoverer decides to keep these items, he will be charged with the same crime as the fugitive. In some cases, a fugitive will sell or lose such items (*idakimono*) during his escape. If someone finds them[40] later and does not know the circumstances of how the items came to be lost or sold, the fugitive's (*genin*) testimony shall not serve as the basis for determining the proper course of action.[41]

Item (49). When suspects (*ikeguchi*) are inadvertently killed during their capture, the apprehender (*torite*) shall be at fault (*oto taru beshi*). Nevertheless, if the confession of another suspect includes the name of the killed suspect (*hakujō ni nosuru ni tsuki*), then the apprehender's position is confirmed.[42]

Item (50). If a captured suspect (*ikeguchi*) does not confess, his captor is at fault. But if one of the captured criminal's compatriots is later apprehended and confesses, while being tortured during the investigation, that he was the previously captured

---

38. These terms mirror clauses 3 and 33 of the 1232 *Jōei Formulary* and suggest how much this code was indebted to those earlier regulations.
39. These items were thought to belong, by right, to the master.
40. This could either refer to the escapees or their items (*idakimono*), which belonged to their master.
41. As to who shall receive the belongings of the escapee.
42. And will not be punished.

10. The Jinkaishū, Laws of the Date

criminal's accomplice and that both they and the captured criminal are guilty, then the captor shall be judged in the right.

Item (51). If a captured criminal disembowels themselves or bites their tongue and dies while being interrogated by the Date's representative (*daikan*),[43] the case shall not be investigated further (*zehi ni oyobu bekarazu*). But such cases can still be adjudicated depending on the particulars.

Item (52). If a captured suspect (*ikeguchi*) being transported along the road is seized by villagers, their lord, relations, or a mob of accomplices, this act will be considered to be theft. But if the suspect shows up in court claiming to have done nothing wrong, they will be questioned and tortured. The truth shall be determined in this matter.

Item (53). Poor planning—such as failure to bring rope—can result in suspects (*ikeguchi*) evading capture. When this happens, the suspects will accuse their captors of being bandits and highwaymen (*hikihagi*); the suspects will claim to be the captors, and both sides will dispute the truth. If neither side can prove their claims, thereby making it difficult to reach a just verdict in the matter, both sides should apprehend further suspects (*ikeguchi*) for interrogation to plead their case in appeal. Then it can be decided which side is in the wrong, and those judged to be in the wrong will be classified as brigands (*akutō*).

Item (54). Anyone who personally punishes a thief shall himself be punished, even if evidence is provided to prove the thief's guilt.[44] But if the thief's captor instead notifies the thief's lord, who then punishes that person, then the right and wrong of the matter should be clear, and no punishment is required.

Item (57). Regarding the blame that falls to the parents and children of thieves: if the parent is guilty, so, too, is the child. But if a thief's children live in a distant area, from which it would be impossible for them to have participated in a crime, they shall not be punished. In similar situations, parents should not be blamed if their children commit crimes. If, however, both parents and children are living under the same roof, they should all be punished in the same manner. Decisions will be made based on the circumstances.

Item (63). Concerning robbers and similar criminals: any accomplices who receive a share of a criminal's stolen booty, even if they did not participate in the crime themselves, shall be punished as thieves. In addition, any accomplices who plotted with criminals but, due to a sudden change of heart, did not show up when the crime was committed, should be considered criminals if their names appear in the thieves' confessions. That is because they aided robbers.

---

43. A euphemism for committing suicide.
44. Only lords could punish their retainers in the Date domains.

Section VIII • *The Rise of Regional Hegemons* (Daimyō)

Item (66). Trespassing—climbing over a fence and entering someone's residences (*zaisho*)—shall be punished just as if it were robbery.

Item (74). When a suspect's confession names a deceased person as an accomplice, the time at which the crime was committed must be determined. If the deceased accomplice's children were under ten years old when the crime was committed, they shall not be punished for their parent's crime. If, however, they were ten years or older at the time, they shall be punished for the same crime as the deceased parent. In addition, the accomplice's son-in-law shall be punished for the same crime if he succeeds to the headship of the family.

Item (75). Arsonists shall be treated as thieves and executed.

Item (76). On the relationship between *jitō* lords and *hyakushō* commoners:[45] if the latter have been retainers to *jitō* for a long time, they should still pay their share of agricultural taxes in full. If they owe back taxes, they will suffer confiscation of their lands. Nevertheless, if the *hyakushō*, claiming historical rights, rely on the authority of central proprietors (*kenmon*)[46] to interfere with tax collection (*zaike*) by the *jitō*, they shall be punished.[47]

Item (83). The opinion of the *jitō* lords shall be followed in settling questions regarding the historical rights of the *hyakushō*. In cases where *hyakushō*, relying on their lord, or based on their ties with central proprietors (*kenmon*), cultivate, harvest, or otherwise interfere with disputed rights, they, along with all other *hyakushō* who support them against the *jitō* shall be punished.

Item (104). A parent's wishes, as expressed in their will, shall be followed in settling a daughter's inheritance.

Item (125). The possessions of craftsmen shall not be sold without good reason (*midari ni*). Both seller and purchaser shall be punished.

---

45. The terms here are somewhat anachronistic. *Jitō*, the signature office of the Kamakura era, continued to remain as a name for local lordship in the far north, where a powerful magnate did not arise, and even the Date continued to delegate important judicial and policing authority to locals. *Hyakushō*, which through the fourteenth century referred to commoners, maintains that residual meaning, as these commoners are described as retainers of military lords, although their cultivator activities are emphasized. By the late sixteenth century onward, this term best describes peasants, but the ambiguity should be evident here.

46. The term *kenmon* traditionally refers to central proprietors, or noble or monastic institutions capable of governing territory through an administrative office called a *mandokoro*. This term is used as such in the 1232 *Jōei Code*.

47. The term *zaike* literally means a dwelling, but in this context refers to the taxing authority for a specific area within an estate.

10. The Jinkaishū, Laws of the Date

Item (130). Concerning revenge for assault and murder: if, in an act of revenge, a resident of our domains is captured or killed in a different domain in an act of vengeance, then anyone living in our domains who is associated with that crime shall be investigated and punished.

Item (131). All the facts of the matter should be considered before revenge is taken on another province's resident who slashed or murdered one of our own. In such cases, a person from the assailant's province should be held hostage, and the office of the protector of that province (*shugosho*) should be notified.[48] But if the assailant has already been punished in another domain, then the hostage shall be immediately released and returned to that province.

Item (132). A warrior killed accidentally on the battlefield by his allies will still be considered to have been "killed in battle" (*uchiji*), and the deceased warrior's relations must not seek revenge in such cases.[49]

Item (151). Concerning the homesteads (*zaisho*)[50] of people punished for their crimes: a suspect's guilt shall be firmly established before our agents (*daikan*) confiscate any of the assets attached to his lands and residences (*tatō*),[51] including such wealth and treasures as cows, horses, and hereditary followers. If a convict flees with the aid of his former lords or anyone else, his assets shall be returned to the previous *jitō*. The province's agents (*daikanshū*) should not squabble over confiscated produce; any agricultural products belong to the *jitō*.

Item (152). The areas surrounding the houses (*zaike*) of convicted criminals should not be burned down as part of their punishment. Anyone who commits such outrages—including the cutting down of trees and bamboo around a criminal's residence or the destruction of the outer walls of the house—shall be punished for their crimes. The guilty parties may have been acting against convicted criminals, but they will have disobeyed the law in their own way, and their punishment shall not be light.

Item (154). If you find a hawk and do not return it, you will be punished as a thief.

Item (156). If a horse or cow runs away and starts eating your produce, you should hold it and fine the owner over the losses you incurred. There is no reason for you to kill or shoot livestock with arrows. If you injure a horse or cow, you should pay

---

48. This is a term for the protector of provinces, the *shugo*, which dates from Kamakura times.

49. The clause is ambiguous and could also mean that the person killed in battle will still be rewarded as if he or she were killed in battle. In other words, this code could refer to rewards for death in battle or limiting of vendettas. As the thrust of the law codes is with the latter, this law has been interpreted thus.

50. This includes lands and residences.

51. In other words, Date representatives could confiscate those properties mentioned above.

compensation. If you kill the animal, you should pay the price of its worth. Those who ignore this law shall have their dwellings confiscated.

Item (157). No one should be punished for killing a dog if they use it for hawk bait. Still, no one should chase a dog onto other's property and kill it.

Item (159). On messengers' lies: if a lying messenger is a *samurai*, their holdings can be confiscated; if they have no holdings, they will be banished to another province. If the lying messenger is of a lower status, they will be summoned and physically punished.

Item (162). A man who secretly has an affair[52] with another's wife will be killed as punishment. This applies to both adulterous men and women.

Item (163). Regarding illicit affairs (*mikkai*): whether forced or gentle encounters, they must occur in a place of assignation (*nakadachiyado*).[53] Those who offer a place of assignation to adulterers will be punished identically to those committing adultery.

Item (164). Regarding adulterers killed by the wronged husband: the laws say nothing about saving the wife. If the husband caught and killed the other man in the bedroom[54] but failed to also kill his wife, he shall not be at fault for not killing her (*oto taru bekarazaru nari*).

Item (168). Attendants should not carry long pikes or quivers when accompanying their retainers. But they can carry quivers or other military accoutrements for falconry, or while accompanying a superior to a different location. These regulations (*sadame*) should be followed henceforth.

Oath: Questions of right or wrong shall be decided at Council meetings.[55]

An individual is liable to make mistakes through defect of judgment, even when the mind is unbiased. They can also, out of prejudice or partiality, reach an erroneous decision while believing they are right. Furthermore, they can claim that proof

---

52. The verb used, however, is *totsugu*, for marriage, which does not, however, make sense in English.

53. For example, whether forcible rape or a consensual encounter. The verb used here is, however, the same as "marriage." As marriage was ill-defined at the time, so determining adultery would have proved difficult. Affairs taking place in a house could merit capital punishment. Hence, the Date tried to limit violence by encouraging affairs to occur in places of assignation.

54. For example, *in flagrante delicto*.

55. The oath at the end of this document is copied directly from Kamakura's 1232 *Jōei Code*, save for one additional clause and some variations with the names of gods and the language concerning divine punishment. Passages copied from the earlier code appear in bold while those unique to this code are reproduced in regular print, and the omissions of gods located near Kamakura are duly noted.

exists, even in cases where there are no facts to be found. Or, even when being cognizant of the facts, they might be unwilling to expose another's shortcomings and therefore refrain from reporting the truth of the matter. When intention and fact are not aligned, catastrophe ensues. Therefore, at meetings of Council, whenever questions of right or wrong arise there shall be no regard for ties of relationship. None shall give in to likes or dislikes, but rather all shall speak out in whatever direction reason pushes and the inmost thought of the mind leads, without regard for companions or fear of powerful houses (*kenmon*). Even when a decision given in a case is perfectly just, it shall be agreed upon by the whole Council in session. The entire Council shall be held accountable for misguided actions taken on the basis of faulty information. Council members will never say to litigants and their supporters, "Although I personally had the right understanding of the matter, so-and-so among my colleagues of the Council dissented, and caused confusion." Should such things be said, the solidarity of the Council would be fractured, and we would be ridiculed. Were an individual Council member to agree to support the appeal of a plaintiff who, because they do not have a legal leg to stand on, was denied a trial by the full Council, such an act would be tantamount to the single Council member declaring that all the others are wrong. Were the Council to agree to hear a direct appeal while burying the appeals of the less worthy (*fushō no tomogara*), they would, in effect, be breaking the law (*hōrei*) themselves. At those times, no one should accept the claims of those in the wrong or agree with them. Likewise, defendants should not rely on clever stratagems to intimidate the thoughtless or inexperienced (*mutenin*); nor should ignorant families (*mōsai*) who have justice (*dōri*) on their side be unable to properly plead [their case in court]. We would be wrong and in violation of the principles of this Constitution (*kenpō*) if we did not carefully distinguish (*ryōken*) between the injustice of the intelligent and the justice of the ignorant.

Such are the reasons for these articles. If in even a single instance we deviate from, or bend or break, them, may the gods Bonten, Taishaku, the four great Kings of the Sky, and all the gods—great and little, celestial and terrestrial of the sixty odd provinces of Japan (Nihon), and especially the Shiogama *Daimyōjin*[56] this [Nishiyama] **Hachiman *Daibosatsu*,** Marishisonten, and **Temman Daijizai Tenjin**—divinely punish us. So may it be, accordingly, we swear a solemn oath as above.

The fourteenth day of the fourth month of Tenbun 5 (1536)

[Names omitted]

---

56. The reference to the "two avatars (*gongen*) of Izu and Hakone, and the Mishima *Daimyōjin*" found in the 1232 code is omitted.

11. Mōri Motonari Oaths

As the tumultuous sixteenth century progressed, warriors resorted to extreme measures to shore up their authority. The following sequence of documents illustrates how Mōri Motonari (1497–1571)—who, at the time, was serving Ōuchi Yoshitaka (1507–51)—ousted and killed the Inoue, a family he believed was preparing to usurp his house. He alludes to similar turmoil among the Yamana and the Akamatsu, with their retainers the Kakiya and Urakami, and provides a comprehensive list of the Inoue crimes—for which they were killed. An oath solidified this organization in 1550 and was reiterated in 1557 after a similar rebellion led to the destruction of the Ōuchi and paved the way for the Mōri becoming a daimyō *in their own right.*

In the first document, Mōri Motonari writes to Lady Ozaki, wife of his son Mōri Takamoto (1523–63). Lady Ozaki (1527–72) was the daughter of Naitō Okimori (1495–1554), a crucial retainer of the Ōuchi. In this document the term comrades *refers to Mōri Motonari's retainers.*

Mōri Motonari's List of the Inoue Group's Crimes (Mōri Motonari Inoue *shū zaijōsho*)[57]

This document provides an excellent overview of what came to be perceived as being intolerable insubordinate behavior to lords.

To: The Honorable Lady Ozaki, respectfully

[From:] Motonari

For thirty years, since the death of Okimoto, the older brother of Motonari, Inoue Kawachi *no kami* (Motokane) has served our house in the following manner:

During councils or times when consultation was required, he did not attend, even when summoned.

He never served for New Year's ceremonies or other established rites.

Without Motonari's permission, he claimed to be retired and refused to respond to our demands of setting up encampments or dispatching messengers on our behalf. Furthermore, he did not pass his benefice lands (*kyūchi*) to his sons but instead continued to control them. He refused to serve the lord (*kōgi*), claiming he was retired.

---

57. *Dainihon komonjo iewake* 8 *Mōri ke monjo*, vol. 2, doc. 398, 8.4 Mōri Motonari Inoue *shū zaijōsho*, 13–18. Translated by Thomas Conlan with Horikawa Yasufumi.

11. Mōri Motonari Oaths

Concerning *tansen*, *tanbetsu* and other taxes.[58] In spite of orders, he refused to survey and assess taxes on all the lands to be dispatched to Motonari. In addition, comrades (*bōhai*) and others never serve as Mōri messengers. These comrades never urge the Inoue to pay taxes to the Mōri; nor, because of their fear of the Inoue, do they cross the boundaries into their lands.

When asked to construct a castle or ordered to provide various levies (*fushin*), Motokane never served at all.

Although appointed as a representative (*daikan*) to Motonari's lands, Motokane refused to collect taxes on these lands. Instead, he occupied them.

Motokane occupied the lands of our comrades (*bōhai*).

He occupied the fields and paddies of temples and shrines.

Regarding seating arrangements, although Watanabe occupied a higher-ranked seat than Inoue Motokane, Motokane unjustly demanded a higher-ranked seat than Watanabe and, in recent years, forcibly occupied it.

Motokane has his retainers (*uchinomono*) engage in unjustified and unwarranted brawls, and allows them to win with no regard for the merits of the case.

Additional violations of recent years:

A man called Yoshirō, the son of Inoue Yozō *uemon no jō*, pummeled the face of Hikoshichirō, son of Mitsunaga Shirō *uemon no jō*, of our same name.[59] Because Yoshirō beat Hikoshichirō, who wears our Mōri crest, Yōzō *uemon no jō* and his son (Yoshirō) were told to disembowel themselves (*harakiri*).[60] [Mitsunaga] Shirō *uemon no jō*, and his son [Hikoshichirō] were also told to disembowel themselves. This was because in the eyes of Motonari they failed to maintain their honor and retaliate against the Inoue as they were expected to do after taking such a beating. But without considering the merits of the case, all with the same Inoue surname objected to this punishment. So to prevent the fracture of my house, I suspended this punishment. Nevertheless, the Inoue killed Mitsunaga Shirō *uemon no jō*.

A man called Kashiwamura Saburō *hyōe no jō*, stabbed his wife to death and killed a person called Inoue Shin *uemon no jō*, whom he declared to be her lover (*megataki*).[61] But the Inoue said they would retaliate against Kashiwamura since he had not caught the lovers in the act before he killed Shin *uemon no jō* and that, furthermore, Inoue Shin *uemon no jō* had not been the lover of Kashiwamura's wife for

---

58. *Tansen* were provisional taxes levied on lands, in units of *tan*, while *tanbetsu* taxes were based on the size of cultivated areas (*tanbetsu*).

59. They were a branch family of the Mōri.

60. Motonari uses the phrase *harakiri* to describe the act which, in later centuries, would be described as *seppuku*.

61. The literal terms for this was "wife enemy" (*megataki*).

several years.⁶² I, Motonari, had no choice but to banish Kashiwamura Saburō *hyōe no jō* from the Mōri domains so as to maintain peace. Already a certain Zen *saemon no jō*⁶³ had killed the mother of one of Saburō *hyōe no jō*'s children. The right and wrong of this matter should be clear (*zehi ni oyobazu*): the Inoue are evil.⁶⁴

At a market, a merchant affiliated with Inoue Gengorō quarreled with a lowly river person from another area and was killed. At that time, a different river person lived in Inokoda, a place in [Mōri] Takamoto's holdings. This other river person had lived on Takamoto's lands for a long time. Saying that this different river person was allied with beggars from elsewhere,⁶⁵ the Inoue gathered in great numbers and killed him⁶⁶ without even consulting Takamoto. Even if a merchant affiliated with Inoue Gengorō had in fact quarreled with and been killed by a river person from Takamoto's holdings, Takamoto should have been notified first, before the Inoue retaliated. Even worse, the beggar,⁶⁷ who actually fought with and killed Gengorō's merchant, came from somewhere completely different. Claiming that the river person from Inokoda was allied with beggars from elsewhere, the Inoue cut him down just below Takamoto's castle without even a word of consultation. It is a great outrage. The right and wrong of this matter should be clear: the Inoue are evil.

Other general issues:

In recent years, the Inoue attitude has been: because they are allied with the Mōri, Motonari and Takamoto can maintain their houses. At the bottom of their hearts, all those named Inoue, whether young or old, harbor the arrogant thought that it's up to them whether to harm the Mōri or not. It is unbearable that they sometimes say such a thing in public. Much as I hate to make the comparison, these statements are similar to those made by the Kakiya, followers (*miuchi*) of the

---

62. In other words, a husband could kill his wife's lover only if he found the lovers in the act. That was not the case here. The Inoue claim that this murder was unjustified had merit, as a husband only had the right to kill a *megataki* if he caught him in the act. Hence, they demanded retribution against Kashiwamura.

63. A retainer of Inoue Motokane.

64. This document justifying the slaughter of the Inoue ends particular outrages with the phrase *zehi ni oyobazu*, which generally means "nothing could be done," but in this case, the original meaning that there should be no need to distinguish right and wrong—e.g., the merits of the case should be obvious—seems in order. The same phrase connotes two diametrically opposed meanings, which has led to much confusion. For example, the warlord Oda Nobunaga used this very phrase just before his death, leading some to think that he was resigned to his end, while others (correctly in the author's view) saw him as aggressively asserting that he was in the right. By implication, he is meaning that the Inoue are in the wrong.

65. In other words, the beggar who had killed the Inoue merchant.

66. In retaliation.

67. A synonym for "river person."

Yamana and the Urakami of the Akamatsu.[68] The right and wrong of this matter should be clear: the Inoue are evil.

The Inoue make it hard for anyone—even commoners (*tami hyakushō*) and village merchants in the markets—to serve our house without first consulting them.

Within our house, our relatives and others with different names favor those who have connections with the Inoue. Those without such connections are harassed by the Inoue on a variety of pretexts. Hence, among the retainers of the highest status (*bunsai*), only three to five do not have such connections with the Inoue. These facts will be of the greatest consequence in the future.

We are forced to make this statement as a result of the countless unprincipled misdeeds done by the Inoue against us, our relatives, and retainers (*hikan*). Because of all this, we asked our lord (Ōuchi Yoshitaka), through the intermediary Hironaka Takakane, that the Inoue should be wiped out with his help. But our request was not granted because the Hiraga—father and son—took up arms against each other at Kashirazaki. As our enemy, the Amako, was strong in Izumo Province, we first needed to complete these difficult campaigns before again asking our lord to strike the Inoue. Yet again, our request went unfulfilled. So this is not the first time we have asked. Please convey this report to your father Naitō Okimori who will notify the Ōuchi.[69]

The fourth day of the eighth month

Kohara Takanobu Letter[70]

A letter from Kohara Takanobu to his lord, Mōri Takamoto, the eldest son of Motonari. Kohara recounts the death of the Inoue, showing how, having justified this course of action in the previous enumeration of the Inoue crimes, Motonari still had to receive the permission of his lord, Ōuchi Yoshitaka, before killing them.

To: The Honorable Mōri Bitchū *no kami*

Kohara Aki *no kami* Takamoto

The other day I presented your report to our lord Ōuchi Yoshitaka and notified him that the Inoue had all been killed. He said he had no problem with you managing

---

68. The Kakiya rebelled against the Yamana as did the Urakami against their Akamatsu lords.

69. Ōuchi Yoshitaka was the lord of the Mōri. One of his retainers was Naitō Okimori. Okimori's daughter, the Lady Ozaki, was married to Motonari's son Takamoto. She is the intermediary for this communication.

70. *Dainihon komonjo iewake 8 Mōri ke monjo* vol. 2, doc. 400, 7.25 Kohara Takanobu *shojō*, 19–20. Translated by Thomas Conlan with Horikawa Yasufumi.

your lands and followers as you see fit. Accordingly, he dispatched Sugi Shinano *no kami* Takemasa as a messenger to you. Since this messenger was sent to you most suddenly, you must arrange all matters in your domain so that all will settle down soon. Sugi Shinano *no kami* shall inform you of the details, so they are omitted here. Respectfully

Twenty-fifth day of the seventh month (Tenbun 19/1550)   Takanobu (monogram)

To: The Honorable Mōri Bitchū *no kami*

Fukuhara Sadatoshi Oath[71]

An oath signed by Fukuhara Sadatoshi and other retainers. In the aftermath of the Inoue killing, Motonari relied on oaths to solidify ties within his organization.

Clauses stated [to those above]

The Inoue have repeatedly belittled Mōri Motonari and in major and minor affairs acted as they wished. Hence, they were ultimately destroyed. We acknowledge this and hence each of us shall not harbor any traitorous intentions.

From now on, all affairs of the house shall be conducted in accordance with the judgment of the lord. We all fervently believe this. Therefore, in all affairs, we shall do as we are ordered to do. In no way shall we be negligent.

Concerning disputes among comrades (*bōhai*): no one shall say or do anything that violates the judgment or orders of the lord (*tonosama*). As for those who ignore who started a quarrel and aid one of the aggrieved parties, all shall follow the commands of the lord.[72] Relatives of the culprits and those who possess familial or other connections shall not intervene in the dispute or say anything about it. In addition, it is henceforth prohibited for retainers to congregate with weapons and armor at the scene of disputes among retainers.

Concerning warfare (literally, *yumiya* or "bow and arrow"), all shall perform outstanding service (*chūsetsu*) as before.

Regardless of which party is in the right, those who engage in disputes with their comrades shall be admonished by both the lord and their comrades.

---

71. *Dainihon komonjo iewake 8 Mōri ke monjo* vol. 2, doc. 401, 7.20.1550 (Tenbun 19), Fukuhara Sadatoshi *ika kashin rensho kishōmon*, 20–43. Translated by Thomas Conlan with Horikawa Yasufumi.

72. Retainers should not aid a party who started a quarrel without the permission of their lord. Those who initiated violence, in other words, were judged to be invariably in the wrong and should not be supported.

Even when unexpected issues arise among comrades, they shall behave appropriately[73] when discussing matters in front of their lord (the *kōgi*) or at times where guests are present.

Concerning fights: once they erupt, the particulars shall be reported. Those mixed up in them should show restraint and obey the commands of the lord.

Concerning the return (*sata*) of people [who have fled]: it applies for both men and women.[74]

Concerning cows and horses that wander onto the lands of others: even if they eat the harvest of others' holdings, they should be returned to the original owner. If they eat such produce without permission three times, the said horses and cows shall be confiscated.

Mountains shall be shared in common as they have before.

Boundaries shall be established in accordance with the flow of rivers.

Concerning deer. Those that come down into villages from the mountains belong to villages and not people from the mountains. Deer that have been shot but crossed boundaries into other jurisdictions shall be taken by those who shot them.

Wells and irrigation ditches belong to the lord (*uesama*).

Clauses ordered from the lord concerning times of war (literally, "bow and arrow").

Military accouterments. Those who are not wearing them in times of war shall have their holdings confiscated.

Arrows.

Additional clauses concerning rewards.

Concerning those who should be rewarded: if the lord has not praised [e.g., rewarded] them, then an appeal shall be launched by the Council of Elders (*toshiyorishū*).

Be prepared for war [literally, times of movement] at all times and respond to orders of mobilization immediately.

Regarding messengers, the same as above.

From now on, those who disobey the above clauses shall be punished [by the lord]. It is fitting then that if we state a lie, the heavenly punishment of Bonten, Taishaku, the Four Heavenly Kings, all of the Great, Middling, and Small Gods throughout the sixty-six provinces of Japan—particularly both Gods (*Daimyōjin*) of Itsukushima, the Ox head Heavenly King of Gion, Hachiman *Daibōsatsu*, the

---

73. And not show their rancor or anger.

74. Often the return of these people, or the dispensation of their abandoned belongings became a source of conflict. This passage is written quite tersely, as the fact that people fled is not mentioned directly. The clause literally reads: "Concerning the distribution of people: both men and women." Most of the later clauses are similarly laconic.

gods of Daiji Zaiten, and various attached gods—shall fall on the bodies of each of us. This oath is such.

The twentieth day of the seventh month of the nineteenth year of Tenbun (1550)

Fukuhara *sakon no suke* Sadatoshi   (monogram)

[The following 237 names are omitted.]

OATH BY FUKUHARA SADATOSHI ET AL.[75]

An oath signed by Fukuhara Sadatoshi and other retainers, written in the aftermath of the destruction of the Ōuchi. In the ensuing chaos, still more oaths were required to keep the Mōri organization intact and ensure compliance to their orders. The strengthening of command authority represents one of the most notable transformations of this time.

The lord's order shall be known by all and spoken by each.

Military forces of this house have continued, unceasingly, to commit outrages, in spite of their prohibition. Therefore, henceforth, those who commit outrages, regardless of their identity or connections, shall be cut down immediately.

From now on, it is unlikely that the lord will order military encampments to be destroyed.[76] The lord shall punish those who ignore this order in the same manner as those mentioned above; they shall be cut down.[77] Orders are most important. Hence, from now all shall sign their names and take this oath. Hachiman *Daibosatsu* and the Itsukushima *Daimyōjin* shall view these words. Thus, this oath is such.

The second day of the twelfth month of the third year of Kōji (1557)

Fukuhara *sakon no suke* (monogram)

The following 240 names omitted

---

75. *Dainihon komonjo iewake 8 Mōri ke monjo* vol. 2, doc. 402, 12.2.1557 (Kōji 3), Fukuhara Sadatoshi *ika kashin rensho kishōmon*, 43–62. Translated by Thomas Conlan with Horikawa Yasufumi.
76. The exact meaning of this is not clear. Often this term refers to abandoning encampments. It is clearly something negative, but whether it refers to the abandonment or destruction of a military encampment, or some other outrage of depredation committed in camp, is not clear.
77. Killed.

SECTION IX
The First European Encounter (1543–87)

Early interactions between the Portuguese, who landed in the country in 1543, and the Japanese were fraught. The gap in understanding between the Portuguese and the Japanese is amply evident in this section's first document, in which Ōuchi Yoshinaga (?–1557) sets aside land for the construction of a Portuguese church. The Japanese text of this commendation reveals that the Ōuchi perceived these newcomers as being reformist Buddhist monks, while the Portuguese believed they were receiving a permanent land grant for their church. But the church was destroyed in 1557 when the Ōuchi fell from power.

The Portuguese brought cannons and gunpowder to Japan. Ōtomo Sōrin (1530–87), a *daimyō* who converted to Christianity, received both cannons and gunpowder recipes from the Portuguese; the latter were quickly disseminated through Japan.

1. Ōuchi Yoshinaga's Commendation[1]

Ōuchi Yoshinaga permitted Cosme de Torres (1510–70) to establish a Christian church in Yamaguchi. Yoshinaga saw the early Portuguese as Buddhist monks from the west, a mix-up possibly caused by the fact that the Portuguese had traveled to Japan from Goa, India. Comparison of the two texts here reveals the gulf in understanding between the Japanese and the Portuguese regarding their diplomatic documents.

Monks from the western regions who came to Japan[2] desiring to revitalize the Buddhist Law wish to build the Temple of the Great Way (Daidōji) in Yamaguchi

---

1. *Nihon kankei kaigai shiryō Iezusukai Nihon shokanshū yakubun hen* 2.2, 207–8 for the 8.28.1552 (Tenbun 21), Ōuchi Haruhide *saikyōjō*. For the original and a facsimile, see *Nihon kankei kaigai shiryō Iezusukai Nihon shokanshū genbun hen* 2 (1996), "Appendix 2" pp. 329–30. This document was originally published in a collection of letters in *Coimbra* in 1570, although the editors thought that the document came from Ōtomo Sōrin. For these insights I am indebted to Patrick Schwemmer. The Japanese was translated by Thomas Conlan, while the Portuguese version was translated and analyzed by Patrick Schwemmer.
2. Literally, "came to the court" (*raichō*), an alternate way to describe Japan.

county (*agata*) Yoshiki district of Suō Province. In accordance with their request, permission is granted thus.

Twenty-eighth day of the eighth month of the twenty-first year of Tenbun (1552)

Suō *no suke* (*gohan*)³

To: The Head of This Temple

2. Portuguese Translation of Ōuchi Yoshinaga's Commendation

> *This document, translated from Portuguese, was published in a collection of letters printed in Coimbra in 1570. In addition to the translation, a facsimile of the Japanese document was reproduced as well. The editors are under the impression that the donor of the Yamaguchi lands was Ōtomo Sōrin, who later converted to Christianity and adopted the name Francisco. That introduction states:*
>
> *"Other than the [land] rent and fields of which the above letters tell— which the King of Bungo gave to the priests in order that they might make churches in the Hakata and Bungo—he gave them another sixty leagues of Bungo in the city of [Y]amaguchi. The donation is put here so that their writings, permits, and script may be seen. And each of these figures means what comes above it." In addition to confusing Ōuchi Yoshinaga with Ōtomo Sōrin, this document claims that the Ōtomo (Ōuchi) exercised authority over all of Japan.*

Donation which the Duke of Bungo and Japan made of a field to the Priests of the Company of Bu [Ya]maguchi

The Duke of the Kingdom of Suō, of the Kingdom of Nagato, of the Kingdom of Buzen, of the Kingdom of Chikuzen and Aki, of the Kingdom of Iwami, of the Kingdom of Bingo, [and] of the Kingdom of Bitchū, concedes Daidōjio⁴ (i.e., Great Way of Heaven) to the Priests of the Occident, who have come to preach a law for making Saints, according to his will, until the end of the world, which is

---

3. Ōuchi Yoshinaga, who took over for Ōuchi Yoshitaka after the coup of the previous year.

4. The manuscript seems to have a capital letter O written and then crossed out. Coimbra 1570 transcribes this as a small e, yielding *Daydogie* (f. 161v), and Évora 1598 apparently corrupts this further to *Daydoige* and scrambles it in with the translation of the name (vol. 1, f. 61r). Translated and analyzed by Patrick Schwemmer.

a plain which is behind [Y]amaguchi, a great city,[5] with privileges, which no one may be killed nor captured in it, and in order that it may be clear to my successors I give them this patent so that at no time may they be able to take them out of this [temple].

The King who now governs the reign of Tembun, year 21, in the eighth month, the twenty-eighth day.

the name   sign

The Duke Daidiki Bosatsu [J. seal]

of the monastery, the Priest who resides in it.[6]

3. Letter by Ōtomo Sōrin[7]

Ōtomo Sōrin wrote and cosigned (along with his heir Yoshimune) this document in 1580, following the rebellion of Tabaru Chikatsura, the head of a different branch of the family. Tabaru Chikatsura revolted after the disastrous battle of Mimigawa, where his forces were devastated by those of the Shimazu. Following Chikatsura's rebellion, Sōrin named one of his sons, Chikaie, at the request of the Tabaru family. Although Sōrin initials this document "FRCO"—for "Francisco"—he signs it using Ensai, his Buddhist name. Sōrin's FRCO seal, rarely used on documents, appears on a saddle and a cannon constructed for his use.

Tabaru *uma no kami* Chikatsura's treachery (*gyakushin*), planned at this time, is unheard of. Words fail me. Nevertheless, the retainers of the Tabaru (*kachū*) were

---

5. A mark made between *grande* and *çidade* and then crossed out, together with the corrections *Bu Manguchi* and *Daydogi O* above, suggests that this is the original manuscript written from dictation in Yamaguchi, presumably on a copy of the document with the seal impression (*go-in*).

6. In the scribe's apparent zeal to preserve the word order of the original, the grammar has become convoluted, but the priest of the monastery is presumably being listed as the party to whom the donation of "Duke Daidiki" is addressed.

7. Ōita ken kyōiku bunka ka, comp., *Ōtomo Sōrin shiryōshū*, vol. 5 (Ōita kyōiku iinkai, 1994), doc. 1744, 2.12 [(Tenshō 8/1579)] Ōtomo Yoshimune Ensai *renshojō*, 99–100. Translated by Thomas Conlan with Horikawa Yasufumi.

united with appropriate judgments (*junro no kakugo*) and defeated Chikatsura's evil bands (*akutō*) and the Nyohōji rebels.[8]

Concerning the head (*katoku*) of the house of Tabaru: they[9] petitioned (*konmō*) us that it will be most appropriate (*kan'yō*) to name [Sōrin's second son] Chikaie as my successor. Therefore, we[10] accept (*ryōsho*) and order Chikaie to become the Tabaru heir in the district. If *Uma no kami*'s evil bands happen to flee to your region, coordinate with people of the district to ensure the bandits will be killed so that they cannot flee anymore. The performance of such service is most important right now. The Shibata *jiuemon* novice (*nyūdō*) shall explain to you the particulars of what we have discussed with Chikaie. Respectfully.

The twelfth day of the second month (Tenshō 8/1580)

[Ōtomo] Yoshimune [monogram]

Ensai (Ōtomo Sōrin) FRCO monogram

To: The Honorable Kōshita *kamon no suke*

4. Photo of Ōtomo Francisco (Sōrin) Saddle with FRCO Monogram

The Japanese warlord Ōtomo Sōrin converted to Christianity in 1578 and took the name Ōtomo Francisco. From the years 1578 through 1580 he used the initials FRCO in his documents (they represented his new name **FR**ansi**CO**) *and had it prominently added to his saddle and cannon. From the cannon it is impossible to distinguish the F, which is superimposed on the letter R, but the seal on his saddle shows the distinct F and R (see below). The diamond shape in the middle of the letter may be the F, as an R would not normally have this shape in the middle of the letter. Ōtomo Francisco's FRCO monogram prominently appears on two artifacts, a saddle and a cannon. His saddle was made of lacquered wood, with his name inlaid in gold.*

---

8. Nyohōji was another name for the Irie, a collateral line of the Tabaru.
9. The retainers of the Tabaru.
10. Sōrin and his son Yoshimune.

5. Photos of Ōtomo Francisco Cannon with FRCO Monogram

An image of Ōtomo Sōrin's saddle. The monogram on the saddle—FRCO—represents "Francisco," the Christian name that Sōrin adopted following his conversion.

5. Photos of Ōtomo Francisco Cannon with FRCO Monogram

This breech-loading cannon, a rare surviving example, dates from the latter half of the sixteenth century. It was created in the Portuguese colonies in the late sixteenth century. It is a three-pound (79 mm) cannon, with a total length of 268 cm. This cannon was cast by the Portuguese for their Japanese ally Francisco (Sōrin), who died of illness in 1587. His heir Yoshimune (d. 1610) sided with Hideyoshi's supporters against those of Tokugawa Ieyasu. The Ōtomo were divested of most of their lands, and it seems likely that sometime, either after the battle of Sekigahara in 1600, or the destruction of Hideyoshi's castle in 1615, the Tokugawa seized their cannon.

We know that the Tokugawa moved this cannon to defend the Kurile Islands against Russian incursions. Lt. Nikolai Aleksandrovich Khvostov (1776–1809) commanded the Juno for an expedition led by N. P. Rezanov (1764–1807). *In retaliation for the Japanese refusal to establish relations with Russia, Khvostov landed at Shana on Iturup (Etorofu) (Syano) and captured several pieces of ordinance. This cannon was donated to the St. Petersburg Military-Historical Museum by the Russian-American Company, founded by Rezanov, in 1822.*[11]

---

11. Explanation courtesy Dr. Sergei Efimov, the deputy director of the Military-Historical Museum of Artillery, Engineering, and Communications Forces.

Section IX • The First European Encounter

Images of Ōtomo Sōrin's cannon, featuring his FRCO monograph. The Portuguese, who manufactured this cannon, gave it to Sōrin after he lost his first cannon in battle.

6. The Dissemination of Guns: The Example of the Takeda

The following two documents are Takeda mobilization rosters dating from 1562 (Eiroku 5). They are called "vermillion seal" documents, a specific genre, because the document was stamped with the seal of the daimyō *but not signed by him. Of the warriors mentioned here, two-thirds (60 out of 90) have pikes; 4 others have spears. Only 10 bows and 2 marksmen are requested—even though the 5 horse riders most likely relied on bows as well. Still, the impact of guns remained quite limited. The Takeda had more bannermen than arquebusiers.*

Vermillion Seal Document of the Takeda House I[12]

[Seal] Regulation

The accoutrements of forty-five people.

Pikes (*yari*): 30.[13] Nevertheless, of this number, five are present in the headquarters and are hereby exempt.

Bows: 5.

Short pikes (*mochi-yari*): 2.[14]

Gun (*teppō*): 1.

Helmet bearer (*kabuto mochi*): 1.

Bannerman (*kohata mochi*): 1.

Battle flag holder (*sashimono mochi*): 1.

Without anything: 4.

In total, forty-five people.

The aforementioned people are to be mobilized thus and shall perform military service. Thus.

The tenth day of the tenth month (*mizunoeinu*) [(1562/Eiroku 5)]

To: The Honorable Ōi *sama no jō*

---

12. *Sengoku ibun Takeda hen*, vol. 1, doc. 803, 10.10 Takeda ke *shuinjō utsushi*, 286–87. Translated by Thomas Conlan with Horikawa Yasufumi.

13. These were 18 feet (3 *ken* in length).

14. These were 12 feet (2 *ken* in length).

Section IX • *The First European Encounter*

Vermillion Seal Document of the Takeda House 2[15]

[Seal] Regulation

Forty-five people, with accoutrements for forty.

Regarding the latter:

Short pikes (*mochi-dōgu*): 2.

Bows: 5.

Gun (*teppō*): 1.

Bannerman (*kohata mochi*): 1.

Horse riders: 5.

Long-handled weapons [pikes] (*nagae*): 31.[16] Nevertheless, of this number, five are in service at the Provincial Headquarters and are hereby exempt.

Thus.

The aforementioned people are to be mobilized thus and shall perform military service. Thus.

The nineteenth day of the tenth month (*mizunoeinu*) [(1562/Eiroku 5)]

To: The Honorable Ōi *sama no jō*

Excerpts from the Vermillion Seal Document from Takeda Katsuyori[17]

Excerpts from a document sent by Takeda Katsuyori (1546–82) to one of his followers, Koizumi Masamune, revealing a change in military organization after the debacle of the Battle of Nagashino. The document dates from 12.16.1575 (Tenshō 3)

Item (10). Since guns (*teppō*) are currently most important, we will start to limit the number of warriors mobilized with long-handled weapons (*nagae*). Bringing guns to a battle will be considered outstanding military service. We will determine the

---

15. *Sengoku ibun Takeda hen*, vol. 1, doc. 804, 10.19 Takeda ke *shuinjō utsushi*, 287. Translated by Thomas Conlan with Horikawa Yasufumi.

16. *Nagae*. Weapons with long handles. Pikes. In Takeda Katsuyori's 1575 document, the two are translated interchangeably.

17. *Sengoku ibun Takeda hen*, vol. 4, doc. 2555, 12.16.1575 (Tenshō 3), Takeda ke *shuinjō utsushi*, 45–46. Translated by Thomas Conlan with Horikawa Yasufumi.

number of guns required after we have investigated the number of pikemen requisitioned in mobilization rosters.[18]

Item (11). No one should bring bows and guns unless they have been trained to use them. In the future, we will be checking within the camps to see who has been trained to use bows and guns and who has not. If we find untrained warriors with bows and guns, their commanders shall be punished.

Item (12). The handles for *nagae* and handheld spears shall be made of wood or rattan (*uchie*). Currently the shafts of these long-handled weapons are of extremely poor quality. From now on, pay attention and prepare only high-quality shafts.

Item (13). Please be consistent in your preparation and use of battle flags so it will be obvious which units are brave or cowardly on the battlefield. It is up to you to decide which crest you use on these battle flags or banners.

Item (15). Battle flags and banners should be made anew.

Item (16). Regardless of rank, those men who prepare a surplus of bullets and gunpowder will be providing great military service.

7. Portuguese Recipe for Gunpowder, Given by Ashikaga Yoshiteru to the *Daimyō* Uesugi Kenshin in 1559[19]

After receiving a gunpowder recipe from Ōtomo Sōrin, Ashikaga Yoshiteru (1536–65) transmitted it to allies such as Nagao Kenshin (1530–78) (who later adopted the name of Uesugi to become Uesugi Kenshin). Strangely, the document from Yoshiteru was carefully sealed, though the gunpowder recipe was visible to all. This recipe reveals that creating a proper gunpowder slurry mattered as much, if not more, than the guns themselves.

---

18. Mobilization rosters, such as the first two documents in "The Dissemination of Guns," translated above. Katsuyori suggests that guns should be levied in proportion to the number of pikes mobilized.

19. These documents were translated by the students in *Sources in Ancient and Medieval Japanese History* with Thomas Conlan. Claire Cooper translated the three documents under "Portuguese Recipe for Gunpowder," while Kyle Bond translated the gunpowder recipe itself. For the documents, see http://komonjo.princeton.edu/uesugi/. Accessed August 27, 2021.

Section IX • The First European Encounter

An Official Letter (GONAISHO) from Ashikaga Yoshiteru

You have been at Sakamoto for quite some time. How has your boil been?

I am concerned, and thus have dispatched *Saemon no suke* Harumitsu. He shall speak to you in further detail.

The twenty-ninth day of the sixth month [(1559/Eiroku 2)]

[Monogram of Ashikaga Yoshiteru]

To: The Honorable Censor (*danjō shōhitsu*) Nagao

A Letter (SHOJŌ) from Ōdachi Harumitsu

Saemon no suke has been dispatched to inquire about the state of your boil.

Recently Ōtomo Shintarō [Sōrin] presented [Ashikaga Yoshiteru] with a scroll on gunpowder.

Please deign to have a look at it; this is a great honor.

As for further thoughts from the *Shōgun*, Teruuji shall speak to you in detail.

Respectfully yours,

The twenty-ninth day of the sixth month [(1559/Eiroku 2)]

[Monogram of Ashikaga Yoshiteru]

To: The Honorable Censor (*danjō shōhitsu*) Nagao

A Gunpowder Recipe (TEPPŌ YAKU NO KATA NARABINI CHŌGŌ SHIDAI)

> *This sophisticated gunpowder recipe was transmitted by the Portuguese to Ōtomo Sōrin, who in turn informed Ashikaga Yoshiteru, who then passed it along to Uesugi Kenshin. In contrast to the previous documents, which were secret in that they could only be opened by Kenshin, this recipe was not protected.*
>
> *The composition of gunpowder determined the power of an explosion and the distance a bullet could be fired. Potassium nitrate, or saltpeter, provided the explosive potential, while sulfur lowered the ignition temperature, and carbon bound the other two ingredients. The ideal ratio of gunpowder was ultimately determined by the German general staff in the nineteenth century to be a ratio of 74 parts saltpeter (potassium nitrate), 12 parts sulfur, and 13 parts coal. The following recipe approaches that ratio. It contains two options: either*

7. Portuguese Recipe for Gunpowder, Given by Ashikaga Yoshiteru

80 parts saltpeter, 12 parts sulfur, and 8 parts coal, or 77 parts saltpeter, 13 parts sulfur, and 10 parts coal—the latter of which closely approximates the ideal ratio. It also describes how to heat and mix the ingredients into a slurry which, when dried, was more effective than a simple mixture of ground sulfur, coal, and potassium nitrate powders. After receiving this recipe, Kenshin engaged in a series of attacks on his rivals. He occupied Kamakura in 1560–61 and used guns effectively at the battle of Kawanakajima in 1562.

Gunpower recipe

Potassium nitrate	2 *ryō*, 2 *bu* (93.75 g)
Charcoal	1 *bu*, 2 *shu* (12.5 g)
Sulfur	1 *bu* (9.37 g)
Or	
Potassium nitrate	1 *ryō*, 2 *bu* (56.25 g)
Charcoal	1 *bu* (9.375 g)
Sulfur	3 *shu* (4.6875 g)

All of the highest quality

Among the Evergreens (*hainoki*) used for making charcoal, the Kawara yellow catalpa [*kisasage, Catalpa ovata*] or the Japanese Sumac (*katsuki, Rhus javanica*) are suitable. It is not good for the wood to be too dried out. Forty to fifty days of drying is about right. Longer than that will result in the wood splitting apart. Old trees are not good. However, if the tree is a new sprout from an old stump, even an old tree is no problem. Cut the wood for charcoal at about 30 cm. Make sure you remove the bark. Remove the inner core, then dry the wood for a day. Since the summer sun is strong, the wood should be well dried in 10, 14, or 15 days. However, if you dry the wood in excess of 20 days, you should dry it in the shade. Next is the roasting of the wood. Dig a hole about two feet deep and cover the bottom with about five inches of cut straw. Pack the wood on top of the straw and light it from below. When the wood starts to burn, keep putting straw on top of the wood to keep the fire from dying down. Smoke should not rise from the bottom if the wood is burning well. When the smoke stops rising, flip over a bucket and, using it as a lid, steam the pieces of wood. When they turn to charcoal, pour hot water on them and let them boil a good amount. Then take them out and roast them. When they dry, they are ready for concoction. This is how to make the charcoal for the best powder. But not all charcoal needs to be done this way. You can abbreviate steps to make a lower grade of powder.

To cook the potassium nitrate, add 9 *tenmoku* [1.8 l] of water to 1 *kin* [about 600 g] of potassium nitrate. Remove an appropriate amount of wood from the fire commensurate with the amount of water added so that it will not overflow. Reduce the slurry down to a third of the original amount. Then put it in a bucket one foot [30 cm] in diameter and store it away. Do not check it for one whole day. Check the mixture the following day, then put the top layer of liquid into a separate bucket. For about a day, dry the potassium nitrate that has congealed on the bottom and then scrape it with a spatula, dry it thoroughly again, and reduce the liquid content to half its original volume. When it cooks down, add one *tenmoku* of water and let it come to a rolling boil again. Then as before, let it cool in a separate bucket. Repeat the process as before: remove the top liquids, dry the bottom solids, repeat. Use a bright yellow sulfur. Green sulfur is not good. If sand and other impurities are mixed with the slurry, scrape them off with a small blade. For a good mixture, it is not a problem to have crumbly, clumpy sulfur so long as the color is good. But firm sulfur is even better. Grind the charcoal, the potassium nitrate, and the sulfur on a mortar. If ash starts to fly up, whisk in some water without soaking the gunpowder. Mix it until you cannot see the sulfur. Then put a bit of the powder on a table and ignite it. If there is no trace of powder remaining after the reaction, then wrap the powder in paper. Additionally, wrap it in three layers of cloth. Seal it up well, place it on a board, and use your feet to pack it together so it becomes firm. Then cut it up finely. Under no circumstances should you light any fires or have open flames at the site producing the powder. If a fire breaks out, it will cause a catastrophe. Even when lighting the powder to test it, be sure there is no other powder nearby. Extra powder should be stored separately. Fire can ignite powder even at a distance of 2 to 3 yards [3.6 m to 4.4 m]. You must be careful. Though these instructions might lead you to believe the process of making powder takes a long time, it actually takes no time at all once you get used to it. Even when you need to make about 5 or 6 *kin*, use the ratios as stated above. Roughly grind the three ingredients together in the mortar [*yagen*]; then blend them together in a stone mortar like a medicine mortar [*yakuusu*]. When the ingredients have been ground to a fine grain powder, pack it into bamboo cylinders and, once the mixture has hardened, split open the bamboo and cut the powder. All the details not recorded here will be transmitted orally by Kashii.

Respectfully

Twenty-ninth day of the sixth month of the second year of Eiroku (1559)

SECTION X

The Late Sixteenth- and Early Seventeenth-Century Transformations: The Creation of the "*Samurai*" (1575–1691)

The first document in this section is an account of the 1575 battle of Nagashino. During this battle, Oda Nobunaga—a powerful *daimyō* attempting to reestablish order in central Japan—defeated his rivals using guns effectively in battle. Also included here is the law code of Chōsokabe (Chōsogabe) Motochika and an account of Fukutomi Han'emon, a Chōsokabe warrior who fought in Korea and the battle of Sekigahara in 1600. At the core of this section are the documents, issued by Toyotomi Hideyoshi and Tokugawa Ieyasu, which essentially established the samurai order. Here, too, are documents pertaining to Hideyoshi's brutal invasion of Korea. Finally, the laws and regulations of the Tokugawa regime are provided. Ieyasu so desired the position of *Sei-i-tai shōgun* that he changed his clan name from Fujiwara to Minamoto, so as to claim that he, too, was in accord with the Minamoto right to rule, established at the time of the Ashikaga. Codes from 1615 and 1635 are translated as well.

1. Ōta Gyūichi, *The Chronicle of Lord Nobunaga* (1610)[1]

Ōta Gyūichi wrote his famous Chronicle of Lord Nobunaga *in 1610. The earliest passages are anachronistic, but otherwise this is an invaluable account of Nobunaga. Here, Gyūichi recounts Nobunaga drinking from the skulls of his enemies before describing the 1575 battle of Nagashino, a decisive victory over the forces of Takeda Katsuyori. The battle is famous for the impact of guns on the battlefield, an understanding drawn from Gyūichi's account.*

---

1. Elisonas and Lamers, trans. *The Chronicle of Lord Nobunaga*, 204, 222, 224–27.

Book VII

Ōta Izumi no Kami composed this.
Tenshō 2 [1574], the Year of Wood Senior and the Dog.

1

On the first day of the First Month, everybody who was anybody in Kyoto and its neighboring provinces presented himself before Nobunaga in Gifu. They were all invited to participate in a toast according to the *sangon* ceremony. After the outsiders (*takokushū*)[2] had retired and only Nobunaga's horse guards were left,

Some novel, as yet unheard-of appetizers were served at a second banquet:

Item The head of Asakura Sakyō no Daibu Yoshikage.

Item The head of Azai Shimotsuke.

Item The head of Azai Bizen.

These had been taken by Nobunaga the previous year in the North.

The banquet began when the aforesaid three skulls, lacquered and gilt, were brought out on white wooden dinner trays as a relish to the saké. The men made merry, reciting lines from plays and disporting themselves in general. Nobunaga was in unbounded, limitless high spirits. He was exhilarated.

Book VIII

Ōta Izumi no Kami composed this.
Tenshō 3 [1575], the Year of Wood Junior and the Boar.

On the thirteenth day of the fifth month, Nobunaga and his son and heir Kankurō took the field with the objective of relieving Nagashino in Mikawa Province by striking at the rear [of Takeda Katsuyori's army].[3]

That day they encamped in Atsuta. Observing that the Hakkengū, an associate shrine of the Atsuta Jingū, was so dilapidated that it had lost its essential character, Nobunaga ordered his chief carpenter Okabe Mataemon to take charge of its reconstruction.

---

2. The term *takokushū*, literally "those from other provinces," in principle, denotes *samurai* who had subjected themselves in vassalage to Nobunaga after his march on Kyoto, as opposed to men from Owari and Mino provinces, who formed the inner core of his vassal group.

3. The site of Nagashino Castle is found in what now is Ichiba, Nagashino, Shinshiro City, Aichi Prefecture. Takeda Katsuyori had encircled the fortress by 5/11.

1. Ōta Gyūichi, The Chronicle of Lord Nobunaga

On the fourteenth day of the fifth month, Nobunaga and Kankurō reached Okazaki and pitched camp. The next day they sojourned there. On the sixteenth they stayed in Ushikubo Castle. Leaving Marumo Hyōgo no Kami and Fukuda Mikawa no Kami on guard in that fort, on the seventeenth they set up a field camp in Nodahara. On the eighteenth they pressed on to the village of Shitara. Nobunaga pitched camp there on Mount Gokurakuji while Kankurō encamped on Mount Niimidō.[4]

Topographically the village of Shitara was a great hollow into which Nobunaga conducted his army of thirty thousand gradually, in such a way that the enemy could not observe them. The position at the forefront is the privilege of the local samurai and was accordingly taken up by Ieyasu, who encamped on the heights of Koromitsu, on Takamatsuyama. Takikawa Sakon, Hashiba Tōkichirō, and Niwa Gorōzaemon likewise advanced up the slope toward Arumihara and deployed facing east, confronting Takeda Shirō. A palisade for repelling cavalry was erected in front of Ieyasu's and Takikawa's positions.

On the left of the field called Arumihara, great peaks stretched westward from Mount Hōraiji; on the right, wild mountains continued from Mount Tobinosu to the west. On the [southern] flank flowed the Norimoto River, winding its way along the mountainsides. The distance between the mountains on the north and south could not have been any more than thirty *chō* [3.25 km]. The Takisawa River flowed north to south from the foot of Mount Hōraiji to its confluence with the Norimoto River. Nagashino was on flat ground bordered by these two rivers on the south and west.[5]

Had Takeda Shirō chosen to go up Mount Tobinosu and occupy a position there, with a river in front of him, nothing could have been done about it. What he did, however, was dispose a siege force under seven commanders against Nagashino,

---

4. Ushikubo now is a township of Toyokawa City, Aichi Prefecture. Nodahara evidently indicates a field outside Noda Castle, which was located in what now is Toyoshima, Shinshiro City, about eleven kilometers to the southwest of Nagashino Castle. Shitara refers to the vicinity of Hirai and Kami Hirai, Shinshiro City. The Gokurakuji site lies about five kilometers to the west of the site of Nagashino Castle.

5. The stream that flows on the south of Arumihara from east to west, then known as the Norimoto River, now is called the Toyokawa. The Takisawa River now is called the Kansagawa and considered to be the headwaters of the Toyokawa. Accordingly, the Arumihara battlefield can be defined in present-day terms as the open space that extended to the north of the Toyokawa and the west of the Kansagawa. The river now called the Uregawa, which joins the Kansagawa immediately below the site of Nagashino Castle, was formerly also known by the name Norimotogawa but no longer is; in short, that name has gone out of use entirely. Mount Tobinosu, 150 meters high, is situated in the Norimoto area of Shinshiro City, about eight hundred meters as the kite flies to the southeast of the Nagashino Castle site, on the opposite side of the Uregawa. Mount Hōraiji, 695 meters high, is situated in the Kadoya area of Shinshiro City, about twelve kilometers to the northeast of the castle site.

Section X • *The Late Sixteenth- and Early Seventeenth-Century Transformations*

cross the Takisawa River, step forward into Arumihara, advance about thirty *chō*, and deploy with a valley in front of him. His army of some fifteen thousand consisted of men from Kai and Shinano, the troop of Obata [Shigesada] from western Kōzuke,[6] and warrior bands from Suruga and Tōtōmi, reinforced by soldiers from Tsukude, Damine, and Busechi in Mikawa.[7] Takeda Shirō moved these troops into thirteen positions for battle, facing west. About twenty *chō* [2,180 meters] separated the two opposing camps.

"That he should bring his troops up this close," thought Nobunaga, "is a gift from Heaven. I shall kill them all." Pondering how to accomplish that without a single friendly casualty, Nobunaga made his plans. He summoned Sakai Saemon no Jō and appointed him captain over some two thousand men selected from Ieyasu's army, skilled archers and harquebusiers. These were augmented by a detachment of Nobunaga's own horse guards and five hundred harquebusiers, and accompanied by Kanamori Gorōhachi [Nagachika], Satō Rokuzaemon, Aoyama Shinshichi and his son, and Katō Ichizaemon [Kagemochi] in the capacity of inspectors. In all, this force consisted of about four thousand men. On the twentieth of the fifth month, at the Hour of the Dog [around 8 p.m.], they crossed the Norimoto River, took the roundabout way through the overgrown mountains on the south, and[8]

On the twenty-first of the fifth month, at the Hour of the Dragon [around 8 a.m.],[9] climbed up Mount Tobinosu above Nagashino and planted their flags there. Raising the battle cry and firing their several hundred harquebuses all at once, they drove away the Takeda siege force, entered Nagashino Castle, linked up with the castle's garrison, and burnt the enemy's hutment. Now that those entrenched in the castle had gained such a swift victory, something the siege force under its seven commanders had never expected, that force fell apart and fled in confusion toward Hōraiji.

Nobunaga went up Takamatsuyama, a low hill located in Ieyasu's camp, to observe the enemy's maneuvers. Having given strict instructions beforehand that action only be initiated on the receipt of orders from him, and having assigned Sassa Kura no Suke, Maeda Matazaemon, Nonomura Sanjūrō [Masanari], Fukuzumi Heizaemon, and Ban Kurōzaemon as his commissioners in charge of about one

---

6. Obata Shigesada was the castellan of Kunimine, located in what now is Kunimine, Kanra Township, Gunma Prefecture.

7. Tsukude is a large, mountainous area that occupies much of the western part of what now is Shinshiro City; Damine now is part of Shitara Township of Aichi Prefecture; and Busechi was located in the area of what now are Busetsu and Inabu townships of Toyota City.

8. The text breaks here. [TDC]

9. Subject of this sentence is missing. [TDC]

1. Ōta Gyūichi, The Chronicle of Lord Nobunaga

thousand harquebusiers, Nobunaga now gave the order for his light infantry to occupy their forward positions close to the enemy lines and watched as they did so. Finding himself under attack from both front and rear, Katsuyori sent his men forward. His first assault wave was led by Yamagata Saburōbyōe [Masakage]. To the beat of their war drums, the Takeda men came charging. Blasted by ferocious gunfire, they withdrew, only to be replaced by the second wave, led by Shōyōken.[10] Shōyōken's men attacked, fell back, pushed forward again; and the harquebuses riddled their ranks, just as Nobunaga had ordered. When more than half of them had been hit, they retreated, but were replaced by the third assault wave— Obata's troop from western Kōzuke, who wore red battle dress. Warriors of the Kantō are skilled horsemen, and these samurai were no exception. Their tactic was to ride their horses straight into the enemy midst. To the beat of their war drums, they came charging. But Nobunaga's men, deployed behind board screens, waited with their harquebuses. More than half of Obata's warriors were felled by the gunfire, and then the degraded force withdrew from the battlefield. The fourth assault wave was Tenkyū's battle group, samurai dressed in black.[11] Thus one enemy unit relieved another, but not even one of Nobunaga's commanders had his troops venture forward of their lines. Nobunaga simply put more harquebuses to work, letting his light infantry deal with everything. So Tenkyū's men, too, were shot down and ground up until they retreated. The fifth wave was led by Baba Mino no Kami [Nobufusa]. To the beat of their war drums, they came charging. But Nobunaga's men were at their posts, and Baba's formation, too, was shot to pieces and retreated just like the rest.

The battle raged from sunrise of the twenty-first of the fifth month to the Hour of the Sheep [around 2 p.m.], the action bearing East by Northeast. The Takeda army attacked in relays, but its soldiers kept being shot down, and its manpower gradually drained away to nothing. Whoever survived gathered around the flag of Takeda Shirō, who realized that the situation was hopeless. All as one tried to flee in the direction of Hōraiji. Now Nobunaga's army broke ranks and set off in hot pursuit.

Among the heads taken, the following were known by sight:

Yamagata Saburōbyōe, Obata from western Kōzuke, Yokota Bitchū, Kawakubo Bingo, Sanada Gentazaemon, Tsuchiya Sōzō, Amari Tōzō, Sugihara Hyūga, Sawa Murinosuke, Nishina, Kōsaka Matahachirō, Okuzu, Okabe, Chikuun, Ekōji, Nezu Jinpei, Tsuchiya Bizen no Kami, Waki Zenbyōe, and Baba Mino no Kami.

---

10. Shōyōken: Takeda Shingen's younger brother Takeda Nobukado (alias Nobutsuna).
11. Tenkyū: Takeda (not Hosokawa) Tenkyū, that is, Nobutoyo, the son of Shingen's younger brother Nobushige.

Among them all, Baba Mino no Kami stood out by his unparalleled bold feats. In addition to these men, about ten thousand Takeda troops, from warriors of standing to common foot soldiers, fell on the field of battle. Countless others either fled into the mountains, to die of starvation, or were cast off bridges into the river, to drown in the water. In his haste to decamp, Takeda Shirō had failed to mount his favorite horse, a steed with an absolutely unequalled reputation for riding easy. Nobunaga had it put in his stable. Then, having issued instructions in regard to Mikawa Province,

On the twenty-fifth of the fifth month Nobunaga returned from this campaign to Gifu in Mino Province.

Exploiting the momentum of this victory, Ieyasu thrust into Suruga, set fires throughout that province, and then returned to base.

Takeda Shirō held on to Takatenjin Castle in Tōtōmi Province, but it was sure to fall in no time at all. The three captains Akiyama [Nobutomo], Ōshima, and Zakōji [Tamekiyo] were entrenched in Iwamura Castle with a force from Kai and Shinano. Kankurō immediately launched an expedition against them and encircled the castle. It was clear that this matter, too, would soon be settled.

Having taken control of the two provinces Mikawa and Tōtōmi, Ieyasu felt happy after years of distress. Things had gone his way. That such a strong enemy should have been destroyed without the friendly side's having been endangered was something unwitnessed in previous ages. Such is the good fortune that befits the prowess of the valiant hero. Just as the bright rays of the sun make the morning dew vanish, so is it true that valor and virtue are like the two wheels of a carriage. Wishing to gain fame in future generations, Ieyasu for years on end made his home in the fields or the mountains and on the shores of the sea. His armor was his pillow. Thus he exerted himself constantly in the pursuit of the profession of Arms. Mere words can never do justice to his labors.

2. Letter by Shimotsuma Rairen[12]

This letter, written by Shimotsuma Rairen, a monk of Negoroji, to the Saika, a group of warriors, reveals the importance of even a small number of gunners in military campaigns. The context is quite complex. Oda Nobunaga fought against, and was defeated by, Uesugi Kenshin and the forces of Honganji in

---

12. *Wakayama kenshi chūei shiryō* vol. 2 (Wakayama 1983) Honganji Saginomori betsuin monjo, doc. 14, 10.11 Shimotsuma Yorikane *shojō*, 427–28. Translated by Thomas Conlan with Horikawa Yasufumi.

2. Letter by Shimotsuma Rairen

Kaga Province. Nobunaga had besieged Honganji's main fortifications at Ishiyama when Matsunaga Hisahide, one of his erstwhile allies, betrayed Nobunaga and returned to his Shigisan castle in Yamato.

On behalf of my lord I am sending this letter by express messenger. When Matsunaga switched from Nobunaga's side to ours,[13] we requested that you send reinforcements and help in Izumi Province. Nevertheless, during this past evening of the tenth, at the hour of the boar [9–11 p.m.],[14] Matsunaga's Shigisan castle fell—a tragedy beyond words—as the result of an unforeseen ruse by Nobunaga. Now we are receiving clear reports that Nobunaga has dispatched his army to our region and our castle at Ishiyama. Please send quickly a force of three hundred gunners (*teppō shū*). My lord is very sorry to be asking again for reinforcements. However, because there are reports that the enemy has already been dispatched to our region, my lord has ordered, in sealed documents, that Nobunaga be punished.[15] It is most important that you gallop forth and aid us.

Next: in response to the fall of Shigisan castle, my lord (Honganji Ren'nyo) will send a fast ship to the Mōri. He will urge them to immediately cross the inland sea and guard the Ishiyama castle so that the rest of our castles will be secured.

In addition, concerning Kaga Province:[16] it has been reported that the army of Nobunaga, our enemy, was defeated following our successful assault on Nanao castle in Noto Province.[17] I am sending two documents: the original report on this as well as an official copy. Please look at these. Finally, Miya Ichibei will explain this more fully. Respectfully.

The eleventh day of the tenth month [(Tenshō 5/1577)]   Rairen (seal)

To: The [Honganji] sub-temple in Saika and its *Sō*[18]

---

13. Matsunaga Hisahide betrayed Nobunaga on 8.17.1577.
14. Depending on the time, between 9 and 11 p.m. or 10 to 12 p.m.
15. Rennyo of Honganji. The reference to a sealed document (*goinpan*) could also potentially refer to a document from the shogun Ashikaga Yoshiaki, who was directing anti-Nobunaga resistance, but the overall context makes the designation of Rennyo more plausible.
16. This refers to the battle of Tedorigawa in Kaga Province on 9.23.1577. During this battle, Uesugi Kenshin, allied with Honganji and Ashikaga Yoshiaki, defeated the armies of the Oda Nobunaga. This happened after the fall of Nanao castle.
17. The battle of Nanao, in Noto, lasted from late in 1576 through the ninth month of 1577, and resulted in the defeat and annihilation of the Noto Hatakeyama.
18. The Saika sub-temples, also known as Saginomori *betsuin*, were where the Saika, a group of local warriors, discussed matters in their executive body, or *sō*.

3. Toyotomi Hideyoshi's Edict Concerning the Collection of Swords (1588)[19]

Hideyoshi's Edict Concerning the Collection of Swords, commonly known as a "sword hunt," the first enacted since the seventh century, established a firm division between agriculturalists and warriors. The term hyakushō, *which previously referred to warriors' retainers, is here used to refer exclusively to agriculturalists; from this point on, the term will be translated as "peasant."*

Clauses:

Item (1). Peasants (*hyakushōra*) of the various provinces are strictly prohibited from possessing swords, short swords (*wakizashi*), bows, pikes, guns (*teppō*), or other types of military weapons.

Needless to say, those who possess unnecessary military weapons and stop paying their annual taxes, disobey officials, and meet in leagues to plot rebellions will be punished.

If such rebellions happen, the harvest from rice paddies and fields of those regions will be ruined and land possession (*chigyō*) will become a heavy burden. It is the responsibility of the provincial lords (*kokushu*), the local representatives (*daikan*) and officials (*kyūnin*) to confiscate the aforementioned weapons and dispatch them here.

Item (2). Confiscated weapons will not be wasted. They will be used to manufacture nails or braces for Hōkōji, with its Great Buddha,[20] currently under planning. Therefore, Hōkōji will aid the future salvation of peasants (*hyakushō*), not to mention improve their current lives.

Item (3). If peasants (*hyakushō*) possess only agricultural tools and devote themselves to cultivation, they and their descendants will live long and peacefully. Because we value the peasants, we are confiscating their weapons. This is the basis for peace in the realm and the happiness of all people. Overseas,[21] Tang Yao[22] was such a god

---

19. *Dainihon komonjo Iewake* 11, *Kobayakawa ke monjo*, vol. 1, doc. 503, Toyotomi Hideyoshi *sadamegaki*, pp. 479–81. See also *Dainihon komonjo iewake* 16 *Shimazu ke monjo*, vol. 1, doc. 353, Toyotomi Hideyoshi *sadamegaki*, 348–49, and vol. 2, doc. 773, Toyotomi Hideyoshi *sadamegaki*, 111–12. Translated by Thomas Conlan with Horikawa Yasufumi.
20. The Cosmic Buddha, Rushana, at Tōdaiji. For more on this, see "Five Swords," particularly swords 3–4.
21. Literally, in foreign courts.
22. Emperor Yao, one of the first rulers of China, who was famed for his benevolent rule, and the fact that he was a simple farmer.

who first pacified the realm, then used his jeweled and sharp swords for agriculture. We do not have such a fine example in the court of Japan. All landholders shall understand and abide by this order. Peasants shall devote themselves to cultivation.

The aforementioned tools should be collected and dispatched here. Do not be negligent.[23]

The eighth day of the seventh month of the sixteenth year of Tenshō (1588)

Hideyoshi [vermillion seal]

4. Toyotomi Hideyoshi's Edict Regarding the Separation of Status (1591)[24]

The following is a famous edict that became the basis for the separation of classes in the later Tokugawa era. Though it was long thought to separate samurai *from peasants, a careful reading of it reveals that it merely prevents warriors of dependent status—whether* samurai, *retainers, or some other kind of lower-ranking followers—from leaving their lord or changing professions.*[25]

A comparison with the previously translated 1536 Date codes shows that many northerners' concerns, such as a lord's claims to his samurai *or other followers, remained in place. A new concern appears to be an increasing interest by lower-ranking individuals, be they peasants or servants of warriors, abandoning agriculture to become wage laborers or merchants. Note the collective punishments.*

Item (1). Now that forces have returned from the campaign in the north (Ōshū) this past seventh month, check to see if any of those servants (*hōkōnin*)—such as *samurai*,[26] middling retainers (*chūgen*), minor followers, or even the lowest-ranking servants—have attempted to change his status, to become either a merchant (*chōnin*) or a peasant (*hyakushō*). The original inhabitants of these regions should investigate

---

23. The final phrase "do not be negligent" appears in the Shimazu versions of this document, but not the Kobayakawa record.

24. *Dainihon komonjo iewake 8, Mōri ke monjo*, vol. 3, doc. 935, Toyotomi Hideyoshi *hatto*, 216–17, *Dainihon komonjo iewake 11, Kobayakawa ke monjo*, vol. 1, doc. 504, Toyotomi Hideyoshi *hatto*, 481–82, and *Dainihon komonjo iewake 2 Asano ke monjo*, doc. 258, Toyotomi Hideyoshi *shūinjō*, 456–57. Translated by Thomas Conlan with Horikawa Yasufumi.

25. This explanation is indebted to Takagi Shōsaku, *Nihon kinsei kokka no kenkyū*, 279.

26. *Samurai* here specifically refers to lower-ranking warriors who served a lord, and not the generic term for warriors it would become in the Tokugawa era (1603–1867).

them and should not shelter such wayward servants. If any inhabitants hide such people, then their whole ward or village will be punished.

Item (2). If in various places, the peasants (*hyakushōra*) abandon their fields in order to take up business or perform wage labor, both wayward peasants and the locals will be punished. It is the responsibility of the local representatives (*daikan*) and officials (*kyūnin*) to investigate and expel anyone who is not a peasant or servant (*hōkōnin*).[27] Should they[28] disobey this law, then they will be recalled; if any townspeople or peasants hide such false people, their whole district or ward will be punished.

Item (3). Do not take, as a servant (*hōkōnin*), any *samurai* or minor follower who left their lord without permission. Guarantors are required to vouch for such servants, and *hōkōnin* should be carefully investigated. If the servant had left an original lord and this person notifies the new lord of this fact, then the servant should be arrested and returned to his original lord. If anyone disobeys this law and lets a wayward servant go, then three people shall be decapitated as compensation for each servant and their heads sent to the original lord. If these three heads are not sent, the right and wrong of the matter will be clear and the [new] lord will be punished.

The aforementioned clauses are hereby established thus.

The twenty-first day of the eighth month of the nineteenth year of Tenshō (1591)

Hideyoshi [vermillion seal]

5. The 100 Article Code of Chōsokabe Motochika[29]

Chōsokabe Motochika put the following law code into effect on 3.24.1597 (Keichō 2), following the land surveys initiated by Toyotomi Hideyoshi. From these laws we can tell that removing warriors from the land enabled daimyō *to exercise more stringent control over their territories. These laws represent an early assertion of what Max Weber—the influential nineteenth-century*

---

27. *Kyūnin* refers to those who were given lands by Hideyoshi, whereas *daikan* were representatives who managed Hideyoshi's lands on his behalf.
28. The *daikan* and the *kyūnin*.
29. Jansen, M. B. "Tosa in the Sixteenth Century: The 100 Article Code of Chōsokabe Motochika," *Oriens Extremus* 10:1 (1963), pp. 95–108. [The works cited in this article are not listed in the bibliography. TDC]

5. The 100 Article Code of Chōsokabe Motochika

German sociologist and historian—would have described as a "monopoly of coercive violence"; the Chōsokabe magistrates and officials are granted rights while commoners are strictly prohibited from engaging in violence.

1: Services and festivals of (Shintō) shrines must be carried on in the manner that was prescribed in earlier years. Furthermore, wherever possible maintenance costs of shrines should be met from their own lands and endowments. In the event of great damage that makes this impossible, Commissioner must be consulted. Failure to report in this manner will be construed as an offence on the part of the shrine priest authorities and families.[30]

2: The functions of (Buddhist) temples must be continued in the way they have come down from the past and must not be allowed to deteriorate. Furthermore, temples should meet their maintenance expenses by relying on income from their own domain.[31]

3: As soon as an order affecting matters of state is issued it must be carried out conscientiously. Any sign of laxity will naturally be punished immediately.[32]

4: It is of course absolutely forbidden for anyone, high or low, to make use of the chrysanthemum-paulownia crest (of the Imperial family).

5: In regard to the reception accorded an emissary or deputy (from Hideyoshi) who comes to our province: every effort must be made to receive him properly. Those who excel in the pains they take in regard to receptions or farewells shall be rewarded. Furthermore, at such a time care must be taken to report everything which the guides or attendants in the emissary's party may have said.

6: Lords and vassals, priests and laymen, noble and mean, high and low, must all keep from allowing the rules of humanliness, righteousness, and propriety to suffer disgrace, but should on the contrary keep them constantly in mind.

7: It should be the primary concern of everyone to train himself unceasingly in military accomplishment. Those who tend to excel their fellows in this should be given additional income. Particular attention should be paid to

---

30. Earlier instructions here declared still in force doubtless refer to ordinances issued by Kira, Ichijō, Hosokawa, and similar authorities, as well as earlier shogunal conventions. They are mentioned in a total of six other articles (2, 14, 31, 45, 58, 75) covering a wide range of subject matter.

31. Father and son the Chōsokabe, who had for a time held the office of Temple *bugyō*, exerted themselves to protect, restore, and regulate the Buddhist establishments under their control; they both entered orders toward the end of their lives.

32. Motochika took his duties to Hideyoshi very seriously and, in provision of wealth, lumber, or armies, showed his respect for *kōgi* matters of state.

musketry, archery, and horsemanship. The military code is contained in a separate document.³³

8: Strive to develop accomplishments appropriate to your status. Furthermore, you must keep always in your mind the study of books and pursuit of arts insofar as these are consistent with your duties.

9: You should try to live up to the teachings of the various (Buddhist) sects. In things like literary studies, those who excel their fellows, according to their achievements, can nourish hopes in whatever their area, whether worldly prosperity or religious life.

10: With regard to (Buddhist) priests: (a) those to return to lay life without reporting this to the lord of the province will promptly be executed. (b) They will no longer go out at night unless there is a compelling reason, and (c) their misconduct, when reported, will bring special reward for the informer. Violations of these points will bring punishment of exile or death, depending on the gravity of the offence.³⁴

11: The Three Commissioners have been appointed to administer throughout the seven districts of this province, and no objections are to be raised against any decisions the Commissioners make. Furthermore, *shōya* have been appointed for each community, and the instructions they announce must not be neglected in any way.³⁵

---

33. Of muskets, in which the Tosa armies were far behind their Honshū contemporaries, Yamamoto writes, "Muskets were first ordered from other provinces, but from Keichō years (1596 on) there were workers known as musket blacksmiths. Manufacture was not restricted within the retainer corps, but it was absolutely forbidden to non-(Tosa) nationals; orders had to be reported, and secret manufacture was a crime punishable by death," *Chōsokabe Motochika*, 210. Inoue notes that the above-mentioned military code has never been found. *Chōsokabe okitegaki no kenkyū*, 438.

34. In these three articles one finds much of the Tokugawa ethic incorporated; emphasis on status, itself as yet imperfectly worked out in Tosa, emphasis on the study of books and civilized and military arts, respect for Buddhist teachings, and encouragement in the struggle for distinction and achievement in walks secular and religious. And, as the last shows, respect for Buddhist teachings did not necessarily extend to Buddhist clerics; no doubt it also reflected experience as *tera bugyō*.

35. Throughout these pages the distinction between the *san bugyō*, a group with overall responsibility chosen from the top *karō* families, and the *sho bugyō*, officials with specific responsibilities who numbered, according to one source, 138, is suggested by rendering the former as commissioners and the latter as magistrates. It is possible, however, that the code may in places mean one of the three instead of one of the 138 when it says only *bugyō*. For make-up, remuneration, and duties of *bugyō*, see Inoue, 380–94. *Shōya* normally supervised a single village, but where feasible and appropriate they might administer several, while a large population might justify appointment of two or three *shōya*. A late sixteenth-century account credits Chōsokabe Tosa with 174 *shōya* and 63 *tone*, the comparable office for coastal (fishing) villages. Inoue, 398–403.

5. The 100 Article Code of Chōsokabe Motochika

12: The words of the *yorioya* and other unit commanders are to be respected at all times, and no one should ever raise the slightest objection to them.

13: As regards lawsuits throughout the realm, they should first be taken up with the unit commander (*yorioya*) and thereafter submitted to the lord. Those who have no unit commander should take it up with the magistrate. Suits cannot be taken up during periods of military service, duty in Kyoto, or absence, although exceptions can be made in cases of emergency. Furthermore, cases will be heard three times a month, on the tenth, twentieth, and last day. Urgent matters requiring immediate attention may be submitted at any time.

14: The official responsible for forwarding cases to the lord should have both parties discuss the issue together and only then submit it to the lord. But, as in the past, he should not interfere with the *rōjū*.[36]

15: Any interference by wives in legal action is strictly forbidden.

16: Once a verdict has been reached the case cannot be submitted to the lord a second time, even if additional arguments exist.

17: It is only natural that services are demanded of those who hold fiefs, and they must be carried out to the letter regardless of whether they are large or small. Anyone late for logging or construction work will be required to repeat the duty period as punishment. And anyone who comes short of the food and provisions requested of him for work details without excuse will be required to supply as much again.

18: In regard to those who abscond: offenders must be punished whatever their excuse and so also their relatives. Proper reward should be given neighbors or friends who report anyone whose behavior causes suspicion that he is planning to desert. Those who have knowledge of such intent and fail to report it will receive the same punishment as the offender. Furthermore, a man who reports late for lumbering or construction and leaves without getting permission from the magistrate will have his land declared forfeit. If a man deserts directly to another province, punishment will also be imposed on his relatives. Similarly, if a man's servant (*hikan*) deserts (from labor duty), the master will be penalized threefold.[37]

---

36. Here, as in civil suits for commoners, the administrators made every attempt to have cases settled out of court, since they had no particular interest in the outcome and much preferred the compromise settlement consonant with Confucian harmony. For persistence of this, Dan F. Henderson, *Patterns and Persistence of Traditional Procedure in Japanese Law*, unpublished dissertation, University of California Berkeley, 1955.

37. *Hikan* was originally a designation of subordination, with *jitō* acting as *hikan* of the *shugo*. The term gradually came to have a more specific connotation of semi-free, indentured service, and signified the hands whereby the extended family carried out agriculture on the *tezukuri* system. In the above instance, *hikan* are sent off to perform the labor.

19: Anyone who performs more service (*kyūyaku*) than required should take it up with the magistrate to obtain the proper reduction. In case of emergency, not only in event of military service, one should increase the number of laborers and exert himself to the utmost. Thereafter it can be taken up with the magistrate for appropriate reductions in services. But in no case can such reductions be divided or shared.

20: Unless there is an explicit statement of release from the authorities, no one can be excused from services, whatever the reasons that are advanced.

21: When a man is sent somewhere on a mission or named as a magistrate, he will be excused from providing personnel for service duty as follows: If he goes to another province, 5 men less; to Hata or Aki, 3 men less; to the 5 central districts, 2 men less. This has no bearing on men of low status.

22: A man who desires to surrender his fief may be permitted to do so if it is clearly beyond his capacity. But to do so from choice and not from necessity is punishable. When cases are under consideration the applicant will in any case be required to perform his obligations until the twelfth month of the year, after which he may be permitted to give up his fief.

23: As regards crossing the borders of the province by people of any rank, in either direction: Under no conditions will anyone who does not have a signed permit from a magistrate or village elder (*toshiyori*) be permitted to pass a mountain or coastal check point. *Shōya* have been appointed in the mountain areas and *tone* have been appointed in coastal areas, and anyone who disregards their instructions and tries to leave or enter without authority shall be punished. If someone without the proper permits boards a ship, the person in charge of the ship will also be punished.[38]

24: As to horses: Anyone with three *chō* should keep (his mount,) saddle and other equipment in a state of readiness. Naturally those with more land should perfect themselves in military arts, and those with less than three *chō* also will, if they keep up their military training, receive reward.

25: Quarreling and bickering are strictly forbidden. Whether in the right or wrong, begin with restraint and forbearance. If instead of this men resort to violence, then both parties should be punished, regardless of the right or wrong of the matter. If one party only raises his hand against the other, regardless of his reasons for having done so he will be punished.

26: With regard to thieves: They should be captured immediately and the magistrate informed. If there is no question about guilt, they will of course be

---

38. Punishment, *seibai*, could include death, Inoue, op. cit., p. 132.

beheaded. If the thief resists arrest, he will be slain. If these rules are not carried out, the *shōya* responsible will be held punishable.

27: As to cutting and wounds: Whatever the circumstances, whoever strikes or hits a fellow retainer must be punished. However, this does not apply to those serving as magistrate.

28: With regard to someone who injures another without reason: The nature of the death penalty which is to be imposed will be determined after careful examination. Further, if punishment is extended to the offender's relatives, the details of the investigation should be made clear.

29: As to cutting a man and then running away: Anyone doing this will be crucified. The *jitō*, *shōya*, and people of the vicinity should immediately pursue and capture the criminal and then report. If they cannot capture him, they should (try to) strike him down. If he escapes the whole community will be punished. If the murderer's relatives had any knowledge at all of the matter they will receive the same punishment as the criminal. If it is clear that they knew nothing, an appropriate verdict will be found. Anyone who was at the scene and failed to intervene will also be punished. Furthermore: with respect to (punishment for) relatives, the exact degree of relationship will be taken into account.[39]

30: With regard to hitting (with shot or arrows) men in hunting areas, at construction sites, and elsewhere, without provocation: Anyone guilty of this will be punished immediately. If he had a prior grudge against his victim he will be sentenced to death, and punishment will extend to his relatives.

31: With regard to bandits and pirates: As has been the rule in the past, it is the responsibility of the area nearest to their hideout to search for and produce these people. If this is not done, the area in question will be penalized.

32: Heavy drinking is prohibited for all people, high and low, to say nothing of all magistrates. Furthermore: With regard to drunkards, the fine for minor offenses will be three *kan* of coins, and appropriate punishment (*seibai*) will be imposed for severe offenses. A man who cuts or strikes others (while drunk) will have his head cut off.

33: As to illicit relations with another's wife: Although it is obvious, unless the guilty pair kill themselves, both of them should be executed. If approval of relatives is obtained, revenge may be undertaken, but unnatural cruelty will

---

39. *Jitō*, which is used six times in the Code (29, 47, 52, 60, 72, 79), meant little more than enfeoffed proprietor in this period, and seems to have been interchangeable with *chigyō* samurai, *kyūnin*. Inoue discusses variant interpretations.

Section X • The Late Sixteenth- and Early Seventeenth-Century Transformations

constitute a crime. If the husband fails to kill the man, or if he is away the time the offense becomes known, the people of the village should kill the offender. In addition: If a woman has a reputation, the (marriage) contract is to be broken.

34: When there is not a man in the house, no males—masseurs, peddlers, travelling *sarugaku* performers and musicians, solicitors for religious contributions (*banjin*) or even relatives—shall set foot in the house. If someone is ill and if the relatives approve, a visit may be made, but then only in daytime. Even the magistrate must carry on his business outside the gate. However, this does not apply to parents, sons, and brothers (of the household head).[40]

35: Also, when a man is not present, a woman is not to go visiting Buddhist temples or Shinto shrines or sightseeing. Furthermore: The annual and monthly rites (for deceased relatives) should be held at the temple.

36: Also, in the absence of a man: It is absolutely forbidden for a priest to go in and out of the house. Furthermore: This does not apply to devotional services.

37: With regard to regulating *fudai* (hereditary servant) status: Men and women who have served their masters for ten years without having been discharged will be considered *fudai*. Similarly their children will naturally be considered *fudai* also. A male child will go with his father, and a girl goes with the mother. Even though a servant may have been told by his master that he is dismissed, unless there is written evidence of this no other master is to take him as his servant. If a master violates this rule the servant's former master should report this and claim his servant again according to law. It will then be his responsibility to decide whether to put the man in service again or to put him to death. If a servant ran away and his whereabouts were unknown, no matter how many years ago it was he should (if discovered) be reported and returned to his master. Furthermore: But if such a servant's whereabouts in a neighboring area were known to the master for more than ten years without his having taken any action, this will not apply. Similarly, as to *fudai* attached to fiefs: If the proprietor (*jitō*) has gone to another province, even though he return, if he does not receive reinstatement of his original fief, he will not regain his powers over the *fudai*.

38: Debts of rice must be returned in the exact amount that was borrowed. It is a crime to return an insufficient measure of rice it were the full measure.

---

40. Yamamoto, noting the instructions to retainers in the *Tenshō shikimoku* of 1574 to "develop arts such as dancing (*rambu*), flute and drum, football, and tea; you should be ashamed to feel inferior on visits to other provinces," suggests that such efforts to popularize the culture of the Kyoto nobility among the ruling class were accompanied by the modest numbers of itinerant performers who toured the countryside. "The attainments of the commoners did not reach a very high level, but this (article 34) illustrates the general trend of the period." *Chōsokabe Motochika*, 22.

39: With regard to loans to petty retainers throughout the realm: Where the retainer, without his master's knowledge, has already been paying out his whole income and has had to give up his house and become a burden on his master, he should not be pressed for payment any longer.[41]

40: In cases in which borrowed goods or things held in trust, or the lord's (tax) rice, are lost by fire or theft while in someone's possession, if that person's own possessions are also lost, he will not be required to make restitution. But if only the goods in his custody are lost, then he will have to make restitution. Also: It is forbidden to lend to others things which have first been borrowed.

41: With regard to pawned articles: Once it is established that an article has been lost because of theft or fire, claims for the borrowed money for which it served as security will be considered forfeit.

42: With regard to delinquent loans: If the borrower makes difficulties after having been pressed to pay, the matter should be reported to the magistrate, and the loan reclaimed without fail. But if the lender has for years failed to press for payment only the principal need be repaid.

43: Lawsuits over *kōryō* (*daimyō* domain) and *myōden* (private, name fields) must stop. Furthermore: land purchases will be validated by special decree, while the quality of service performed will be the criterion for (transfer) of land for which no validation papers previously exist.[42]

44: It is a punishable offense to convert rice paddy field into dry field or house sites. Where this has been done the taxes will be kept at the same rate as those for paddy.

45: With regard to purchasing land: Even if someone has a contract providing for transfer in perpetuity, if the rice produced (by the plot) is less than ten *hyō* (about one acre of normal paddy) the land remains redeemable (by the seller). Even if it is claimed that a plot was clearly sold permanently, if there is no documentary evidence to support this the plot can be reclaimed by its seller (with restitution of price). And if despite claims there is no documentary evidence to establish even such redeemable status for land, the land will be considered as *toshige* (redeemable from crop yield). The above rules are established in accordance with previous regulations. When a contract provides that land will be

---

41. The word here is *matahikan*. *Mata* ("again, next") was a prefix added to terms for petty retainers to indicate they were attached to rear vassals, *baishin*, e.g., *matahikan, matakomono, matawakato*. Inoue, p. 186 foll.

42. *Tokusei*, here rendered as "special decree," was normally an edict canceling retainer debts; in this instance, it permits alienation of land already registered in another's name, and hence also constitutes special intervention in the retainer's interest. Inoue, 281; for discussion of the fact that both retainers and the *daimyō* himself purchased land, Yokogawa, "Hisatake Kuranosuke," loc. cit.

held in pledge at the rate of 1 *tan* per borrowed *hyō* of rice (about one fifth the yield of average paddy), if the lender has enjoyed crop rights for three years the original owner will no longer be required to repay the loan; he is also entitled to the return of his land. Furthermore: Land alienated under provisions of perpetual or of conditional sale will revert to the original owner if the purchaser's family dies out. But if someone succeeds to this family within ten years the land must again be returned to the purchaser. If, however, it is more than ten years before a successor takes over, their claims lose effect and the land will be considered part of the original owner's fief. The same rule holds for lenders and loans. Furthermore, if the seller's family dies out, except for lands specially registered earlier, all three classifications—perpetual sale, conditional transfer, and terminal option—are to be declared forfeit and confiscated.[43]

46: With regard to abandoned and waste land throughout the realm: *Shōya* in the area must warn their people against letting it grow rank. If the *shōya* is unable to deal with it alone he should consult the magistrate about initiating reclamation measures. If the abandonment has been caused by negligence, the *shōya* of that place must assume responsibility for paying the tax in place of the tillers.

47: As to fiefs throughout the realm: The crop yield, as ascertained by the fall survey of fields ready for harvest (*kemi*) should be apportioned, two-thirds to the vassal samurai (*jitō*) and one-third to the farmer. If farmers object to this, the samurai will have to use his own judgment. He must, at any rate, take care lest the land be abandoned and ruined. Furthermore: Cultivation rights applying to lands which have changed hands in recent years will be determined at the discretion of the vassals holding the fiefs.[44]

---

43. It is not surprising that sixteenth-century Japan, in which land was the chief form of wealth, had a vocabulary rich in terms to indicate degrees of ownership and tenure. The terminology adopted above is for the terms *kyūchi* (permanently alienated land), *honmono* conditional transfer, which can return to the principal (*hon*) owner, and *toshige*, at present "yield," but then used in the sense of land "purchased" under an arrangement whereby the seller-borrower paid interest and principal in kind from the fields, so that after a given period of time—usually ten years—it returned into his possession. Violation of this "option" would presumably result in loss of land. Furthermore, the sudden use of the word *fief* (*chigyō*) halfway through the article makes it clear that Motochika's concern here lies with his *samurai*, probably with the *ichiryō gusoku*. It may be noted that this article is included in a volume of excerpts from feudal land law by the Ministry of Agriculture (*Dai Nihon Nōshi, Tōkyō*, 1891, II, p. 156, 7). The net effect of these regulations would be to discourage and slow alienation of land so that the article is, as Inoue (p. 287) points out, a step in the progress toward the Tokugawa prohibitions on alienation of any kind.

44. "Although the Chōsokabe were unable to make a really thorough change," Yamamoto writes, "their aim, as seen in Motochika's Article 47, must surely have been to change the nature of the *ichiryō gusoku*, protect their fief holders, and build a new retainer corps on the basis of the separation of soldiers and farmers," *Chōsokabe seiken no henshitsu to ichiryō gusoku*, loc. cit., p. 74.

48: With regard to forestation, reclamation of abandoned land, development of waste land, and salt fields: Such reclamation must be reported to the lord, and work may be started after receiving his approval. The practice of keeping the existence of reclaimed land secret must absolutely be stopped. Supplement: The first year after reclamation the *tanmai* tax will be paid, and from the following year on regular taxes will be levied. Such fields are, after all, the lord's lands.[45]

49: With regard to the waste land of fief holders (*kyūnin*): There can be no excuse for having allowed land to go to waste since the land survey.

50: As for the paddy, dry, and dwelling fields which came in dispute at the time of the land survey: As long as these are unresolved, the *shōya* of those areas will have to deliver the exact amount of tax due.

51: With regard to irrigation duty: The irrigation magistrate and *shōya* of the areas concerned must place particular emphasis on allowing nothing to obstruct the irrigation channels. If large-scale damage beyond the capacity of the people dependent on the water takes place, it should be reported to the magistrate, who, after consultation, should call out all the people to repair the damage.

52: Whoever discovers that anyone, whether vassal or farmer, is concealing the existence of (untaxed) fields and reports it to the lord, will be rewarded strikingly. Acting on such information, the magistrate will base his ruling on the land survey register. If it becomes clear that a vassal concealed the field, he will be severely punished. And if it was a farmer who concealed it, he will be made to pay double the tax due since the land survey, after which he will be banished. If he pleads hardship at this, he will have his head cut off.

53: With regard to disputes over property lines: In all cases such disputes will be decided in accordance with the register of the land survey. After a case has been heard with the arguments of both parties stated, the person found to be at fault will be fined five *kan* (i.e. 5000 copper coins) to punish him for his carelessness. If both parties refuse to listen to reason, the disputed area will be confiscated.

54: Within the lord's own domain, not even one grain of rice may be taken away in payment for loans or purchases before the date set for the payment in full of the fall harvest tax. If this ruling is not observed, both the *shōya* and the farmers involved will be severely punished.

---

45. Salt fields, *shiota*, can refer either to salt flats or reclamation of marsh land. Around Urado much reclamation took place, and, as can be seen, its profits ended in the *daimyō*'s coffers. *Tanmai* was a tax levied on rice paddies in addition to the regular tax.

55: In regard to the annual tax (*nengu*): It must all be paid in hulled rice. The decision to plant *taimai* or *kichimai* rice will depend upon the soil. Planting *taimai* on soil more suitable to *kichimai* is strictly prohibited. If this order is violated the tax will be collected at the *kichimai* rate.[46]

56: With regard to units of measure: Throughout the realm measures will be standardized to *kyōmasu*. However, long measure will be used for the annual tax and loan repayments, and short measure for private transactions.[47]

57: Throughout the realm, *tanmai* must be paid each year as assessed.

58: In certain areas the tithe must be paid exactly as it was done in the past.[48]

59: Whether it is hulled or unhulled rice, one *hyō* must contain five *to*.

60: With regard to farmers throughout the realm: The *jitō*, *shōya*, and magistrates must foster them solicitously in their official capacity. Do not require extra taxes and work in addition to the regular exactions from them. But of course, the regular annual tax must be paid strictly. If it comes even a little short, *shōya* and land owners of the lord's own domain will receive prompt and severe punishment.

61: It is strictly prohibited for a magistrate to develop private or abandoned fields.

62: If anyone discovers that a magistrate who has been sent to some part of the realm speaks irresponsibly or shows favoritism he should report the facts of the case, and, no matter how low his position, he will be rewarded handsomely as a result. After receipt of this report and in the light of an examination of the matter, that magistrate will be punished severely.

63: With regard to a magistrate or *shōya* anywhere in the realm who shows favoritism or partiality or indulges in any other unjust practices whatever, it makes no difference whether complaints come from someone in the offender's area (of jurisdiction) or not. Details should be forwarded to the authorities, and they will be rewarded. After an investigation, punishment will be meted out.

---

46. *Kichimai*, standard paddy rice, was superior to *taimai*, a southern, soft rice with higher yield. *Kichi* was considered synonymous with rice, and paddy land was often referred to as *kichi chi*. See the articles by Yamamoto Takeshi, in *Nihon rekishi daijiten* (Tōkyō, 1956), vol. 5, p. 316, and Vol. 12, p. 69.

47. In this article one sees Motochika following Hideyoshi's orders for standardization of weights and measures. The *kyōmasu koku* was more than 10% smaller than that earlier in use, and the unit measure also smaller, so that the traditional generalization that Hideyoshi's smaller unit measure meant higher taxes requires further examination in the case of Tosa.

48. Both the *tanmai* and the tithe (*jūbunichi*) were traditional taxes continued Chōsokabe; the former had its origins in a tax on paddies inaugurated by Kamakura *shugo* and was designed as additional income for enfeoffed retainers, while the tithe survived into Tokugawa times as an impost on goods and especially shipping. Yokogawa discusses the *tanmai* and related problems in *Ōsato shō no kenkyū*, p. 187–91.

5. The 100 Article Code of Chōsokabe Motochika

64: A magistrate is forbidden to post or issue regulations for even a single area without reporting it.

65: Throughout the realm, if messengers for officials such as magistrates request horses or labor services on their way, they should be accommodated, provided they have official authorization with them. If they do not, they do not have to be obeyed.

66: It is absolutely forbidden to sell horses of this province to other provinces. If anyone attempts to send out horses illegally, the horses will be confiscated. The barrier keepers (at border crossings) must keep particularly close watch in view of this.

67: Artisans should have confidence in the things that magistrates and group leaders say and should not raise any objections to their instructions.

68: Wages for artisans including carpenters, sawyers, cypress bowl makers, blacksmiths, silversmiths, sharpeners, lacquerers or painters, dyers, leatherworkers, tilers, cypress dyers, wall plasterers, mat (*tatami*) makers, armorers and the like should be, per day, 7 *shō* of unhulled rice, *kyōmasu* measure, for skilled workers, 5 *shō*, *kyōmasu* measure, of unhulled rice for average workers, and 3 *shō* of unhulled rice, *kyōmasu* scale, for unskilled workers. The classification into skilled, average, and unskilled categories must be approved by the magistrate. Supplement: The wages for a boat-builder will be one to of unhulled rice, *kyōmasu* scale, per day.[49]

69: The standard length of cotton cloth, irrespective of quality must be 7 *hiro*, taking one *hiro* as 4 feet 5 inches (*shaku*, *sun*) on the carpenter's measure. Coarse sacking will be standardized at 6 *hiro*.

70: With regard to trading boats: They should operate as much as possible, but the traders should realize how important it is that they stay within the borders of the province.

71: With regard to runners: The local *shōya* should dispatch or reserve them with due regard to the distances involved. If, when there is urgency, the runner is late, he should be decapitated.

72: The width of the main roads is to be 2 *ken*, each *ken* being 6 feet, 5 inches (*shaku*, *sun*). In regard to roads, *shōya* must see to it that they are maintained, whether in mountain, countryside, or coastal areas. If a road is bad, it is the *shōya*'s responsibility to collect one *kan* of coins from the landed samurai and farmers as a fine and turn it over to the magistrate's office.

---

49. As was noted above Motochika's efforts to attract merchants and artisans to his castle town were not very successful, and it is apparent in this article that the Code is directed largely to *goyō shōnin*, merchants favored by the regime, as it is the magistrates who make the key decisions about quality and pay.

Section X • The Late Sixteenth- and Early Seventeenth-Century Transformations

73: With regard to linear measurements: In castle construction and all other work, use the standard *ken* of 6 *shaku* 5 *sun*. However, rice paddies are an exception.

74: It is strictly forbidden to travel along side roads. Anyone who breaks this regulation will be fined 1 *kan* of coins.

75: As for the fishing tax (*katsura zeni*): It will be maintained as in the past.

76: It goes without saying that it is strictly prohibited to cut bamboo, cedar, cypress, camphor, pine and all other trees which have been registered for official use. It is also forbidden to cut down a bamboo of which one has need, even though it is within the confines of his own fief, without first reporting it to the magistrate's office. It is an important resource for all areas, country, mountain and coastal, to have bamboo trees growing.

77: It is strictly prohibited to break off bamboo shoots. Anyone who violates this rule will be fined 1 *kan* of coins, which will be given as reward to the informer who reports the offense.

78: It is forbidden to let cattle and horses wander freely at any season. Anyone who violates this rule will be fined 100 *mon* of coins. If there has been damage caused to harvest in the fields, an additional 100 *mon* will have to be paid to the owner.

79: If a man builds a house on leased land and moves away, if he has paid the annual tax, the house, whether board or thatched roof, belongs to him. But if he has been sentenced for a crime then the master (land owner) will take over his property as well as the house. If there is some question about his having paid his tax, the landowner will have to pay it to the enfeoffed proprietor in his stead. If, however, a landless laborer is convicted of a crime his house and property will be confiscated. In such a case the annual tax, if still outstanding, will be remitted to the (enfeoffed) land owner.[50]

80: Between father and son, if either acts against the will of the lord, he will receive separate punishment according to his offence and what it deserves. But each case should be considered on its own merits.

---

50. This important article shows gradations of tenure and dependence among non-samurai. The first case, of the man who leases land from another, finds the Code giving the tenant substantial rights provided he has had no record of punishment; it represents, in other words, a step toward an undifferentiated body of agriculturalists. Yet the tenant is still subordinate (*hikan*), as seen from the compulsion on his landlord the tenant is still subordinate (*hikan*), as seen from the compulsion on his landlord (*shunin*) to pay his tax to the enfeoffed proprietor (*jitō*). On the bottom rung, the landless laborer (*mōto*) gets less consideration, and the concluding phrase (for the interpretation of which this follows Inoue, p. 309) seems to protect the fief holder against loss. Yamamoto discusses this article at some length in "Chōsokabe seiken - ," *Nihon Rekishi*, loc. cit., p. 73-74. A general view of stratification in village life of the period can be found in T. C. Smith, "The Japanese Village in the 17th Century," *Journal of Economic History*, XII, 1, (1952).

81: With regard to transferring the headship of a temple throughout the realm: Suitable persons should be recommended to the lord and the transfer arranged in accordance with his instructions. Even though the candidate is a disciple (of the head), selection must necessarily be based on capability.

82: With regard to family succession: It is necessary to notify the lord and receive his permission, even if the heir is the head's real child. It is strictly forbidden to decide succession matters privately. Furthermore: One must also request and receive permission to become a guardian for a minor.[51]

83: Anyone who succeeds to two houses without getting the approval of higher authority will be punished as soon as it becomes known.

84: As regards family name and succession designation for loyal retainers: If a vassal commits a crime and has to be punished, his family name will not be affected if the offence was a minor one. But if he commits a major crime, his punishment should include the loss of his family name.

85: With regard to the marriage of samurai: It is strictly prohibited for samurai who receive over 100 *koku* to arrange a marriage without the lord's approval. Supplement: Whether one's status be high or low, matters of marriage must not be broached at any time if the understanding of both families has not been arranged.

86: Private contract is prohibited in all matters.[52]

87: It goes without saying that anyone who speaks or proposes evil things without regard for what is in the interest of the realm will be punished; in addition anyone in his company will receive the same punishment.

88: Those who start groundless rumors shall immediately be punished by death by crucifixion. It is also wrong to write irresponsible things on walls or gates. Anyone discovered to be doing this will be put to death.

89: It is absolutely forbidden to employ *rōnin* without notifying the lord and obtaining permission.

---

51. Alternatively, the last phrase could refer to selection of a child as heir or of a temporary family head. Inoue, p. 161 and 270, prefers "name a child as heir." The code, which reads *yōshō myodai*, permits either construction.

52. This provision would operate both to reinforce the previous article and, more particularly, to guard against the organization and consolidation of new power groups in the countryside. In the fifteenth century contractual agreements among groups of *myōshu* led to the formation of semi-military bands out of which the *ichiryō gusoku* developed. For examples drawn from the Ōsato shō, Yokogawa, *Ōsato shō no kenkyū*, p. 58–62, discussed also by Irimariji, op. cit., 212–13. By the 1590's, Yamamoto concludes, "it is probable that remnants of the old *myōshu* alliances had ceased to exist." "Chōsokabe seiken no henshitsu," op. cit., p. 75.

90: As regards *matawakato* and *matakomono:* they are strictly forbidden to associate in public or in private with the lord's own retainers.[53]

91: With regard to documents concerning paddy and dry fields: precedence (between conflicting documents) will be established by the date indicated.

92: As to false accusations: Punishment will depend on whether the offence is minor or serious. If it is a minor matter, the fine will be 3 *kan* of coins.

93: Regardless of rank, the practice of dismounting (in deference to superior) should be stopped. However, when an envoy or deputy from above (i.e., Hideyoshi) passes, he should receive this courtesy.

94: In matters large or small and good or bad, the lord's chamberlain must at all times transmit the sentiments of all the people, whatever their status to the lord. When there is an urgent matter and there is no one to transmit it, it should be submitted at once on paper. If an official fails to transmit anything, regardless of what it is, he will be punished immediately.

95: Anyone who has something on his heart should report it freely, whether his status is high or low. If he keeps it within himself until he develops evil ideas, he will be punished severely.

96: No one, high or low, is permitted to change his seal.[54]

97: No one may change his family name, his official title or office, or his given name. However, an official title may be changed once in accordance with provisions with the lord's permission.[55]

98: With regard to fire, it is essential to be vigilant at all times. If fire breaks out in a neighborhood, the owner of the house in which the fire first started will be fined according to his status. If the fire is confined to one house, the owner will be banished. Furthermore if responsibility for arson becomes clearly established, severe punishment will extend even to the relatives of the incendiary.

99: When someone in this realm, whatever his social standing, takes a long trip, there should be no objection raised against providing him a night's lodging. If a man of low rank steals or damages some of the things in his lodgings, he

---

53. This separation of rear vassals from direct vassals would contribute both to peace and order and to consciousness of class and status distinctions.

54. Miura Hiroyuki, *Hōseishi kenkyū*, (Tōkyō, 1924) p. 1089, explains that seals were substituted for hand-written signatures at about this time.

55. These references to official title and office are to the honorific designations awarded by the imperial court, in return for service or payment. For a brief review of the way in which territorial titles like "lord of ..." became separated from place and function, see Inoue, op. cit., p. 164–5. Similarly family names, which had their origin in place, were by this time disassociated and therefore changeable.

must make restitution. Supplement: The fee for the accommodations shall be determined by both parties.

100: With regard to the division of family property among relatives: Allocate one-tenth of the property to the father, and one-twentieth to the mother. But if both father and mother live together they should be satisfied with the father's share. The service (*kyūyaku*) required of a man who retires must be performed carefully by his successor. However, an exception can be made if different arrangements have been made by agreement between parent and son. Settlement of rights of brothers, uncles, nephews and other family members will be decided on the basis of their degree of relationship. But in all cases, whether between elder and younger brothers, or uncles and nephews, or others with the same surname, judgments will be handed down on the basis of propinquity of relationship.

These articles will provide the rule throughout this realm from this time on. All people, whether noble or base, must observe them strictly and in good faith. Any violation, even one word, is subject to immediate and severe punishment. Accordingly, it is promulgated as here set forth.

Twenty-fourth day of the Third Month,

Second Year of Keichō (1597)

Morichika

Motochika

6. A Receipt of Noses[56]

Under Hideyoshi's rule, the warriors of Japan became involved in the country's campaigns in Korea. This document, dating from 1597, shows that warriors seeking restitution for their service in battle were required to produce "proof" of their participation. In this case, noses were substituted for heads.

Concerning the noses of heads taken in Jinwon district:

In total, 870.

---

56. *Dainihon komonjo Kikkawa ke monjo*, vol. 1, doc. 138, 9.21 [(Keichō 2/1597)], Hayakawa Nagamasa *hoka ni rensho hana uketorijō*, 105. Translated by Thomas Conlan.

Section X • The Late Sixteenth- and Early Seventeenth-Century Transformations

The aforementioned have certainly been received.

Twenty-first day of the ninth month. The second year of Keichō (1597)

Kumagai *Kuranojō* [Naomori] (Monogram)

Kakimi Izumi *no kami* [Kazunao] (Monogram)

Hayakawa *shume no kami* [Nagamasa] (Monogram)

To: The Honorable Kikkawa *kurōdo no tō* [at the] Military Encampment

7. The Memoir of a Unification Era Warrior, Fukutomi Han'emon[57]

Here Fukutomi Han'emon Masachika (1576–1656), a warrior from Tosa, site of the Chōsokabe domains, recounts the campaign in Korea, as well as the battle of Sekigahara.[58] Fukutomi was on the losing side of this battle, and this defeat resulted in the Chōsokabe losing their domains. Fukutomi survived the transition and later fought for the Tokugawa against Toyotomi forces in the siege of Ōsaka in 1615.

In the first year of Bunroku [1592].3.8 at the time of the invasion of Korea, my lord Motochika sailed from Urado port in Tosa Province. At that time I was called Fukutomi Shichirōbei. I was seventeen at the time. At first we sailed to Katoku island [K. Kadŏk island] in Korea and then proceeded to the Pusan sea area. Pusan is the place from which one travels from Korea to Japan. We then sailed to the port of Takeshima [K. Chukto] where many *daimyō* had their vessels. From there we marched by three routes to the capital called Akakuni Rajun. The northern route was led by Lord Konishi Yukinaga, the middle route by lord Katō Kiyomasa and the southern route by Lord Motochika. The overlord Toyotomi Hideyoshi assigned the inspector Kakimi Kazunao to Lord Motochika's forces.

In the same year [1592].12.5 Motochika ordered that we should send out two or three small units for five or six *ri* [about 20–24 kilometers if he is using Hideyoshi's *ri*] and if we encounter foreigners we should kill them and cut off their noses to bring back as proof to be recorded in the books of service. However we should return to camp before sunset. If we did not return by sunset we would be punished

---

57. Translated by Luke Roberts.
58. The Chōsokabe name is also transcribed as Chōsogabe.

7. The Memoir of a Unification Era Warrior, Fukutomi Han'emon

severely even if we brought back noses. At that time I was in Hisatake Kuranosuke's unit. Our unit consisted of sixteen men. Our camp was at a place called Sosen [K. Sach'ŏn] and we set out around 3 in the morning. About twenty-four kilometers from it we spotted about twenty Korean horsemen. They saw us and fled into a pine woods so we could no longer see them. We got off our horses to search and found a cave into which it seemed they had gone. Even if we fired our guns into the cave we would not know if we hit them. At that Hiroi Kaemon said that if we just chased them into a cave and left it at that we would likely be criticized later so we should go into the cave to hunt them out. Because the entrance to the cave was narrow we removed our armor and planned to go in just with our short swords. At this point my retainer Kuzaemon whispered into my ear that this was my time and I should crawl in first. I thought this a good idea and I started crawling into the cave, but then Hiroi Kaemon crawled in after me and grabbing my waistband started to pull me out. Hisatake Kuemon told Kaemon "If Shichirōbei in his youthful ambition crawled in first, even if you pull him out now, later investigations will reveal this and Shichirōbei will be counted as first entry so just let him go!" So Hiroi Kaemon came in second and Hisatake Kuemon came in third. No one else came in. Inside the cave, Kaemon drew his short sword. Inside the cave it was narrow but it gradually widened further in and was probably about twenty or so meters long but bending as it climbed upwards. If we had just fired our guns into the cave we would have hit no one. The foreigners must have feared the possibility of guns and did not face us. Every one of them escaped out of another exit, but the men outside captured all of them and bound them up. There were seventeen of them including leaders and servants. We cut off their heads and took their noses dividing them among the three of us. I got seven noses. Hiroi Kaemon got six noses and Hisatake Kuemon got four. Well, it was after midnight when we returned to the main camp. Because we broke camp law, the three of us who had entered the cave were sentenced to kill ourselves by *seppuku*. We had resigned ourselves to this, but on the third day our lord declared that only ten out of every hundred warriors of Tosa came to Korea, and these warriors were very precious to him, so he ordered to his confidant Nakauchi Shōsuke that we should be spared. Then on the ninth we were granted audience with the lord.

Lord Motochika returned to Japan and the twenty-three members of our unit went home from Pusan before him. When Lord Motochika arrived back he sent word praising that I had been the first to enter the cave and also noting his appreciation of my grandfather and father he granted me a fief.

Lord Motochika passed away in the third year of Keichō [1598].8.19 in Ōsaka in Settsu province.

Section X • The Late Sixteenth- and Early Seventeenth-Century Transformations

At the time of the battle of Sekigahara in Mino Province in the fifth year of Keichō [1600].9.15 Lord Motochika's son Lord Morichika allied with Ishida Mitsunari and arrayed his forces at Kurihara south of Nangū Mountain. Mitsunari's forces lost, and without engaging in the fight Morichika's forces retreated to the town of Kaitsu that evening in the hours before midnight. However a riot occurred, the town set aflame and our forces fell into disarray. Fukura Sukebei said "The enemy is chasing us. On our left is a river and on the right is a mountain. This is a place difficult to flee from." He yelled out "Wherever you ask directions, kill them all!" Fukura Sukebei named himself to lead the rear guard. Yasunami Genba, Hirose Matabei, Yoshimura Sakonbei and I then exchanged words with Sukebei and formed a rear guard. On that occasion Sukebei's appearance was as follows: He had armor laced *kebiki* style, and his breastplate was decorated in gold lacquer with an Amida triad. His had a studded helmet with a front crest that was whitened with silver, and it had deer horns protruding out left and right. He had a red crepe canopy banner on his back and the decoration was a golden fan. His horse was black as ink and armored in vermillion. His appearance was finer than any man there.

When my lord Morichika arrived at Tenman in Ōsaka Fukura Sukebei presented his report on the retreat. The lord then called to himself Yasunami Genba, Hirose Matabei, Yoshimura Sakonbei and myself. He declared that our service was admirable and gave three pieces of silver to each of us. After staying at Tenman three to five days he ordered that all the forces return to Tosa, which we did.

Lord Tokugawa Ieyasu confiscated Tosa [from the Chōsogabe][59] and bestowed it to lord Yamauchi Katsutoyo. He had already ordered Ii Naomasa to take control of Tosa, who sent his retainer Suzuki Heibei to take over the castle. Heibei arrived at the port of Urado in the same year in the middle of the tenth month with a hundred warriors and followers. When it came time to hand over the castle, a major conflict developed between the Chōsogabe senior retainers and the common housemen. Heibei was in the place called Mimase, and the elders decided to lead him inside at night and hand over the castle. The common housemen disagreed and formed a league refusing to turn over the castle. They gathered to contest at the place called Nukatsuka on the south of Urado. The common housemen were defeated there. I and my relatives were elders. Negotiations then quieted things and I and my companions retreated to a place known as Tsuzumidani.

Among the leaders of the resisting housemen there was a Kitaoka Rokubei and his son Genshichi. The elders decided that they needed to be killed and directed

---

59. In his translation of the 1597 codes, Jansen transcribes Chōsogabe as Chōsokabe. They are the same family.

7. The Memoir of a Unification Era Warrior, Fukutomi Han'emon

Kumano Mataemon, Maeda Kyūemon, Sawaragi Rihei, Kitaoka Sōemon, Kariya Kozaemon, Utsuno Magoemon, Mitani Rokuemon, and myself—eight of us—to go do the job. I arrived first and then Kumano Mataemon so we took the road at the front of the house and decided the rest would go back behind the house. So Mataemon and I went up to the front entrance. Genshichi came charging out in attack and he and I fought. Rokubei then came out swinging and fought with Mataemon. Things went well for me and I cut open Genshichi's head with my Dōtanuki sword killing him. Rokubei had been cut by Mataemon in the arm and lower thigh and had fallen down. Mataemon had a cut on his head and the blood flowed down into his eyes. He said he could not see. I had killed Genshichi about six meters away. I ran straight from there and finished off Rokubei. The others came running from the back and stated their regret at not participating. Well, I gave the long and short swords that I had won to a local samurai from there named Takahashi Heiemon. I told him "I will be spending all of my time drifting and working around other provinces, and I may come back so be a witness for what happened here!" Yet how quickly even children of the next generation have no knowledge of this incident.

I departed Tosa in the sixth year of Keichō [1601].3.3 together with Maeda Kyūemon. We went to Masaki in Iyo province to stay with Katō Yoshiaki. Hōno Saburōemon sponsored us so that we could ask Yoshiakira's house elder Tsukuda Jirōbei for employment. Around that time they constructed a new castle [in the east] near the borders of Awa, Sanuki and Tosa provinces at a place called Kawanoe in Uma county of Iyo province. Kawamura Gonshichi was appointed castellan. Maeda Kyūemon and I were assigned to Gonshichi's unit, and we went to Kawanoe in the same year 4.26. Gonshichi's fief was 6,500 *koku*. Kawanoe was about eighty-four kilometers away from Katō Yoshiakira's castle at Masaki.

In the same year [1601] 8.16 one of Kawamura Gonshichi's servants committed a crime and ran off. Twenty-six people were assigned to hunt him down towards Awa, Sanuki and Tosa provinces. They were divided up into groups of three to five and sent out to chase him down. Yagi Kuzaemon and I went into Sanuki province. At Ōji village Kuzaemon entered by the high road and I entered by the coast. Happily I encountered the servant near the coast and captured him, and then took him back to Kawanoe. On that day I received a stipend of fifteen *koku* of rice so I could maintain a horse. Near the end of that year Akiyama Kahei sponsored me to marry into Terao Kiemon's house as adopted heir. Kiemon had a number of recognized feats of arms and was someone I knew about. At the time I was called Fukutomi Den'emon.

263

8. The *Buke Shohatto* of 1615[60]

Following his victory over Toyotomi Hideyoshi's supporters, Tokugawa Ieyasu (1543–1616) issued the laws to the court and warriors. The latter, directed to warriors, are translated here. The laws set the foundation for the Tokugawa regime and regulated the regime and culture for the next two and a half centuries.

Item (1). Warriors should devote themselves to civil and military affairs, archery, and horsemanship.

Item (2). Drinking in groups and carousing is prohibited.

Item (3). Lawbreakers should not be hidden or protected in the provinces.

Item (4). Great lords (*daimyō*), lesser lords (*shōmyō*) of various provinces, and anyone who receives benefice[61] should not shelter any soldiers who were reported to have rebelled or committed murder. Such soldiers should instead be dispelled from that province (domain).[62]

Item (5). From now on, people from other domains should not live in your domain.

Item (6). Lords may repair the castle in which they live, but only after being granted permission to do so. It goes without saying that new construction is prohibited.

Item (7). Those who plot[63] with groups in neighboring provinces must be immediately reported.

Item (8). Self-selected marriages[64] are prohibited.

Item (9). *Daimyō* lords should follow established custom when they service in Edo.

Item (10). Clothing conventions must not be confused.[65]

Item (11). Low-ranking people (*zōnin*) should not ride in palanquins.

Item (12). *Samurai* of the various provinces shall practice frugality.

Item (13). "Lords of the Provinces" (*kokushu*) should select men of ability.

---

60. For the 1615 and 1635 *buke shohatto* codes (Documents 8–9), see Ishii Shirō, ed., "Buke shohatto," *Kinsei buke shisō*, 454–52. Translations by Thomas Conlan with Horikawa Yasufumi.
61. This could refer to any benefit from their lord, be it lands or a stipend.
62. Although the old term for province is used, it refers to domains, which were more fragmented than the older provinces.
63. The term here is *shingi*, or innovation, which means fomenting rebellion.
64. Marriages privately determined.
65. Status distinctions shall continue to be displayed by distinct clothes.

9. The Revised *Buke Shohatto* of 1635

The original codes were clarified and expanded upon in 1635 by Tokugawa Ieyasu's grandson Iemitsu (1604–51). The revised codes clearly stipulated the principle of alternate attendance in Edo.

Item (1). Warriors should devote themselves to civil and military affairs, archery, and horsemanship.

Item (2). Great lords (*daimyō*) and lesser lords are to serve in Edo alternatively. They should proceed there in the fourth month of every year. Recently the excessive number of followers attending to this duty has created a burden on the provinces and districts and become a source of hardship for the people. These numbers should be reduced commensurate with their status in the future. But when visiting the capital, the *daimyō* should still follow orders and dutifully perform the public [military] service in accordance with their status or resources.

Item (3). The construction of a new castle is strictly prohibited. If the moats or stone walls of castles require repair, the *daimyō* should contact the magistrates' office and receive permission for repairs. Castle towers, walls, and gates should be repaired in accordance with precedent.

Item (4). If some disturbance arises in Edo or the provinces, people of the affected provinces (domains) should remain there and follow our orders.

Item (5). Only officials should attend executions. Nevertheless, all matters of attendance depend on officials' judgments.

Item (6). Forming plots[66] and swearing oaths with a group is strictly prohibited.

Item (7). The lords of various provinces or domains should be careful and not engage in quarrels. Magistrates should be notified of any lingering disputes.

Item (8). Lords of provinces or castles, warriors controlling over ten thousand *koku*[67] of revenue, personal attendants, and unit leaders (*monogashira*) should not establish marriages on their own.

Item (9). Recently the following have become excessive: ceremonial visits, the exchange of goods, weddings, banquets, and the construction of new residences. These are to be curtailed from now on; frugality should be practiced in all matters.

---

66. Literally, *shingi* or innovation.
67. A *koku* was the nominal amount one grown man required in a year.

Item (10). Styles of clothing should not be mixed. Undyed patterned silk (*shiro-aya*) can be worn only by the high nobility and above. White silk robes (*kosode*) can be worn only by those with the rank of *taifu* (grandee).[68] Purple-lined robes, white glossy silk robes, or robes with no crests must not be worn without good reason. The old regulations do not expressly grant the followers and warriors of a given house permission to wear silk, damask, or brocade embroidery; therefore, they may not wear these items.

Item (11). Those who may ride palanquins: high-ranking people of Tokugawa lineage, lords of provinces, lords of castles, warriors possessing over ten thousand *koku*, the sons of provincial lords, the heirs of lords of castles, the heirs of those with the rank of adviser (*jijū*) or higher, anyone over fifty years of age, doctors or *yin-yang* specialists, and sick people. Only these people may ride in palanquins; any violation (*ransui*) is prohibited. Nevertheless, anyone who has been given special permission to ride palanquins can do so. In each province, people from notable houses can be selected to ride in palanquins. Of course, these regulations do not apply to nobles, members of the monastic nobility (*monzeki*), and other high-ranking monks.

Item (12). Anyone who has had troubles with their original lords should not be employed by others. If a retainer is discovered to be a rebel or murderer, they must be returned to their original lord. Any uppity retainers should be returned to their original lord or banished.

Item (13). A lord must receive a magistrate's permission before banishing or executing his followers who provided hostages to the *bakufu*.[69] If a hostage is cut down unavoidably in the heat of the moment, details of the incident must be reported to a magistrate.

Item (14). Local administration must be fair and impartial. Illegalities[70] are prohibited; otherwise, the provinces and districts will decay.

Item (15). Do not block roads or bridges, hinder the passage of station horses or boats, or otherwise interfere with traffic.

Item (16). Do not create private toll barriers or create new regulations that interfere with the circulation of goods.

Item (17). Ships capable of transporting over five hundred *koku* of cargo are prohibited.

---

68. This generally refers to high-ranking warriors.
69. The Tokugawa wanted to retain authority over those who provided hostages to them. Otherwise, those who provided hostages would only depend on their lord.
70. Presumably this refers to bribery but also local officials placing themselves above the law as well.

Item (18). Temples and shrines have possessed lands in the provinces since ancient times; they should not be confiscated.

Item (19). The laws of Edo should be followed in all matters and in all provinces and places throughout Japan.

10. Kumazawa Banzan, "Abolition of the Separate Soldier Class"[71]

Kumazawa Banzan (1619–91) astutely criticized the removal of samurai from the land, and the burdens of alternate attendance as enervating the military power of Tokugawa domains. He realized that for a region to be powerful, warriors needed to reside on the land, while peasants had to be prepared to fight for the domain. These conditions were only met in the largest tozama domains. Banzan justified these policies according to the Confucian-inspired notion of jinsei, *or benevolent government.*

CHAPTER XII: ABOLITION OF THE SEPARATE SOLDIER CLASS

Question: For a long time there have been two classes of subjects, the *samurai* (soldiers) and the farmers. Is it not possible to join them again into one class as in olden times?

Answer: If the Way of reason does not prevail, it will be hard to do. If the Way does prevail, it will be easy. Even a lord of benevolent and receptive heart, if he should govern with laxity and inefficiency, could hardly expect to reunite them. That would not be the *jinsei* to which I have referred.

Question: What do you mean by laxity and inefficiency?

Answer: Even though all the *daimyō* were ordered to conform to the old rule of living at Yedo [Edo] fifty days during every three years, if they were at liberty, at other times, to lead a life of extravagance, it would be a case of "winning in the East and losing in the West" there would be no net gain. The benevolent policy of which I have spoken can be effectively carried out by command of the Government, just as a father directs his family affairs. After the Government has investigated and found that it had even more grain than it could store, it could easily return rice to the farmers and soldiers, and thereby greatly please them.

---

71. Kumazawa Banzan, "Abolition of the Separate Soldier Class," from Fisher, trans., "A Discussion of Public Questions in the Light of the Greater Learning," in *Transactions of the Asiatic Society of Japan*, 313–17.

Section X • The Late Sixteenth- and Early Seventeenth-Century Transformations

First of all, let the Government adjust the debts of the people, returning mortgaged rice-fields to their owners, and buying back the fields at the original price, so as to return them to the sellers. Then most of the rice-fields bought should go back to a small number of sellers. But if the number of the rice-fields sold is larger than the number of buyers, then the fields should go to the buyers. Next, let the *samurai* live among the farmers and release the farmers from a tenth of the tribute ordinarily due, and gradually this would lead to a larger tax reduction. The backwardness of the farmers is due to their separation from the *samurai*. Therefore, let the *samurai* stick to residence in the country districts, always remembering that the people from generation to generation, in life and in death, are their hereditary vassals, for whose betterment they ought to be solicitous. In time of war, let the *samurai* take the farmers with them to the battlefield, but not too many of them in ordinary times. Two or three will be enough.

When the *samurai* are not on guard or official duty, and go to visit other *samurai* in nearby towns and villages, let them enter by the kitchen and talk and avoid being treated as guests. This will save time and expense. If they do a little farming and weed the garden, it will be recreation for themselves and lend a helping hand to the villeins. But it better fits *samurai* to hunt in the mountains and fish in the streams, regardless of rain and wind, to cultivate martial and literary arts, and to guard the lord's castle in time of need. These various duties should be defined in rules drawn up as occasion demands.

When a *samurai* of higher rank has many children he may not have enough property to go around among them. The time may come when their descendants will have to become *samurai* farmers, paying taxes at the rate of one-tenth of their income.

The duties of commissioners of the *Shōgun* (*bugyō*) and deputies (*daikan*, higher representatives) are important, but nowadays some deputies cannot control the people, and it may be well for a general commander of retainers and a company captain to divide responsibility for a number of villages and hamlets, and become in a real sense deputies of the *Shōgun*.

Question: A lord of a castle of 100,000 *koku*, a medium-sized fief, would pay a tax of 50,000 *koku* at the rate of 50 per cent, or 10,000 *koku* at the rate of ten per cent. Is it right for him to pay as much as 50 per cent?

Answer: The tax of 50,000 *koku* of rice really becomes a 40 per cent tax, when the 10,000 *koku* stored for food and reserve has been deducted. This is not enough to pay the expense of living at Yedo. If he borrows and runs into debt, he must pay the interest and pile up a larger debt. Gradually the family estate will be mortgaged and they will be guilty of such inhumanities as turning out retainers. If *jinsei* were applied, and a *daimyō* were to spend at Yedo fifty days during every three years, returning to the old rule, then he could save 1,000 *koku* a year, which would be

10. Kumazawa Banzan, "Abolition of the Separate Soldier Class"

3,000 *koku* in three years, an amount ample to meet the expense of the Yedo service. A reserve of 9,000 *koku* of rice laid by each year is more than he would need. A good way to save expense on castle maintenance would be to summon men from the surrounding villages to serve as guards, the only expense being their rations. The castle would he well protected in fact by the central and second citadels, so that a tenth of the present *samurai* living quarters would suffice. The area thus cleared could he turned into rice-fields, which would benefit both *samurai* and commoners. The larger compounds should be given to the *samurai* who are serving in the castle. Let them plant bamboo hedges across the fronts, and mulberry trees along the side boundaries, so that their wives and children can raise silkworms.

Question: What shall be done with the *daimyō* around Yedo (within the barrier)?

Answer: It may be all right for them to cultivate the soil in Yedo like farmer-*samurai*. Under *jinsei*, all the *daimyō* would be held in check, and their mothers, wives and children would be sent back to their respective provinces. Then one mansion in Yedo would suffice for a *daimyō*, and one-tenth of the present tributary buildings would he enough for all needs. All of the direct feudatories of the *Shōgun* (*hatamoto*), and the others of high rank should return to their respective domains. A general should be despatched to command the guard of the Shogunal treasury. The wide area in Yedo left vacant by the removal of the unnecessary buildings could be used for rice-fields, if there were a plentiful water-supply, and if level, they could he flooded. Realizing the peace and happiness of the life of a farmer-soldier, there may be many *samurai* of lower rank who would like to go to such farms.

Schools should be established where the duties of superior and inferior would be taught and the character of the people be improved. The carrying out of this plan calls for consultation. Let the *samurai* officials be given mansions with large grounds on the four sides of the castle, with hedges along the front, and mulberry trees along the back boundary, and they will always enjoy a pleasing landscape. The foreman of the lower workers should withdraw them five or ten *ri* away from the castle, but they should be brought back to act as guards around the castle during fifty or a hundred days a year. The use of the bow and the musket and the art of fighting should be taught, especially to the guards. They should go to school and learn the Way of virtue, so that they would do their duty gladly.

Three hundred able *samurai*, far removed from their wives and children, are worth more than a thousand *samurai* with their wives and children around them at the castle town.

If peace prevails as a result of *jinsei*, there is nothing to be anxious about, but military preparations and literary studies must never be forgotten, lest virtue and culture should suffer.

Section X • The Late Sixteenth- and Early Seventeenth-Century Transformations

Question: After the situation has been examined and the ten per cent rate of tribute has been restored, is there no danger that the Government stores of rice would run short?

Answer: In the present state of things, there is no advantage in giving the rice either to the various *daimyō* or to the higher officers of the Shogunate. Nor would it help to let the common people waste it. If it were withheld from high and low alike, the Shogunate would have plenty. If the Shogunate should run short, then let the old regulation be revived by which *daimyō* had to pay one-fiftieth of their income as tribute during the two years they stayed at home. Let the matter be adjusted after due investigation. The old requirement would mean a tribute of two hundred *koku* out of an income of ten thousand *koku*, and two thousand *koku* out of an income of 100,000. There might be some additional tax on miscellaneous income.

The guard for Kyoto, Ōsaka and Suruga should be abolished; the number of temples and shrines should be reduced and repairs be made only after close scrutiny. By these means the Government expenses could he reduced. Men of character should be given appropriate posts, and if perchance the Government lacks the means to pay them, then all the *daimyō* should confer and somehow find a way to do it. Even if the *daimyō* were reimbursed by the Government for most of their official expenses, a slightly higher rate of tribute would yield enough to pay them. When the *Shōgun* treats the *daimyō* like his sons, then the *daimyō* will regard him as their own father.

Question: If it is true that wealth should he used to develop the country until storage space for the harvest runs short, will the Government always have enough?

Answer: National wealth is to be used for the whole people. If overflowing harvests are used for culture and martial equipment, there will never be lack. After everything has been regulated, poverty and distress will cease, and wealth will not be wasted. When the old system of farmer-soldiers is restored and a tribute of one-tenth is paid, and wealth is used for the sake of the people, their hearts will he won. When plenty prevails and it is the custom to spend wealth with kindness and sympathy, then the people will know no lack. When the *samurai* become farmer-soldiers, the martial spirit of the nation will be greatly strengthened and it will deserve to be called the country of *samurai*. Since the *samurai* and farmers became separate classes, the *samurai* have fallen sick and become weak in hands and feet. It avails nought to boast if the warrior plays out when he confronts an enemy or if he dies of disease. His young retainers of lower rank will lose all respect for such a *samurai* and want to quit the service in a year. This will surely weaken the military forces. On the whole, a noble and lasting social order can only be built on a farmer-*samurai* basis. Now is the time to restore the farmer-soldier of olden times.

SECTION XI
The *Samurai* of the Tokugawa Era (1603–1867)

With the onset of peace in Japan, debates arose over what to do with the *samurai*, and the warrior culture more generally. Some early thinkers, such as Kumazawa Banzan (1619–91) (see Kumazawa Banzan, "Abolition of the Separate Soldier Class," p. 267), argued that warriors must be tied to the land in order to be effective fighters. To Banzan, life in newly founded capital cities made the *samurai* soft and ineffectual. The autobiography of Confucian scholar Arai Hakusei (1657–1725) (Arai Hakuseki's *Autobiography*, p. 272), ably recounts changes in *samurai* attitudes and status by describing his father and grandfather, who lost his land holdings. In addition, Hakuseki's account of a fugitive *samurai* reveals that warrior violence still lingered for decades after the establishment of a Tokugawa peace.

Yamamoto Tsunetomo (1659–1719) wrote privately that the way of the *samurai* was found in death; he advocated that *samurai* focus on that which they could control—their end (see *The Book of the Samurai Hagakure* by Yamamoto Tsunetomo, p. 276). He also voiced skepticism regarding earlier morals and beliefs. Other *samurai* relied on ruses and the threat of committing suicide to squeeze taxes out of peasants (*Musui's Story: The Autobiography of a Tokugawa Samurai*, p. 280). Fukuzawa Yukichi (1835–1901), a *samurai* who gained knowledge of European affairs, was critical of *samurai* ideals and mores, rejecting most of them entirely (see *The Autobiography of Yukichi Fukuzawa*, p. 291). Shiba Gorō (1860–1945), the young son of a *samurai* family, fought valiantly, and his mothers and sisters killed themselves in the battles of 1869, which closely followed the collapse of the Tokugawa regime (see *The Testament of Shiba Gorō*, p. 292). This section closes with two warriors' petitions, written in an archaic fourteenth-century style, for reward (Two Petitions for Reward Submitted in 1869, p. 297).

Section XI • *The Samurai of the Tokugawa Era*

1. Excerpts from Arai Hakuseki's *Autobiography*[1]

Arai Hakusei compares his way of life with that of his grandfather, who experienced the last great battles of the early seventeenth century. He also shows how his grandfather lost status and power and was forced to give up one of his younger sons (Hakuseki's father) to adoption. Hakuseki's account also reveals how commoners remembered and at times aided fugitive ancestral lords or their descendants.

Book 1.

My father said that as he lost his mother at the age of four and his father at the age of nine, he knew little about his parents. Grandfather's name was Kageyu, and grandmother was the daughter of someone called Someya. Both ended their days in Shimozuma-no-Shō in Hitachi Province.

The Arai sprang from the Minamoto clan of Kōzuke Province. The Someya were descended from the Fujiwara of Sagami Province, but for some reason they moved to Hitachi Province. There is a traditional explanation, but as it was not positively stated by my father, I cannot accept it.

My father told me; "Your grandfather said he lost his fief for some reason and went into hiding on the estate he used to possess. I remember that his eyes were large, his beard thick, and his expression stern. When he died, his hair had not yet turned white."

Whenever grandfather ate, he always took his chopsticks from a black lacquered box, decorated in gold with irises, and when he had finished eating, he put them back in the box and placed it by his side. When father asked his old nurse about it, she told him that once, after grandfather had taken a good head in a battle, the general said to him when he presented himself: "You must be weary with fighting. Eat this." He pushed forward his dinner-tray and gave it to grandfather with the chopsticks. This became a famous incident at the time, and so grandfather would never let them leave his side. My father added: "Since I was a child when I heard the story, I am not certain when she said it happened, where the battle took place, or who the general was."

My father once said: "One other thing I remember. When I was playing with a companion of the same age, your grandfather heard me say to him: 'You're the fellow who called me a fool.' Your grandfather said to me: 'It is a great insult for a man to be called a fool. Though just now you were only speaking in jest, it was as bad as if you insulted yourself. You should not say such things.'"

---

1. Ackroyd, *Told Round a Brushwood Fire*, 37–40, 49–50.

1. Excerpts from Arai Hakuseki's Autobiography

Father told me: "After your grandfather's death, by an arrangement made by my elder brothers, I was brought up in the house of a certain man. He was not like your grandfather, but was very rich and had many servants and a great collection of bows, muskets, long spears, etc. He was very fond of me, but when I was thirteen, a friend I had had a quarrel with said: "What can a fellow understand who does not know that he has become the son of his own retainer?" I could not understand, and since there was no one else to ask, I went to the house of my old nurse and asked her about it; she told me not to bother myself about such things. More and more perplexed, I persisted. Then she wept and said: "Since those you now regard as your parents were mindful of past kindnesses, your father died peacefully. Now, this man is rich. He could adopt anyone's son, but he has adopted you and loves you better than his own son because he bears in mind that you are the son of his lord. You must devote yourself to serving him dutifully."

When I heard this, I felt a deep resentment against my elder brothers, and so I went to the priest who taught me calligraphy and borrowed copper coins. Fastening up some clothes in wrapping paper, I hung them on my sword hilt, did up the coins in my belt, and set off. Having gone two or three *ri*, I fell in with two couriers on their way from Mito to Edo. I inquired about the road to Edo, and they said: "If a young fellow travels alone, he will be in danger of robbery. Come along with us." Thinking this was so, I went with them. When they asked where I was from, whose son I was, and whose house I was going to in Edo, I did not reply immediately, but as they were kind, and let me ride when I was tired, I thought there was no reason to be so fearful and told them how things were. They were sorry for me, took me to Edo, and looked after me. With their help, I found a master.

Twenty-five years after your grandfather's death, desirous of visiting his grave, I returned to my native village. My three elder brothers were dead, and my elder sister alone survived. My sister told me that my second eldest brother, grieved at not knowing my whereabouts, had gone to Edo every year inquiring for me everywhere, again and again, but now he was dead. Later I heard that she too had died shortly afterward. After that, there was no one to visit in my native village.

My father's mother died on the 2nd April 1604, and his father died on the 25th September 1609. My father was born in 1601. He left his native province in 1613.

A man called Ryōya, a former abbot of Kōtokuji, told me that when he was still a child, in the time of the abbot who preceded him, someone called Arai Kansai visited this temple. Ryōya took word to my father, who came to meet the visitor, and the two stayed together all day. The visitor sometimes came every year, and sometimes after an interval of several years. Ryōya heard he was a cousin but was not sure, nor did he know where he came from. I do not know whether my mother knew about this, much less did she dare tell me. Why were people in olden times so reticent? Even Ryōya did not tell me of this until thirty years or so after my father's death.

Not long after the civil wars, when my father was still young, men were chivalrous and were accustomed to setting a high value on nobility of spirit, in contrast to the situation today. My father spent some years wandering no one knows where. At the age of thirty-one, when he first entered the service of Mimbu-no-Shō Minamoto Toshinao (Tsuchiya), three foot-soldiers (at that time called *kachizamurai*) were accused of night burglary. They were arrested and confined above the firing gallery in the gate-tower and placed in the sole charge of my father. On being informed of this, father said: "If these men are committed to my custody, I hope their long and short swords will not be taken away from them." My father's request was granted, and their weapons were handed over to him. Giving them to a servant to carry, he climbed up to the floor above the gallery and returned them to the three men, saying: "If you intend to escape, cut off my head and go. I alone am no match for the three of you, so my own weapons are useless." Then he wrapped his two swords in a piece of toweling and laid them aside, and so he slept and ate with the men. After about ten days, the charge against them was proved baseless. Nevertheless they were dismissed from the Kohō's House on the grounds that he did not want such men in his service. When that time came, they said to my father: "We felt that the lord committed us to the charge of only one man because he considered us contemptible. We intended to prove otherwise, but if we had killed you, unarmed as you were, he would have concluded that we were as despicable as he had thought, which would have been unbearable. There was nothing for us but to wait for death, but still we planned, if by some lucky chance our lives were spared, to take our revenge. Owing to your kindness, our weapons were not confiscated, and now we can take our place in the company of warriors again. We do not wish to be unmindful of your kindness, and we feel that our resentment has been done away with." With this they parted. This is the story as my father told it to me.

Shortly afterward, he was selected for special duties, and at last became a permanent retainer in the Kohō's House, Later he was appointed a surveillance officer (at that time called a *metsuke*).

The events which I now relate are my own recollections dating from the time when I first began to understand things.

My father's daily routine was always the same and never varied. He always rose early at about four o'clock, bathed in cold water, and dressed his own hair. When the nights were cold, my mother wanted him to use warm water, but he would not countenance putting the servants to this trouble and forbade it. When he was past seventy, my mother said that she too was getting on in years and could no longer endure the cold nights, so hot coals were placed on the ashes in the hearth, and they

1. Excerpts from Arai Hakuseki's Autobiography

lay down with their feet toward it. A kettle of water was placed by the side of the fire, and when my father got up, he bathed with the hot water.

Both my parents were devout Buddhists. My father never neglected to make obeisance to Buddha each morning, after he had done up his hair and put on his clothes. On the anniversaries of his parents' deaths, he prepared rice and placed it on the altar with his own hands, without troubling the servants. While the night was still dark, he sat up waiting for the dawn, and as soon as it was light, he went on duty.

**

My father said that when he was young, there was a certain man named Takataki who served in the House of the Lord of Shisawa, in Harima. (He was commonly called Kichibei; I do not know his given name.) This man suddenly disappeared. After some days had passed, the story went about that, being fond of fishing, he had gone out with what is called a casting net, and, taking off his clothes by the riverside, had told his servant to guard his two swords carefully while he himself, carrying the net, went into the water. As he walked along catching trout, he crossed the border of the territory of Hayashida. The lord of that region had forbidden fishing in that place, and Kichibei was seized by two guards. When they went to tie him up with a rope, he pleaded piteously with them; they grudgingly let him go free, and off he went.

He then disappeared, perhaps because he thought that the affair would eventually become known. It was being said that he had suffered this misadventure because of his fondness for so frivolous a pastime when that year drew to a close. On the day of the lunar New Year of the following year, he cut down one of the chief samurai among the large number on duty in front of the great gate of the Hayashida mansion. He left a card describing in detail the circumstances of what he had done, stating that it was in order to wipe out his shame, and fled. Thinking that he had not fled far, they sent out parties to search for him, but they were unable to find him. The next day he cut down another man and left his card as before. Although no time was lost in making a search, once more he could not be found. Five days later he cut down yet another man, left a card, and fled as before. Despite a thorough search, they were never able to discover where he had gone. People said that to do such a deed once was easy, but to do it twice and three times proved his courage beyond a doubt. My father said: "After I went to serve in the Kohō's House, I used to relate this incident. Later, when I went to take charge of affairs in Kazusa, my companions and I came to a place called Takataki where we stopped in at the house of the headman. When night fell, a crowd of villagers came in and one of them, a man close to sixty, who was seated at the other side of the fire that was burning in a long hearth, caught my eye and then averted his face.

His glance seemed peculiar, so I stared in his direction, and he also looked back at me and then away, two or three times. I was puzzled and got up from my seat, went across to him and asked him who he was. At first he turned away saying only that he was a native of that place. Afterward he said: 'How can I conceal myself in this way? I am the ruin of that Takataki whom you once knew.' I was astonished, and exclaimed: 'How do you come to be living here?'

"Thereupon he said: 'I am descended from the Kazusa branch of the Takataki who were retainers of the Kamakura Bakufu. I am a grandson of the Takataki who bore the title of Sakyō-no Jō at the time of the Satomi of Awa who annexed this province. When the House of Satomi was destroyed, I entered the House of the Lord of Shisawa. After that incident occurred, I fled here. My ancestors had held this place for generations, and the people here sheltered me for the sake of the past. When I heard that a man called Arai had come here, I wondered if it was the man I had met. I came to see, but you were surprised and spoke in an embarrassed way, and so I was ashamed.'

"When my companions asked me if I knew the man, I said: 'He is the Takataki who, it is said, cut down three men in Harima Province in the space of seven days, and each time set up a card.' They were all astounded. How hard it is to foresee the vicissitudes of a man's life."

2. Excerpts from *The Book of the Samurai Hagakure* by Yamamoto Tsunetomo[2]

Yamamoto Tsunetomo (1659–1719) was a samurai from the Saga domain of Hizen Province, which was controlled by the Nabeshima. After his lord Nabeshima Mitsushige died in 1700, the forty-two-year-old Tsunetomo, disappointed that he could not follow his lord in death, retired. His sayings were recorded by Tashiro Tsuramoto, a fellow samurai, and published with the title "Hidden Leaves" or "Hidden by Leaves" (Hagakure). This work was kept secret, circulated among samurai of the domain, and only became widely known in the nineteenth and early twentieth centuries as the notion of Japan's warrior culture, and "samurai spirit" came to be popularized. Yamamoto's famous opening passage is included here, as are other passages critiquing the forty-seven rōnin—masterless warriors who engaged in an elaborate vendetta and were elsewhere lauded as exemplars. Though Yamamoto's quotes are

---

2. Yamamoto Tsunetomo, *The Book of the Samurai*, 17, 28–29, 38–39, 43–44, 144–45.

2. Excerpts from The Book of the Samurai Hagakure by Yamamoto Tsunetomo

often used to promote the concept of "unthinking action," he also focuses on the importance of training and concentration. He also related an anecdote about a warrior who refused high status in order to remain able to act as he pleased.

The Way of the Samurai is found in death. When it comes to either/or, there is only the quick choice of death. It is not particularly difficult. Be determined and advance. To say that dying without reaching one's aim is to die a dog's death is the frivolous way of sophisticates. When pressed with the choice of life or death, it is not necessary to gain one's aim. We all want to live. And in large part we make our logic according to what we like. But not having attained our aim and continuing to live is cowardice. This is a thin dangerous line. To die without gaining one's aim is a dog's death and fanaticism. But there is no shame in this. This is the substance of the Way of the Samurai. If by setting one's heart right every morning and evening, one is able to live as though his body were already dead, he pains freedom in the Way. His whole life will be without blame, and he will succeed in his calling.

*

At the time when there was a council concerning the promotion of a certain man, the council members were at the point of deciding that promotion was useless because of the fact that the man had previously been involved in a drunken brawl. But someone said, "If we were to cast aside every man who had made a mistake once, useful men could probably not be come by. A man who makes a mistake once will be considerably more prudent and useful because of his repentance. I feel that he should be promoted." Someone else then asked, "Will you guarantee him?" The man replied, "Of course I will." The others asked, "By what will you guarantee him?" And he replied, "I can guarantee him by the fact that he is a man who has erred once. A man who has never once erred is dangerous." This said, the man was promoted.

*

A certain person was brought to shame because he did not take revenge. The way of revenge lies in simply forcing one's way into a place and being cut down. There is no shame in this. By thinking that you must complete the job you will run out of time. By considering things like how many men the enemy has, time piles up; in the end you will give up.

No matter if the enemy has thousands of men, there is fulfillment in simply standing them off and being determined to cut them all down, starting from one end. You will finish the greater part of it.

Concerning the night assault of Lord Asano's *rōnin*, the fact that they did not commit *seppuku* at the Sengakuji was an error, for there was a long delay between the time their lord was struck down and the time when they struck down the enemy. If Lord Kira had died of illness within that period, it would have been extremely regrettable. Because the men of the Kamigata area have a very clever sort of wisdom, they do well at praiseworthy acts but cannot do things indiscriminately, as was done in the Nagasaki fight.[3]

Although all things are not to be judged in this manner, I mention it in the investigation of the Way of the Samurai. When the time comes, there is no moment for reasoning. And if you have not done your inquiring beforehand, there is most often shame. Reading books and listening to people's talk are for the purpose of prior resolution. Above all, the Way of the Samurai should be in being aware that you do not know what is going to happen next, and in querying every item day and night. Victory and defeat are matters of the temporary force of circumstances. The way of avoiding shame is different. It is simply in death.

Even if it seems certain that you will lose, retaliate. Neither wisdom nor technique has a place in this. A real man does not think of victory or defeat. He plunges recklessly towards an irrational death. By doing this, you will awaken from your dreams.

*

According to the situation, there are times when you must rely on a person for something or other. If this is done repeatedly, it becomes a matter of importuning that person and can be rather rude. If there is something that must be done, it is better not to rely on others.

*

There is something to be learned from a rainstorm. When meeting with a sudden shower, you try not to get wet and run quickly along the road. But doing such things as passing under the eaves of houses, you still get wet. When you are resolved from the beginning, you will not be perplexed, though you still get the same soaking. This understanding extends to everything.

*

In China there was once a man who liked pictures of dragons, and his clothing and furnishings were all designed accordingly. His deep affection for dragons was brought to the attention of the dragon god, and one day a real dragon appeared before his window. It is said that he died of fright. He was probably a man who always spoke big words but acted differently when facing the real thing.

*

---

3. The incident involving Lord Asano's retainers (dramatized in the Kabuku play *Chūshingura*) is regarded as an example of true loyalty. Tsunetomo disagrees, feeling that the retainers should have taken revenge immediately, rather than wait a whole year to be sure of the killing of Lord Kira. The Nagasaki Fight resulted from a man's accidentally splashing mud on a *samurai* of another clan. Tsunetomo feels that the men involved acted properly, because they took revenge immediately, without pausing to consider the cause or the consequences of what they were doing.

2. Excerpts from The Book of the Samurai Hagakure by Yamamoto Tsunetomo

There was a certain person who was a master of the spear. When he was dying, he called his best disciple and spoke his last injunctions: "I have passed on to you all the secret techniques of this school, and there is nothing left to say. If you think of taking on a disciple yourself, then you should practice diligently with the bamboo sword every day." Superiority is not just a matter of secret techniques. Also, in the instructions of a *renga* teacher, it was said that the day before the poetry meeting one should calm his mind and look at a collection of poems. This is concentration on one affair. All professions should be done with concentration.

*

Although the Mean is the standard for all things, in military affairs a man must always strive to outstrip others. According to archery instructions the right and left hands are supposed to be level, but the right hand has a tendency to go higher. They will become level if one will lower the right hand a bit when shooting. In the stories of the elder warriors it is said that on the battlefield if one wills himself to outstrip warriors of accomplishment, and day and night hopes to strike down a powerful enemy, he will grow indefatigable and fierce of heart and will manifest courage. One should use this principle in everyday affairs too.

*

There is a way of bringing up the child of a samurai. From the time of infancy, one should encourage bravery and avoid trivially frightening or teasing the child. If a person is affected by cowardice as a child, it remains a lifetime scar. It is a mistake for parents to thoughtlessly make their children dread lightning, or to have them not go into dark places or to tell them frightening things in order to stop them from crying.

*

You cannot tell whether a person is good or bad by his vicissitudes in life. Good and bad fortune are matters of fate. Good and bad actions are Man's Way. Retribution of good and evil is taught simply as a moral lesson.

*

Because of some business, Morooka Hikoemon was called upon to swear before the gods concerning the truth of a certain matter. But he said, "A samurai's word is harder than metal. Since I have impressed this fact on myself, what more can the gods and Buddhas do?" and the swearing was canceled. This happened when he was twenty-six.

*

Master Ittei said, "Whatever one prays for will be granted. Long ago there were no *matsutake* mushrooms in our province. Some men who saw them in the Kamigata area prayed that they might grow here, and nowadays they are growing all over Kitayama. In the future I would like to have Japanese cypress grow in our province. As this is something that everyone desires, I predict it for the future. This being so, everyone should pray for it."

*

When something out of the ordinary happens, it is ridiculous to say that it is a mystery or a portent of something to come. Eclipses of the sun and moon, comets, clouds that flutter like flags, snow in the fifth month, lightning in the twelfth month, and so on, all are things that occur every fifty or one hundred years. They occur according to the evolution of Yin and Yang. The fact that the sun rises in the east and sets in the west would be a mystery, too, if it were not an everyday occurrence. It is not dissimilar. Furthermore, the fact that something bad always happens in the world when strange phenomena occur is due to people seeing something like fluttering clouds and thinking that something is going to happen. The mystery is created in their minds, and by waiting for the disaster, it is from their very minds that it occurs. The occurrence of mysteries is always by word of mouth.

*

Calculating people are contemptible. The reason for this is that calculation deals with loss and gain, and the loss and gain mind never stops. Death is considered loss and life is considered gain. Thus, death is something that such a person does not care for, and he is contemptible. Furthermore, scholars and their like are men who with wit and speech hide their own true cowardice and greed. People often misjudge this.

*

Hirano Gonbei was one of the Men of Seven Spears who advanced straight up the hill at the battle of Shizugadake. At a later date he was invited to become one of Lord Ieyasu's *hatamoto*. Once he was being entertained at Master Hosokawa's. The master said, "Master Gonbei's bravery is not a hidden matter in Japan. It is truly a shame that such a man of bravery has been placed in a low rank such as you are in now. This must be contrary to your wishes. If you were to become a retainer of mine, I would give you half the domain." Giving no answer at all, Gonbei suddenly got up from his seat, went out to the veranda, stood facing the house, and urinated. Then he said, "If I were the master's retainer, it would never do to urinate from here."

3. Selections from *Musui's Story: The Autobiography of a Tokugawa Samurai*[4]

This account by Katsu Kokichi (1802–50), a marginal samurai, ruffian, and charlatan, provides a remarkable window onto the late Tokugawa world. The first selection recounts episodes in his youth, while the later extended passage

---

4. Craig, *Musui's Story*, 16–17, 128–42.

3. Selections from Musui's Story: The Autobiography of a Tokugawa Samurai *reveals a remarkable moment later in his life, after he had taken Buddhist vows. When a friend gambled away the tax revenue he had collected from Goganzuka village, Katsu employed a variety of stratagems, detailed here, to force the villagers to pay still more taxes. Other sources confirm that he did, in fact, manage to con the villagers in this way. Katsu Kokichi's son became one of the last generals of the Tokugawa regime.*

When I was nine, my father told me to take judo lessons with Suzuki Seibei, a relative of the Katsu family in Yokoami-chō. Suzuki served as the head of the office of procurements and was reputed to have many students, among them *daimyō* from provincial domains and from the great houses of Hitotsubashi and Tayasu. The classes I attended were held on the third, fifth, eighth, and tenth days of each month. I behaved myself at first but soon got into mischief. My fellow students strongly disliked me and ganged up against me all the time.

On my way to class one day I found to my great surprise that a crowd of boys from Mae-chō and their parents were lying in wait for me near the Hannoki riding ground. "Here comes that troublemaker Otani—let's beat him to a pulp!" they yelled, and flourishing bamboo spears and sticks, they quickly closed in on me. I drew my sword, slashed my way out, and clambered up the embankment of the riding ground. Just below was a muddy ditch that surrounded the shogunate lumberyard. I jumped in. I spattered my *haori* and *hakama*,[5] but at least I had escaped. The gatekeeper of the lumberyard was a friend of mine—I often went there to play—and knowing he was a brave man, I had him walk me home. Forty or fifty people were still waiting. Did we get a thrashing!

For two months I avoided that section of Kamezawa-chō. Then one day I caught Tatsu, the son of an embroidery craftsman in Kamezawa-chō, walking by our house. I ran out and struck him with my sword until one of our retainers had to come out and restrain me. He told me later that he had taken Tatsu home and explained to his parents that I was only trying to get even for what had happened near the riding ground. In any case, no one in Kamezawa-chō crossed me after that.

As I said, everyone in judo class hated me. On the day that an all-night midwinter session was to be held, we received permission from the teacher to bring food. We took a break at midnight. I had packed a lacquer box full of bean jam cakes and had been looking forward all day to this moment when we would share the food. My classmates had other plans. They got together and tied me up with an obi, hoisted me to one of the rafters, and began eating, even helping themselves to my

---

5. A *haori* is a kimono-like jacket, and a *hakama* is a divided skirt worn over a kimono. Both are worn when formal dress is required.

cakes. So I pissed on their heads, spraying the food that had been spread out, and naturally, everything had to be thrown away. Served them right, too.

*

I then persuaded Jizaemon a village headman in the fief, to lend me forty *ryō* for my travel expenses to Settsu and said I'd return it by the end of the year. Earlier in the seventh month I had submitted a request to my commissioner to become a lay Buddhist priest and change my name. I received permission from Wakisaka Nakatsukasa Shōyū on the seventeenth day of the tenth month. I took the religious name of Musui, but as my shaved samurai hairdo had not yet grown in, I decided to travel under my samurai name as a retainer of Okano Magoichirō.

I asked Toranosuke to tend to my affairs in my absence. On the ninth day of the eleventh month I set off on the Nakasendō post road.[6] Accompanying me were Hotta Kisaburō, Iyama Yūhachi, and two other men.

At the post station in Kumagaya, Jizaemon was waiting for me with the forty *ryō*. I was feeling none too well, but I pushed my men to cover as much distance as possible. We arrived at last at the Hakken'ya[7] in Osaka. We rested for several days and then went to Sonezaki, to the north of the city, to call on a friend, Kagatora. He was fortunately at home, and when I explained to him the purpose of my trip, he readily agreed to my request for a loan.

We arrived the next day at the village of Goganzuka, Magoichirō's fief in Settsu. It was about six miles from Osaka. We were put up at the residence of Yamada Shin'uemon, the manager of the fief. I lost no time in filling him in about the details of the situation in Edo.

In the morning I called together the villagers and told them of the urgent need for money. Shin'uemon said, "As you know, the rice yield of the village is assessed at five hundred *koku*, and the villagers have already lent over seven hundred *ryō*. I doubt if they can put up another penny." I had been told by Magoichirō and his retainers that the amount lent by the village came to five hundred *ryō* and had undertaken the trip on that assumption. This huge discrepancy was a complete surprise. I was extremely annoyed but said nothing and dismissed the villagers for the day. If I set my mind to it, I knew there would always be a way.

I spent the next few days walking around the village. The villagers seemed relatively prosperous—a good sign. I asked Shin'uemon how much it cost the villagers to accommodate official visitors. He replied that whenever a retainer came on business, he usually came with only one man, and daily expenses amounted to eighteen silver *monme*. There were five of us. We would have to be very frugal.

---

6. The post road connecting Edo and Kusatsu, a town just east of Kyoto; it was more circuitous and less traveled than the Tōkaidō.

7. Landing place for boats on the Yodo River; it had accommodations for travelers.

3. Selections from Musui's Story: The Autobiography of a Tokugawa Samurai

I told my men to decline all side dishes and to take them instead to Shin'uemon's mother. Each day I reminded them how important it was to cut down on expenses, though now and then I slipped them some money to sneak off to Itami for food and drink. Within several days, looking very pleased, Shin'uemon reported that our daily upkeep came to only ten *monme*. I refrained from bringing up the subject of money and took trips to Osaka for my own diversion as well as to gather information on the sly about the villagers. The rumor was that they had no intention of putting up the money. "They're simply waiting for you to get so bored that you'll leave," someone said.

To pass the time, every evening I invited Shin'uemon and the villagers and their children to hear me tell stories about the exploits of famous generals and brave warriors. They were very much taken and listened absorbed until late at night.

One day I again raised the subject of money. The villagers protested, "But we don't have any money." I dropped the matter. It then came to light that my man Iyama Yūhachi had on his own been pressuring the villagers to put up money. Feelings ran high. The angry villagers met day after day for discussions and began milling around our living quarters waving bamboo spears and shouting abuses. My men were afraid and said they wanted to go back to Edo. I gave them a piece of my mind.

The villagers continued to hold their daily meetings, rushing to the local temple at the sound of the bell. And all because of Iyama's stupid demands.

I wasn't a bit fazed. Now and then I put on my kimono with the shogunal crest[8] and marched around the village with a retainer in tow. This never failed to send the villagers scurrying. Every morning I had Hotta Kisaburō give readings on the *Greater Learning* and the *Book of Filial Piety* and invited Shin'uemon and his family to join us. Shin'uemon, a well-meaning and upright soul, appreciated this and offered to negotiate with the villagers on his own. I said no. For I had a plan up my sleeve—something so startling that the villagers would hand over the money, even while foaming at the mouth. I bided my time.

I came down with scabies and commuted daily to Koyama Hot Springs in Itami. But I set a man to spy on developments in the village. He found out that the village officials were cooking up various evil plots. I pretended not to know.

We had been in Goganzuka for some time. I thought I would pay a visit to Shimoyama Yauemon, a friend who was in the service of Hori Iga-no-kami, the magistrate of Osaka. I had done several favors for him back in Edo and was sure I could count on him. I talked to him in private—he already knew all about Magoichirō and his troubles—and returned to Goganzuka.

---

8. Presumably the kimono given to Katsu's adoptive father on the occasion of an audience with the shogun in 1792.

Shin'uemon was curious about my trip. "May I ask who you visited in Osaka?" he asked.

"Oh, Iga-no-kami, the magistrate—we used to take fencing lessons together."

"You don't say!" He looked intimidated.

Several days later a messenger arrived from Osaka with a train of bearers. He delivered an oral communication from the magistrate and presented me with boxes filled with fish and other delicacies. The villagers were struck dumb. "Little did we know, Katsu-sama, that you were friends with the Osaka magistrate." They put away their bamboo spears and gave up surrounding our lodgings. It was really funny.

I distributed the fish to the village officials and gave the rest to Shin'uemon and his family. It was reported that they all ate the food reverently, bowing their heads and murmuring, "A gift, a precious gift from the magistrate himself." They were also apparently chastened and willing to talk about money. I could carry out my scheme any day.

One morning I announced to Shin'uemon that I wished to make a pilgrimage to Nose Myōken Shrine and that I would be taking with me my man Kisaburō and two or three of the villagers who had been particularly troublesome. I wore the kimono with the shogunal crest and took along a spear box.[9] I said to the group, "Today I go not as a retainer of Okano Magoichirō but as a pilgrim." Just before leaving I said to Shin'uemon, "Could you get me a complete set of rainwear?"

"Oh, that won't be necessary," he said. "The weather's been fine for the past few days, and I'm sure it won't rain for at least five or six days."

"Then let me tell you that I've been devoted to Myōken-sama for many years and that every time I pray, it pours. So get some rainwear, will you?" He grudgingly provided a porter to carry the rainwear.

We set off, stopping at Ikeda long enough for the porter to go back and fetch a covering for my palanquin. The weather remained clear, and as we climbed uphill toward Mount Nose, we could see in the distance Osaka, Amagasaki, and further down the coastline of Settsu. For winter it was unusually warm and even with only one layer of clothing, we perspired. No one imagined for a moment that it would rain. The porter grumbled and complained.

I left my palanquin at a teahouse at the foot of Mount Nose and walked the last stretch to the peak. We purified ourselves with water from the shrine well and climbed the flight of steps leading to the main prayer hall. The other worshippers scattered in all directions when they saw the crest on my kimono, and we were left to pray undisturbed.

---

9. Part of the equipment for a *daimyō* procession; Katsu took it to lend an air of formality to the trip.

3. Selections from Musui's Story: The Autobiography of a Tokugawa Samurai

We took refreshments in the teahouse outside the main gate and began our descent. Halfway down I saw banks of rain clouds drifting over from Mount Rokkō in Arima.

"You're in luck," I said to the porter. "Any moment now it'll rain and your load will be lighter."

Everyone disagreed. "Just because there are rain clouds, it doesn't mean it's going to rain."

"I wouldn't want it to rain before we got to the inn anyway," I said, but urged them, nevertheless, to hurry.

No sooner had we reached the foot of the mountain than it began to pour. There was still some distance to the inn. The men were drenched, but I was nice and dry in the palanquin.

It stormed through the night and let up only around four in the morning. I stayed awake, warming myself at the hearth—you could never tell what the villagers might do, though there was no question that they had been impressed. "Katsu-sama," they said. "You are a man of truly strange and wondrous powers. You knew all along it was going to rain. It can mean only one thing—that the gods pay special attention to your prayers. Yes, indeed, the honorable bannermen of the *shōgun* are really different. The likes of us could pray for a hundred days, and this would never happen." I thought to myself, "I've got them now."

We made a brief detour to the Tada Gongen Shrine and arrived back at Goganzuka about four. That night Iyama came stealthily to my bedside. He said, "Katsusama, the whole village is agog about the rain. I have a feeling they've had a change of heart and that you'll be getting the money after all." I was heartened.

The next evening I had Iyama scout the situation again. He reported that the villagers were divided in two—those willing to put up the money and those who were not. Leaving Horta Kisaburō in charge, I decided to make another trip to Osaka and left early in the morning. I took in a play at Nipponbashi, had another talk with Shimoyama, and stayed overnight at the Hakken'ya.

The following day once again a messenger came from the Osaka magistrate with a letter and gifts of food. I had the food cooked and invited Shin'uemon, his staff, and the village headman. When we had finished eating, I read aloud the letter from the magistrate. Everyone looked subdued.

"Now about the money—" I began.

"We are doing our very best, but so far it's been impossible," they said. I left it at that and went to sleep.

In the morning I called for Shin'uemon. "Today I have a special reason for celebrating, and I would like to invite all the village officials for some sake around four. Order some particularly tasty dishes from Amagasaki—I'll pay for it—and see to it that the soup and all the other dishes are prepared with extra care." I gave him a copy of the menu I had planned and asked to have water heated for a bath. I had Kisaburō fix my hair and bathed while the men cleaned up the sitting room.

Then, leaving word that we were going to Gozu Tennō Shrine in Itami, I took my men to a kimono shop in Itami called the Shirokoya. I ordered three sets of ceremonial robes in linen and two sets of white *haori* and kimono dyed with the Okano family crest. "And have them ready by two this afternoon." The shopkeeper said he would, as long as he didn't have to dye in the crest. I paid for the goods and told him that someone would be by to pick them up.

On the way back I gave my men the particulars of the big farce I proposed to put on that evening. We returned to the village sometime past noon.

I had Kisaburō arrange a few sprays of white camellias in a vase to place in the alcove. It was close to five by the time we had attended to all the details. The food was ready to be served and the village officials had gathered in Shin'uemon's office. I asked everyone to come into the sitting room. "As you've no doubt heard, I have a special reason for inviting you here today. It was good of you to come. Now if you would just make yourselves at home and drink—" I poured sake for everyone. "And if there's anyone here with a hidden talent, please feel free to perform."

I started off with a popular ditty I had picked up during my wilder days in the Yoshiwara. I kept replenishing their cups and urged them to relax and forget formalities of rank. Unlike previous meetings at which money had been mentioned, the villagers were in high spirits, laughing and singing and saying the first thing that popped into their heads. Having satisfied myself that the sake had taken its effect, I ordered tea and rice to conclude the meal. The villagers finished eating, thanked me, and rose to leave.

I hurried out to the garden and washed myself with the buckets of water that had been set out according to plan. I quickly changed into one of the white kimono and wore over it the kimono with the shogunal crest. I piled several cushions in the center of the room flanked them with a pair of candlesticks, and sat down.

"Kisaburō," I called out. "Tell Shin'uemon and the village officials to come back. I have something important to say."

The villagers demurred. "Couldn't we wait until tomorrow? We've all had too much to drink—"

"No, I can't. I have a previous commitment to go to Osaka tomorrow and will probably be away four or five days. Since you're here anyway, you might as well sober up and listen to this message from your lord and master in Edo."

They straggled back to the adjoining room, and when everyone had been seated, Kisaburō threw open the partitions. The villagers bowed low.

3. Selections from Musui's Story: The Autobiography of a Tokugawa Samurai

"What I have to say is no less than this," I began. "For the past month all of you have conspired to ignore the repeated request from your lord for funds to settle the Jōsuke affair. It is inexcusable that you should think only of yourselves and look the other way when your lord makes an appeal. Be that as it may, be informed that I herewith call off all talk of money."

The villagers looked grateful and relieved. I went on. "I'll have you know that I made this trip expressly at the request of your lord and at great risk to my health. Time and again I appealed to you for help, but you turned a deaf ear, as if I were just another ordinary retainer. It was the height of rudeness. And then, for reasons I fail to understand, you threatened me and my men with bamboo spears. Pray tell me why you did this. Depending on your answer, I may have to take it up with the Osaka magistrate tomorrow and request a hearing."

Everyone remained huddled on the floor speechless. At length one of them spoke up in tears. "We are entirely to blame. Please have pity and forgive us."

"If you insist—what are you but poor benighted peasants?"

I turned to Shin'uemon. "Since they seem to be genuinely sorry, I will forgive them. There is one request, however, that I would like to make to you and the villagers. You will grant me this, I hope—"

The villagers said, "Anything, anything that we can possibly do. After all, you were good enough to overlook our offenses."

"My request is none other than this. As you know by now, the affair in Edo has involved Magoichirō's relatives, the senior councilor Ōta Bingo-no-kami, and several other high government officials. The fact is, it's much more serious than you imagine. Jōsuke is bargaining for all he's worth, nothing's been resolved, and the case threatens to be brought to the shogunate court any day. I, Kokichi, could not stand by idly, but try as I might, without money there was really nothing I could do. And that is why I came to you.

"I realize the amount Magoichirō wants to borrow is enormous and puts you in a difficult position. It isn't that I don't understand your reasons for refusing. All the same, you would do well to remember the debt you owe your lord from the time of his father, Gōsetsu. Indeed, it goes back several generations. Would it be right to forget it? In my opinion to abandon your lord when his family name and honor are in danger is behavior unworthy of even beast or fowl.

"Oh, one or two thousand *ryō* I could have easily borrowed from the Osaka magistrate. But what would be the point then of having been entrusted with the land by Gōsetsu? Just think if it were known that Magoichirō had bypassed his own fief and borrowed from another to restore his family fortune. In the first place it would be most unfilial to his ancestors. Or supposing it were bruited about that he had done this because he couldn't control the peasants on his own land—he would be hard put to revive his family name, much less show his face to his friends and peers.

"I came to Osaka in the hope that you would come forward—that lord and follower together would put things right and set an example of devotion that no one could criticize. But I, Kokichi, failed to raise the money, and having accomplished nothing, I cannot go back to Edo. In atonement I have decided to commit harakiri tonight. My request is simply this—that all of you here see to it that my corpse is delivered by the appropriate officials to my son in Edo. Yūhachi will take this letter immediately to Magoichirō. Kisaburō has already agreed to administer the final blow with his sword[10] and explain everything to my wife and children when he returns to Edo. As for the other two who accompanied me here from Edo, I thank them for all they've done. They may keep whatever money I gave them and leave tomorrow or do as they wish. I have nothing further to say. Ah yes, this kimono from the shogun—I leave with the village officials. Treat it with respect."

I took off my kimono and put it on a large tray. Handing Kisaburō my long sword, I said, "Use this to cut off my head." I ordered one of my men to bring the container in which to place my decapitated head—I'd brought it from Edo—and as I unsheathed my dagger and wound its handle with a strip of cloth, I reminded everyone to carry out my instructions. I looked around the room. "You may raise your heads now. Behold how Katsu Kokichi commits harakiri!" I held up the dagger.

"Stop. Please stop!" Crying out, the villagers crawled toward me.

"Kisaburō, are you ready?"

He remained bowed to the floor.

"Must I ask someone else?"

Kisaburō slowly got up and went behind me. Several villagers clung to him and wailed. "Please wait—we have something to say."

"Quickly then," Kisaburō said.

"Katsu-sama, we'll do whatever you say. Yes, even if we have to sell our possessions."

I said, "It's too late now."

"Please—we beg of you not to take your life. Please."

They beseeched me weeping and sobbing. I returned the dagger to its scabbard.

Shin'uemon tottered forward on his knees in a daze. "It is all my fault for not discharging my duties as manager of the fief. At the very least please cut off my head and send it to Edo."

---

10. In ritual harakiri another man stood by to administer the final blow by decapitation.

3. Selections from Musui's Story: The Autobiography of a Tokugawa Samurai

"That won't be necessary. The blame lies with everyone for being selfish and wanting in respect for their master. As far as I'm concerned, I've retired and don't ask much of this world. It doesn't matter what happens to me, though I was hoping that I might help a lot of people and that even Jōsuke might come round once he heard of my death. But since you insist, I will not take my life. Instead, I will ask you to sign a pledge that you will furnish the money."

The villages drew up a note immediately and signed their names. "When would you like to have the money?"

"By ten in the morning."

"Yes, yes, anything you say."

As they shuffled out of the room, Kisaburō spoke to them in a stern voice. "Be sure you get the money, because if anything goes wrong, then I'll commit harakiri."

The money was collected in a frenzy and presented on a tray the next morning at ten—all of 550 *ryō*, with a promise to have the remaining 50 *ryō* delivered to the House of Shimaya in Edo before we ourselves had returned. The villagers asked that their contribution to Magoichirō's living expenses be reduced from 330 *ryō* to 200 for the coming year. I told them that it was out of the question.

"Would you grant us this request, then?" they said. "Your man Iyama Yūhachi has extorted close to 400 *ryō* over the past year. We would appreciate it if you would hand him over to us so that we can hold an inquiry." I said, "As soon as the work's done." I could see Yūhachi shaking with fright, so after they had left, I told him not to worry.

The next order of business was to punish the villagers. I demoted the village officials who had been particularly defiant to the status of plain water-drinking peasants and replaced them with men who had served in Gōetsu's time. To those who had lent money, I granted the privilege of bearing surnames, and to Shin'uemon, I gave a set of ceremonial robes, a house, and a plot of land with a yield of almost one *koku* of rice.

By evening all the business had been completed. I told Shin'uemon that my men and I would be going to Kyoto for some sightseeing the next day. "Send some coolies ahead to make the necessary arrangements, and have everything we brought from Edo packed and ready. I'll be needing Yūhachi for a while yet, but I'll send him back from Kyoto." I turned to Yūhachi and said, "You're coming with me, do you hear?"

That night we were chatting and taking our ease when we were told that two village officials, Uichi and Gen'uemon, had come with a written petition claiming they had a note from Magoichirō promising to repay 150 *ryō* by the end of the year. "Tell them to extend the deadline to the coming year," I told Shin'uemon.

I could hear the two protesting in the next room so I went in and demanded to see the petition. Pretending to read it, I held the paper up to the candle and burned it. Uichi and Gen'uemon blanched and muttered something under their breath.

"Are you criticizing me?" I shouted. "It has come to my attention that you two have been the worst of the lot. I've tolerated it so far, but this time—" They both cringed. "And the note. I'll keep it thank you." I snatched the document and walked out. With one phrase I had disposed of a debt of 150 *ryō*. I thought then how important it was in life to strike at the right moment.

We left for Kyoto at four in the morning. The villagers didn't say a word. We rested up for three days at an inn near Sanjō Bridge and then set off for the Tōkaido. During the stop at Ōiso, I had my hair trimmed and combed back to fall behind the ears. At Kawasaki, I sent word ahead that we were returning. A crowd was waiting for us in Edo. It was the ninth day of the twelfth month.

I went straight to Magoichirō's house with the money. The entire family came out and talked as if I were a living god. Two days later I summoned Jōsuke and handed him 339 *ryō*, obtained a receipt that included the signatures of his relative, and gave it to Magoichirō.

My adoptive grandmother died the next day. I made arrangements for her funeral.

The peasants on Magoichirō's fiefs in Musashi and Sagami had said that I'd be lucky if I came back with one hundred *ryō*. They were amazed, and as for Magoichirō's relative who'd said he would resign from office if I got as much as fifty—well, I guess I put him in his place. My friend Toranosuke was very pleased. Jōsuke himself couldn't have been happier. "Katsu-sama," he said, "as long as I live, I won't sleep with my toes pointed in your direction."[11] He stops by my house even now.

Only a few days remained until the end of the year. I dashed around settling Magoichirō's affairs. His grateful family invited me to dinner, saying, "It's really the first time since Magoichirō became family head that we've had such a pleasant year's end."

All the people involved in the affair were in awe of me. The truth was, I'd never worked so hard to raise money. The expenses for the trip came to sixty-seven or sixty-eight *ryō*—I'd treated my men to palanquins for the trip back—and though Magoichirō offered me the remainder of the money, I declined. I knew that he had barely enough to see him through the year. My friends also said I should take at least one hundred *ryō*, but I had my own reasons for refusing. I finally accepted a bolt of cotton cloth from the Okano family.

The mourning period for my grandmother was completed early in the new year. I gave myself up to fun and pleasure as it if were my business and flitted about from place to place. If I ran short of pocket money, I could always sell swords for people or come up with one scheme or another.

---

11. A common figure of speech for showing respect and gratitude.

4. Selection from *The Autobiography of Yukichi Fukuzawa*[12]

This autobiography shows that, in contrast to warriors of earlier ages, some samurai of the late Tokugawa period were skeptical regarding earlier patterns of belief.

One day when I was twelve or thirteen years old, I ran through the room in one of my mischievous moments and stepped on some papers which my brother was arranging on the floor. Suddenly he broke out in disgust: "Stop, you dunce!" Then he began to speak solemnly. "Do you not see what is written here?" he said. "Is this not Okudaira Taizen-no-Tayū—your lord's name?"

"I did not know it," I hastily apologized. "I am sorry."

"You say you did not know," he replied indignantly. "But if you have eyes, you should see. What do you think of trampling your lord's name under foot? The sacred code of lord and vassal is . . ."

Here my brother was beginning to recite the samurai rules of duty. There was nothing for me to do but bow my head to the floor and plead: "I was very careless, please forgive me."

But in my heart there was no apology. All the time I was thinking: "Why scold about it? Did I step on my lord's head? What is wrong with stepping on a piece of paper?"

Then I went on, reasoning in my childish mind that if it was so wicked to step on a man's name, it would be very much more wicked to step on a god's name; and I determined to test the truth.

So I stole one of the charms, the thin paper slips, bearing sacred names, which are kept in many households for avoiding bad luck. And I deliberately trampled on it when nobody was looking. But no heavenly vengeance came.

"Very well," I thought to myself. "I will go a step further and try it in the worst place." I took it to the *chōzu-ba* (the privy) and put it in the filth. This time I was a little afraid, thinking I was going a little too far. But nothing happened.

"It is just as I thought!" I said to myself. "What right did my brother have to scold me?" I felt that I had made a great discovery! But this I could not tell anybody, not even my mother or sisters.

When I grew older by a few years, I became more reckless, and decided that all the talk about divine punishment which old men use in scolding children was a lie. Then I conceived the idea of finding out what the god of Inari really was.

---

12. Kiyooka Eiichi, *The Autobiography of Yukichi Fukuzawa*, 15–17.

There was an Inari shrine in the corner of my uncle's garden, as in many other households. I opened the shrine and found only a stone there. I threw it away and put in another stone which I picked up on the road. Then I went on to explore the Inari shrine of our neighbor, Shimomura. Here the token of the god was a wooden tablet. I threw it away too and waited for what might happen.

When the season of the Inari festival came, many people gathered to put up flags, beat drums, and make offerings of the sacred rice-wine. During all the round of festival services, I was chuckling to myself: "There they are worshipping my stones, the fools!"

Thus from childhood I have never had any fear of gods or Buddha. Nor have I ever had any faith in augury and magic, or in the fox and badger which, people say, have power to deceive men. I was a happy child, and my mind was never clouded by unreasonable fears.

5. Selection from *Remembering Aizu: The Testament of Shiba Gorō*[13]

> *This testament of the young samurai Shiba Gorō (1860–1945) of Aizu, a domain which was defeated during the Bōshin War (1868–69), reveals how women upheld the same samurai values as the men. In this case, all of the women of the Shiba household committed suicide when defeat loomed, while all of the men survived. Gorō, the youngest of the family, did not take part in the fighting, but was disguised as a peasant. At the same time, some peasants, such as Jinmori Heizō, fought valiantly. Heizō's actions suggests that a kind of "domain nationalism" existed, whereby peasants, like warriors, identified with and were willing to fight to defend* tozama *domains.*

A Night of Despair

In Omokawasawa, I found the house overrun by refugees. Complete strangers—at least a hundred—filled the rooms, huddled under the eaves, or stood in the garden drenched by the rain. Several had even cajoled my great-aunt Kisa and Tomekichi's wife to cook rice for them and acted as if they owned the place. Among the crowd I recognized Ina Hanroku, a samurai of distinguished lineage, who had come with his retainers, but I could not find my mother or other members of the family anywhere.

---

13. Craig, *Remembering Aizu*, 54–59.

5. Selection from Remembering Aizu: The Testament of Shiba Gorō

My aunt and Tomekichi's wife ran to me as soon as they saw me. They asked for news of the family, but of course I could tell them nothing. Several refugees noticed us talking and realized that I was the young master of the house. They bowed deferentially and tried to cheer me up: "Oh, your family is bound to come soon." Clinging to a glimmer of hope, I stood by the entrance and searched the gathering crowd for a familiar face. Though it was almost midday, I had no desire to eat.

At about two, my maternal aunt Hinata Hide arrived with her five children—Oyoshi, Orin, Shinsaburō, Shinshirō, and Shingorō. But my aunt, too, did not know of the family's whereabouts. Presently, my great-uncle Shiba Seisuke (seventy years old), who lived in Omokawa Village, came with his wife, Tada. They looked utterly exhausted. I asked for news of the family, but my uncle merely answered in a low voice, "Wait till later," and went into the house.

My uncle cleared the inner room of the refugees and beckoned me to come and sit in front of him. Drawing himself up straight, he began to speak. "It happened this morning. The enemy was already in the city, but your mother and the rest of the women in the family refused to leave the house. They committed suicide—yes, all five—your mother, your grandmother, your sisters Soi and Satsu, and Taichirō's wife, Toku. I administered the final blow at their request.[14] I then set fire to the house and came here. As her last wish, your mother asked me to take care of you."

"I realize that this is very painful for you, but you and I both know that this is the lot of samurai. You must not become distraught or give in to unseemly grief. You are to resign yourself and accept your fate with grace and fortitude. I want you to know that your own little sister killed herself with great courage and determination. From this day forward, you are to bear up and do as I say."

I looked at my uncle blankly, too stunned to speak, even to cry. Suddenly, my head began to swim, and I fainted away. I have no idea how long I remained unconscious, but in the middle of the night, I was awakened by someone tapping me on the shoulder. It was my uncle Seisuke. He lit the oil lamp and told me to sit up.

"Enemy troops have burned down the city and laid siege to the castle. They are certain to look for samurai outside the castle precincts. They're the kind of scoundrels who think nothing of killing the womenfolk of townsmen and peasants. They even leave the corpses of women strewn along the streets, though the peasant men have been covering them with straw mats as they flee. You never know what those good-for-nothing potato samurai will do next. The way you look now, anyone can tell right away you're from a samurai family. And since your mother asked me to

---

14. When a person commits ritual suicide, the final blow is administered by decapitation.

take care of you, I've decided to have you dress like a peasant boy for your own safety."

Although I remained silent, my uncle motioned to my aunt Kisa to come in and help him cut off my topknot. They cropped my hair close to the skull, dressed me in an old kimono and pair of leggings that belonged to Tomekichi's son. They stowed my Western suit and pair of swords in the loft. "This should do. But do not go outside without my permission." With these words, my uncle left the room. I lay down on the quilts and fell asleep to the sound of rain. It was to be the last day in my life as a samurai son.

The days passed, and one by one, the refugees drifted away. My aunt Hide's family and ten or so acquaintances stayed on. In a while, my aunt's family left, too, but unable to find anyone willing to take them in, they soon returned.

Uncle Seisuke's grandson Arakawa Toranosuke and I were the same age. Tomekichi's son Tometarō was a couple of years younger, and my cousins Hinata Shinsaburō and Shinshirō were a year older and a year younger. They made perfect playmates. I played with them during the day, and the distraction momentarily eased the pain, but at night, for a full two months, I dreamed about my mother and sisters—about the family sitting happily together—and woke up each time with a start.

It was the middle of the ninth month. The sound of shelling from Wakamatsu had not ceased. In fact, one day, Satsuma soldiers had come all the way to Omokawasawa in pursuit of Naitō Kain, a domain elder, who had taken shelter with his family at the Taiunji Temple. Surrounded, he and his family committed suicide.

Then, unexpectedly, on the twentieth, my brother Taichirō arrived, carried on a stretcher by Jinmori Heizō and several subordinates. Under orders from castle headquarters, he had been fighting near Ichinoseki but had been shot in the leg. I had long since given him up for dead, and I was so happy to see him that I ran around the house announcing the news. My uncle and everyone in the Hinata family rushed out to greet my brother and took him inside to tend to his wound. Unable to stand, he barely managed to crawl across the tatami mat with his hands and one leg. The same day, my uncle told him what had happened to the family; I knew only too well the sorrow and pain my brother must have felt.

My brother worried that he would be captured if he stayed on in the house. So after dismissing his other men, he asked Heizō and me to carry him to a ravine eight hundred yards deep in the mountains. The ravine was rather ominously called Dead Man's Gorge, but it was secluded and well hidden. We chose a spot near a spring, laid down a bed of boards about the size of two tatami mats, covered it with

5. Selection from Remembering Aizu: The Testament of Shiba Gorō

rough straw mats, and put a thick layer of green branches overhead. Here the three of us would stay, safe from enemy eyes.

Heizō's job was to nurse Taichirō's wound. Each day, he drew springwater into a water pistol he had fashioned from a length of bamboo, squirted the wound, and covered it with a piece of white cotton. I easily passed for a peasant boy, so my job was to wait until dark, when no one was around. Then I would fetch food from the house and bury the soiled bandages in the ground.

One day, we received a warning that enemy troops were in the vicinity. The Hinata family came to join us, and we helped Taichirō along as we all went farther into the mountains. Taking shelter under our umbrellas, we pitched camp in a grove of pine trees.

Meanwhile, the sound of gunfire from Wakamatsu continued without even a moment's pause. We felt much anxiety as we speculated about the outcome. My aunt Kisa and Uncle Seisuke's wife, Tada, were of the opinion that when the shooting stopped, it meant all was lost—that the *daimyō* and everyone else in the castle had died. But Heizō, who was young and hotheaded, would have none of this, and whenever he heard of enemy troops approaching, he would run out with his gun and sword, only to be restrained by my brother.

Heizō came from the village of Nigorigawa in Echigo Province. He was fond of sumo and had been the champion wrestler in his village. He was also fond of gambling and regularly got into fights. But at the same time, he was a man of strong loyalties and considered himself a friend of the weak and downtrodden. In the fifth month, he had been hired as a servant by my uncle Shiba Morizō (later Kōzuki Sagonosuke), who was fighting on the Echigo front. Heizō came to relish the experience of war and eagerly fought at the front line of battle. My uncle sustained a wound, however, and Heizō had to nurse him. As soon as my uncle recovered, Heizō returned to Echigo to fight, this time under the command of my brother, the region's military commissioner.

The Aizu forces had to retreat, and on the morning of the twenty-third of the eighth month, my brother and his men reached Tabanematsu, on the outskirts of Wakamatsu. They looked in the direction of the castle, but saw only fire and smoke. My brother pointed at the scene and said, "Wakamatsu has fallen into enemy hands. Our only course is to join the men in the castle and fight to the death. But you, Heizō, have no ties whatsoever with Aizu and are under no obligation to die with us. Go home, quickly." Handing some money to Heizō, he bid him farewell.

Heizō was furious. "This comes as a terrible shock, sir. I cannot believe that my own master would say anything so pitiless and unkind. I may be a lowly gambler, but I am not the sort to forget a favor, whether it is a night's lodging or bowl of rice. At a time when my master's domain is in grave danger, I consider it my duty to offer up my life in its defense. Yet I now hear that I am to leave because my master is returning to the castle in its hour of need. This would be an act of sheer ingratitude and heartlessness. These may be your orders, sir, but I must refuse." With this, Heizō sat himself down on the ground, red with indignation and determined not to budge an inch. My brother relented. They did not go to the castle, but instead the two fought on various fronts until my brother was wounded at Ichinoseki on the nineteenth day of the ninth month.

I am jumping ahead with my story, but after the end of the hostilities, Taichirō was taken to a hospital. Assured that his master was in good hands, Heizō asked for permission to leave Taichirō's service. He would once again become a gambler and roam about as he wished. Wearing one sword, he then took off without further ado.

After that there was no news from Heizō, but five years later, in Meiji 6 [1873], when I was a student at the Army Cadet School, I unexpectedly received a letter from him. The envelope was addressed to Shiba Gorō, Institute of Learning, Former Residence of the Honorable Ii Kamon-no-kami [Naosuke]. He asked about the family, and I immediately wrote back. Instead of answering, Heizō himself came to see me. I took him to see my brother, who was staying temporarily at the Sensōji Temple in Asakusa. Our reunion made us shed tears of joy at having come through the years unharmed. Heizō said he had settled down, found a place to live opposite the Kichijōji Temple in Komagome, taken a wife, and opened a rice-husking shop. Heizō came to visit from time to time, and in the autumn following our reunion, he invited my brother and me to dine with him at the home of a farmer living near Dangozaka in Komagome. It was the height of the chrysanthemum season. The meal was simple but served in a most hospitable manner. After we had finished eating, Heizō bowed low and pressed his hands together on the tatami. "As you know, I decided to mend my ways and make an honest living. I have somehow managed until now, but I am really not cut out for it. I don't think I can last much longer. You see, a gambler's only happy when he's with his cronies. And besides, it doesn't look as though there'll be another war. I really have nothing to look forward to. I have made up my mind to pull up stakes and wander about again, and that is why I asked you here today. I cannot tell you how very honored I am to have you here this evening."

Taichirō tried to dissuade him, but some time later, when I went by his house, I saw no trace of the shop. Heizō was thirty-six at the time of the Boshin War, so he must have been forty-one or forty-two when we met that evening. He was a good man, and I very much regret not seeing him again.

6. Two Petitions for Reward (*gunchūjō*) Submitted in 1869[15]

Chōshū domain (comprised of the old provinces of Suō and Nagato) and ruled by the Mōri played a crucial role in leading armed resistance in the wars that brought an end to the Tokugawa regime. The Chōshū forces, famously known as kiheitai, *were drawn from warriors and peasants. Narazaki Raizō (1845–75), a Hagi samurai, was a guard for Mōri Motonori (1839–96); Raizō followed Motonori to Kyoto in 1864 and fought in battles from 1865 onward. Raizō's petition for reward, below, reveals an underappreciated side of the Bōshin War of 1869, which followed the collapse of the Tokugawa regime. Raizō's petitions describe campaigns conducted after the fall of the Tokugawa in the far north, where the forces of Aizu Wakamatsu were defeated. Raizō was eventually dispatched to France to learn military science. While there, he must have witnessed the Franco-Prussian War. He died in France in 1875.*

Such petitions for reward—often written in an archaic, fourteenth-century style, even after two hundred years of peace—reveal a conservative side to the Mōri domain. Its warriors unusually looked back to the documents of the fourteenth century as a template. Unlike most other clans, the Mōri never relocated; their unusually long residency in Chōshū generated an equally unusual level of support from the locals. In spite of the old style of these documents, the Mōri's military organization was quite original and new. Raizō's actions were recognized by Mōri Takachika (1819–71), the penultimate daimyō *of the domain, who signed his name to the document. In 1869, Takachika passed the headship of the domain to his son Motonori, who held it only for that year before it was abolished. The name Shirakawa refers to a location in the domain of Aizu Wakamatsu.*

Narazaki Raizō Keifuku Petition for Reward

Received. (Seal) [Mōri Takachika]

During the previous year, the first of Meiji (1868), from the ninth day of the third month through the twenty-second day of the ninth month, after fighting battles in various places, the wounds suffered by Keifuku are as follows:

---

15. These documents were introduced by Kurushima Noriko, "Senkō no kiroku: Chūsei kara kinsei e," *Kokuritsu rekishi minzoku hakubutsukan kenkyū hōkoku* no. 182 (1.2014), 167-80. Documents translated by Thomas Conlan. For more on Narazaki Raizō (in Japanese), see https://sites.google.com/site/hagijinbutsu/list/35, accessed May 16, 2020.

On the first day of the fifth month, at Shirakawa in Ōshū,[16] Keifuku was wounded: One place. Right wrist.

While serving as the First Battalion Second Company Commander (*Dai ichi daitai niban chūtai shireikan*) in the eastern provinces (Kantō), I was ordered to report this information to my superiors. This petition for reward is thus.

The second year of Meiji (1869)

Narazaki Raizō

Second Month   Keifuku (monogram)

To: The Honorable Censor (*danjō no suke*) Masuda [Chikayoshi]

Narazaki Raizō Keifuku Petition for Reward

Received.   (Seal) [Mōri Takachika]
The Commander of the First Battalion Second Company Narazaki Raizō Fujiwara Keifuku respectfully states:

I desire to be granted a monogram quickly so that my military service will serve as a model for the future.

Since the ninth day of the third month-dragon-of the first year of Meiji (1868), through the twenty-second day of the ninth month, at a variety of battles fought at Bushū's[17] Yanada station, Sōshū's[18] Iwai village, Yashū,[19] and Ōshū, my squad's (*taichū*) casualties—killed and wounded—were as follows:

On the ninth day of the third month, at Bushū's Yanada station, Itō Jūrō, from the first platoon (*shōtai*), was wounded. Later, at Bushū's Kumagai station, Itō Jūrō died while his wounds were being treated.

On the twentieth day of the fourth month at Sōshū's Iwai village, Tanaka Jinkichi, of the first platoon, was killed. Scout (*Kyōdō eki*) Momura Hatsuzō, of the first platoon, was wounded.

[abbreviated]

Killed: 16[20]

---

16. The far northern province of Mutsu. Here refers to the domain of Aizu-Wakamatsu.
17. Musashi province.
18. This refers to the two old provinces of Kazusa and Shimōsa.
19. Shimotsuke province.
20. Corrected from 17.

6. Two Petitions for Reward (gunchūjō) *Submitted in 1869*

Wounded: 43

Died while being treated: 5[21]

Thus.

The second year of Meiji (1869)

Narazaki Raizō

Second month

Keifuku (monogram)

To: The Honorable Censor (*danjō no suke*) Masuda [Chikayoshi]

---

21. Corrected from 4.

SECTION XII
Abolishing the *Samurai* (1868–77)

After the collapse of the Tokugawa regime, the new Meiji government (1868–1912) attempted to centralize and transform Japan, ushering in a period of rapid reform. Following the lead of domains such as Chōshū, which was dissolved in 1869, other domains (*han*) were abolished in favor of prefectures and the *samurai* status was ended as well. *Daimyō* and high-ranking warriors were given generous stipends and made into a new nobility, and supported the Meiji government, but the new regime abolished the samurai status and granted them the virtually meaningless class status of *shizoku*. The government struggled to pay the stipends of all *samurai*, leading to resentment, and ultimately revoked the warriors' right to wear swords. The official government edict is reproduced below (see *The Japan Mail: Abolishing of the* Samurai *Right to Wear Swords*). After the government created a conscripted army, Saigō Takamori (1828–77) of Satsuma seized an armory and attempted an uprising. He tried and failed to capture Kumamoto castle; his defeat by the Meiji government's new army represented the last gasp of the samurai as a fighting force. *The Diary of Kidō Takayoshi* (p. 302) describes this uprising and how it was fought primarily with rifles and cannon.

1. *The Japan Mail:* Abolishing of the *Samurai* Right to Wear Swords[1]

The 1876 edict ending the samurai*'s right to wear swords also effectively ended the order as a whole. The edict is reproduced below, along with commentary from the 1876* Japan Mail. *The social position of* "samurai" *lingered in the Ryūkyū Kingdom, which was incorporated into Japan. Although the Ryūkyū equivalent to the* samurai, *the* gozoku *order, was abolished on 1.9.1872,[2] it*

---

1. This order, reproduced from the *"Nichi Nichi Shinbun"* on April 4, 1876, was published in English in the *Japan Mail* on April 10, 1876.

2. See the 1872 (Meiji 5) *Daijōkan-fu* no. 29. https://ja.wikipedia.org/wiki/%E5%A3%AB%E6%97%8F For this reference, I am indebted to Mark Ravina. Accessed August 26, 2021.

1. The Japan Mail: Abolishing of the *Samurai* Right to Wear Swords

was not until 1914 that people could no longer register as having higher status; this was the final, official end to the samurai *order.*[3]

Abolution of the Practice of Wearing Swords
(From the "Nichi Nichi Shimbun," April 4, 1876)[4]

Memorial from the Minister of War respecting the abolition of the wearing of swords—(taken from No. 4 of the Native and Foreign Army News).

It has for years been the established custom for the military class (i.e., the *samurai*) in this country to gird on two swords, the reason therefore being that though the advantages of the sword, it being a weapon used in war, were limited to repelling enemies and protecting one's self, still, on the conclusion of war, it was impossible in view of the habits relevant under the feudal system that it should be laid aside. However, times having changed, the *samurai* are released from the necessity of military studies, the *Han* have restored their lands to the Government, and, in 1873—greatest change of all—the conscription was enjoined and is now in force throughout the whole country. Previous to that measures had been taken against foreign war or internal disturbance by the establishment of the Imperial Guard for the protection of the Court, and of garrisons for controlling the seven circuits. The safety of town and country, too, had been provided for by the organization of a police force in each *ken* and *fu* and evildoers were arrested by it. By these measures human safety has been sufficiently provided for and the Emperor's behests are observed, and not the smallest distrust of them aroused. Notwithstanding all this, however, a large number of the nobles and entry throughout the country still continue to wear the sword in accordance with the old custom. These obstinate and unpolished men, unobservant of the changes which have occurred in the spirit of the times and in the military system, trust to themselves to keep off their enemies by the sword and to ensure thereby their own safety. Not only, however, is this practice of wearing dangerous weapons of no advantage to the empire, but owing to it the habit of assassination and wounding lingers under the false name of military spirit. As long as the wearing of the sword is not put a stop to serious trouble may arise to the Government at any time. The fact, besides, of there being persons not soldiers wearing military weapons considerably affects the latter's privileges, and

---

3. https://kotobank.jp/word/%E9%83%B7%E5%A3%AB-62146. I am indebted to Gregory Smits for this information.

4. The Meiji government adopted the Western calendar in 1873.

Section XII • Abolishing the Samurai

I therefore beg that orders may be speedily issued abolishing the sword, and the Japanese people thus caused to advance in the path of civilization.

I reverently await your order.

(Signed) Yamagata Aritomo,

Minister of War.

December 7th, 1876.

2. Selections from *The Diary of Kidō Takayoshi*[5]

Kidō Takayoshi (1833–77), the son of a doctor from Chōshū domain, became an important leader of the Meiji Restoration. He helped establish an alliance with Satsuma, which brought down the Tokugawa bakufu. In the passages selected below, he describes the 1877 rebellion of Saigō Takamori, another Meiji leader from Satsuma. Takamori, dissatisfied with Meiji policies, decided to rebel and seized arms and cannons from the local armory. Meiji forces, which were conscripted, relied on modern guns and ammunition and held off the rebellion at the castle of Kumamoto. As Takamori's forces ran out of ammunition, this new army advanced inexorably and utterly annihilated his rebel forces. With their ammunition supplies dwindling, some futilely relied on their swords to attack the enemy, and this led the revolt to have been mischaracterized as one in which Saigo and his men were the "last samurai," who eschewed modern weapons.

5 February 1876. Fair. Those who came to visit were Kusaka Yoshio, Sugiyama Takatoshi, Kawachi Naokata, Yamada Akiyoshi, Ōkura Kihachi (concerning Narushima), Assistant Minister Kodama, Kodama Jun'ichirō, Okudaira Shōsuke, and Onda Jinsuke. Ga Noriyuki brought over his translation of *The Spirit of Laws*. Hiraoka Michiyoshi . . . went with me to look for some land to build my new house. Two other visitors came.

---

5. Brown and Hirota, *The Diary of Kidō Takayoshi*, vol. 3, February 5, 1876, p. 258; March 18, 1877, pp. 465–66, 21; March 21, 1877, pp. 467–68; March 24, 1877, p. 469; March 28–29, 1877, pp. 471–72; March 31, 1877, pp. 472–73; April 2–6, 1877, pp. 475–78; April 10, 1877, pp. 480–81; April 17, 1877, pp. 484–85; April 22, 1877, 488–89.

2. Selections from The Diary of Kidō Takayoshi

18 March 1877. Fair. Several dozen visitors. Ōzaki Saburō who has arrived from Tokyo brought me a letter from Minister of the Right Iwakura. He also brought Prime Minister Sanjō's order to me to go up to Kyoto. I have been a strong advocate of an attack from the rear in the Yatsushiro sector, but as this is outside my control I could not bring it about. Moreover, at Tabara we have been attacking the forts for seventeen or eighteen days; we have expended 600,000 to 700,000 rounds of ammunition daily; and casualties are running at 160 to 170 a day. Ours cannot be called a successful strategy. In the end we have made a big change in direction of policy with the adoption of the strategy of attacking from the rear, and I am a bit relieved. Consequently, Yamada Akiyoshi who has advocated this policy from the first has been ordered on the Nagasaki to take command of the forces attacking from the rear. We had been unable to convince others to take this step until today. I have no regrets; and I am satisfied to see him reach his objective, and to see this indication of cooperation and unity. I only hope, day and night, that this tragedy will yield quick results, and that it will sweep away the poisoned atmosphere and make the people rejoice.... With Shimaji Mokurai I went to Yamada Akiyoshi's; then I went to Nakajima Nobuyuki's, and at 11 I returned to my inn. The Public Procurator was given orders to day to strip Ōyama Tsunayoshi of his court rank. Nakahara Hisao and others went to Tokyo today with Okauchi. Kitashige came to talk.

21 March 1877. Rain, then clearing. Kawada Kagetomo, Akamatsu Renjō, and Nagayasu Wasō came to talk. At 10 I went to the Imperial Palace. I reported to the throne our decision to make the attack from the rear, and to send round a large force to the Yatsushiro sector in groups as the men arrived, and on correspondence from the front and intelligence reports. I requested that the Emperor go to the Imperial Study every day to receive the daily report on the state of the battlefront and other matters. I also reported in detail on the consumption of ammunition and on casualties. There were more than ten telegrams, one of which reported that our forces had launched a general offensive from Tabarazaka at 6 a.m. on the twentieth, seized Ueki, put it to the torch, and captured a number of enemy soldiers. Four big guns were taken, and 200 rifles; an ammunition dump was set afire. It was reported, however, that the rebel forts to the right and left have not been taken, and that the battle still rages around them. The situation with regard to the force attacking from the rear is still the same as reported yesterday.

The Emperor received a report from Iwamura... on the case against Maebara Issei and the other rebels in Yamaguchi prefecture last year.

At 4 I withdrew from the Palace. Shimaji came to my place with Ōzu Tetsuzen, who was arrested on suspicion in Kagoshima on 6 February, and experienced great difficulties for a time. He returned from there with the Imperial Envoy, and today he related to me the situation as it developed after 30 January. I sent a letter to Itō Hirobumi today.

Section XII • Abolishing the Samurai

(Note) Tetsuzen travelled with the Imperial Envoy as far as Nagasaki, and returned on his own to Kyoto yesterday.

24 March 1877. Rain, then clearing. Itō Hōsei came to give me medical treatment. Iwakura Tomosada came to talk. At 10 I went to the Palace. Today I pleaded with Prime Minister Sanjō to send me to the Yatsushiro front. We have already dispatched more than five million soldiers to Yatsushiro for the offensive, in accordance with our resolution of a few days ago; consequently, some local civil government is necessary. Those in Yatsushiro have also requested it from the government. I withdrew from the Palace at 4; and, after withdrawing, I visited Priest Mokurai, and Renjō came to talk with us. On the way back I went to the Kyūkyodō, then to the Keika. As I had an appointment with Sugi Chō'u, I had dinner with him at a restaurant. Several telegrams came.

28 March 1877. . . . Several telegrams came, reporting that about 500 *shizoku* in Fukuoka appeared to be ready to rise. We took prompt steps to suppress them. Letters arrived from Sugi Magoshichirō and Hiraoka Michiyoshi.

29 March 1877. Cloudy. Visitors came throughout the day. Among the telegrams was one reported on the fighting around Kidome and Ueki. There was a great many casualties in Kidome, and we have been unable to take the forts in that area, and have withdrawn to the earlier battle line. I can imagine the desperate fighting going on there, and believe that we must plan our strategy for the future, so discussed it with Itō Hirobumi. This morning Ōkubo Toshimichi came to talk; and Nakano Goichi also came to visit.

At night a letter arrived from Torio. In regard to the Imperial visit which we have discussed in the past, I believe that it should be undertaken without delay, since the troops stationed in Osaka are soon to be dispatched to the front. I proposed this to Kyoto by telegram.

31 March 1877. Fair. At 7 I went to the Palace. The Imperial party had already left, so I went to the railway station and began my attendance on the Emperor there for the trip to Osaka, where we arrived at 9:20. The Emperor rode horseback from the station to the Osaka garrison where he inspected the officer's hospital, and took a short rest. Afterwards the garrison troops passed in review for His Majesty. (There were more than three battalions, two of which are to be dispatched to the front today together with four guns and their mounts. One of the battalions consists of recruits who are in their prime, and their spirit was especially high. This group is headed for the Udo front.)

Afterwards the Emperor made a tour of the hospital for enlisted men. (Out of 670 wounded men here, 300 arrived today. Further there were seventy men who

2. Selections from The Diary of Kidō Takayoshi

had been wounded in the Kumamoto garrison during the Jimpūren rising last year. All had suffered serious injuries, but the wounds of most have now healed. The Emperor also inspected them.) After the Emperor had his noon meal in the place prepared for his relaxation, and left for the railway station at 2. Ōkubo and Itō welcomed the Emperor today, and sent him off. They consulted me about the return of Yanagihara, member of the Chamber of Elders, in Tokyo in connection with the trail of Nakahara . . . , and about the proposal which I made yesterday.

The Emperor returned to Kyoto on the 3:40 train. There I withdrew from the Palace at 6; and I stayed at Hōjō Tai'ei's tonight. Today the Emperor presented me with *sake,* fish, and cakes in recognition of my services in going to Osaka to work day and night on the dispatch of the expeditionary force.

2 April 1877. Cloudy. Nakajima Nobuyuki came to talk. I went down to Osaka on the 10:55 train. The performance of the Imperial Army in recent days has differed substantially from our expectations at the beginning, as I see it. If the situation continues for ten more days, the Kumamoto garrison may fall. If that happens, it is difficult to know how the situation in the nation may change. At present the prefectures have quieted down; but we must be prepared with counterplans in case things go wrong. Consequently, I discussed my six-point proposal with Ōkubo, Itō, and Torio. They agreed with my proposal, so we shall start working on it at once. Makimura Masanao came down from Kyoto in connection with the matter which I had entrusted to him last night concerning the movements of *shizoku* in Wakayama, Hikone, Tottori, Tamba, and Tango. Fukuchi Gen'ichirō who has returned from the battlefront in Kyushu gave me a detailed report on the present situation there. . . . I visited Tsukuda Motokiyo to discuss the matter of Hagi Castletown. Chamberlain Kataoka and Ōgi, and official of the ninth rank, are being dispatched to the battlefront in Yatsushiro; and they came to talk with me. I sent a letter to Yamada Akiyoshi. . . . Magobei returned from Tokyo, and brought me letters from my home, from Harada Isoemon, Sōbei, and Kawase Shinkō.

3 April 1877. Fair. Ōkubo Toshimichi and Itō Hirobumi came. As there have been some miscalculations in the last few days, I strongly hope that the government will give attention to the worst possible developments, and make preparations for handling them. Its members, however, to my great regret, swing from depression to euphoria in an instant. The plan on behalf of which I busied myself all day yesterday, and on which a tentative decision was reached, was wrecked because of a single telegram from Udo, and this was not even a report of a decisive victory. Even if it be considered a minor victory, the enemy has retreated to a position at Kawajiri with the ultimate intention of fighting a major defensive action at the Midori River. We must not hold them in contempt. Fukuchi Gen'ichirō and Narushima Ryūhoku

came to walk with me. Kōno Togama who has recently returned from Kōchi told me about the current situation there. Togama is soon to be dispatched to Kyushu to join the staff of the Commander-in-Chief, and to serve also as judge. Nakajima Nobuyuki and . . . came to talk. I went to Torio Koyata's place, and I find that the decision about the matter which I discussed with him last night has gone altogether against my position. Ōkubo and Itō have changed their minds; and my efforts have come to naught. Here is an example of the saying "The promises of yesterday are as ephemeral as smoke." It is strange that telegrams should change minds in this way. I alone have lost face in this affair. . . . Several telegrams arrived.

I went to Ōkubo's, but he was away. I put down in writing the feelings which I can no longer suppress. A letter came from Minister of the Right Iwakura.

4 April 1877. Fair. Visitors without a break. A letter arrived from Prime Minister Sanjō. I went up to Kyoto on the 12:30 train, aboard which were Nakamura Kōki and Sakuma Kazusuke. After arriving I went directly to Prime Minister Sanjō's to tell him my idea on recruitment of the ablest soldiers and other things. From there I met Makimura Masanao and went with him to the Secretariat, where Nakajima Nobuyuki joined us. I went to Prime Minister Sanjō's again to continue our discussion, and then I went to Makimura Masanao's to confer with Kawada Kagetomo. We completed our talk which began several days ago. I sent a letter to Ōkubo and Itō today. Then I wrote to Ōkubo and Itō again intending to send Matatarō out with the letter tomorrow evening. After 11 I went to Hōjō's to stay for the night.

5 April 1877. Fair. I went to Makimura's at 10, and from there to the Palace. Prime Minister Sanjō came to the Palace. In observing the present situation, I have made advance preparations these last few days in case the worst should happen. Consequently, I instructed Kagawa Keizō to make secret. . . preparations for the Emperor to travel light. I withdrew at 1. I went to Makimura's again, and took the noon meal with Fukuchi Gen'ichirō. Toda Saburō came to see me. From there I went with Makimura to Tani Tesshin's place where we had a long talk about the direction things are taking. Tani's views are not completely in accord with mine. Makimura and I left there to go to see Miura Kyūtarō whose views are substantially the same as mine with minor differences. I have gone about the city this way to argue on behalf of a firm course of policy hereafter. Itō Hirobumi came up to Kyoto to visit me; and we went to the Ikegami for a long confidential talk. On the way back I visited Nakajima Nobuyuki, went to Makimura's again, visited Chō Sansu, met Sugi Magoshichirō, and returned to my inn before 10. I entrusted Nakajima Nobuyuki with letters to the Minister of the Right Iwakura, my family in Tokyo, Okudaira Nisui, Kawano Michinobu, and Harada Isoemon.

2. Selections from The Diary of Kidō Takayoshi

Among the several telegrams which arrived, one reported that Miura Gorō had launched a strong offensive from the Yamaga front, and finally reduced Tosu fort. This was the first news of victory in a long while. Now that we have reduced Kidome, and also Tosu, we must be approaching the garrison in full strength. This link-up of our forces will have an incalculable effect on the course of the war. Judging from the rate of advance of our armies up to the present, and the number of days it has taken, we must be careful about predicting when it will occur. I was very much pleased to be informed by Fukuchi the other day that Miura Gorō's military camp, from his observations, maintains strict order, and is very different from other camps. Miura is a sincere man, reserved in speech, my true friend; and he reveres me as an elder brother. I have long deplored that his ability has remained undiscovered while sycophants of clever words were promoted in office. That today, when we face a formidable enemy, Miura's ability has become known to the world for the first time is not solely a matter for personal gratification. It is a stroke of good luck for all.

6 April 1877. Fair. I went to Makimura's and from there I went to the Palace, arriving at 10. Fukuchi Gen'ichirō accompanied me; and he was summoned into the Emperor's presence to give a detailed report to the Throne on his observations of the state of the war, the relative strength of the Imperial Army, the condition of the enemy troops, the achievements of the officers, the terrain, and the hardships of the people.

10 April 1877. Rain all day. Takasaki Seifū, who was dispatched to the war front last month to give recognition to those who gave distinguished service, returned to Osaka last night; and he told me about the situation at the front, and the recent condition of things in Kagoshima. He says that the whole of Kagoshima is rebel territory now. When Lieutenant General Kuroda went down there, he destroyed arsenals, and disposed of any ammunition he could find. But after he withdrew, the situation returned to what it was earlier; and a certain Ikebe and a certain Beppu raised 1,500 men and set out for the Yatsushiro front. He says that when the Imperial Envoy and Lieutenant General Kuroda went to Kagoshima to meet Shimazu Hisamitsu and his son, the General was treated exactly as if he were still a retainer, and could not sit on the same level with Shimazu. Hisamatsu waited for him in a haughty manner. This is a very deplorable thing from the standpoint of the Imperial government; and that is why I proposed sending Major General Yamada to Kagoshima in the first place. The decision we came to some time ago was changed around completely by the personal relationships involved. If Lieutenant General Kuroda should meet Hisamitsu and his son as a private individual, it is proper that Kuroda should greet him with the utmost courtesy because of their old relationship. But to behave like this when Kuroda had gone to Kagoshima under Imperial orders and through his own request in order to clarify that one's highest loyalty is to the national state seems as

if it were deliberate disobedience to the Emperor. At present, not a single one of the purposes of the Imperial government has been accomplished. Kagoshima having made such a move as this has prolonged the hardships which the people will able to endure. This is the most regrettable thing that has happened in my lifetime. Once I proposed that we dispatch a large force to Kagoshima with all speed; but Torio flatly refused to do this on the grounds that it would harden the rebels' determination, and would accomplish nothing. But the problem of Kagoshima, with its arms and with its ammunition, does not allow us to delay any more. I tried my best to make a start on my plan for speedy dispatch of troops, but the majority was not with me. From what I heard from Takasaki today the battle for Higo is proving more difficult than the rebels expected. After the fighting started they shipped in an enormous amount of ammunition, having brought along a very small quantity at first. . . . He said that most of the guns were sent in afterwards. As Takasaki left the battlefront before Fukuchi Gen'ichirō, he had little new to report.

(One line is blank.)

Mayahara Akira. . . (the following is blank.)

(Note) The number of casualties which Takasaki reported from his battlefield investigation was 7,340.

17 April 1877. . . . Deep into the night I thought about our troubled times; year after year blood flows, and the people are in distress. We must reflect on the source of these difficulties. But the men who govern the country have grown accustomed to their long-practiced abuses, and none shows signs of self-examination.

22 April 1877. . . . Telegrams have been arriving since yesterday from Kuroda, the Chief of Staff, reporting that the battle for Mifune opened at 8 o'clock on the twentieth. Kawaji attacked from the rear, Yamada from in front and an angle, and Takashima provided support on the right flank. The rebels finally abandoned their fort, and suffered a great defeat. They even abandoned their dead as they took flight. The Imperial Army took over Mifune at 9, seizing arms and ammunition, and taking the severed heads of a large number of enemy soldiers. On this front was a large contingent of Satsuma soldiers, and twenty-five platoons of men put up a stout defense of the fort. (The number of men in each platoon is uncertain.) At 12 the two forces of Yamada and Kawaji took Mount Iida, Occupied Togama, and attacked Kiyama from the rear. The rebel moral was broken, it is reported. . . . At 4 a.m. on the seventeenth one battalion and one company of our forces opened the fighting at Ogiwara, Miyanohara, and Mukōzaka, taking the rebels unaware so that they have abandoned their arms and ammunition. Rebel casualties were enormous; those of our troops numbered thirteen.

GLOSSARY

Akutō (悪党). "Evil bands" or brigands. This pejorative term describing those who resorted to violence regardless of their social status.

Ashigaru (足軽). A term for foot soldiers, common in the fifteenth century, which in the seventeenth century came to designate low-ranking warrior retainers.

Ashikaga bakufu (足利幕府). Otherwise known as the *Muromachi bakufu*, Japan's second warrior government. It was closely linked to the court and lasted from 1338 through 1573.

Azukari dokoro (預所). Name for an estate manager, usually an official who attained the right to manage lands that were originally commended to a central proprietor. They were of a higher rank, more closely connected to the proprietor than *gesu* (see *gesu*), and did not necessarily need to reside on the estate.

Bakufu (幕府). Literally meaning "tent government," this term describes three warrior governments of Japan: the Kamakura (1185–1333), Muromachi or Ashikaga (1338–1573), and Tokugawa (1603–1867) regimes. Each varied in character, with Kamakura being a limited judicial government that governed in tandem with the court, while the Ashikaga governed Japan and fused with the court (although it devolved authority to regional lords). Finally, the Tokugawa governed Japan most successfully and severely constrained the court.

Bōhai (傍輩). "Comrades," a term used to describe warriors of equal status or rank.

Bonge (凡下). People of low status who did not possess surnames and were incapable of autonomy.

Chinjufu shōgun (鎮守府将軍). "Pacification general." This office was one that suggested control over the north and was a competing, and less prestigious, office to the more famous "barbarian subduing general" (*sei-i-tai shōgun*). This office lapsed in the mid-fourteenth century.

Chinzei (鎮西). Another name for Kyushu. Site of the Chinzei *tandai*, an administrative organ of the Kamakura shogunate, which lasted from the time of the Mongol invasions through 1333.

Chūgen (中間). Low-ranking followers. Those men obligated to serve a lord in battle or perform various menial duties, but lacking a surname.

Da (駄). Unit of weight that constitutes roughly 240 pounds.

Daimyō (大名). A provincial magnate. This autogenic term described powerful warlords from the mid-fourteenth century onward. By the seventeenth century, the term referred to any lord controlling ten thousand or more *koku* of revenue, with *koku* constituting the amount of rice one person required in a year. During the Tokugawa era, their lands were known as "domains" (*han*).

Dōri (道理). A notion "justice" or "reasonableness," or the idea of following the spirit, rather than the letter, of codified law.

Emishi (蝦夷). "Barbarians," or those inhabitants of the northern regions of the Japanese archipelago who did not recognize the authority of the Japanese court.

Genin (下人). A member of the "base" orders, lacking a surname and generally unfree, although they could be granted a name and rise in status through their battle service.

Gesu (下司). A local manager, appointed to an estate (*shōen*), who could be removed from his office by the proprietor. This office was similar in function to a *jitō*, but the latter was more desirable.

Gesu shiki (下司職). The office of *gesu*. See above.

Gokenin (御家人). "Honorable housemen," a social status drawn from the ranks of provincials. An amorphous designation, they could be selected by *shugo* for the performance of guard duty. The advantages of this status were initially unclear but by mid-thirteenth century, the benefits associated with *gokenin* status outweighed its burdens. This term continued to be used after the fall of the Kamakura *bakufu*.

Han (藩). Domains. The territories of a *daimyō* during the Tokugawa era (1603–1867). Abolished in 1871.

Hanzei (半済). The "half tax" initiated in 1351. It allowed half of a province's taxes to be used for military provisions by *shugo*. This enabled *shugo* to create larger armies and break down the autonomy of provincial warriors. It directly contributed to the rise of regional magnates (*daimyō*).

Hikan (被官). A retainer, or follower.

Hyakushō (百姓). Literally "the hundred surnames," originally a generic term for commoners (e.g., those having no court office or rank). As late as the fourteenth century, some were armed and owned horses. The first reference to *hyakushō* as designating cultivators appears in the late thirteenth century, but even as late as the mid-fifteenth century, one still sees powerful provincials with surnames referring to themselves as *hyakushō*.

Hyōjō (評定). Council meeting designed to determine policy or adjudicate disputes among either members of the court or one of Japan's warrior governments.

Ikki (一揆). A verb originally meaning "to be in accord," this word became used as a noun to designate military units during the fourteenth century. Later in the Tokugawa era the term became associated with peasant uprisings.

Jitō (地頭). A land steward, or one who was invested with this power in the aftermath of the Genpei War (1180–85) by Minamoto no Yoritomo. Possessing powers of taxation and policing and difficult to confiscate by court officials, the post was very desirable. After the destruction of Kamakura, this term lost its original meaning, but it still became associated with powers of local ownership and possession of land.

Kamakura bakufu (鎌倉幕府). The warrior government, nominally of eastern Japan, that was responsible for policing and providing order and adjudicating disputes among *jitō*.

Kanrei (管領). The post of shogunal chancellor, which superseded the office of *shitsuji* in 1367. It became the hereditary prerogative of three families: the Hatakeyama, Hosokawa, and Shiba.

Kassen bugyō (合戦奉行). Administrators who inspected the veracity of battle reports.

Kebiishi (検非違使). Capital, or imperial, police, an office dating from the ninth century, whose members were responsible for guarding the capital and adjudicating disputes.

Kenin (家人). Housemen. Any servant or follower in a particular house could use this term. By being a member of the house, they were not expected, or allowed to act autonomously.

Kenmon (権門). A "gate of power." This term describes institutions with their own house organ of governance, or *mandokoro*, capable of transmitting orders.

Kessho (闕所). Lands declared "appropriable" by those in authority as a result of "crimes" or "rebellions" by either their proprietor or manager.

Kōgi (公儀). Public affairs or authority. The term could also refer to powerful lords.

Koku (石). The amount of rice one person required in a year. A crucial unit of income in the seventeenth century, which determined warrior status.

Kokujin (国人). "Men of the provinces," or autonomous warriors. An autogenic and generic designation for warriors appearing in the thirteenth century and becoming more popular from the mid-fourteenth century onward.

Kuni no miyatsuko (国造). A district, or prominent district chieftain during the time of the Yamato court (circa fifth to sixth century).

Mandokoro. (政所). A secretariat of a ranking official or courtier.

Miuchi (御内). Term used to describe all dependent warriors. By contrast, autonomous warriors were known as *tozama*.

Muromachi bakufu (室町幕府). Japan's second warrior government, lasting from 1338 until 1573. Also known as the *Ashikaga bakufu*.

Myōshu (名主). Literally "lord of the *myō*." *Myō* represented a unit of taxation. During the eleventh and twelfth centuries, some powerful locals (*zaichō kanjin*) secured the right to assess taxes. They became known as *myōshu*. Not all became *gokenin* or *jitō* in the Kamakura age. Some became conflated with the higher ranks after the fall of Kamakura.

Nobushi (野伏). Skirmishers.

Rōjū (郎従). A generic term for retainer.

Rokuhara tandai (六波羅探題). Post established after 1221, whereby two Kamakura deputies resided in the capital, overseeing its affairs and engaging in preliminary judicial decisions, primarily for western Japan. Rokuhara was a region located in eastern Kyoto and the former mansion of Taira no Kiyomori. The last *tandai* were killed in 1333 shortly after they fled the capital.

Rōnin (浪人). "Wave men," or masterless samurai. A term that came into being only during the Tokugawa era, when *samurai* became a distinct status that required ties to a lord.

Rōtō (郎等). Term for retainer, follower, or armed servants.

Rōzeki (狼藉). An outrage. Open defiance of authority, frequently resorting to military force after the promulgation of an order to cease and desist.

Ryōke shiki (領家職). Proprietary rights of income, which were granted to temples or ranking members of the nobility. Proprietors with this office could divest *gesu* and secure a preponderance of *shōen* income. They could not, however, divest *jitō* of their rights. Although *shiki* represented status-based rights to income, this practice started to break down in the fourteenth century, and some provincial figures were invested with this title, something that was inconceivable in earlier ages.

Samurai (侍). Arising originally from the ranks of "commoners" (*hyakushō*), they possessed surnames and were obligated to a lord, who was generally of *zaichō kanjin* status. They should be conceived as a warrior's retainer and possessed considerably greater rights than did "the base" (*genin*) (i.e., immunity from torture). With the breakdown of warrior autonomy and the reforms of Toyotomi Hideyoshi in the 1590s, *samurai* became a generic term for a sword-wielding social order of warriors.

Samurai dokoro (侍所). An administrative office of the Ashikaga (Muromachi) *bakufu*, concerned with granting rewards for its warriors.

Sei-i-tai shōgun (征夷大将軍). An eighth-century office, originally designed to quell barbarians. Coveted because of its assumed unilateral ability to engage in military campaigns. Sakanoue no Tamuramaro was first appointed to this office. Minamoto no Yoritomo was appointed to this post in 1192, but he passed it to his son so as to ensure succession. After their deaths, Fujiwara Regents and imperial princes staffed this office. With the downfall of the Kamakura *bakufu* in 1333, Ashikaga Takauji started laying claim to the post again and was appointed as *sei-i-tai shōgun* in 1338. His descendants continued being appointed to this position until 1573. Tokugawa Ieyasu was appointed to the office in 1603 and it was held by his descendants through 1867.

Shiki (職). Status-based rights of income.

Shikken (執権). The chief of the Hōjō family during the Kamakura age. Often this term has been translated as "regent," due to the ease with which the Hōjō deposed *shōgun* between the years 1226 and 1333, but adjunct or "shogunal chief of staff" better describes this role. Head of the shogunal administrators staffing his *mandokoro*.

Shitsuji (執事). A term used to describe the chief of staff for early Ashikaga *shōguns*. Superseded by the post of *kanrei*.

Shizoku (士族). A social class created in the aftermath of the abolishment of the *samurai* order by the Meiji government (1868–1912) of Japan. In contrast to high-ranking warriors (ex-*daimyō*) who were made into an aristocracy, this class had no particular prerogatives and was functionally the equivalent to that of commoners. It was abolished in 1947.

Shōen (莊園, 庄園). Estates that existed, in principle, from the eighth through the late sixteenth century, although in actuality most survived for relatively short periods of time. Units of governance, territory, and population, they were characterized by distinct boundaries. Crucially, their rights were status based, with the proprietor and members of the capital getting most of the revenue, while managers received less. These status-based rights blurred after the mid-fourteenth century. See also *azukari dokoro, gesu, ryōke,* and *jitō.*

Shugo (守護). Provincial constable. Although assumed to have originated in the 1180s, it became a prominent official in the Kamakura *bakufu* after Yoritomo's death in 1199. A policing office during the Kamakura age, it became far more powerful after the promulgation of the *hanzei* edict under Ashikaga rule. This act allowed these figures to secure access to half of a province's revenue for military provisions. Many *shugo* had to reside in the capital during the Ashikaga heyday and in the later fifteenth and sixteenth centuries, some were supplanted by their deputies. In time, the more amorphous designation of *daimyō* came to be preferred by magnates over this appointed office.

Sōjitō (総地頭). An over-*jitō*. This chief, or over-*jitō*, was a Kyushu institution and refers to a warrior from the east who was appointed to oversee lands that already had a *jitō*. Contributed to much tension and litigiousness in this island during the Kamakura age (1185–1333).

Sōtsuibushi (惣追捕使). A policing officer appointed to estates, who often resided on the lands he was responsible for protecting.

Teichū (庭中). Court of Appeals.

Tennō (天皇). The sovereign of Japan, a term used to describe the occupant of the throne from the seventh century onward. At times they could be surpassed by Retired Emperors, who overshadowed these figures on occasion ritually and administratively from the latter eleventh through the fourteenth centuries.

Tokusei (徳政). Literally "virtuous government," a policy of debt relief that was initially enacted in the 1240s, it ultimately became less binding and more favorable to creditors over time.

Tozama (外様). Literally an "outsider," this term refers to warriors who were capable of behaving with autonomy, receiving their own petitions for reward, and fighting for whomever they pleased. Later came to designate more powerful *daimyō* during the Tokugawa era (1603–1867). See also *miuchi.*

Tsuitōshi (追討使). Envoy to pursue and punish. Warriors from the capital were appointed to this position on an ad hoc basis to conquer rebels or criminals.

Tsukushi (筑紫). Ancient name for the island of Kyushu. See also *Chinzei.*

Wakatō (若党). Retainers possessing surname, but not exercising any autonomy. They were capable of riding horses, but not submitting their own petitions for reward.

Zaichō kanjin (在庁官人). Prominent local individuals, holding managerial office. Initially they aided provincial governors with the collection of taxes. Few commended their lands into estates. Many *zaichō kanjin* were appointed to the office of *jitō* during the Kamakura era. They were the most prominent warriors of the provinces.

Zuryō (受領). A provincial governor who served as a tax farmer from the ninth century onward. Often famed for rapacity. Collected taxes by relying on *zaichō kanjin*.

BIBLIOGRAPHY

"Abolishing of the *Samurai* Right to Wear Swords." *Japan Mail*, April 10, 1876.

Ackroyd, Joyce, trans. *Told Round a Brushwood Fire*. Princeton: Princeton University Press, 1979.

Adolphson, Mikael. *The Gates of Power: Monks, Courtiers, and Warriors in Premodern Japan*. Honolulu: University of Hawaii Press, 2000.

———. *The Teeth and Claws of the Buddha: Monastic Warriors and Sōhei in Japanese History*. Honolulu: University of Hawaii Press, 2007

———. "Weighing in on Evidence: Documents and Literary Manuscripts in Early Medieval Japan." In *Manuscripts and Archives: Comparative Views on Record-Keeping*, edited by in Alessandro Bausi et al., 297–318. Berlin: De Gruyter, 2018.

Amino Yoshihiko. *Rethinking Japanese History*. Ann Arbor: University of Michigan Center for Japanese Studies, 2012.

Anzawa, Wakao, and Manome Jun'ichi. "Two Inscribed Swords from Japanese Tumuli: Discoveries and Research on Finds from the Sakitama-Inariyama and Eta-Funayama tumuli." In *Windows on the Japanese Past; Studies in Archaeology and Prehistory*, edited by Pearson et al., 375–95. Ann Arbor, MI: Center for Japanese Studies, 1986.

Arntzen, Sonja, trans. *Ikkyū and the Crazy Cloud Anthology*. Tokyo: University of Tokyo Press, 1986.

Ashikaga Takauji: Sono shōgai to yukari no meihō. Tochigiken hakubutsukan, 2012.

Benesch, Oleg. *Inventing the Way of the Samurai—Nationalism, Internationalism, and Bushidō in Modern Japan*. Oxford: Oxford University Press, 2014.

Berry, Mary Elizabeth. *The Culture of Civil War in Kyōto*. Berkeley: University of California Press, 1994.

———. *Hideyoshi*. Cambridge, MA: Harvard East Asian Monographs, 1982.

———. "Public Peace and Private Attachment: The Goals and Conduct of Power in Early Modern Japan." *Journal of Japanese Studies* 12 no. 2 (Summer 1986): 238–71.

Birt, Michael. "Samurai in Passage: The Transformation of the Sixteenth Century Kantō." *Journal of Japanese Studies* 11 no. 2 (Summer 1985): 369–99.

Brazell, Karen, trans. *The Confessions of Lady Nijō*. Stanford: Stanford University Press, 1973.

Brown, Delmar, trans. *The Future and the Past: A Translation and Study of the Gukanshō, an Interpretive History of Japan Written in 1219*. Berkeley: University of California Press, 1979.

Brown, Sidney Devere, and Akiko Hirota, trans. *The Diary of Kidō Takayoshi*. 3 vols. Tokyo: University of Tokyo Press, 1983–86.

Buc, Philippe. "Sectarian Violence in Premodern Japan and Europe: Jōdo Shinshū and the Anabaptists." *Viator: Medieval and Renaissance Studies* 50 no. 2 (2019): 351–86.

Butler, Kenneth Dean. "The Heike Monogatari and the Japanese Warrior Ethic." *Harvard Journal of Asiatic Studies* 29 (1969): 93–108.

Clulow, Adam. *Amboina, 1623: Fear and Conspiracy on the Edge of Empire*. New York: Columbia University Press, 2019.

Conlan, Thomas D. *From Sovereign to Symbol: An Age of Ritual Determinism in Fourteenth Century Japan*. New York: Oxford University Press, 2011.

———. *In Little Need of Divine Intervention: Takezaki Suenaga's Scrolls of the Mongol Invasions of Japan*. Ithaca, NY: Cornell University East Asia Program, 2001.

———. "Instruments of Change: Organizational Technology and the Consolidation of Regional Power in Japan 1333–1600." In *War and State Building in Medieval Japan*, edited by John Ferejohn and Frances Rosenbluth, 124–58. Stanford: Stanford University Press, 2010.

———. "Largesse and the Limits of Loyalty in the Fourteenth Century." In *The Origins of Japan's Medieval World*, edited by Jeffrey Mass, 39–64. Stanford University Press, 1997.

———. "Myth, Memory, and the Scrolls of the Mongol Invasions of Japan." In *Archaism and Antiquarianism in Korean and Japanese Art*, edited by Elizabeth Lillehoj, 54–73. Chicago: Center for the Art of East Asia, University of Chicago and Art Media Resources, 2013.

———. "The 'Ōnin War' as Fulfillment of Prophecy," *Journal of Japanese Studies* 46, no. 1 (Winter 2020): 31–60.

———. *State of War: The Violent Order of Fourteenth Century Japan*. Ann Arbor: University of Michigan Center for Japanese Studies, 2003.

———. "Traces of the Past: Documents, Literacy and Liturgy in Medieval Japan." In *Currents in Medieval Japanese History: Essays in Honor of Jeffrey P. Mass*, edited by Gordon Berger et al., 19–50. University of Southern California East Asian Studies Center: Figueroa Press, 2009.

———. "The Two Paths of Writing and Warring in Medieval Japan." *Taiwan Journal of East Asian Studies* 8, no. 1 (2011): 85–127.

———. "Warfare in Japan, 1200–1550." In *The Cambridge History of War*, vol. 2, edited by Anne Curry and David A. Graff, 523–53. Cambridge: Cambridge University Press, 2020.

———. *Weapons and the Fighting Techniques of the Samurai Warrior, 1200–1877*. New York: Amber Press, 2008.

Cooper, Michael. *They Came to Japan: An Anthology of European Reports on Japan, 1543–1640*. Berkeley: University of California Press, 1965.

Bibliography

Craig, Teruko, trans. *Musui's Story: The Autobiography of a Tokugawa Samurai.* Tucson: University of Arizona Press, 1991.

———, trans. *Remembering Aizu: The Testament of Shiba Gorō.* Honolulu: University of Hawaii Press, 1999.

Dainihon kokiroku Hekizan nichiroku (Unsen Taikyoku). 2 vols. Compiled by Tōkyō daigaku shiryōhen sanjo. Tokyo: Iwanami shoten, 2013–17.

Dainihon komonjo iewake 2. Asano ke monjo. Compiled by Tōkyō daigaku shiryōhen sanjo. Tokyo: Tōkyō daigaku shuppankai, 1906.

Dainihon komonjo iewake 19 Daigoji monjo. 17 vols. to date. Compiled by Tōkyō daigaku shiryōhen sanjo. Tokyo: Tōkyō daigaku shuppankai, 1955–present.

Dainihon komonjo iewake 9. *Kikkawa ke monjo.* 3 vols. Compiled by Tōkyō daigaku shiryōhen sanjo. Tokyo: Tōkyō daigaku shuppankai, 1925-32.

Dainihon komonjo iewake 11. Kobayakawa ke monjo. 2 vols. Compiled by Tōkyō daigaku shiryōhen sanjo. Tokyo: Tōkyō daigaku shuppankai, 1927.

Dainihon komonjo iewake 8. *Mōri ke monjo.* 4 vols. Compiled by Tōkyō daigaku shiryōhen sanjo. Reprint edition. Tokyo: Tōkyō daigaku shuppankai, 1920–24.

Dainihon komonjo iewake 16. Shimazu ke monjo. 6 vols. Compiled by Tōkyō daigaku shiryōhen sanjo. Tokyo: Tōkyō daigaku shuppankai, 1952–2019.

Dainihon komonjo iewake 15 Yamanouchi Sudō ke monjo. Compiled by Tōkyō daigaku shiryōhen sanjo. Tokyo: Tōkyō teikoku daigaku, 1940.

Dainihon shiryō series 6. Compiled by Tōkyō daigaku shiryōhen sanjo. 50 vols. to date. Tōkyō daigaku shuppankai, 1901–present.

Dainihon shiryō series 8. Compiled by Tōkyō daigaku shiryōhen sanjo. 42 vols. to date. Tōkyō daigaku shuppankai, 1913–present.

Elisonas, J. S. A., and J. P. Lamers, trans. *The Chronicle of Lord Nobunaga.* Leiden: Brill, 2011.

Farris, Wayne. *Heavenly Warriors: The Evolution of Japan's Military 500–1300.* Cambridge, MA: Harvard East Asia Series, 1993.

Fisher, Galen, trans. "*Daigaku wakumon* [The Great Learning] by Kumazawa Banzan." *Transactions of the Asiatic Society of Japan,* 2nd ser., vol. 16 (1938): 259–336.

Friday, Karl. *The First Samurai: The Life and Legend of the Warrior Rebel Taira Masakado.* Hoboken, NJ: John Wiley and Sons, 2008.

———. *Hired Swords: The Rise of Private Warrior Power in Early Japan.* Stanford: Stanford University Press, 1992.

Garrett, Philip. "Crime on the Estates: Justice and Politics in the Kōyasan Domain." *Journal of Japanese Studies* 41, no. 1 (Winter, 2015): 79–112.

Gay, Suzanne Marie. *The Moneylenders of Late Medieval Kyoto.* Honolulu: University of Hawaii Press, 2001.

Gerhart, Karen. "Akahashi Nariko: A Force to be Reckoned With." *Journal of Asian Humanities at Kyushu University* 4 (March 2019): 1–20.

———. "Reconstructing the Life of Uesugi Kiyoko." *Japan Review* no. 31 (2017): 3–24.

Goble, Andrew. "War and Injury: The Emergence of Wound Medicine in Medieval Japan." *Monumenta Nipponica* 60, no. 3 (Autumn 2005): 297–338.

Goodwin, Janet R., and Joan R. Piggott, eds. *Land, Power, and the Sacred: The Estate System in Medieval Japan*. Honolulu: University of Hawaii Press, 2018.

Grossberg, Kenneth. *Japan's Renaissance: The Politics of the Muromachi Bakufu*. Rev. ed. Ithaca, NY: Cornell East Asia Program, 2001.

———, trans. *The Laws of the Muromachi Bakufu*. Tokyo: Sophia University Press, 1981.

Hagihara Daisuke. "Ashikaga Yoshitada seiken kō." *Historia* 229 (2011): 78–103.

Hall, John Cary. "Japanese Feudal Law: The Institutes of Judicature: Being a translation of 'Go Seibai Shikimoku'; the Magisterial Code of the Hojo Power-Holder." *Transactions of the Asiatic Society of Japan* vol. 34, 1906: 1–44.

Hall, John Whitney, and Toyoda Takeshi, eds. *Japan in the Muromachi Age*. Reprint. Ithaca, NY: Cornell East Asia Program, 2001.

Hasegawa Tadashi et. al., eds. *Taiheiki (Jingū chōkokanbon)*. Ōsaka, Izumi shoin, 1994.

Hayashi Yuzuru. "Yoritomo no kao ni tsuite—sono keitai henka to Jishō Jūei nengo no shiyō o megutte." *Tokyo daigaku shiryōhensanjo kenkyū kiyō* 6 (March 1996): 1–21.

Hino Shishi Hensan Iinkai, comp. *Hino shi shi shiryōshū Takahata Fudō tainai monjo hen*. Hino, 1993.

Hosokawa Shigeo. *Kamakura Seiken tokusō senseiron*. Tokyo: Yoshikawa kōbunkan, 2000.

Hyōdo Hiromi, ed. *Taiheiki (Seigeninbon)*. 6 vols. Tokyo: Iwanami shoten, 2014-16.

Hyōgo kenshi shiryōhen Chūsei 4. Hyōgo, 1991.

Hyōgo kenshi shiryōhen Chūsei 9. Hyōgo, 1997.

Ikegami, Eiko. *The Taming of the Samurai: Honorific Individualism and the Making of Modern Japan*. Cambridge, MA: Harvard University Press, 1997.

Inryōken Nichiroku (Kikkei Shinzui). 5 vols. *Dainihon bukkyō zensho*, no. 133–37. Bussho kankōkai hensan, 1912–13.

Ishii Shirō, ed."Buke shohatto." *Kinsei buke shisō, Nihon shisō taikei* vol. 27. Tokyo: Iwanami shoten, 1974.

Ishii Susumu et al., eds. *Chūsei seiji shakai shisō*, vol. 1. *Nihon shisō taikei* vol. 21. Tokyo: Iwami shoten, 1972.

Jansen, Marius B. "Tosa in the Sixteenth Century: The 100 Article Code of Chōsokabe Motochika." *Oriens Extremus* 10, no. 1 (1963): 95–108.

Bibliography

Kamikawa chō kyōiku iinkai, Kyōto furitsu daigaku bungakubu kokōgaku kenkyūshitsu comp. *Fukumoto Dōyashiki ni okeru hakkutsu chōsa no seika* (March 2017).

Kanazawa bunko, comp. *Kamakura Hōjōshi no kōbō*. Kanazawa, October 2007.

Kanmon gyoki. Zoku gunsho ruijū hoi 2. Third revised edition. Tokyo: Zoku gunsho ruijū kanseikai, 2000.

Keene, Donald, trans. *Essays in Idleness*. New York: Columbia University Press, 1967.

———. *Yoshimasa and the Silver Pavilion: The Creation of the Soul of Japan*. New York: Columbia University Press, 2003.

Keirstead, Thomas. "Inventing Medieval Japan; The History and Politics of National Identity." *Medieval History Journal* 1, no. 1 (1998): 47–71.

Kimbrough, Keller, and Haruo Shirane, eds. *Monsters, Animals and Other Worlds: A Collection of Short Medieval Japanese Tales*. New York: Columbia University Press, 2018.

Kiyooka Eiichi, trans. *The Autobiography of Yukichi Fukuzawa*. New York: Columbia University Press, 1966.

Koakimoto Dan. *Taiheiki Baishōron no kenkyū*. Tokyo: Kyūko shoin, 2005.

Kurushima Noriko. "Senkō no kiroku: Chūsei kara kinsei e." *Kokuritsu rekishi minzoku hakubutsukan kenkyū hōkoku* no. 182 (January 2014): 167–80.

Lamers, Jeroen et al., trans. *The Chronicle of Lord Nobunaga* (Ōta Gyūichi). Leiden: Brill, 2011.

———. *Japanius Tyrannus: The Japanese Warlord Oda Nobunaga Reconsidered*. Leiden, Neth.: Hotei Publishing, 2000.

Lurie, David. *Realms of Literacy: Early Japan and the History of Writing*. Cambridge, MA: Harvard University Asia Center, 2011.

Matsuoka Hisato, comp. *Nanbokuchō ibun Chūgoku shikoku hen*. 6 vols. Tokyo: Tōkyōdō shuppan, 1987-95.

Mass, Jeffrey P. *Antiquity and Anachronism in Japanese History*. Stanford: Stanford University Press, 1992.

———. "Bakufu Justice: A Case Study." In *The Development of Kamakura Rule*, 270–76. Stanford: Stanford University Press, 1979.

———. *The Kamakura Bakufu*. Stanford: Stanford University Press, 1976.

———. *Lordship and Inheritance in Early Medieval Japan*. Stanford: Stanford University Press, 1989.

———. *Yoritomo and the Founding of the First Bakufu: The Origins of Dual Government in Japan*. Stanford: Stanford University Press, 1999.

McKelway, Matthew. *Capitalscapes: Folding Screens and Political Imagination in Late Medieval Kyoto*. Honolulu: University of Hawaii Press, 2006.

Bibliography

Miyazaki, Fumiko. "Religious Life of a Kamakura Bushi: Kumagai Naozane and his Descendants." *Monumenta Nipponica* 47, no. 4 (Winter 1992): 435–67.

Morris, Ivan. *The World of the Shining Prince: Court Life in Ancient Japan*. New York: Duff Cooper, 1964.

Nihon kankei kaigai shiryō Iezusukai Nihon shokanshū yakubun hen 2.2. Compiled by Tōkyō daigaku shiryōhen sanjo. Tokyo: Tōkyō daigaku shuppankai, 2000.

Ōita ken kyōiku bunka ka, comp. *Ōtomo Sōrin shiryōshū*. 5 vols. Ōita kyōiku iinkai, 1994.

Okami Masao, comp. *Gukanshō*. Tokyo: Iwanami shoten, 1967.

Oxenboell, Morten. "The Mineaiki and Discourses on Social Unrest in Medieval Japan." *Japan Forum* 18, no. 1 (March 2006): 1–21.

Perkins, George, trans. *The Clear Mirror: A Chronicle of the Japanese Court During the Kamakura Period (1185–1333)*. Stanford: Stanford University Press, 1998.

Pitelka, Morgan. *Spectacular Accumulation: Material Culture, Tokugawa Ieyasu, and Samurai Sociability*. Honolulu: University of Hawaii Press, 2016.

Rabinovitch, Judith N. *Shōmonki: The Story of Masakado's Rebellion*. Monumenta Nipponica Monographs. Tokyo: Sophia University, 1986.

Ravina, Mark. *The Last Samurai: The Life and Battles of Saigō Takamori*. Hoboken, NJ: John Wiley and Sons, 2004.

Roberts, Luke. *Performing the Great Peace: Political Space and Open Secrets in Tokugawa Japan*. Honolulu: University of Hawaii Press, 2012.

———. "A Transgressive Life: The Diary of a Genroku Samurai." *Early Modern Japan* (December 1995): 25–30.

Sather, Jeremy. "A Critique by Any Other Name: Imagawa Ryōshun's *Nan Taiheiki*, an Introduction and Translation (Part 1)." *Japan Review* no. 29 (2016): 39–68.

———. "A Critique by Any Other Name: Part 2 of Imagawa Ryōshun's *Nan Taiheiki*." *Japan Review* no. 31 (2017): 25–40.

Satō Shin'ichi and Ikeuchi Yoshisuke, comp. *Chūsei hōsei shiryōshū*. 7 vols. Tokyo: Iwanami shoten, 1955-2005.

Satō Shin'ichi. *Nanbokuchō no dōran*. Tokyo: Chūō kōronsha, 1972.

Sawyer, Ralph. *The Seven Military Classics of Ancient China*. Boulder: The Westview Press, 1993.

Sekijō chōshi, shiryōhen III, chūsei kankei shiryō. Sekijō chō, 1985.

Seno Sei'ichirō, comp. *Nanbokuchō ibun Kyūshū hen*. 7 vols. Tokyo: Tōkyōdō shuppan, 1985–92.

Shapinsky, Peter. *Lords of the Sea: Pirates, Violence, and Commerce in Late Medieval Japan*. Ann Arbor: University of Michigan Center for Japanese Studies, 2014.

Shibatsuji Shunroku, comp. *Sengoku ibun Takeda hen*. 6 vols. Tokyo: Tōkyōdō shuppan, 2002–6.

Shinoda, Minoru. *The Founding of the Kamakura Bakufu 1180–85*. New York: Columbia University Press, 1960.

Shizuoka kenshi shiryōhen vol. 5, *Chūsei* 1. Shizuoka, 1989.

Souyri, Pierre. *The World Turned Upside Down*. New York: Columbia University Press, 2001.

Spafford, David. *A Sense of Place: The Political Landscape in Late Medieval Japan*. Cambridge, MA: Harvard University Asia Center, 2013.

Stavros, Matthew. "Military Revolution in Early Modern Japan." *Japanese Studies* 33, no. 3 (2013): 243–61.

Steenstrup, Carl. "The Gokurakuji Letter. Hōjō Shigetoki's Compendium of Political and Religious Ideas of Thirteenth-Century Japan." *Monumenta Nipponica* 32, no. 1 (Spring 1977): 1–34.

———. *Hōjō Shigetoki (1198–1261) and His Role in the History of Political and Ethical Ideas in Japan*. London: Curzon Press, 1979.

———. "Hōjō Sōun's Twenty-One Articles." *Monumenta Nipponica* 29, no. 3 (Autumn 1974): 283–303.

———. "The Imagawa Letter: A Muromachi Warrior's Code of Conduct Which Became a Tokugawa Schoolbook." *Monumenta Nipponica* 28, no. 3 (Autumn 1973): 295–316.

———. "*Sata Mirensho:* A Fourteenth-Century Law Primer." *Monumenta Nipponica* no. 4 (Winter 1980): 405–35.

Taiheiki (Kandabon). Tokyo: Kokusho Kankōkai, 1907.

Takagi Shōsaku. *Nihon kinsei kokka no kenkyū*. Tokyo: Iwanami shoten, 1990.

Takeuchi Rizō, comp. *Heian ibun*. 15 vols. Tokyo: Tōkyōdō shuppan, 1963–80.

Takeuchi Rizō, comp. *Kamakura ibun*. 51 vols. Tokyo: Tōkyōdō shuppan, 1971–97.

Tamai Kōsuke, ed. *Towazugatari*. Tokyo: Iwanami bunko, 1968.

Tonomura, Hitomi. *Community and Commerce in Late Medieval Japan: The Corporate Villages of Tokuchin-chō*. Stanford: Stanford University Press, 1992.

Tsang, Carol. *War and Faith: Ikkō Ikki in Late Muromachi Japan*. Cambridge, MA: Harvard East Asian Monographs, 2007.

Tsuji Zennosuke, ed. *Kūge nichiyō kufū ryakushū* (Gidō Shūshin). Kyoto: Taiyōsha, 1939.

Tyler, Royall, trans. *Before Heike and After: Hōgen, Heiji, Jōkyūki*. CreateSpace Independent Publishing Platform, 2012.

———, trans. *From the Bamboo-View Pavilion: Takemuki-ga-ki: Fourteenth-Century Voices I*. Australia: Blue Tongue Books, 2016.

———, trans., with Shuzo Uyenaka. *Fourteenth-Century Voices II: From Baishōron to Nan-taiheiki*. Australia: Blue Tongue Books, 2016.

———, trans. *Iwashimizu Hachiman in War and Cult: Fourteenth-Century Voices III*. Australia: Blue Tongue Books, 2017.

———, trans. *Tale of Genji*. New York: Penguin Classics, 2002.

———. *The Tale of the Heike*. New York: Penguin Classics, 2012.

Vaporis, Constantine. *Samurai. An Encyclopedia of Japan's Cultured Warriors*. New York: ABC-CLIO, 2019.

———. *Tour of Duty: Samurai, Military Service in Edo, and the Culture of Early Modern Japan*. Honolulu: University of Hawaii Press, 2008.

———. *Voices of Early Modern Japan: Contemporary Accounts of Daily Life during the Age of the Shoguns*. New York: Routledge, 2021.

Varley, H. Paul, trans. *A Chronicle of Gods and Sovereigns: Jinnō Shōtōki of Kitabatake Chikafusa*. New York: Columbia University Press, 1980.

———. *The Chronicle of the Ōnin War*. New York: Columbia University Press, 1967.

———. "Oda Nobunaga, Guns, and Early Modern Warfare in Japan." In *Writing Histories in Japan: Texts and their Transformations from Ancient Times through the Meiji Era*, edited by Baxter et al., 105–25. Kyōto: Nichibunken kaigai shinpojium hōkokusho, 2007.

———. "Warfare in Japan, 1467–1600." In *War in the Early Modern World, 1450–1815*, edited by Jeremy Black, 53–86. London: UCL Press, 1999.

———. *Warriors of Japan as Portrayed in the War Tales*. Honolulu: University of Hawaii Press, 1994.

Wada Hidematsu, ed. *Shūtei Masukagami shōkai*. Tokyo: Meiji shoin, 1910.

Wada Hidemichi, ed. *Ōninki*. Tokyo: Koten bunko, 1978.

Wakayama kenshi chūei shiryō 2. Wakayama 1983.

Wakita Haruko. "Ports, Markets and Medieval Urbanism in the Ōsaka Region." In *Ōsaka: The Merchants' Capital of Early Modern Japan*, edited by McClain and Wakita Osamu, 22–43. Ithaca: Cornell University Press, 1999.

Washio Junkei, ed. *Taiheiki (Seigen'in bon)*. Tokyo: Tōkō shoin, 1936.

Wert, Michael. *Samurai: A Concise History*. Oxford: Oxford University Press, 2019.

Wilson, William Richie. "The Way of the Bow and Arrow: The Japanese Warrior in Konjaku Monogatari." *Monumenta Nipponica* 28, no. 2 (Summer 1973): 177–233.

Yamamoto Tsunetomo. *The Book of the Samurai Hagakure*. New York: Kodansha International Press, 1979.

Yonekura Michio. "Reassessing the Jingō-ji Portraits: Personage and Period." *Impressions* 39 (2018): 11–49.

SOURCE AND IMAGE CREDITS

Unless noted below, all sources and images are in the public domain. Images are listed in order of appearance; sources are listed alphabetically by author/translator.

IMAGES

Images 1–2. Musashi Saitama Inariyama sword (*Inariyama kofun shutsudo tekken*), possession of the Agency of Cultural Affairs (*Bunkachō*). Photographs and permission, Agency of Cultural Affairs and the Saitama Prefectural Museum of the Sakitama Ancient Burial Mounds.

Images 3–5. Eta Funayama tomb sword (*Eta Funayama kofun tekken*), possession of the Tokyo National Museum. Photographs and permission, Tokyo National Museum e-museum DNP Art Communications.

Images 6–9. Tōdaiji Kondō gold and silver ceremonial Bright (yang) sword (Tōdaiji Kondō *chindangu kingin sō no tachi yōhōken*), possession of Tōdaiji. Tōdaiji Kondō gold and silver ceremonial Shadow (yin) sword (Tōdaiji Kondō *chindangu kingin sō no tachi inhōken*), possession of Tōdaiji. Tōdaiji Kondō gold and silver ceremonial Bright (yang) sword (Tōdaiji Kondō *chindangu kingin sō no tachi yōhōken*) X-ray. Tōdaiji Kondō gold and silver ceremonial Shadow (yin) sword (Tōdaiji Kondō *chindangu kingin sō no tachi inhōken*) X-ray. Photographs and permission, Tōdaiji and the Gangōji Research Institute (Gangōji bunkazai kenkyūjo).

Image 10. Nishinoyama Tomb sword (*Nishinoyama kobo tōken*), possession of The Kyoto University Museum. Photograph and permission, The Kyoto University Museum.

Image 11. A Scene Depicting Takezaki Suenaga's Audience with Adachi Yasumori (*Mōko shūrai ekotoba*, Volume 2 [1916]). Photograph courtesy of the George J. Mitchell Dept. of Special Collections & Archives, Bowdoin College Library.

Image 13. Francisco *goji mon-iri wachigae-mon maki-e kura* (Francisco lacquered saddle with interlocking letter crest), possession of The Kyoto University Museum. Photograph and permission, The Kyoto University Museum.

Images 14–16. Late sixteenth-century breech-loading cannon, Portuguese colonies in South-Eastern Asia, possession of the Military-Historical Museum of Artillery, Engineer and Signal Corps. Photographs and permission, Sergei Efimov, Deputy Director, Military-Historical Museum of Artillery, Engineer and Signal Corps.

Source and Image Credits

Sources

Ackroyd, Joyce, trans. *Told Round a Brushwood Fire*. Princeton: Princeton University Press, 1979, 37–40, 49–50. Reprinted by permission of Princeton University Press and University of Tokyo Press.

Arntzen, Sonja, trans. *Ikkyū and the Crazy Cloud Anthology*. Tokyo: University of Tokyo Press, 1986, 139–40.

Brown, Sydney Devere, and Akiko Hirota, trans. *The Diary of Kidō Takayoshi*, vol. 3, 1874–77. Tokyo: University of Tokyo Press, 1986; February 5, 1876, 258; March 18, 1877, 465–66; March 21, 1877, 467–68; March 24, 1877, 469; March 28–29, 1877, 471–72; March 31, 1877, 472–73; April 2–6, 1877, 475–78; April 10, 1877, 480–81; April 17, 1877, 484–85; April 22, 1877, 488–89.

Craig, Teruko, trans. *Musui's Story: The Autobiography of a Tokugawa Samurai*. Tucson: University of Arizona Press, 1991, 16–17, 128–42. © 1988 Arizona Board of Regents. Reprinted by permission of the University of Arizona Press.

———, trans. *Remembering Aizu: The Testament of Shiba Gorō*. Honolulu: University of Hawaii Press, 1999, 54–59.

Elisonas, J. S. A., and J. P. Lamers, trans. *The Chronicle of Lord Nobunaga*. Leiden: Brill, 2011, 204, 222, 224–27.

Fisher, Galen, trans. "Abolition of the Separate Soldier Class." "A Discussion of Public Questions in the Light of the Greater Learning." *Transactions of the Asiatic Society of Japan*, 2nd ser., vol. 16 (1938): 313–17.

Jansen, Marius B. "Tosa in the Sixteenth Century: The 100 Article Code of Chōsokabe Motochika." *Oriens Extremus* 10, no. 1 (1963): 95–108.

Kiyooka Eiichi, trans. *The Autobiography of Yukichi Fukuzawa*. New York: Columbia University Press, 1966, 15–17.

Komonjo.princeton.edu documents. Translated by *Sources in Ancient and Medieval Japanese History* course graduate students (Megan Gilbert, Kyle Bond, Mai Yamaguchi, Claire Cooper, Skyler Negrete, David Romney, Nate Ledbetter, Caitlin Karyadi, Gina Choi, Kentaro Ide, Antonin Ferré, Michelle Tian, Joseph Henares and Filippo Gradi).

Mass, Jeffrey. "Bakufu Justice: A Case Study." In *The Development of Kamakura Rule*, 270–76. Stanford: Stanford University Press, 1979. ©1976 by the Board of Trustees of the Leland Stanford Jr. University. All rights reserved. Used by permission of the publisher, Stanford University Press, sup.org

Roberts, Luke, trans. "The Memoir of a Unification Era Warrior, Fukutomi Han'emon." Unpublished manuscript. Used by permission.

Schwemmer, Patrick, trans. Ōuchi Yoshinaga's commendation translated from the Portuguese version. Unpublished document. Used by permission.

Steenstrup, Carl. "Letter to Nagatoki." *Hōjō Shigetoki (1198–1261) and his Role in the History of Political and Ethical Ideas in Japan*. London: Curzon Press, 1979, 143–57.

Tyler, Royall, trans. *Before Heike and After: Hōgen, Heiji, Jōkyūki*. CreateSpace Independent Publishing Platform, 2012, 211–13.

———, trans. *From Baishōron to Nantaiheiki: Fourteenth-Century Voices II*. Australia: Blue Tongue Books, 2016. Excerpts from the *Baishōron* (with Shuzo Uyenaka) and *Nantaiheiki*, 32–34, 47–52, 79–83, 85–90, 92–93, 97–98, 99–100, 102–5, 116–19, 236–38.

———, trans. *Iwashimizu Hachiman in War and Cult: Fourteenth-Century Voices III*. Australia: Blue Tongue Books, 2017, 55–56.

———, trans. "Mine'aki." Unpublished manuscript. Used by permission.

Wilson, William Richie. "The Way of the Bow and Arrow: The Japanese Warrior in Konjaku Monogatari." *Monumenta Nipponica* 28, no. 2 (Summer, 1973): 222–31.

Yamamoto Tsunetomo. *The Book of the Samurai Hagakure*. New York: Kodansha International Press, 1979, 17, 28–29, 38–39, 43–44, 144–45. ©1979, 2002 by William Scott Wilson. Reprinted by arrangement with The Permissions Company, LLC on behalf of Shambhala Publications, Inc., Boulder, Colorado, www.shambhala.com.

INDEX

abatis (*hashiriki*), 106
Abe no Munetō, 22–24
Abe no Sadatō, 9, 12, 17–18, 20–24, 134
Abe no Yoritoki, 9, 18–19
absconding, 56, 247
Adachi Yasumori, 33, 81–82, 84–86, 93–95, 97n138, 120
adjudication, 46 52, 58, 60. *See also* Jōei Formulary
administrative reforms, xiv, xvii, xxi
administrators (*bugyōnin*), xxvii, 34, 81, 83, 94–95, 107, 127, 128n30, 129n32, 132n42, 152, 155, 193, 196, 198, 203, 247n36, 268, 311, 313
adoption, 51, 65, 67, 263, 272. *See also* succession
adultery, 99n144; determination of, 53–54, 214, 214n53; punishment of, 53–54, 198–99, 214, 218n62, 249–50. *See also* marriage
affairs. *See* adultery
agents (*daikan/shū*), 68n78, 213. See also *daikan*
Aizu Wakamatsu, xxviii, 292–98
Akamagaseki, 132, 201–203
Akama-no-seki, 132. *See also* Akamagaseki
Akamatsu, xxiv,124n21; residence, 178–80; messenger, 180; retainers, 109, 113, 175, 179, 216, 219; castle, 113–14
Akamatsu Enshin (Norimura), 109, 112–13, 124, 128–29, 131, 138
Akamatsu Mitsusuke, xxiv, 178–80
Akasaka (castle), 175
Akasaka (harbor), 133, 202
Aki (province), 28, 89, 131, 224, 248
akoda-bachi, 204
akutō (evil bands), xxi, 53, 103–6, 116, 211, 226, 309
Amagasaki, 113, 284–85

Amaterasu, 116
amendments (*tsuikahō*), 33, 61–62, 85, 93–96
Amida, 176, 262
Amidaji, lands, 202
ammunition, 302–3, 307–8; dump, 302; rounds of, 302
Andō Renshō, 104–5
Ankokuji, 125n25, 142
Aoyanagi Saburō, 161, 161n35, 162. *See also* Yamanouchi Tsuneyuki
appeals, 83, 95; procedure regarding 45, 52, 59, 211, 215, 221
apprehender (*torite*), 210
Arai, family (of Hitachi), 156–57, 166–67, 272; later movement, 272–74
Arai Hakuseki, xxviii, 271
archery tower (*yagura*), 106. *See also* watchtowers
arihan (monogram copy), 36, 89
armies: conscription, xiv, xxviii, xxix; mobilization, xxiii–xxiv, xxvii, 37–38, 87–91, 112–13, 124–26, 129–30, 142–43, 149, 182; size of, 20, 31–32, 124, 129–30, 133–34, 146, 153, 155–58, 237–38, 241; speed of, 33, 35–38, 41, 132, 307; supplies for, xxiii, 160, 182–83, 201–2, 310. See also *hanzei*; *kiheitai*; Six-District Army
armor, xvi, xxii, xxvii, 19, 26–27, 87, 90–91, 100–1, 105, 123, 132–36, 139, 175, 175n66, 176, 177, 204–5, 220, 240, 261–62; iron, xiv; suits of, xiv, 26, 26n6, 90, 132, 134–35, 137. See also *kebiki* armor; *haramaki*; *sode*; *yoroi*
armor chests, 105, 202. *See also* chests
armor sleeves. See *sode*
armorers, 255
armory, xxix, 300, 302
Army Cadet School, 296

Index

arrows, 17–20, 26–27, 87, 90, 103, 105, 110–111, 126, 128, 134–37, 139–140, 175; wounds by, 184–85, 213, 220–21, 249; fire arrows, 188
arson, 22–23, 179, 258, 293, 295
arsonist, 53, 196, 212
Asahara Tameyori, 33, 100–2
Asano, Lord, 277, 278n3
Ashikaga Ietoki, 118–21
Ashikaga lineage, 110, 118, 121–122
Ashikaga shogunate (*bakufu*), 144, 173, 181n15
Ashikaga Tadayoshi, 17, 118, 120–22, 129–130, 132–137, 139–146, 168–69
Ashikaga Takauji, xxii–xxiii, 99n147, 109–111, 115, 118–148, 150, 152, 168–169, 172–73, 204, 313; mother and birthplace, 125n25
Ashikaga Yoshiakira, 119
Ashikaga Yoshimasa, xxiv–xxv, 13, 89, 131, 178–81, 184, 186
Ashikaga Yoshimitsu, xxiii–xxiv, 176, 178
Ashikaga Yoshimochi, xxiii–xxiv, 13, 40, 178
Ashikaga Yoshinori, xxiii–iv, 178–80
Ashikaga Yoshiteru, 22, 231–32
Aso Harutoki (Tokiharu), 114, 126n27, 128, 128n31
Aso Koresumi, 171–72
assassination attempts, 33–34, 100–2, 178–180
assault, 209, 213, 239, 241, 277
Atsuta (shrine), 134n48, 236
attendants (*kannushi*), 43, 214, 245, 265; shogunal, 97; imperial, 99, 101
audience, 81–82, 84–86, 94, 142, 261, 283n8
Awa (province), 15, 130, 142, 263, 276
Awaji, 26, 139
Awazu (family), 190–92
Awazu Kiyonori, 190–91
azukari dokoro (manager), 54n37, 66n68, 67, 89–90, 309, 314
Azuma Kagami, 30–31, 35

Baishōron, 41–42, 118, 122–43, 145
bamboo, 106, 213, 234, 256, 269, 295; blinds, 75, 98; cylinders, 234; grass, 133, 135; swords, 279; spears, 105, 281, 283–84, 287; quivers, 104
Banba (Ōmi province), 111, 115, 127–28, 143
bandits, 103–4, 127, 226, 249
banditry (*sanzoku*), 43, 47, 104, 210–11
bannermen, 82, 91, 175, 229–30, 285
banners, 138–39, 174, 231; imperial, 110, 129–30, 138–39
Barbarian-Subduing General. *See* Sei-i-tai shōgun
barbarians, xv, 7, 20, 61, 98, 112, 117, 310
barricades, 27, 110
base (*genin*, *bonge*), 47, 91, 96, 197, 210, 259, 310, 313
bathing, 81, 136–37, 274–75, 286
battle axe, xiii
battle camp, 106, 110, 125–26, 133, 136–37, 146, 152, 175, 188–89, 200, 216, 222, 231, 236–38, 260–61, 295, 307
battle cries, 101, 110, 135, 140, 175, 238
battle flags, 229, 231
battle reports, 82–83, 91, 171, 311
battle service, xxii, 38, 84, 87–88, 91–92, 113, 153, 259, 310
battlefield, 82n112, 112, 118, 213, 231, 235, 237n5, 239, 268, 279, 308
battlefront, 303, 305, 308
battles, xiv, xviii, xxii, xxv–viii, 13, 16–17, 19, 21–23, 25–27, 38–39, 49, 81–84, 87, 91–92, 109–11, 115, 123–24, 126–30, 132, 134–142, 146, 149, 152–54, 159–61, 163–67, 171, 173–78, 182–86, 189–90, 213, 225, 227–28, 230, 233, 235, 238–40, 241n16, 260, 262, 271–72, 280, 295, 297–98, 303–5, 308, 310
beatings: people, 47, 207, 217, 281; drums, 138, 140, 239, 292
benefice lands (*kyūchi*), 197, 216, 252n43
bettō. *See* intendants
Bingo (province), 131, 224
Bitchū (province), 32, 224
Bizen (province), 125, 131, 137
blood, xxviii, 100, 136, 263, 308

Index

boats, 89–90, 103, 130, 199n7, 201, 203, 255, 266, 282n7. *See also* ships
bōhai. See comrades
bonge, 47, 48n31, 96, 197, 309. *See also* base
Book of Filial Piety, 283
borrowing: accoutrements, 160, 163; goods, 251; horses, xxii, 160; money, 157, 159, 164, 251, 268, 273, 287; rice, 250, 252
Bōshin War, 292, 296–97
bow and arrow, 70, 135, 220–21; honor of, 82, 84–85, 177; way of, 15, 73, 81
bows, xiv, 26, 87, 90, 105, 195, 229–31, 242, 273
Brahma (Bonten), 59, 110, 169, 215, 221
branding (of horses), 204
brigands. See *akutō*
bright, sword, xv, 4–6
brothers, xx, xxiv, 8, 10, 13, 15, 17, 21, 24, 27, 32, 38, 41, 51, 64, 69, 92, 98n142, 101, 116, 120, 122, 131, 139n59, 140, 143–46, 168, 169n56, 179n3, 200, 208, 216, 239n10–11, 250, 259, 273, 291, 294–96, 307
Buddhism, 141; Nichiren, xxvii; relationship to state, xiv, xx, 4; rites, xvii
Buddhist law, 13, 148, 223
Bugyō, 155n8, 245n31, 246n34–35, 311. *See also* administrators
buke shohatto, xxvii–xxviii, 264–67
Bungo (province), 90–91, 224
buntori (decapitation), 91
burglary. *See* theft
Bushidō, xxix
Buzen (province), 224

calendars, xiii, xxix, 2, 301n4; doctors of, 15
camp. *See* battle camp
campaigns, xix, xxii–iii, 35, 41n23, 87, 113, 149, 159–65, 167–68, 168n53,187n30, 200, 204, 219, 240, 243, 259–60, 297, 313
cannon, xi, xxvi–xxviii, 223, 225–28, 300, 302
cape (horo), 123, 139, 139n60
capital. *See* Kyoto

Capital Police (*kebiishi*), xvi, 34, 55, 107
castle towns, xxvi, 255n49, 269
castles, xxvii, xxix, 105,111, 113–14, 117n92, 131, 138, 159, 163, 166–68, 174–75, 188, 218, 236n3, 237–38, 240–41, 262–63, 265–66, 268–69, 293–96, 300; construction, 105, 217, 256, 263, 265; repairs, 264–65, 269; sieges, 149, 152, 154, 163, 166–68, 174–75, 188, 227, 241, 262, 293, 295, 300, 302, 305
catapults, 182, 188, 189n39
Catfish tail (Namazu-o), sword, 101
cattle (cows), 54, 57, 213, 221, 256
cedar, 133, 256; branches, 133
chakushi. See main heir
chakutōjō. See report of arrival
Chang An (scribe), 3–4
charcoal, 233–34
chestnuts, 133, 160
chests (storage; Chinese style; *karabitsu*), 105, 190, 202
chigyō (possession), 46, 50–51, 62, 168, 242, 249n39, 252n43
Chihaya (castle), 114
Chikugo (province), 92, 129
Chikuzen (province), 32, 132, 191, 224
child, 15, 24, 129, 198–99, 208, 211, 250, 257, 272–73, 279, 292; child name, 63n58; child *shōgun*, 107; childish, 291; childhood, 292
children, xiv, xxviii, 18, 44, 46, 49–52, 56, 61, 70, 76, 103, 180, 199–200, 208, 211–12, 218, 250, 257, 263, 268–69, 279, 283, 288, 291, 293. *See also* grandchildren
China, xxiii, xxv, xxvii, 3–4, 12, 41, 87, 133, 141, 143, 242, 278. *See also* Ming
Chinjufu *shōgun*, xv, xxii, 7, 13, 25, 120, 309
Chinzei. *See* Kyushu
Chinzei Eastern Administrator, 33, 87–88
chiten no kimi, 25
chopsticks, 272
Chōshū (domain consisting of Suō and Nagato provinces), xxviii, 297, 300, 302
Chōsogabe. *See* Chōsokabe

Chōsokabe, family, 235, 244, 252n44, 260n58, 262, 262n59; domains, 260
Chōsokabe Morichika, 259, 262
Chōsokabe Motochika, 235, 244, 245n32, 252n43, 254n47, 255n49, 259, 260–62
Christianity, 223; banning, xxvii; conversion, xxvi, 224, 226; establishing churches, 223; names, 227; uprising, xxviii
Chrysanthemum Turtle (Kamegiku), 39–40
chūgen, 70, 81, 184, 190, 243, 310
Chūgoku (region), 129
chūkin. See battle service; military service
chūsetsu. See battle service; military service
clan (*ichimon*), 16, 63n57, 82, 122n8, 150, 170, 235, 272, 278n3, 297
coal, 232–33, 274
coins, 104, 202n24, 249, 253, 255–56, 258, 273
commissariat rice. See *hyōrōmai*
commissioner (*Tale of Genji*), xvi, 8–10, 12
commoners: *hyakushō*, xiv, xxii, xxvi, 56, 98, 149, 154–56, 160, 165, 198, 199; *heimin, domin*, 206, 212, 219, 242–43, 245, 247n36, 250n40, 269, 272, 310–11, 313
compensation, 40, 45, 149, 153, 210, 214, 244
comrades (*bōhai*), 45, 54, 57, 110, 161, 174, 216–17, 220–21, 309
confessions, 206, 210–12
confirmation edict (*ando no onkudashibumi*), 51
confiscation, xxi, xxiv–xxv, xxvii, 40, 44, 46–47, 53–54, 56–57, 61–62, 84, 95, 159, 183, 197, 203, 208–9, 212–14, 221, 242, 252–53, 255–56, 262, 267, 274, 311
Confucian scholar, 108, 271
Confucianism, xxvii
conscription, xiv, xxviii, xxix
cosigned document (*rensho shojō*), 63, 153
cosigner (*rensho*), 105n164
Cosme de Torres, 223
Cosmic Buddha (Rushana). See Great Buddha
cotton, 295; cloth, 255, 290

Council of Elders (*toshiyorishū*), 221
counties (*kōri*), 44
court cases, 155, 158
Court Lady's Communiqué (*nyōbō bōsho*), 190–91
Court of Appeals (*teichū*), 52, 81, 83–84, 314
courtiers, xvii, xx–xxi, xxiii–xxiv, 8–9, 11, 28, 73n91, 77.n100–1, 97, 100, 109–110, 127, 129n32, 190–91, 312
cows. See cattle
cowardice, 70, 231, 277, 279–80
craftsmen, 188, 195, 212, 281
crest, familial, 27, 85–86, 99, 130, 137–39, 204, 217, 231, 245, 262, 266, 283–84, 286
crimes, 44, 46–48, 53–54, 56–58, 60, 72, 80n108, 98.140, 198–99, 206–13, 216, 219, 246n33, 250, 256–57, 263, 311
criminals, xix, 37, 105, 202, 207–8, 211, 213, 314
crossroads, 182, 184, 189, 194
Crunchbone (sword), 134
cut seal (*kirifu*), 160n31, 191, 192

Daidōji, xi, 223–24
Daigoji, 120, 121n6
daikan (representative/agent/deputy) 27, 44, 47, 53, 88, 202, 211, 213, 217, 242, 244, 244n27, 268
daimyō (great lords), xxiii, xxvi, xxvii–xxviii, 97–99, 179, 193, 216, 223, 229, 231, 235, 244, 251, 260, 264–65, 267–70, 281, 284n9, 295, 297, 300, 310, 313–14
Daishinbō, 159, 164
Dannoura, battle of, xviii
Date: family, 193; laws, 206–15, 243
daughters, xviii, 8, 11, 99n144, 216, 219n69, 272; inheritance, 49, 51, 63–66, 68, 99, 212
Dazaifu, 10, 26, 34, 67n72, 69n83, 84, 129n33, 132–33, 136–37, 138n54
death, xv, xix, xxiv–v, xxvii, 1, 4, 7–9, 19–21, 25–26, 30, 41n21, 46, 48, 51, 53, 65n65, 71, 85n113, 93, 96, 103, 107, 122, 124, 124n20, 125–26, 128, 139n60, 140,

144–46, 148, 161, 163, 173, 176–77, 179, 185, 200, 208n33, 213n49, 216–17, 218n64, 219, 246, 248n38, 249–50, 257, 268, 271, 273–78, 289, 295, 313–14
decorum, 11, 94
deer, 60, 221; horns, 262
defendant, 48, 54, 215
desertion, 161
Dewa (province), 21, 24, 95
Dharma Emperors. *See* Retired Emperors
directive (*mikyōjo*), 36–37, 83, 87n115, 88, 105, 106, 108, 121
disinheritance, 50, 63
disown. *See* disinheritance
district (*gun*), xiv, 15, 19, 21, 24, 28–30, 35n5, 44, 89, 102, 107, 115, 161, 164n40, 191, 224, 226, 244, 246, 248, 259, 265–66, 268, 312
divorce, xxvi, 62
document (*kakikudashi*), 82, 87n115, 89–90, 145
Document of Damages/Loss (*funshitsujō*), 115, 172–73
Document of Praise (*kanjō*), 114, 153, 182–83, 185–86
dogs, 103–4, 187, 202, 214; archery practice on, 80, 80n109; dog's death, 179–80, 277
dog temple, 103
domain, xxv, xxvii–xxviii, 41, 53, 90, 193, 198–99, 206, 208, 213, 218, 220, 245, 251, 253–54, 260, 264–65, 267, 269, 276, 281, 292, 294, 296–98, 300, 302, 310
dōri (justice), 53, 72, 215, 310
dragons, 106, 278; dragon god, 130, 278; name of wind, 130
dreams, 17, 85, 110, 138, 144–46, 278, 294
drums, 138, 140, 174n65, 239, 250n40, 292
drunkards, 207–8, 249
dry fields, 106, 251, 258
dwelling (*zaike*), 44, 155, 158, 197, 212n47, 214; dwelling fields, 253
dyed robes, 158

earthworks, 188–89
Eastern Army, xxv, 182, 184, 188

Eastern barbarians, 61, 112, 117
ebisu, 98. *See also* barbarians
eboshi (cap), 96, 104
Echizen (province), 8, 26, 37, 37n15
Echū (province), 37, 37n15
edict. *See inzen*; *kudashibumi*; *rinji*
Edo (city) (Yedo), xxvii, 264–65, 267–69, 273, 282, 282n6, 283, 286–90
emishi, xv, 7. *See also* barbarians
encampment. *See* battle camp
enemies, xxvii, 16, 20, 36, 117, 122, 124n19, 126, 129, 141, 143, 174, 187, 208, 235, 301
Envoy to Pursue and Capture. *See tsuitōshi*
Envoy to Pursue and Punish. *See tsuitōshi*
envoys, 105, 258
estates. *See shōen*
etiquette, 108
execution, 207, 265
experts of law (*hōke*), 49
Europe, 223, 271
eyes, 71, 99, 103, 106, 121, 143, 180, 217, 263, 272, 291, 295

falcons, 197, 214. *See also* hawks
falconers, 197
family (*ichizoku*), 153, 168–69
father, xvii, 8–9, 13–14, 17, 28, 40–41, 46, 49–52, 56, 63n57, 66n69, 69–70, 75n95, 77, 98, 99n144, n147, 120, 125, 125n22, 132, 143, 164, 187n30, 208, 219, 245n31, 250, 256, 259, 261, 267, 270–75, 281, 283n9, 287
father-in-law, 19
fencing, 284
ferrymen, 202
feudalism, xix, 70n86, 252n43; system, 303
feuds, 206, 208n35
filial piety: book on, 283; seven rites of, 108
fire arrow (*hiya*), 188
fire spear (*hihō hisō*), 189
firearms, 186. *See also* guns
fish, 77, 97n137, 284, 305
fishing, 275; tax, 256, 268
Five Circuits, 34–35

331

five phases, 4
followers. See *chūgen*; *hikan*; *kenin*; *miuchi*; *rōtō*; *shojū*; *wakatō*; *yoriki*
forgery, 29, 47–48
Former Nine Year's War, 9
fortifications, 15, 105n161, 174, 174n65, 188–89, 241
forty-seven *rōnin*, 276–77
fowl, 77, 287
Franco-Prussian War, 297
frugality, 77n100, 93–95, 264–65, 282
fudai (hereditary servant), 250
Fujiwara Fuhito, 141
Fujiwara Hidesato, 16–17
Fujiwara Kiyohira, xv, xviii
Fujiwara Nobuyori, 26
Fujiwara of the north, 9, 25
Fujiwara Regents (*sesshō*, *kanpaku*), 25, 96, 99, 100, 313
Fujiwara Sumitomo, xvi
Fujiwara Tametoki, 8, 19
Fujiwara Tsunekiyo, 19, 21, 23–24
Fujiwara Yasuhira, xv, xix
Fujiwara Yoritsuna, 107
Fukakusa (region), 110
Fukuchi Gen'ichirō, 305–8
Fukuhara Sadatoshi, 220, 222
Fukuoka, 304
Fukutomari (harbor), 104, 105n163
Fukutomi Han'emon Masachika, 235, 260, 263
Fukuzawa Yukichi, 271, 291
Funabashi, battle, 183
Fushimi: emperor, 100; region, 125n24

garrison, xv, 19, 238, 301, 304–5, 307
gates, 18, 108, 257, 265
gechijō, 38–39, 58n.45, 67, 67n.71, 172
genealogies, 172
genin. See base
Genji (Minamoto) lineage, 37, 107, 110, 153
Genjō (lute) 101
Genpei War, xvii–xviii, 28, 118, 311
gesu, xvii–xviii, 25, 28, 33, 44, 48, 172, 309–10, 312, 314

gesu shiki (managerial rights), xvii, 28, 310
gifts, xiv, 1, 18, 21, 50, 74–75, 94, 141, 179, 187, 238, 284–85
Gifu, 236, 240
Gion Festival, 198
Go-Daigo (emperor), xxi–xxii, 109–111, 114, 116, 117n92, 118, 122, 124–28, 129n32, 144, 150
Go-Fukakusa (emperor), 98, 98n42, 99
Go-Fushimi (emperor), 101, 109–111, 117n192, 126n26, 127n28, 129, 129n32
Go-Hanazono (emperor), 190
Go-Murakami (emperor), 171
Go-Reizei (emperor), 17
Go-Sanjō (emperor), xvi, 25
Go-Shirakawa (emperor), xvii–xviii, 26, 28, 32, 41
Go-Toba (emperor), xx, 26, 33–35, 37–41, 48n32, 107n171, 112n181
Goa, 223
Goganzuka (village), xxviii, 281–83, 285
gojisō. See protector priests
gokenin (householders), 36, 38, 44, 48, 51, 54, 61–62, 81–83, 89–91, 95, 102, 105, 108–9, 115, 172, 196, 310, 312
gold, xv, xviii, 7, 9, 18, 105, 107, 138, 141, 226, 262, 272
Golden Pavilion, xxiv
Gongen, 59, 59n46, 215n56, 285
Goseibai shikimoku. See Jōei Formulary
Gotō islands, 153
gozoku, 300
grandchildren, 64, 199
grandfather, xvii, 17, 42, 46, 50, 63, 120, 148, 191, 208, 261, 271–73
grandmother, 8, 10–11, 208, 272, 290, 293
Great Buddha (Rushana), xv, 242
Greater Learning, 267n71, 283
guard duty (service), xiv, xix, xxi, 44, 62, 161, 165–66, 310
guests, 71–72, 77–79, 105, 193, 209, 221, 268
gunchūjō. See petition for reward
gunfire, 239, 261, 295
gunpowder, xxvi, 223, 231–32, 234

Index

guns, xxvi, 182, 186–89, 223, 229–31, 233, 235, 242, 261, 302–4, 308

Hachiman, 9, 15, 21, 59, 81, 84, 97, 110, 120–22, 125, 133, 136, 138, 147, 169, 183, 215, 221–22; three gods of, 21, 147
Hachiman-dono (Yoshiie), 120
Hachiman Tarō (Yoshiie), 20
Hagi (castle town), 199n17, 297, 305
hair, 24, 111, 272, 274–75, 282, 286, 290, 294; shaving as punishment, 54
hakama (trousers), 104, 281
Hakata, xxi, 81–82, 89–90, 132–33, 136–37, 224
Hakone, 59, 135, 215n56
Hakozaki: harbor, 81, 136–37; Hakozaki Hachiman shrine, 133, 136; temple, 136
half-tax. See *hanzei*
Hanazono (emperor), 110–11, 117n192, 126n26, 127n28
haniwa, xiv
hanzei (half-tax), xxiii–xxiv, 178, 310, 314
haori, 195, 281, 286
haramaki (simplified armor, corselet), 26, 90, 105, 105n160, 204
harakiri, 217, 288, 288n10, 289. See also *seppuku*
harbor, creation of, 104
hardship, 138, 253, 265, 307–8
Harima (province), 39, 102–4, 106, 109, 113, 124–25, 129, 131, 138, 275–76; road, 139–40
Harimanada, 130
harvesting, 221, 242, 252–53, 256, 270; illegal, 106, 212
Hatakeyama, family, xxiv, 120, 241n17, 311
Hatakeyama Masanaga, 189
Hatakeyama Yoshihiro (Yoshinari), 189, 189n42
hatamoto (bannerman), 269, 280. See also bannermen
Hatano Kageuji, 150, 152–53
hats, 104, 195
hawks, 213; bait, 197, 214
headman, 282, 285

headquarters, xxvii, 14, 18, 24, 29, 40, 68n78, 132, 158, 168n53, 175, 229–30, 294
heads, 18, 21, 23–24, 40, 42, 82–84, 114, 128, 175, 179–80, 236, 239, 244, 259, 263, 274, 282, 284, 286, 291, 293, 308; as cups, 236; beheading, 17, 19, 23–24, 82–84,114, 136, 179–80, 183, 249, 253, 261, 288, 308
headship, 107, 212, 257, 297
Heavenly Kings, 110, 169, 221
Heiji Disturbance, xvii–xviii, 26, 28
heimin (commoner), 198–99
helmets, 27, 42, 130, 134–35, 163, 204, 229, 262
Higo (province), 8, 10, 32, 81, 89–90, 114, 171, 308
Hikamisan, 197
hikan, 92, 185, 195–96, 219, 247, 247n37, 251n41, 256n50, 310
hiki (cash), 210
Hiraizumi, xviii, 9
Hirohashi Kanehide, 191–92
Hiromine (warrior family), 102
Hironaka Takakane, 219
Hitachi (province), 13–17, 154, 157, 159, 166–67, 168n53, 272
hitatare (robes), 27, 96–97, 132, 134–35
Hizen (province), 8–9, 63–64, 67, 82–83, 91–92, 276
Hōgen Disturbance, 28
Hōjō (Osaragi) Koresada, 105, 105n164
Hōjō Masako, xix, 41, 41n22, 45, 45n30
Hōjō Nagatoki, 33, 69, 70n85
Hōjō Nakatoki, 111, 117, 127–28
Hōjō Sadatoki, 93–94, 98–99
Hōjō Shigetoki, 33, 61n51, 64, 69, 70n85, 73n91
Hōjō Takatoki, 112, 125, 125n23, 129
Hōjō Tokifusa, 41, 41n23, 60
Hōjō Tokimasa, 42, 112
Hōjō Tokimasa (Rokuhara *tandai* who dies 1333), 111
Hōjō Tokimune, 89, 93
Hōjō Tomotoki, 37, 37n14, 125

333

Index

Hōjō Yasutoki 33, 36n9, 37–38, 41–42, 60–61, 69
Hōjō Yoshitoki, 33–34, 36–37, 38n16, 40–42
Hōki (province), 106, 110, 125
Hōkōji, 242
hōkōnin. *See* servant
Hokuriku (district), 34, 125
honesty, 61, 106, 142, 202, 279, 296
Honganji, 240–41
Honganji Ren'nyo, 241
honjo (proprietor), 45, 47, 57
honryō (original owner; homelands), 45, 159, 171
Honshu, xv, 7, 132n41, 202n23, 246n33
honshu (original holder), 45–46, 48, 50
horsemanship, 246, 264–65
horses, xiv, xvi, xix, xxii, 16–18, 20, 27, 32, 37, 39, 41, 54, 56n42, 57, 75, 81–82, 84, 89–90, 95–96, 99, 109, 117, 122–23, 127, 129, 132, 134–36, 138–41, 149, 154, 159–61, 163, 175–76, 181, 202, 204, 213, 221, 229, 239–40, 248, 255–56, 261–63, 266, 311, 315; branding of, 204; characteristics of, xiv, xix; as gifts, 75; pastures (*maki*), 95
Hosokawa, 120, 129, 131, 138, 140, 175, 179, 280, 311
Hosokawa Akiuji, 131, 142
Hosokawa Katsumoto, 181, 183–87, 189, 190n46, xxv
Hosokawa Kazuuji, 125, 127, 131
Hosokawa Kiyouji, 173, 175
Hosokawa Masamoto, xxv
Hosokawa Sumimoto, 204–5
Hosokawa Takakuni, xxv
Hosokawa Yoriharu, 131
Hosshōji, 110, 152, 188
hostages, 213, 266, 266n69
hot springs, 194, 283, 285
husband, 24, 39, 46–47, 50–51, 61–62, 63n57, 67n74, 214, 218n62, 250
hyakushō, xxii, xxvi, 56, 56n42, 149, 154–56, 160, 165, 206, 212, 212n45, 219, 242–43, 310–11, 313. *See also* commoners; peasants

Hyōgo Island, 104, 113, 129, 132, 138–39, 152
hyōgu (generic term for armor), 91
hyōrōmai (military provisions, commissariat rice), 157, 164

Ichijō (avenue), 182, 184
Ichijō (family), 245n30, 100
Ichinoseki, 294, 296
Ichinotani, 139
Iga (province), 127
Iga Mitsusue, 41, 41n21
ikeguchi. *See* suspect
ikki (agreement; military unit), 153, 164, 168, 170, 174–75, 311
Ikkyū, 180–81
Imagawa Ryōshun, 118–19, 120n2
Imperial Guard, 39, 301
In no chō. *See* Office of the Retired Emperor
Inaba (province), 106
Inari: festival, 292; god, 291; shrine, 292
India, xxvi, 4, 12, 87, 223
inheritance, xx, 50–51, 63, 93, 103, 212
Inoue (family), 216–20
Inoue Motokane, 216–17, 218n63
inshi, 35
intendants (*bettō*), 107
intermediaries, 52, 94, 201, 219
interrogation, 155n8, 211
inzen, 38, 109, 129, 144
irrigation, 221, 253
Ise (province), 25, 127
Ise (shrine), 107
Ishida Mitsunari, 262
Itami, 283, 286
Itawa (sword maker), 4
Itō Hirobumi, 303–6
Itsukushima shrine, 28, 221–22
Iwakura Tomomi, 303, 306
Iwashimizu Hachiman Shrine, 97, 97n137, 107, 147
Iyama Yūhachi, 282–83, 285, 289
Iyo (province), 38, 263
Izu (province), 15, 30, 59, 112, 142, 179, 215n56

334

Index

Izumi (province), 114, 172, 174n64, 188, 236, 241
Izumo (province), 219

Jien (*gojisō*), 26
Jimyōin (imperial line), 124, 129, 129n32, 131n40
Jingū (early ruler), 133, 147
Jinkaishū. *See* laws, Date
Jinmori Heizō, xxviii, 292, 294–96
Jinsei, 56, 267–69
jitō, xviii–xxiii, xxv, 28, 33–37, 39, 42–45, 53–55, 57–58, 61, 89, 92, 102, 105, 107–8, 172, 206, 212–13, 247n37, 249, 249n39, 250, 252, 254, 256n50, 310–312, 314–15
Jizō (*Sanskrit* Kṣitigarbha), 145–46
Jōei Formulary, 33, 42–62, 198–199, 206, 210, 210n38, 212n46, 214–15
Jōkyū War, xx–xxi, 33, 41, 107n171
judicial authority, xx, 212n45
judo, 281
justice. *See dōri*

kaburaya (humming arrows), 126, 134, 137, 140
Kaga (province), 37, 37n15, 241, 241n16
Kagoshima 303, 307–8
Kai (province), 31, 238, 240
Kakiya (family), 176–77, 183, 216, 218, 219n68
Kakogawa, 104, 138
Kamakura (city), 9, 30, 34, 64, 77n100, 81, 96–97, 99, 105–7, 111, 114, 118, 121, 123, 126n27, 154–55, 158; law, 33, 42–69, 84–85, 91, 93–96, 193, 198, 233, 311
Kamakura shogunate (*bakufu*), xvii–xxii, 33–42, 82, 84–85, 87–88, 91–92, 97–98, 100, 102–3, 105n164, 106, 107n169–173, 108–9, 111–12, 114–15, 118, 121, 124n21, 129n32, 132, 180, 198, 214, 254n48, 276, 309–14; era, 103, 206, 212n45, 213n48, 214, 312–15
Kamegiku. *See* Chrysanthemum Turtle

Kameyama (emperor), xxi, 100–101, 101n152, 109, 116, 116n189, 127n29
Kamigata (region), 278–79
Kamo Shrine, 183
Kanesawa Sadaaki, 111
Kaneyoshi (prince), 171
kanmon (unit of cash), 158–59
Kannō no jōran (*Kannō Anarchy*), 122, 145, 154, 168–72
Kannonji, 127
kanrei. *See* shogunal chancellor
Kantō, 34, 39, 41, 43, 45n29, 47–49, 51, 54–55, 64n62, 66–67, 85, 88, 112n179, 124, 127, 129–30, 132, 135, 239, 298. *See also* Kamakura
karabitsu (Chinese chests). *See* chests
Kasagi, 109, 125
Kashii Shrine, 133
Kashiwabara (emperor), 13–14
Kasuga Shrine, 183
katana. *See* swords
Katō Kiyomasa, 260
Katsu Kokichi, 280–81, 284–85, 288, 290
Kawachi (province), 111, 174, 174n64
Kawajiri *hyōe no jō* (*ōryōshi*), 90
Kawajiri Shichirō, 171–72
Kawanakajima (battle), 233
Kazusa (province), 14–15, 17, 99n147, 130, 275–76, 298n18
kebiishi. *See* Capital Police
kebiki armor, 262
keisei. *See* prostitutes
kenin, 311
kenmon, 52, 57, 59, 212, 212n46, 215, 311
Kenshun (Sanbōin, monk), 124, 131, 131n40, 146–48
Khvostov, Nikolai Aleksandrovich, 227
Kibi-tsu Daimyōjin, 169
Kidō Takayoshi, 300, 302–8
kiheitai, 297
Kii (province), 26, 172
Kikkawa (family), 184–86, 189–90, 259–60
Kikkawa Mototsune, 184–85, 189–90
killing, xxi, 46, 97n138, 128, 136, 179, 196–99, 214, 219–20, 263, 278n3, 293

335

King of Japan, xxiii–xxv; Ryūkyū King, 187, 187n30. *See also* Yūryaku
Kinkakuji. *See* Golden Pavilion
Kira (family), 136, 245n30, 278, 278n3
kirigami, 185, 185n25
Kitabatake Akiie, xxii, 124n20
Kitabatake Chikafusa, 154, 154n6, 168, 168n53
Kitano Shrine, 183
Kitaōji (avenue), 189
Kitayama, xxiv, 279
Kiyohara, 9, 135
Kiyowara (Kiyohara) Mitsuyori, 21
Kō no Morofuyu, 154, 157–59, 164, 167–68
Kō no Moronao, 142–43, 145
Kō no Morouji, 121, 131
Kō no Moroyasu, 134, 145
Kobayakawa family, 131
Kōfukuji, 141
Kōga district, 24
Koga Michimitsu, 34
Kōgon (emperor), 109–11, 114, 117n192, 124, 126n26, 128, 129n32, 131, 143–44
koku, xxvi, 196, 254n47, 257, 263, 265n67, 266, 268–70, 282, 289, 310–311
Kokubunji, 95, 141
kokujin, 53, 168–69, 312
Kokura (harbor), 202
Kokushi (provincial governor), 44
Koma (castle), 159, 163, 167
Kōmyō (emperor), 144
Kōmyō (empress), xv, 4
Konishi Yukinaga, 260
Kōno Michinobu, 38, 38n17
Korea: interactions with, xiii, xxv, 3; invasion attempt, 33, 87, 87n115, 88–90; invasions of, xxvii, 133, 235, 259–61
Koromogawa, 17, 19, 21–22
Kōsa Shrine, 85
Kōzei (Sanbōin, monk), 146–47
Kōzuke (province), 15, 238–39, 272
kudashibumi, 28–30, 46, 51, 55–56, 67, 67n71, 84–85, 95
Kujō (district), 115
Kujō (street), 126

Kujō Kanezane, 31
Kumamoto castle, xxix, 300, 302, 305
Kumano, 26–27
Kumazawa Banzan, xxvii–xxviii, 267–70
kuni no miyatsuko, xiv, 312
Kuroda Kiyotaka (Lt. General), 307–8
Kushida shrine, 137
Kusunoki, 124, 126, 126n27, 174
Kusunoki Masanori, 174n64, 175n67
Kusunoki Masashige, 111, 126, 128, 139–40
kuwagata, 27
Kyoto, xv–xvi, xxiii–xxv, 7, 27, 37–38, 54, 73n92, 75n96, 77n100, 80n110, 97, 97n136, 99n144, 106, 114–15, 121, 125n24, 127, 129, 132n42, 152, 182, 186, 201, 236, 236n2, 247, 250n40, 270, 282n6, 289–90, 297, 303–6, 312
kyūnin, 46, 242, 244, 244n27–28, 249n39, 253
Kyushu (Chinzei, Tsukushi), xxi, xxvi, xxvi, 1, 3, 8, 26, 55n38, 84–85, 88, 95, 123, 126, 128–29, 131–32, 132n41, 136n52, 137–38, 143, 146, 150, 153, 201, 202n23, 305–6, 309, 314

labor tax, xiv
language: proper, 8; abusive, 47
Latter Age, 141, 143
Latter Three Years War, 9
lawsuit, 45–48, 52–54, 56, 57n44, 58, 64–66, 66n69, 67, 68–69, 247, 247n36, 251
letters, 10, 14, 33, 45, 69, 149, 154–55, 157, 159, 163, 165, 167, 187, 223n1, 224, 304–6
loitering, 197–98, 208
Lord of the Ten Good Acts, 41, 98n143
lordship, 208, 212n45
loyalty, notions of, xxii, 121, 130, 278n3, 307
laws: Chōsokabe, 244–59; Date, 206–15; Kamakura, 42–69, 82–85, 93–96; Ōuchi, 193–204; Tokugawa, 235, 264–67

Index

magistrates, 52, 102, 114, 116, 245, 246n35, 247–56, 265–266, 283–85, 287
Magna Carta, xx
Magoichirō. *See* Okano Magoichirō
maidate, 204
main heir (*chakushi*), 51
managerial rights. See *gesu shiki*
mandokoro, xix, 28, 52n36, 63n57, 107n169, 212n45, 311–13
Manzei (Sanbōin, monk), 147, 147n74, 148
marriage: determination, 214n53, 69n82; inheritance and, 50–51, 61–62, 65, 67–69
martial arts, 8
Mass, Jeffrey P., 62
Masuda Michihiro, 63–64, 67n74, 67–69.
  See also Yamashiro widow
Matsunaga Hisahide, 241
Matsura, lady of, 133
matsutake mushrooms, 279
Meiji government, xxviii, 300, 313
menoto (wet nurse), 162. *See also* nurse
merchants, 104, 218, 218n65, 219, 243, 255n49; merchant ships, 201, 203
messengers, 12, 19, 26, 94–95, 105, 108, 117, 124, 131, 137–38, 155, 158–59, 164, 166, 180, 197, 214, 216–17, 220–221, 241, 255, 284–85
Mikawa (province), 27, 158, 164, 236, 238, 240
Mikita (family), 114, 128n31, 174
Mikita Masatake, 174n64
Mikita Sukehide, 114n186
mikyōjo. *See* directive
Military Envoy of Mutsu Province, 9
military manuals, 149, 174, 188
military service (*chūkin*, *chūsetsu*), xix, 38, 83–84, 88, 109, 122n9, 130n36, 143–45, 152–53, 167–68, 171–72, 185–86, 229–31, 247–48, 265, 298
Mimasaka (province), 102
Mimigawa (battle), 225
Minamoto (kin group), xviii, xxii, 29, 31, 63, 65–67, 96–97, 107, 118, 121, 143, 235, 272, 313
Minamoto Hiroshi, 63, 65, 67

Minamoto Koreyasu, 93n127
Minamoto Mamoru, 13, 16
Minamoto Sanetomo, 45n30, 110n176
Minamoto Takauji, 122, 147–48
Minamoto Tametomo, 119–120, 136
Minamoto Tameyoshi, 119, 136n52
Minamoto Tasuku, 13, 16
Minamoto Tsunemoto, 14, 17
Minamoto Yasuuji, 119–120
Minamoto Yoriie, 45n30
Minamoto Yorimasa, 134n47
Minamoto Yorimitsu, 141
Minamoto Yoritomo, xviii–xx, 7, 9, 28–31, 33, 45n30, 96, 107, 110n176, 119–120, 130, 134, 134n46, 141–42, 311, 314–15
Minamoto Yoriyoshi, 9, 12, 17–18, 134–35
Minamoto Yoshiie, 20, 25, 119–120
Minamoto Yoshikane, 119–120
Minamoto Yoshikuni, 119–20
Minamoto Yoshinaka, 31, 121
Minamoto Yoshitomo, 26, 26n4, 27
Minamoto Yoshitsuna, 18, 22, 24
Minamoto Yukiie, 30–31
Minatogawa (battle), 123–24, 128, 138–40
Ming (Dynasty of China), xxiii, xxvii
Minister of War, 301–2
Mino (province), 115, 127, 236n2, 240, 262
Mirror God of Matsura, 11
Mishima deity (*Daimyōjin*), 29–30, 59, 215n56
Mishima island, 198–99
Mishima shrine, 29–31, 81
Mito (region), 273
miuchi, 84, 197n12, 218, 312, 314
moats, 189, 265
mobilization, xxiii–xxiv, xxvii, 37–38, 87–91, 112–13, 124–26, 129–30, 142–43, 149, 182
mobilization directives (*mikyōjo saisoku*), 106
Mochihito (prince) (Takakura no miya), 28–30
Moji (harbor), 202
Mokurai (prince), 303–4
monastic nobility, 266

Index

money, 157, 159n26, 164, 180, 251, 282–90, 295
Mongol Invasions, xxi, 81, 86–87, 91, 123, 309
Mongols, 33, 81, 87–88, 91–92
monks, 21–22, 26n6, 54, 79n105, 87, 103–4, 111, 146, 147n74,75, 156–57, 164, 180, 186, 188, 204, 240. *See also* protector priests
monme (unit of cash in Tokugawa times), 282–83
monogram, xxvi, 29–30, 36–37, 39, 64, 66–67, 69, 88, 91–92, 102, 113–14, 116, 121–22, 145, 148, 150, 152–53, 161–63, 167–69, 172–73, 182–86, 190–91, 199, 203n26, 220, 222, 226–27, 232, 260, 298–99
monopoly of coercive force, 248–49; clauses, 25, 27
monzeki, 107, 111n178, 146, 266. *See also* monastic nobility
Mōri (family), xxvii–xxviii, 193, 216–22, 241, 297
Mōri Motonari, 216–20, 241
Mōri Motonori, 297
Mōri Okimoto, 216
Mōri Takachika, 297–98
Mōri Takamoto, 216, 218–19
Moriyoshi (prince) (son of Go-Daigo), 34, 109, 111–13, 127n29
Moriyoshi (prince) (son of Kameyama), 109, 116–17, 127n29
mothers, 8, 45n30, 49, 56, 64n61, 98, 98n143, 99, 125n25, 158, 161–62, 165, 180n12, 199, 218, 250, 259, 269, 271–74, 283, 291–94
Mt. Hiei, 27, 107, 152
Mt. Kongō, 110, 114
Mt. Maya, 114, 129
Mt. Rokkō, 285
mulberry trees, 269
Munakata shrine, 118, 123, 132, 132n42, 133–35
Murasaki Shikibu, xvi, 8–9
murder, xxviii, 43–44, 47, 85n113, 206–9, 209n37, 213, 218n62, 249, 264, 266. *See also* killing

Muromachi mansion, 180, xxiv; street, xxiii
Muromachi shogunate. *See* Ashikaga shogunate
Muro-no-tsu (Muro harbor), 129–31
Musashi (province), 14–15, 36, 99n146, 158, 164n40, 290, 298n17
mushrooms. See *matsutake* mushrooms
music, 15; musicians, 195, 250
Musō Soseki, 141–42
Mutsu (province), xv, xviii–xix, 7, 9, 18–19, 21, 24–25, 34, 80, 95, 105, 105n164, 120, 134n46, 206, 298n16
myōden, 251
Myōken. *See* North Star God
myōshu (lords of the land), 48n31, 55, 55n38, 57, 95, 257n52, 312

Nabeshima Mitsushige, 276
nagae (long-handled weapons), 230, 230n16, 231
nagamaki, 204–5
Nagasaki, 278, 278n3, 303–4
Nagashino: battle of, 230, 235–38; castle, 236n3, 237n4–5, 238
Nagato (province), 131–32, 198–99, 224, 297
Nagoe Takaie, 125
nainai, 197n12
Naitō Okimori, 216, 219, 219n69
Nakajima (Settsu province), 180
Nakajima Nobuyuki, 303, 305–6
Nakasendō post road, 282
Nankai (district), 89, 105
Nanyō (district), 34
Nanzenji, 187, 187n31
Nara, 107, 128, 174n64
Narazaki Raizō, 297–99
Negoroji, 240
Nejime family, 35, 35n5, 36, 150–51; oaths, 150–51
Nejime Kiyoshige, 35–36
nenbutsu, 96, 176–77, 195
nengu (annual tax), 45, 57, 95, 254. *See also* taxation
New Emperor. *See* Taira Masakado
night attacks, 36, 43, 47

338

Nihongi, 103
Nijō (avenue), 101, 110, 126
Nijō (family), 100
Nijō, Lady, 96–99, 121
Niki Yoshinaga, 135–36
ninja, 100
Nitta Yoshisada, xxii, 130n36, 138, 139n59, 140, 144
Noh (play), 178
North Star God (Myōken), 197, 284
Northern Court, 123n11, 146
noses, 259–61
notice (*fuda tally for taxes*), 21, 156
Noto (province), 37, 37n15, 241, 241n17
nurse (wet-nurse), 8, 10–11, 161–62, 272–73, 295. See also *menoto*
nyozai, 43
nyūdō (novice), 35, 64, 67–68, 91, 97, 104–5, 109, 112, 117, 120, 124, 156, 179, 226

oaths (*kishōmon*), 21, 58–59, 65, 83, 92, 105, 109, 118, 121, 149–50, 168–69, 193, 203n36, 206, 214, 214n55, 215, 216–22, 265
observation, 14, 22, 24, 32, 40, 69, 123, 134–39, 139n61, 174, 188, 237–38, 253, 307
Oda Nobunaga, xxvi–xxvii, 218n64, 235–41
Office of the Retired Emperor (*In no chō*), 34–35
Okano Magoichirō, 282–84, 287–90
Oki Island, 109, 111–12
okibumi (testament), 120. See also testament
Okinawa, xxix, 187n30, 189n39. See also Ryūkyū, kingdom
Ōkubo Toshimichi, 304–5
Okudaira Taizen no Tayū, 291
Ōmi (province), 24, 35, 111, 116
Ōmiya (avenue), 110, 126, 182
Omokawa village, 292, 294
Ōnin War, xxiv–xxv, 178, 181–92, 200
order. See *gechijō*; *inzen*; *kudashibumi*; *rinji*
original holdings. See *honryō*
original lords. See *honshu*

ōryōshi (military envoy), xv, xviii–xix, 9, 25, 90. See also Military Envoy of Mutsu Province; *tsuibushi*
Ōsaka, 174n16, 261–62, 270, 282–88, 304–5, 307; siege of, 260
Ōta Bingo-no-kami, 287
Ōta Gyūichi, 235
Otokoyama, 30
Ōtomo Chiyomatsu [maru], 129, 143
Ōtomo family, 88, 134
Ōtomo Francisco. See Ōtomo Sōrin
Ōtomo Sōrin (Francico), xi, xxvi, 223–28, 231–32
Ōtomo Yoriyasu, 88, 90
Ōtomo Yoshimune, 225–27
Ōuchi family, 131, 193, 199, 201–3, 6
Ōuchi forces, 177
Ōuchi laws, 193–204, 206, 216
Ōuchi Masahiro, 181, 187–89, 196, 200
Ōuchi Mochiyo, 179
Ōuchi Nagahiro, 131
Ōuchi Norihiro, 193n2, 194, 196n10, 198
Ōuchi Yoshinaga, 223–24
Ōuchi Yoshioki, xxv, 201
Ōuchi Yoshitaka, xxv, 216, 219, 219n69, 224n3
outrages. See *rōzeki*
over-*jitō* (*sōjitō*), 55, 107, 314
Owari (province), 120, 125, 131, 134n48, 187, 187n32, 236n2
oyoroi. See *yoroi*
Ozaki, Lady, 216, 219n69

Pacification General. See Chinjufu *shōgun*
paddies, 44, 166n49, 171, 217, 242, 253n45, 254n48, 256
pagodas, xxiv, 43, 103, 189
palanquins, 98–99, 101, 202, 264, 266, 284–85, 290
parents, 46, 49–51, 61, 161, 200, 208, 211, 250, 272–73, 275, 279, 281
payment, 45, 56, 251, 253–54, 258n55
peasants, xxvi, xxviii, 56n42, 124, 154, 206, 212n45, 242–44, 267, 271, 287, 289–90, 292–95, 297, 311

Perfection of Wisdom Sutra, 148
petition, 44, 47–48, 57, 69, 91, 152, 159, 182, 226, 271, 289, 297
petition for reward (*gunchūjō*), xxviii, 33, 87, 91, 113, 115, 150, 171, 271, 297–98, 314–15
pike, 182, 184–85, 189, 195n7, 214, 229–30, 230n16, 231n18, 242
piracy (*kaizoku*), 44, 47, 104, 210
pirate ships (*zokusen*), 85
plaintiff, 46–47, 52, 54, 59, 63, 155n8, 215
poems, 11, 180–81, 279
Portuguese, xxvi, 223–25, 227–28, 231–32
possession, xviii, 1, 4, 15, 36, 44–46, 48, 54, 56–57, 62, 65, 67, 93, 95n132, 101, 168, 208, 212, 242, 251, 252n43, 288, 311
precedent (*hikake*), 14, 25, 44, 46–47, 53–56, 60, 73, 83, 98, 98n140, 108, 201, 265
Prince Okiyo, 14–15, 17
Princely Priests. See *monzeki*
prohibitions, 193, 195–98, 203, 222, 252n43
proprietary rights. See *ryōke shiki*
proprietor (*ryōke*), xvii, 35, 44, 44n27, 45, 103, 172, 215, 312, 314
prostitutes, 180, 199, 199n16
protector priests (*gojisō*), 26–27, 99n144, 124, 146–47
provincial governors, xvi–xviii, 8–9, 14, 17, 21, 29, 35, 44–45, 55, 99, 107, 315
provincial headquarters, 14, 29, 158, 230
provincial office holders. See *zaichō kanjin*
punishment, xxiv, 17, 39, 43, 48–49, 53–56, 61–62, 71, 141, 143, 150, 169, 197, 199, 201n20, 206–8, 211, 213–14, 214n53, 55, 217, 221, 243, 246–47, 248n38, 249, 254, 256, 256n50, 257, 258–59, 291
Pure Land, 176, 180
purification, 81, 196–97

quiver, 90, 104, 135, 195, 214

ranso (spurious/slanderous suits), 46, 52–54, 65, 67–69
ransui (violation), 266
rape, 16, 53, 214n53

rebellion, xvi, xxix, 7, 12–14, 26, 29–31, 35, 43–44, 99n144, 106, 109–11, 117n193, 118, 124, 125n25, 128n31, 141, 150, 216, 225, 242, 264n63, 302, 311
remarriage, 61–62, 65, 67, 69n82
renga, 279
rensho. See cosigner
report (*onchūshin*), 82, 88, 91
report of arrival (*chakutōjō*), 102, 168
residents (*jūnin*), xv, 29, 31, 49, 122, 126, 201
retainers, xxv, 20, 24, 41, 47, 50, 57, 61, 71, 72n90, 88, 92, 97, 108, 128–29, 142, 161, 175, 179, 182, 186, 195–96, 197n12, 199, 200–1, 203, 206, 212, 214, 216–17, 219–20, 222, 225, 242–43, 250n40, 251, 254n48, 257–58, 262, 266, 268, 270, 276, 278n3, 281–82, 292, 309, 315. See also *hikan*; *wakatō*
Retired Emperors, xvi–xvii, xx–xxi, 25–26, 32–35, 40–42, 99–101, 108–11, 117, 127–28, 129n32, 143–44, 190, 314
revenge, 14, 198–99, 208, 210, 213, 249, 274, 277, 278n3
rewards, 4, 17, 24, 38, 42, 45, 48–50, 57–58, 81, 83–85, 91–92, 95, 108, 113, 143–44, 149, 153, 168–69, 171, 184, 191, 213n49, 221, 313
Rezanov, N. P., 227
rice, xxvi, 13–14, 21, 30n14, 157, 203, 242, 250–56, 263, 267–70, 275, 282, 286, 289, 292, 296, 310–11
riding grounds, 281
rifles, 300, 303
rinji, 122
river people, 218
roads, 18, 21–23, 32, 37n15, 108, 126–27, 139–40, 145, 211, 255, 263, 273, 278, 282, 282n6, 292
rocks, 8, 11–12, 22, 104, 187–89; rock throwers, 8, 196; wounds caused by, 189–90
Rokuhara, 27, 47, 63, 64n61, 65n65, 66n68–69, 69n83, 100–2, 105n164, 109–111, 115–17, 123n15, 124, 126–28,

129n32, 143, 312; orders (*gechijō*), 3–39, 58n45, 67, 67n71, 172
Rokuhara *tandai* (administrators), 105n164, 115, 127, 172n62
Rokuonin, 180, 186, 188–90
rōnin (wave men), xxvi, 257, 276–77, 312
Roster of Wounds (*teoi chūmon*), 184
rōtō (followers), 27, 312
rōzeki (outrages), 53, 58, 312
rumors, 12, 22, 32, 35, 53, 57, 61–62, 68, 98, 99n144, 101, 109, 126, 159, 180, 200, 257, 283
Rushana. *See* Great Buddha
ryō (unit of cash in Tokugawa times), 202, 233, 282, 287, 289–90
ryōke shiki, xvii, 35, 44–45, 103, 172, 312, 314
ryōsho (land holdings), 46, 171, 226
Ryūsenji, battle, 173–75
Ryūkyū: *gozoku*, 300; islands, 300; kingdom, 186, 187n30

Sadafusa (prince), 179, 180n6
saddle, xxvi, 84, 160, 175, 225–27, 248
Sado (province), 37n15
Saga: province, 276; region in Kyoto, 126
Sagami (province), 15–17, 20, 99n146, 272, 290
Saigō Takamori, xxix, 300, 302
Saika, 240–41, 241n18
Saitama: district, 164n40; province, 1
Sakamoto, 152, 232
Sakanoue no Tamuramaro, xv, xix, 7, 141, 313
sake, 23, 30n14, 52, 73, 77n101, 79, 155, 179, 199n16, 236, 270, 276, 285–86, 305
saltpeter, 232–33
samurai, xiii, xxvi–xxviii, 26–27, 47, 48n31, 70, 70n87, 109, 197, 209, 214, 236n2, 237, 239, 249n39, 252, 252n43, 255, 256n50, 257, 263–64, 268–69, 271, 275–80, 282, 291–94, 297–98, 300–2, 312–13; abolishment, xxix, 267–69; creation of order, 235, 243–44; *samurai* farmers, 268–70; potato *samurai*, 293

Sanbōin Kenshun. *See* Kenshun
San'in (district), 125
Sanjō (avenue), 26
Sanjō (bridge), 290
Sanjō (family), 101, 179
Sanjō Sanemasa, 179–80
Sanjō Sanetomi, 303–4, 306
Sanjō Tadako, 180
Sanuki (province), 140, 179, 263
Sanyō (district), 34
sarugaku, 178–79, 250
Satomi (family), 276
Satsuma (province), xxviii–xxix, 33, 36, 294, 300, 302, 308
Scrolls of the Mongol Invasions, 81–85
seal, vermillion, 229–30, 243–44
Sei-i-tai *shōgun*, xv–xvi, xix, xxii, xxiv, xxvii, 7, 33–34, 43n26, 96, 122, 235, 309, 313
Seki (castle), 154, 168
Sekigahara, battles, xxvii, 227, 235, 260, 262
Sengakuji, 277
seppuku (death by disembowlment), 106, 111, 179, 217n60, 261, 277. *See also harakiri*
servants (*hōkōnin, rōtō, shojū*), 31–32, 66, 66n69, 68, 68n80, 70–71, 75–76, 79, 79n107, 83, 98–99, 108, 137, 156, 243–44, 247, 250, 261, 263, 273–75, 295, 311–12
Seta (bridge), 110, 127
Settsu (province), 40, 113, 129, 180, 261, 282, 284
Shadow Sword, 4–6
Shiba Gorō, 271, 292–96
Shiba Taichirō, 293–96
Shibuya (family), 102, 105
Shichijō (avenue), 12, 110, 115
Shigisan castle, 241
shikken. *See* shogunal chief of staff
Shikoku, 126, 129, 131, 138, 140
Shimabara, xxviii
Shimazu (family), xxvii–xxviii, 33, 36, 134, 225, 243n23
Shimazu Hisamitsu, 307
Shimazu Hisatoki, 87n115, 89
Shimazu Tadatoki, 36n8

Index

Shimokōbe estate, 159–60
Shimonoseki, Straits of, xviii, 132n41, 201, 202n23
Shimōsa (province), 13–16, 167, 298n18
Shimōsa (Taira) Yoshikane, 13
Shimotsuke (province), 14–15, 17, 19, 179, 298n19
Shimotsuma Rairen, 240–41
Shimoyama Yauemon, 283, 285
Shimozuma-no-Shō (estate), 272
shin guards, 176
Shinano (province), 31, 36–37, 161, 238
Shinomura shrine, 121–23, 125, 125n25, 126
Shintō shrines, 245, 250
Shiogama *Daimyōjin*, 215
shipping: ammunition, 308; taxes on, 254n48
ships: and armies, 129–32, 138, 201–3, 241; battles with, 92; creation of ports and harbors, 104; fast ships, 241; limits on size, 266; permission to board, 248
shirabyoshi, 39–40
Shirakawa (emperor), xvi, 17, 25
shizoku, 300, 304–5, 313
Shō Dynasty, 187n30
shōen (estates), xvi–xvii, 43–45, 310, 312–13
shogunal chancellor, xxv, 179, 181, 311
shogunal chief of staff (*shikken, shitsuji*), 93, 96, 107–8, 145, 313
shojū (followers), 57, 66, 68n80, 90
shōkan (estate official), 44, 48
Shōkokuji, 186, 188n36, 189
Shōmu (emperor), xiv, 4, 141
shomu sōron (administration), 83, 104
shōmyō (lesser lords), 264
Shōmyōji, 111n177
Shōni Kagesuke, 33, 82, 87, 92
Shōni Myōe, 132
Shōni Sadatsune, 129n33
Shōni Tsunesuke, 88
Shōni Yorinao, 132, 134, 137, 139
shoryō (land holdings), 45, 47, 50–51, 54, 58, 61–63, 65–66, 95n133
Shōshi (Empress), 8

Shōtoku (prince), 141
shoulder boards. See *sode*
shōya, 246, 246n35, 248–49, 252–55
shrine administrators (*kannushi no shikken*), 107
shrine attendants (*kannushi*), 43
shrine households (*ufu*), 43
shrine priests (*saishu*), 107
shrines, 28–31, 40, 43, 45, 55, 81, 84–85, 95, 97, 107, 116–18, 121–23, 125, 132–137, 146–47, 171, 183, 196, 236, 245, 284–86, 292
shugo, xix, xxi, xxiii–xxiv, 30, 34–36, 43–45, 53, 61, 67n72, 68n78, 81, 88, 90, 99n147, 105n162, 105–8, 149, 172, 178, 182, 198, 213n48, 247n37, 254n48, 310, 314; *shugosho*, 213
Shun, 143
Siberia, xxvi
sieges, 114, 126–28, 159, 174–75, 189, 237–38, 241, 260, 293
sightseeing, 142, 198, 250, 289
silkworms, 269
silver, 3, 19, 105, 107, 141, 262, 282
Silver Pavilion, xxv
silversmiths, 255
sisters, xx, 18, 180n11–12, 198, 198n13, 271, 273, 291, 293–94
Six-District Army, xv, xviii, xix, 7, 9
skirmishers, xv, xvii, xxiv, 25, 114, 125, 127, 174, 312
skulls, 235–36, 294
slander, 19, 50, 52, 57, 179, 208
slanderous suit. See *ranso*
smallpox, xiv, 4
snakes, 106, 197
sode, 130n36, 133, 134, 176–77
sōjitō. See over-*jitō*
Soma district, 15
Southern Court, xxii–xxiii, 123n11, 154, 168, 168n53, 169, 169n56, 171, 173, 174n64, 175n67
Spirit of Laws (Montesquieu), 302
St. Petersburg, xxvi, 227
stables, 75, 84, 95, 240

status, viii, xx, xxvi, xxviii, 3, 8, 35n2, 36, 44n27, 48n31, 52n36, 55, 64n60, 69, 72, 72n89, 73, 76, 79, 91, 95, 98, 98n143, 104n159, 109, 121, 154, 180, 214, 219, 243, 246, 246n34, 248, 250–51, 257–58, 258n53, 258n65, 264–65, 271–72, 277, 289, 300–1, 309–14
stepmothers, 50
stepping, on paper, 291
stipends, 263, 264n61, 300
succession, xxiv, 25, 28, 57, 75n95, 107–8, 257, 313. *See also* adoption
Sue (family), 203, 203n28, 204
Sugi Takamasa, 120
suicide. See *seppuku*
suit, Western, 294. *See also* armor; lawsuit; *ranso*
suitors, 8, 52
Sukō (emperor, crown prince), 111
sulfur, 232–34
Sumiyoshi shrine, 137
summons, 13, 84, 129; *meshibumi*, 33–34, 47, 54, 87–88; in a suit, (*toijō*) xxi, 58, 64–65
sumo, 39, 194, 295
Suō (province), 131, 224, 297
surrender, 42, 122n9, 130, 146, 248
Suruga (province), 35, 37n13, 238, 240, 270
suspect (*ikeguchi*), 210–11
Suwa, 169
Suzuka, 101
swimming, 39
swords, xiii, xv, 1–6, 15, 23–24, 76, 76n97, 77–78, 90, 101, 130, 133, 134n47, 135–37, 176, 181, 185, 281, 295–96, 313; bamboo, 279; banning, 300–1; bearer, 2–3, 176; blunt, 23; fittings, xv, 135, 273; hunt, 242–43; inscriptions, xiii, 1–6; *katana*, 204–5; killing with, 23, 263; long, 3, 78, 176, 204, 288; named, 4–6, 101, 134 (*see also* Bright; Crunchbone; Catfish tail; Shadow); *nagamaki*, 204–5; rust and, 77–78; short, 77, 204, 261; smith, 2, 4; *tachi*, 90, 179, 204–5; *wakizashi*, 242; wearing and status, 300–1
swordsmiths, 2, 4

Tabara, 303
Tabaru (Ōtomo) Chikaie, 225–26
Tabaru Chikatsura, 225
tachi. *See* swords
Tada Gongen Shrine, 285
Taga, fort, 7
Taga Shrine, 116–17
Taiheiki, 121–24, 139n59, 149, 173–75
Taihō (castle), 154, 168
Taira (kin group), xviii, 31, 191
Taira Ietsuna, 28
Taira Kiyomori, xvii–xviii, 26–29, 41, 107, 312
Taira Masakado, xvi, 8, 12–15, 17
Taira Munemori, 26
Taira Sadamori, 13, 16–17
Taira Shigemori, 27
Taira Sukemori, 31–32
Taira Yorimori, 27
Taira Yoritsuna, 85n113, 97n138, 98n139
Taisanji, 112–13
Taishaku, 59, 169, 215, 221
Tajima (province), 106
Takahata Fudō, 154–67; monk (Shōshin), 156
Takakura (avenue), 184, 189
Takakura (emperor), xviii
Takakura (Prince Mochihito), 30. *See also* Mochihito
Takashima: battle, 91; island, 260
Takataki Kichibei, 275–76
Takatenjin Castle, 240
Takeda (family), xxvi, 164, 229–30, 235–40
Takeda (region), 110, 124, 126
Takeda Katsuyori, 230–31, 235–40
Takeda Kenshin, 189
Takeda Nobutaka, 152–53
Takeda Shingen, 239n10–11
Takezaki Suenaga, 33, 81–86, 123n13
Takikawa, 237–38
Tale of Genji, xvi, 8–12
Tale of Heike, 121, 180n13
Tamakazura, 8–9, 12
Tanba (province), 106, 122, 125, 305
tanbetsu (taxes), 217, 217n58

343

Index

Tango (province), 125, 305
Tannowa (family), 145, 172–73, 182
tansen (taxes), 217, 217n58
Tatarahama (battle), 123, 124n19, 128, 133–35
tax collection, 212, 254; tallies, 21
tax collectors, xvi, xxviii
taxation, xiv, xxii, 201, 251–54, 256, 268, 270–71, 281, 310–12; annual, 57, 95, 254, 256; on debt, 181; exemption, 171; fishing, 256, 268; land, 45, 47, 56, 171, 253–54; provisional, 155; rate and reduction, 268; revenue, 166n49, 281. See also *hanzei*; *nengu*; *tanbetsu*; *tansen*; *tokubun*
tea, 112, 158, 160, 250n40, 286
teichū. See Court of Appeals
telegram, 303–8
Temman Daijizai Tenjin, 59, 138n54, 215
temples, xv, xviii, 4–5, 35, 40, 43, 45, 55, 80, 97, 103–4, 107, 111n17, 113, 115, 120, 128, 136, 142, 144, 152, 154, 156, 160, 162, 165n44, 166, 180n6–7, 183, 186, 198, 207, 223–25, 241, 245n31, 250, 257, 273, 283, 294, 296
Tenjin. See Temman Daijizai Tenjin
Tenryūji, 141
testament, xxviii, 36, 52, 62–65, 67, 75n95, 118, 120–21, 146, 271, 292–96. See also *okibumi*; *yuzurijō*
theft, 53, 104, 211, 251. See also punishment
thieves, 60, 196, 211–12, 248
Toba (region), 124, 126
Tōdaiji, xv, 5–7, 141, 242n20
Tōgan Ean, 33, 87
toijō. See summons
Tōji-in, 180
Tōkai (district), 34
Tōkaidō, 41n23, 282n6, 290
Toki (family), 174–75, 179, 179n4, 189
tokubun (taxes), 94, 156
Tokugawa Iemitsu, xxvii, 265
Tokugawa Ieyasu, xxvii, 227, 235, 237, 240, 262, 264, 313
Tokugawa shogunate, xvi, 270, 264–67, 281, 302

tokusei (debt relief), 180, 251n42, 314
tolls, 202, 210; toll barriers, 99, 266
tombs, xiv, 1–3
topknots, 76, 294
Tosa (province), 246n33, 254n47, 260–63
Tōtōmi (province), 112, 240
Tottori, 305
tower. See archery tower; watchtowers
towering (*jō takaku*), xv, 10, 100
towns, xxvi, xix, 193, 255n49, 262, 268–69, 282n6, 301
Toyotomi Hideyoshi, xxvi–xxvii, 235, 242–45, 258, 260, 313
Tōzan (district), 34
treason, 35, 46–47
trespassing, 197–98, 212
trial, 47, 58–59, 63–65, 68, 215
Tripitaka, 142
tsuibushi (Envoy for Pursuit and Capture), 107
tsuitōshi (Envoy to Pursue and Punish), 32, 314. See also *tsuibushi*
Tsukiyama lord. See Ōuchi Norihiro
Tsukiyama Shrine, 196, 198
Tsukushi. See Kyushu
Tsuruoka Hachiman Shrine, 81
turtles (*tochigame*), 197
tutoring (*gogakumon*), 93

Udo, 304–5
Uesugi Kenshin, xxvi, 231–33, 240, 241n16
Uesugi Kiyoko, 125n25, 138n54
Uesugi Shigeyoshi, 125
Uji (river, bridge), 31, 32, 32n17, 39, 110
Unoha (Cormorant Feathers), 178
Unsen Taikyoku, 188–89
Urakami (family), 216, 219, 219n68

vassals, 37, 62–64, 67, 236n2, 252–53, 257, 291; use of term, 37, 62
vendetta, 276. See also feuds
vengeance, 199, 213, 291. See also vendetta; feuds
villages, xxviii, 113, 122, 139, 219, 221, 237, 244, 246n34–35, 250, 256n50, 263, 268–69, 273, 281–86, 288–89, 293, 295,

298; village elders, 248; village officials, 289
violence, xxi, 43–44, 80n108, 100, 104, 113, 193, 198n15, 214n53, 220n72, 245, 248, 271, 309. *See also* monopoly of coercive force

Wakamatsu. *See* Aizu Wakamatsu
Wakasa (province), 37n15
Wakatakeru. *See* Yūryaku
wakatō (retainer, follower), 82, 98, 115, 164, 315
Wakayama, 305
wakizashi. See swords
Wall Writings (*hekisho*), 193–94, 196–98, 200–1, 206
Watanabe (family) 217
watchtowers, 188–90, 265, 274
Way of the Bow and Arrow, 15, 73, 81, 84–85, 87, 177, 220; training in, 70
Way of the Samurai, 267, 271, 277–78
Way of the Warrior. See *Bushidō*
wayo (compromise; gifts), 50, 50n35
wealth, xxiii, 9, 63–64, 66, 66n69, 181, 213, 245n32, 252n43, 270
Weber, Max, 244
Western Army, xxv, 183, 188, 191
widows, 39, 51, 63–67, 67n74, 68, 68n80
willfully (*watakushi ni*), 203, 207, 209
witnesses, 67–69, 82, 91–92, 175, 177, 263
wolves, 106
women, xiv, xx, xxviii, 10, 16, 23, 43, 49, 51, 53–54, 61–62, 63n57, 64n30, 73, 94, 101, 137, 250, 292–93
worship, 13, 43, 93, 122, 137, 156
writings, xiii, 37, 61, 70, 74, 74n93, 88, 157–58, 161–62, 166, 190, 193–94, 196–98, 200–1, 206, 224, 257, 306

yagura. See archery tower
Yakushiji *Nyorai*, 113
Yamada Akiyoshi, 302–3, 305, 307–8
Yamada Shin'uemon, 282–89
Yamagata Aritomo, 301–2
Yamagata district, 28

Yamagata Masakage, 239
Yamaguchi: prefecture, 303; town, xxv, 193–96, 202, 203n26, 223–25, 225n5
Yamakawa (region), 160–61
Yamamoto Tsunetomo, 271, 276–280
Yamana (family), xxiii, xxv, 176, 179, 181, 183, 187, 189, 216, 219, 219n68
Yamana Koretoyo, 189
Yamana Sōzen, xxv, 181, 183, 187–89
Yamana Ujikiyo, 176
Yamanouchi Sudō (family), 167–68
Yamanouchi Tokimichi, 168, 170
Yamanouchi Tsuneyuki: 149, 154–68, 171; Etchū Hachirō, 161; Gorō, 158, 166; Hachirōshirō, 155, 166; Hikosaburō, 156, 161, 166; Hikoshirō, 161–62; Kiheiji, 161, 164, 164n40; Kosaburō, 156, 163; Matakesa (son), 154–66; Shirojirō, 158; Tarō Hachirō, 162; Tarōjirō, 156; wife, 154, 158, 160, 165–66; Yasaburō, 163; Yatsu, 161–62. *See also* Daishinbō; Aoyanagi Saburō
Yamashina, 190–91
Yamashiro Katashi, 63–68
Yamashiro (province), 183
Yamashiro widow (Hō-Amidabutsu), 63–68
Yamataishi (prophecy), 187
Yamato (province), 174, 174n64, 241
Yamauchi Katsutoyo, 262
Yamazaki, 15, 110
yamiuchi (assassination), 209
Yao, 143, 242
Yasuda estate, 39
Yatsushiro, 303–5, 307
Yawata (castle), 152–53
Yedo. *See* Edo
yin-yang, 4, 266, 280
yoriki (followers), 105
yoroi, 90, 105, 105n160
Yoshida Tsunefusa, 31–32
Yoshikawa Shinji, 7
Yoshiki district, 224
Yoshino, xxii
Yoshiwara, 286
Yuasa Muneshige, 26

Index

Yuasa Yajirō, 184–85
Yuigahama, 97
Yuinohama, 81
Yūki Chikamitsu, 129
Yukichi Fukuzawa. *See* Fukuzawa Yukichi
Yūryaku (early king), xiii, 1–3
yuzurijō (will, testament), 35, 35n3, 63

zaichō kanjin, xvi–xviii, 25, 112, 312–13, 315
zaike. *See* dwelling
zaisho. *See* dwelling
zasu (temple chief), 107, 111, 111n178
zōshiki, 70
zuryō (provincial governor), xvi, 55, 315